Tutu

Tutu

The Authorised Portrait

Allister Sparks and Mpho A. Tutu

Foreword: Bono

Introduction: His Holiness the Dalai Lama

Edited by Doug Abrams

MACMILLAN

in association with PQ Blackwell

"SOMETIMES STRIDENT,
OFTEN TENDER, NEVER AFRAID
AND SELDOM WITHOUT HUMOUR,
DESMOND TUTU'S VOICE WILL
ALWAYS BE THE VOICE OF
THE VOICELESS."

NELSON MANDELA

CONTENTS

FOREWORD

Everybody is trying to figure out their way in the world, their way through the world. How do you carry yourself? How can you be humble, yet not get walked upon? How do you hold your head up but not be fearful? For most it's not easy ... for me it's impossible. And in my struggle to sort it out, Archbishop Desmond Tutu – "the Arch" to his friends – has been a role model like no other.

His leadership, his bravery and the change he has brought to the world mark him out as extraordinary. Quite unlike the rest of us. But when you meet him, what strikes you is his very humanness, his humour, his humility. All echoes of the Latin "*humus*" – earth that has reached its natural settling point. Earthiness, combined with elevation: that's some dance to pull off. To be that serious and that silly. To carry the weight of injustice, yet remain so light on his feet. To have so much faith and so little religiosity.

Surely laughter is the evidence of freedom. When the archbishop laughs, you hear and you feel his freedom. For me, he's not just a graceful man but the embodiment of this most radical and transformative of words – grace – a quality impossible to define and difficult to evoke, but we know it when we see it, and we see it in him.

All this makes me quite willing to do whatever he tells me to do. He really leaves me no other choice. The last time I was slow in responding to one of his requests I was told in an email that I would "not be let into heaven". The Arch plays hardball and he's got the Lord on his side. So it's no wonder I consider him my boss. People ask how I got so involved in the fight against extreme poverty and why my singing voice has some-times turned into town crier. Well, it would be nice to say that I work on behalf of the voiceless, the poor and the vulnerable but, actually, I do this because the Arch asked me to. He was my wake-up call – mine and many others'. Not the shrill, ear-splitting sound of a fire alarm, but more like a church bell ringing out: a clear, beautiful note that hangs in the air and resonates in your bones.

Wake up to what, exactly? Wake up to what the world can be. A world truly at peace. And peace, from the Arch's point of view, is not the absence of war. What he seeks is a shift in the battleground – forsaking armed conflict for the longer and more ennobling struggle against complacency, against selfishness, against revenge and other, darker aspects of human nature. To follow him in this fight is to have your life turned upside down turning the world right side up. To follow him is to join that ongoing march, the journey of equality.

BONO

INTRODUCTION

I remember first meeting Archbishop Desmond Tutu over two decades ago. Since then, the better I have got to know him, the greater has been my respect for him as a sincere spiritual practitioner, one who sets great store by the power of faith. There is a remarkable, frank and mutual respect between us.

I have immense admiration for the great work he and Nelson Mandela accomplished with the Truth and Reconciliation Commission. The genuine reconciliation they achieved not only allowed South Africa to make a new start less burdened by the past than it might have been, but also served as a tremendous model for other communities emerging from extended periods of conflict. It was likewise the archbishop's important suggestion that spiritual leaders should visit places of conflict together to offer good counsel.

As a spiritual leader and a freedom fighter committed to non-violence, his achievements have been wonderful. Archbishop Tutu's sharp and piercing eyes reflect his realistic assessment and astute judgement whatever the situation, but I've also noticed that his nature is gently teasing. His easy-going joviality brings a pleasant atmosphere to any meeting he attends, no matter how serious the matter under discussion.

His commitment to reconciliation, not simply as a spiritual ideal but in actual practice, has been exemplary. I can only hope that, when the time comes, I too can show as much commitment and strength. When we first met, Archbishop Tutu was not much interested in the cause of Tibet, but he has since become one of our staunch supporters, for which I am grateful. He is a man of principle who has spoken up on the Tibetan people's behalf even when it meant criticising his own government. China often likes to suggest that it is only white Americans and Europeans who criticise it for its conduct in Tibet. I cannot emphasise enough the impact of such criticism when it comes from a distinguished black African of his stature. In a similar vein, he and Václav Havel recently wrote a ringing defence of the imprisoned Chinese human rights activist and fellow Nobel laureate Liu Xiaobo.

It gives me great pleasure to know that Archbishop Tutu's daughter, the Reverend Mpho A. Tutu, a warm and beautiful person like her father, has compiled this affectionate portrait of him. It is a fitting tribute to a great man.

HIS HOLINESS THE FOURTEENTH DALAI LAMA

EDITOR'S NOTE

Desmond Tutu looked out from the raised pulpit at St Mary's Cathedral in Johannesburg unable to speak. The standing-room-only crowd of more than a thousand had gathered to hear him preach on the occasion of his seventy-fifth birthday. He gazed out at the congregation that he had led during the struggle to end apartheid, and the rest of us who had gathered from around the world. Three-quarters of a century of his impossibly rich life was flashing before him and it rendered him speechless. From the self-described "township urchin" to the Nobel Peace laureate, archbishop and healer of a nation, his life had been as unimaginable as the transformation of his beloved country. And yet, he had imagined it, believed in it and orchestrated it with a fist-pounding confidence that this is a moral universe.

The man who is known around the world for his laugh – that warm chuckle that deepens into a belly roar and concludes with a mischievous giggle – began to sob deep body-shaking sobs. The congregation spontaneously broke out into song, singing their love for him. His wife, Leah, without pause, left her pew and, despite her aching, aged knees, hobbled up the stairs and into the pulpit. Tutu turned around to face her and buried his head in her chest as she wrapped her arms around him. He continued to sob, the congregation raising them both up with their song. After several minutes, he was finished. Leah stepped down out of the pulpit and Tutu turned back to the congregation, completely renewed, and proceeded to deliver a passionate and brilliant sermon on the struggle to end apartheid, and this particular congregation's role in ending that oppressive system. During those moments, we witnessed a kind of leadership for which our world is desperate: a leadership based on recognising our shared humanity and our shared vulnerability, and on recognising that our need for one another is not weakness but strength.

This authorised portrait, published on the occasion of Tutu's eightieth birthday, celebrates one of the great moral leaders of our time. We see the pivotal roles he played in the liberation of South Africa, both at home and abroad, as leader, liberator and healer – roles he often played in the face of his own hesitation and uncertainty.

Tutu, as he himself has often said, was simply responding to the needs of his suffering flock while the real leaders of the struggle were in jail or in exile. Less well known is what a reluctant prophet he was. Tutu calls his fatal flaw his "need to be loved". As a result he is conflict-averse, which is why God had to drag him practically kicking and screaming into one of the most brutal and dehumanising conflicts of the twentieth century, during which time he was vilified, harassed and declared public enemy number one of the apartheid government. Only his international stature kept him safe from the bludgeoning violence of that time, and then only just barely. Again and again he was called to stop the country from falling into chaos and revolution, while at the same time becoming an ambassador for a free South Africa, endlessly travelling to convince the world to isolate and sanction the apartheid regime.

It is true that Tutu did not do it alone, nor could he have done it alone. He will be the first to tell you of our interconnectedness, of our dependence on one another, of the profound African teaching of *ubuntu* – of our being who we are only in relation to one another. Through the eyes of family, friends, colleagues, comrades and opponents included here, Tutu's life is refracted so luminously that it reveals as much about humanity as it does about one man.

Tutu has never aspired to sainthood, to some exalted station outside of the anguish and rapture of being human. By contrast he is perhaps the most human human I have ever met: the most extraordinary example of what is possible for each of us if we are willing to answer the call of our times and turn to one another with the laughter-filled, tear-stained eyes of the heart.

DOUG ABRAMS
EDITOR

CHAPTER ONE

....

OUR REAL LEADERS ARE IN
PRISON AND IN EXILE

South Africa has a way of producing exceptional individuals. It is no small miracle that in the space of a single century it has produced three such figures, in Mohandas Gandhi, Nelson Mandela and Desmond Tutu: men assured of immortality in the history of humankind's long and still-unfinished struggle to free the wretched of the earth from the bondage of colonialism, racism, poverty and prejudice.

It is, of course, the moral challenge presented by a culturally and racially diverse society that has been at

Left: Tutu speaks at a mass funeral in KwaThema township, near Johannesburg, July 1985. He condemns the practice of "necklacing", a horrific method of killing suspected informers where a tyre filled with petrol is placed around the victim's neck and set alight.

> ## "Our real leaders are in prison and in exile. The government must release them and bring them home to negotiate a new constitution."
>
> Desmond Tutu

war with itself over all those issues, more intensely than almost any other, that has fired the furnace that forged these remarkable individuals. For if you are imbued with what Hannah Arendt called the passion of compassion, you cannot remain neutral in a moral crisis – and these three exceptional individuals were certainly transfused with that passion. Nor is it misappropriation to claim Gandhi for South Africa, for it was his struggle for human rights during the twenty-one years he spent in South Africa as a young lawyer that forged him into the iconic figure he became back home in India. It was here that Gandhi developed the philosophy of *satyagraha* (non-violent resistance) which he used so effectively on his return. As a senior Indian diplomat once put it during an official visit to South Africa: "We sent

you Mohandas Gandhi, and you sent us back the mahatma" – the special honorific he was given meaning "great soul".

Tutu will no doubt disclaim any such bracketing of himself with the likes of Gandhi and Mandela, for he has always insisted he was neither a politician nor a leader of the black struggle in South Africa. "Our real leaders," he would say repeatedly in those dark days, "are in prison and in exile. The government must release them and bring them home to negotiate a new constitution." His own role, as he saw it, was to fulfil the mandate vested in him as a pastor of the Christian Church, to combat the evil of apartheid and follow God's intention that his people should be led out of bondage into full liberation.

The truth, though, is that Tutu was in fact an interim leader of special importance, for he filled the void caused by the absence of those in prison and exile or otherwise legally silenced at a time when South Africa was under the rule of its two most tyrannical leaders: Balthazar Johannes Vorster from the mid-1960s to the late 1970s and Pieter Willem Botha – better known by his initials, P. W., or his Afrikaans nickname, die Groot Krokodil (the Great Crocodile) – in the 1980s. Tutu was pitched into that tough role when he returned to South Africa in 1975 as dean of St Mary's Cathedral in Johannesburg, after serving on the staff of the World Council of Churches in Britain. Young black South Africans in particular were in a state of high tension at the time and, within a year of Tutu's return, were to erupt into a nationwide revolt when the apartheid regime ordered that all black schools had to use Afrikaans as a parallel medium of instruction with English. The students objected: few could speak Afrikaans, but their primary objection was that they saw it as the language of the oppressor. The majority of the white-minority population were the Dutch-descended Afrikaners whose ethno-nationalist movement dominated the government which was imposing the apartheid policy.

The conflict exploded in Johannesburg's huge black dormitory complex of Soweto on 16 June 1976 when thousands of black students decided to march to a big soccer stadium in the complex to stage a protest demonstration against the language decree. The police opened fire and, in a series of running skirmishes, killed twenty-three students by nightfall that first day. The carnage set off a chain reaction of protest demonstrations around the country, which raged on until the end of the year, leaving a death toll of more than six hundred. Thousands were injured and some thirty thousand detained, interrogated and often tortured by the security police.

The uprising was eventually quelled but it was a turning point in the black liberation struggle. Until then it had been fought outside the country, in Rhodesia (later to become Zimbabwe), South West Africa (later to become Namibia) and Angola but, from the Soweto uprising onwards, the struggle became internal – not so much a guerrilla war, but a campaign of civil unrest aimed at rendering the black townships ungovernable.

Significant though these events were, black political leadership was shredded at the time. Nelson Mandela's African National Congress (ANC), the main black resistance movement, had been outlawed fifteen years earlier and Mandela himself, along with the entire top leadership of the ANC, had been sentenced to life imprisonment after deciding in desperation to form an armed wing and continue the struggle underground. A breakaway movement, the Pan Africanist Congress (PAC), had likewise been banned and a range of lesser movements with it. The multiracial South African Communist Party (SACP) had been put out of action even earlier.

The outlawing of these movements had created a decade of silence in the black community through the sixties, with only the voices of a handful of courageous white liberals and newspapers opposing the onward march of the grand apartheid scheme and exposing the oppressive and often cruel effects of its implementation on the black population. The regime's strategy was to crush all black nationalist resistance to this plan, subsequently creating time and space for the compliant black tribal leaders it had put in place in these supposedly emergent states, known as bantustans, to establish themselves and build support bases.

But the process was interrupted as the sixties drew to a close with the emergence of the powerful Black Consciousness Movement led by a charismatic, young medical student, Stephen Bantu Biko. This movement spread like a grass fire and was animating the black youth particularly, just as Desmond Tutu and his family returned from Britain. But even its activities were circumscribed by the "banning" of its leader – banning being a particularly ingenious legal device used by the apartheid regime to neutralise political activists. It involved confining the recipient of a document signed only by the minister of justice to the small magisterial district where the victim lived, prohibiting him or her from being in the company of more than one other person at a time and from writing or publishing anything at all, and, above all, prohibiting the media or anyone else from publishing or broadcasting anything the banned person might say or write currently or had expressed at any time in the past. In other words, it was a comprehensive gag. No evidence was required, there was no trial and no appeal was possible. It was all done with the single stroke of a pen by one all-powerful member of the apartheid government. Whole organisations could also be banned, as had been done with the ANC, PAC and SACP and was to be done eventually with the Black Consciousness Movement and its affiliates as well. And to add to the ferocity of the times, Biko was himself arrested a year later for breaking his banning order and beaten to death by his interrogators in one of the most appalling acts of racist brutality and callousness in apartheid's sordid history.

It was into this black leadership vacuum that Tutu landed as he came home. There was nothing for him but to fill the gap as best he could, which he did with courage and verve for the next fifteen years until the historic day on 2 February 1990 when the Great Crocodile's successor,

President Frederik Willem de Klerk, stunned the world by announcing the unbanning of all black political movements and the impending release of Nelson Mandela and all other political prisoners, so setting South Africa on the road to what many saw as a miraculous transformation.

Above: Tutu at a United Democratic Front rally, 1986.

Those fifteen years, during which Tutu was effectively the interim leader of the black liberation struggle and its primary voice at home and abroad, were among the stormiest in the history of this tempestuous land. There were other key figures in the struggle too, of course: notably the Reverend Allan Boesak, whose leadership of the mixed-race branch of the segregated Dutch Reformed Church put great moral pressure on the Afrikaner establishment; and later a united front of nearly a thousand civic bodies was formed to give organisational shape and thrust to the internal struggle. But Tutu was the principal figure throughout who gave focus to the struggle and articulated its issues most clearly. Those were also the years in which the struggle was won and apartheid finally ended. It was a passage in Tutu's life that won him international acclaim and the Nobel Peace Prize.

It was no easy role to fill. Tutu had to tread the finest of lines. He had to sound radical to maintain credibility among blacks but, in doing so, he risked being regarded as a dangerous revolutionary by the repressive white government. Even to call for "one person, one vote", the minimum necessary to retain credibility in the black community, particularly among the fired-up youth in those overheated days, was to risk criminal prosecution or one of the disabling banning orders. Universal suffrage was the most basic of all the banned ANC's demands – and the apartheid regime's battery of security laws made it a criminal offence, punishable by long imprisonment, to further any of the aims or objectives of a banned organisation.

Right: Armed only with a Bible, Tutu confronts South African police as they attempt to break up a demonstration in Soweto, Johannesburg, 1985.

The ANC's commitment to armed struggle and the formation of its armed wing, Umkhonto we Sizwe (Spear of the Nation), presented Tutu with an even trickier dilemma. He abhorred violence. The whole thrust of his prophetic ministry was to campaign and plead for the abandonment of apartheid so as to avoid the racial bloodbath he believed would otherwise engulf his beloved South Africa. Yet he never decried the ANC's armed struggle. Again this was necessary to retain credibility among the militant youth to whom he was trying to give leadership and guidance. But this was not just an opportunistic attempt to wriggle out of a tight corner; Tutu genuinely believed in, and was able to justify theologically, the principle of a just war in the face of intolerable oppression. "I will never tell someone to pick up a gun," he once said in an attempt to explain the ambiguity of his position, "but I will pray for the man who picks up the gun, pray that he will be less cruel than he might otherwise have been, because he is a member of the community."[1] Careful though he was, it inevitably meant once again that he sailed close to the wind, stopping just short of inviting the capital charge of treason.

But, ironically, it was among the militant "comrades" that Tutu ran into the most vehement criticism for his position on violence. For all his intellectualising of the legitimacy of a just war, such was his abhorrence of violence, his deep sense of the inherent sanctity of all human life, that he sometimes flung himself with reckless courage into the way of militant mobs intent on wreaking terrible revenge on individuals they regarded as police informers, sell-outs or simply those termed "system blacks", performing jobs within the apartheid bureaucracy.

The ranks of the broad liberation movement were riddled at the time with informers, often young activists who had been captured and "turned" by the security forces – either through torture, the threat of execution or just plain bribery – into spies for the apartheid state and informers on their erstwhile comrades. The security forces called them *askaris*; to the comrades they were *impimpis*. This fabricated word has no known linguistic derivation but seemed to resonate with the special odium of a pimp, with a prefix and suffix added. As far as the comrades were concerned, impimpis had to be killed, and the chosen method of execution in the adrenalised fury of those days was by a cruel method known as necklacing, which involved putting a car tyre around the victim's neck, filling it with petrol and setting it ablaze.

On at least two occasions, Tutu, a small and quite frail man, then in his fifties, stopped the executions by plunging into the frenzied crowd and rescuing the intended victim. The first occasion was when Tutu and a colleague, Bishop Simeon Nkoane, came upon a mob attacking a man some accused of being an informer as mourners were leaving the funeral of four comrades who had been killed the previous week in what looked like security force assassinations. Yelling, "Impimpi! Impimpi!" the mob beat the man to the ground, doused him with petrol and were about to set him ablaze when Tutu reached the victim and, with Nkoane's help, pulled him away and put him in Nkoane's nearby car. When Tutu admonished the crowd, telling them theirs should be a noble and righteous struggle, they shouted back at him, "Why don't you let us deal with these dogs the way they treat us?"

The second rescue was at the funeral of a prominent civil rights lawyer, Griffiths Mxenge, who had been butchered by state assassins (led by an *askari* named Almond Nofomela) who hacked him to death with pangas, knives and daggers late at night on a football field in Durban. Mxenge's terrible death aroused intense anger throughout the liberation movement and, again, as mourners left the makeshift platform where Tutu had delivered the funeral oration outside a tiny Eastern Cape hamlet, the cry of "Impimpi" went up from the crowd, and a group of youths pounced on a man among them. As they pummelled him to the ground, a tyre appeared seemingly from nowhere. But before it could be slipped around his neck, Tutu burst through the group and flung himself across the bleeding man's prostrate body, calling to the crowd to back off. They withdrew reluctantly and, as Tutu stood up, his cassock stained with the man's blood, he called to aides to carry the man to a car and drive him away. They did so but, later that night, to Tutu's dismay, the avengers tracked the man down and completed their execution.

Tutu, appalled by the continuation of necklace killings and frustrated by his inability to stop them, threatened at one point to leave the country if the incendiary comrades did not heed him.

TUTU: THE AUTHORISED PORTRAIT

The young radicals were unimpressed. "Let him go," a group of them declared after meeting in Soweto to discuss his threat, "then we can get on with the revolution without him restraining us."

Tutu again felt the hostility of the youths to his pleas for moderation when he addressed a huge funeral rally of some forty-five thousand in the Johannesburg township of Alexandra at the height of the violence in February 1986. He had tried to intercede by conveying the community's grievances to the government, and had to report back that the authorities had done no more than undertake to look into their objections. The anger of the crowd was directed at him. For once his sparkling rhetoric failed to stir them. Sullen faces stared at him as he delivered his address and there were even some shouted interruptions. Afterwards a smaller group surrounded him and tried to prevent him from leaving as they bombarded him with questions about how he expected them to redress their injustices. Eventually an aide muscled his way through the crowd and pushed Tutu into a car.

The government, meanwhile, continued to accuse him of condoning violence. Yet it was Tutu's advocacy of the seemingly milder issues of economic sanctions and disinvestment that made life even more difficult for him, prompting a furious reaction in the white community and, most painfully for him, disapproval within the body of his own Anglican Church and among his white liberal supporters as well. Such eminent figures as Alan Paton, the celebrated author and leader of South Africa's Liberal Party, and Helen Suzman, who for thirteen tough years was the sole human rights voice speaking out forcefully in the all-white and overwhelmingly male Parliament in Cape Town, opposed him vigorously. "I do not understand how your Christian conscience allows you to advocate disinvestment ..." Paton wrote angrily to Tutu. "It would go against my deepest principles to advocate anything that could put a man, and especially a black man, out of a job."[2] But Tutu was steadfast, insisting that the vast majority of black people would willingly endure such hardships if it would bring an end to the system of apartheid under which they all lived.

Tutu triggered this surge of condemnation during a visit to Denmark when he chastised the Danes in a television interview for buying South African coal. When the interviewer asked whether a boycott would not cause black workers to lose their jobs, Tutu replied that such suffering would be temporary, while the suffering caused by apartheid looked as though it was "going to go on and on and on".[3]

The government went ballistic. Interior minister Alwyn Schlebusch, who was responsible for issuing passports, expressed his "disgust" and summoned Tutu to Pretoria to tell him he was guilty of economic sabotage and should retract or apologise.[4] Police minister Louis le Grange delivered a furious speech in Parliament, accusing Tutu of promoting disinvestment, the evasion of military service, labour unrest and furthering the aims and objects of the ANC – all crimes under South Africa's security legislation. President Botha denounced him as "public enemy number one" and called on church members to repudiate him.[5]

But Tutu remained unrepentant, arguing that economic pressure was necessary to bring about change in the country. When a group of business leaders who were members of the Anglican Church met with Tutu to remonstrate with him, he listened carefully and then – according to the Reverend Njongonkulu Ndungane, who was the church's public relations officer at the time and later Tutu's successor as archbishop of Cape Town – responded with a challenge of his own: "If you can tell me of an alternative non-violent strategy that will bring an end to apartheid," he said, "then I will abandon my commitment to sanctions and go round the world pursuing your approach until we reach our goal. But if you cannot, then I will stick with sanctions."[6] According to Ndungane, the businessmen had nothing to suggest.

For several years, egged on by sustained vilification from the right-wing press and the pro-government national broadcasting service, Tutu was the subject of blind hatred in the mainstream white population. He received abusive phone calls and death threats. Crude graffiti appeared on walls. One day a group of right-wing extremists wearing crash helmets burst into his office, yelled abuse at him and flung thirty silver coins at his desk. A special dirty tricks unit of the state security service, called the Strategic Communications (Stratcom), started a smear campaign through pamphlets and planting of whispered slanders to members of the pro-government media

– culminating in a bizarre operation when Stratcom agents hung the foetus of a monkey outside Tutu's home in an apparent attempt to make supposed superstitious township folk think he was under some kind of witchcraft spell. In fact, all it did was bemuse them.

The hate campaign reached a climax on 31 August 1988 when President Botha ordered his most ruthless special operations unit to bomb the building housing the South African Council of Churches (SACC) headquarters, called Khotso House (House of Peace), in downtown Johannesburg. The bombing, carried out at night, destroyed the multistoreyed building but fortunately injured no one. Moreover, Tutu had left the SACC by that time and was serving as archbishop of Cape Town, but the fact that the head of state had gone to such lengths as to personally order so dramatic an attack reflected the visceral hatred he and his government felt for Tutu and the organisation he had mobilised to arouse the conscience of the world against what they bluntly called the "evil" of apartheid.

The great irony of the South African story, of course, is that the white establishment's vicious attacks on Tutu helped him retain credibility in the black community despite his moderation. Not only the youth but many adult blacks were often irritated by Tutu's calls for moderation in the polarised passions of the time, and felt he took his message of Christian forgiveness too far, but the government's malicious harassment of him and his family kept bringing them back to his side and entrenching his leadership status. Without that, Tutu might well have lost his credibility, especially after making two fruitless visits to President Botha to plead for an easing of the regime's heavy crackdown on activists during a state of emergency in the mid-1980s. He could easily have been dismissed as a sell-out and suffered the fate of Zimbabwe's Bishop Abel Muzorewa, who faded into obscurity after being drawn into a coalition with that country's despised white leader, Ian Smith. Instead, thanks to Vorster, Botha and their thuggish security goons, Tutu was able to sustain his interim leadership and carry his non-racialism into the transition process, where its principles were embedded in the country's new constitution, and his idealistic vision of a "rainbow nation of God" became the popular slogan of the new South Africa.

Eventually the government reluctantly yielded to diplomatic pressures and reissued him a passport, which Schlebusch had seized earlier, to enable him to accept an invitation to attend the

9 April 1985

The Hon. F.W. de Klerk
Minister of National Education
  and Home Affairs
P.O. Box 15
CAPE TOWN.
8000.

Dear Mr. Minister,

<u>re : South African Passport</u>

As you are no doubt aware, I travel on a South African
Document for travel purposes whose validity is extended
on an ad hoc application on my part.

I think the situation in which I am placed is in fact
a ridiculous one.   The State President announced that
the matter of our citizenship was being reconsidered.

In the meantime I travel with facilities which quite
preposterously describe my nationality as "undeterminable
at present".   When I announce this fact at meetings
overseas I do not need to comment any further.   It is
such a blatantly ridiculous and utterly unjust situation
that my overseas audiences are left aghast at the enormity
of what the policy of denationalising blacks actually entails.

It is a gratuitous embarrassment to our country.   I have
travelled on a South African passport before and request
that you reissue me with one valid for all countries and
for the normal period.

I retain my known opinions about the policy of apartheid as
utterly evil, unChristian and immoral which I have expressed
and will continue to express here and abroad.   I will continue
to call for pressure to be exerted on your Government as yet
not a call for disinvestment.   When I am prevented from
travelling, my viewpoint gains wider publicity than if I had
been permitted to travel.   You may recall the publicity that
surrounded my not being permitted to go to New York to receive
an honorary degree from Columbia University.

I therefore urge you as a matter of expediency and good sense and
equity to issue me with a South African passport now.   I have
applied to be allowed to go to the United States of America
in May to speak at our daughter's graduation.   I hope to hear
positively from you on both counts.

God bless you.

Yours sincerely,

national convention of the Episcopal Church in New Orleans in September 1982. Tutu struck a chord with his American audiences, which grew with time and established him in their eyes as the authentic voice of South Africa's oppressed black masses, whose cause until then had seemed distant and somewhat abstract to Americans, since there was no leading figure to personify it in the popular imagination. Suddenly Tutu filled that gap.

His warm humanism and unique preaching style – a combination of evangelical energy and theological intellectualism delivered in plain, down-to-earth language strewn with colloquialisms and self-deprecating humour – charmed and captivated American audiences. Americans began seeing television newscasts night after night of police breaking up the mass funeral rallies in South Africa's black townships in the mid-1980s: baton-charging, tear-gassing, beating up and shooting the young demonstrators. Tutu was there among them, looking small and vulnerable in his clerical robes. It evoked images of America's own civil rights struggle, with Bull Connor and his dogs attacking the marchers in Selma, Alabama. For many, and especially students, Tutu began to take on the mantle of the martyred conscience of America: Dr Martin Luther King Jr. Suddenly the American public was able to identify with the anti-apartheid struggle; model squatter camps sprang up on university campuses, built by impassioned students who could barely pinpoint where South Africa was on the global map but for whom the anti-apartheid struggle had become a tangible moral cause with an identifiable and very human leader. The result was a political tsunami. When President Ronald Reagan, following his passive policy of constructive engagement towards South Africa, vetoed a congressional vote to impose sanctions on the country, the legislators, responsive as always to such waves of popular passion, overrode the veto.

It was another critical moment in the liberation struggle, mobilising international pressure to add to the intensifying internal crisis. Within a year of the veto override, forty American companies had pulled out of South Africa, with another fifty following suit in the next year. The crunch came when Chase Manhattan Bank refused to roll over short-term loans to South Africa, sparking a chain reaction as other international banks followed suit. As the rand currency plunged 35 per cent overnight and the government found itself facing a financial crisis, even the Great Crocodile flinched. President Botha and his cabinet cobbled together a constitutional reform arrangement, giving the country's Indian and mixed-race "coloured" communities the right to vote for

representatives of their own in separate and subservient chambers of Parliament, while leaving the black African majority still with no more than their Potemkin bantustans and the merest smidgen of local government rights in the black townships of so-called "white" South Africa. It was intended as a conciliatory gesture but it elicited even greater pressure, for the activists rightly saw it as a sign of weakening resolve. Looking back, it is clear that although there was still a decade and a half to go, that was the key turning point that marked the beginning of the decline and fall of apartheid.

In the years that followed, we watched the influence of this remarkable man expand, both directly and vicariously, until it infused the entire nation. We watched the reluctant admiration that his courage evoked from even his bitterest enemies as he stood up to the extremists on both sides, spoke truth to power and chastised the excesses of his own people. We watched in awe as he linked arms with clerics of other faiths to lead great liberation marches of tens of thousands of people past the guns and armoured vehicles of the formidable, nuclear-armed apartheid government.

An ecumenical army of theological crusaders marching as to war.

And then to peace.

When at last that memorable day arrived, and Nelson Mandela and the other black political leaders walked out of prison and returned from exile, Desmond Tutu, true to his word, left his political leadership role, his warrior role in the liberation struggle, to become the country's principal champion of peace: the crusader for reconciliation with the people who had harassed and humiliated him and his family and his entire race for so long.

It was as chairman of South Africa's Truth and Reconciliation Commission (TRC), itself perhaps the most remarkable process of a national public confessional ever undertaken, that Desmond Tutu reached the apex of his career. The TRC has its critics, but on one thing all are agreed: it was a triumph for Tutu, the consummation of his role as a Nobel laureate of peace, and his emergence as the moral conscience of the new South Africa. It also completed the transformation of his public image from Botha's "public enemy number one" into an icon of national affection.[7]

But Tutu's role does not end at the borders of his own country. In his years since retirement he has assumed a new and more universal importance as he has plunged into conflict areas around the globe with an urgent message to governments to follow the South African example and negotiate with groups they regard as terrorists. In his role as a member of The Elders, a group of eminent retired leaders, and through his own personal international ministry, Tutu has involved himself in the conflicts of Northern Ireland, the Middle East, Burma, Tibet, Rwanda, Darfur, Cyprus, Kenya and Sri Lanka – always with the same message: "There can be no future without forgiveness".

Nor is it just empty rhetoric. Tutu brings to these debates not only the moral authority of his own record but an evolving, all-embracing theology: a respect for all religious faiths that acknowledges the moral and spiritual validity of each. It is an all-inclusive ecumenism that contrasts sharply with the trend towards a regressive fundamentalism in religions and cultures across the world and that lies at the heart of so many of today's conflicts.

Our turbulent priest is not just a man for all South Africa, but for all humanity.

Left, above: Tutu is greeted by placard-holding demonstrators as he arrives at Jan Smuts International Airport (now O. R. Tambo International Airport), Johannesburg, 19 May 1988.

Left, below: Tutu, flanked by Bishops Sigisbert Ndwandwe (left) and Simeon Nkoane (right), leads a group of white priests on a procession through the streets of Johannesburg. Both bishops worked closely with Tutu: Simeon Nkoane presided over the Duduza funeral with Tutu in July 1985, and between them they managed to save a man from the awful fate of "necklacing".

At the height of the hate campaign against Tutu, a small cameo event occurred that foreshadowed the emotional instability of white South Africans that has seen them shift from the hatred of the apartheid years to a point today of near hero-worship of both Tutu and Mandela. When – after repeated ballots and in the face of strong opposition from an organised group of lay Anglicans – the elective assembly of the Johannesburg Diocese finally chose Tutu to be their new bishop, a former mayor of the city, Cecil Long, issued a press statement announcing that he, a devout Anglican all his life, was leaving the church in protest. I read the report on the front page of the *Star* newspaper with a mixture of amusement and outrage.

On impulse, I sat down at my desk and penned a brief two-sentence rejoinder, which I faxed to the editor of the *Star* saying that I, an ex-editor of one of the city's leading newspapers and a lapsed Anglican who had turned my back on the church because of the vacuous ritualism of so many of its white clergy who for years had nothing meaningful to say in the face of the great moral challenges facing the country, was going to rejoin the church now that it had elected a bishop who was prepared to speak truth to power.

The next day the paper splashed my brief statement on its front page, presenting it as a rejoinder to ex-mayor Long. I was frankly startled, then a little alarmed. "Gosh," I said to my wife Sue, "I'll have to live up to this now." So I called some Anglican friends, who directed me to the rector of a church in the affluent suburb of Bryanston, who they assured me would make my wife and me welcome. Father Arnold Hirst did more than that: he proposed a special welcoming service for us the following Sunday morning and we planned a surprise event for the congregation. I phoned a friend, George Mxadana, who was the leader of a wonderful Soweto choir called Imilonji KaNtu that I had heard perform on a number of occasions and greatly admired. I asked George whether he and his choir could perform at the Bryanston church next Sunday morning, and he agreed.

It was with some trepidation that Sue and I approached the lovely little stone church on the day. Congregants were trickling in to find that the thirty-odd members of the choir had already occupied pews at the back. There were a few thin-lipped faces and some quick backward glances as the suburban congregants filled the pews upfront. For many, if not all, it was probably the first time they had seen black faces in their church. It turned out to be an unusually large gathering and by the time the service started there was standing room only. Father Hirst welcomed Sue and me to the parish, then introduced the choir, which he said would sing a special hymn.

He did not name the hymn, which was indeed special: a dramatic piece of indigenous music composed by an eighteenth-century Xhosa spiritualist named Ntsikana, who was converted to Christianity but remained largely indigenous and blended Christian liturgy with African symbols and music. His triumph, which the choir was to sing here, is simply called the "Great Hymn", a powerful call-and-response praise song to God performed as an exchange between the lead singer and the choir facing each other along the full length of the aisle. George Mxadana and his choir had sung this hymn by candlelight outside the Tutus' home in Soweto when Senator Edward Kennedy had visited there during his 1984 tour of South Africa, and much later Leah Tutu was to choose it for her seventieth birthday celebration. But, to white South African suburbia, it was a cultural jewel of their own land as distant as Outer Mongolia.

As George began the great hymn in his rich, deep baritone – bowing and making sweeping motions with his arms as he backed through the nave of the church – and the big choir responded in its exquisitely harmonised cadences, the sounds echoing off the walls of the little stone church, the effect on the congregation was electrifying. They were riveted, entranced, visibly elevated by the sheer power and spiritual impact of the "Great Hymn". As the music ended, the church fell silent. One generally doesn't applaud in a church but, in any case, the congregation seemed choked still, with emotion. As the congregation began to file out, there were tears in a number of eyes. Some shook hands emotionally with George and members of the choir. Some came over to thank Sue and me, and tell us they had never heard anything so powerful and moving before.

As Sue and I looked at each other alone afterwards, we realised something in our country had been touched.

Ntsikana's "Great Hymn"

Ulo Thixo omkhulu, ngosezulwini;
Ungu Wena-wena Khaka lenyaniso.
Ungu Wena-wena Nqaba yenyaniso.
Ungu Wena-wena Hlati lenyaniso.
Ungu Wena-wen' uhlel' enyangwaneni.
Ulo dal' ubom, wadala phezulu.
Lo Mdal' owadala wadala izulu.
Lo Menzi weenkwenkwezi noZilimela;
Yabinza inkwenkwezi, isixelela.
Lo Menzi wemfaman' uzenza ngabom?
Lathetha ixilongo lisibizile.
Ulongqin' izingela imiphefumlo.
Ulohlanganis' imihlamb' eyalanayo.
Ulomkhokeli wasikhokela thina.
Ulengub' inkhul' esiyambatha thina.
Ozandla Zakho zinamanxeba Wena.
Onyawo Zakho zinamanxeba Wena.
Ugazi Lakho limrholo yini na?
Ugazi Lakho liphalalele thina.
Le mali emkulu-na siyibizile?
Lo mzi Wakhona-na siwubizile?

Thou art the great God – the one who is in heaven.
It is thou, thou Shield of Truth,
it is thou, thou Tower of Truth,
it is thou, thou Bush of Truth,
it is thou, thou who sittest in the highest,
thou art the creator of life,
thou madest the regions above.
The creator who madest the heavens also,
the maker of stars and the Pleiades –
the shooting stars declare it unto us.
The maker of the blind, of thine own will didst thou
    make them.
The trumpet speaks – for us it calls,
thou art the Hunter who hunts for souls.
Thou art the Leader who goes before us,
thou art the Great Mantle which covers us.
Thou art he whose hands are wounded;
thou art he whose feet are wounded;
thou art he whose blood is a trickling stream –
    and why?
Thou art he whose blood was spilled for us.
For this great price we call,
for thine own place we call.

CHAPTER TWO

....

LIBERATOR OF THE EXODUS

The most remarkable feature in the life of someone who has reached such heights as a theologian is that Tutu did not become a clergyman until he was thirty years old, by which time he was already married and had children. He had not even thought of the priesthood as a career in his youth. He wanted to be a doctor and had applied to and been accepted by the medical school of the University of the Witwatersrand in Johannesburg, but he couldn't raise the tuition fees. So he became a teacher instead and practised that profession until 1957. He quit in disgust when the apartheid government seized control of all the black mission schools, which had delivered quality education to blacks for years, and subjected them to its notorious Bantu Education system aimed at equipping black people for an inferior station in life. That was when Tutu turned to the priesthood as the only alternative career readily available to an educated black man.

Left: The editorial staff of *Normalife*, a publication produced by the students of the Pretoria Bantu Normal College. From left to right: Isaac Sibanyoni, Dee Sechele, Tutu and the Reverend Stanley Mogoba (standing at the back).

Nor was he even particularly religious in those early years. He had been a regular churchgoer, even a Sunday school teacher and a lay preacher in his local Anglican church in his early twenties, but he never thought for a moment of becoming a priest. To this day, he cannot remember any moment of epiphany that awakened his religious passion. It seems it just grew on him as he immersed himself in his faith after beginning his theological studies. That incremental transformation, from lukewarm interest to the deeply prayerful and disciplined regimen of spiritual life that Tutu leads today, is an amazing story of personal evolution.

Moreover, as Tutu's faith deepened and strengthened it drove him more and more to political action. For, unlike Karl Marx, Tutu did not see religion as the opiate of the masses. Not for him the notion of the wretched of the earth enduring the whips and scorns of everyday life in prayerful submissiveness while awaiting their reward in the hereafter. For him, life itself was sacred. If men and women were made in the image of God, if they were truly God's children, then to demean them was to demean their maker. "When you treat any human being as if they were less than a child of God," he said, "you are not just doing wrong – you are being sacrilegious. You are desecrating something that is holy. You are like someone who spits in the face of God."[1]

For Tutu, therefore, there could be no such thing as keeping politics out of religion, as the government and many of his own congregants kept insisting he should, for the two were interwoven in his concept of divine intention. God was the liberator of the Exodus, and those who served him were under an obligation to lead his people out of every kind of bondage: spiritual, political, social and economic. From that it followed, in Tutu's exegesis, that Jesus Christ was emphatically on the side of the poor, and that the Bible was "the most revolutionary, the most radical book there is".[2]

So it came about that the mainstream English-language churches, under Tutu's leadership, became a collective political force at the cutting edge of the struggle against apartheid during those confrontational years of the seventies and eighties when the black leadership was silenced inside the country.

If Nelson Mandela's life was a long walk to freedom, Tutu's was a highly compressed one. Once he became a priest at the age of thirty, things happened fast, propelling him swiftly up the ladder of seniority in his church and into the thick of the anti-apartheid struggle. By the time he was thirty-six, he was a lecturer in theology, at forty-four he was dean of the largest cathedral in South Africa, at forty-five he was bishop of Lesotho, at forty-six he was bishop of

This page:
Tutu's father,
Zachariah Zelilo Tutu.

Opposite: Tutu's mother,
Aletta Dorothea Tutu
with Tutu's nephew,
Eudy Zamille Morrison,
the son of Tutu's
sister Sylvia.

Johannesburg, playing a leading role in the struggle, and at fifty-four he was archbishop of Cape Town and primate of all southern Africa.

Desmond Tutu was born in a black township outside the modest "white" town of Klerksdorp, 120 kilometres west of Johannesburg, on 7 October 1931. His father, Zachariah Zelilo Tutu, commonly known as ZZ, was a member of the Xhosa tribe from the Eastern Cape Province. His mother, Aletta Dorothea Mavoertsek Mathlare, was a Motswana from the Sotho-Tswana linguistic group. So Tutu was literally born into defiance of apartheid's ethnic categorisation, for he could not be assigned to one of its designated "nationalities". When eventually the government reluctantly reissued him with a travel document (not a passport, having withdrawn it when he began speaking out politically), the space for his citizenship bore the incongruous words "Undeterminable at present".

Tutu was a frail child who contracted polio in infancy and nearly died. His second name, Mpilo, meaning "life" in the isiXhosa language, expressed his parents' hope that he would survive, the more so because his birth followed the death of an infant sibling. The polio left Desmond with a weakened right hand, forcing him to learn to write with his left. He later contracted tuberculosis as a teenager, and spent twenty months in a sanatorium, but eventually developed a robust constitution which has carried him into his octogenarian years.

Zachariah Tutu was a teacher educated at Lovedale, a mission school in the Eastern Cape that produced many of South Africa's black intellectual elite. ZZ instilled in his children a discipline of study and a love of books. He had a stern demeanour and occasionally drank too much and beat his wife, to young Desmond's great distress. Tutu's mother, known to everyone as Matse, had an elementary school education followed by some training in domestic science. She was a short, dumpy woman with a big heart, and Tutu contends it was from her he inherited his strong sense of compassion and humanitarianism, as well as his large nose – a physical feature he likes to use in his witty, self-deprecating way to illustrate the absurdity of racial discrimination. To be born black, he points out, is as existentially indeterminate a condition as to be born with a large nose. Therefore, to discriminate against people because of their skin colour is as irrational as to decree that people with big noses are inherently superior to those with small noses.

The Tutu family left Klerksdorp when Desmond was four, moving to the black township outside a western Transvaal town called Ventersdorp where ZZ was appointed headmaster of the black primary school. (Ventersdorp was to acquire a singular notoriety in later years, when an extreme racist named Eugene Terre'Blanche established the headquarters of his neo-Nazi Afrikaner Weerstandsbeweging (Afrikaner Resistance Movement) there, from where he tried to launch his own armed struggle against South Africa's transition to non-racial democracy.) Desmond began school there as a barefoot kid living in a spartan three-roomed house with no electricity, and attending

"My earliest and strongest recollection of my mother was of her amazing generosity. I remember as if it were yesterday how she never cooked a meal that would be sufficient just for her family. She always had to run the gauntlet of my father's criticism that she was being wasteful for cooking such large meals. But my mother ignored those strictures and continued to expect that someone or someones would pitch up and we should be able to extend

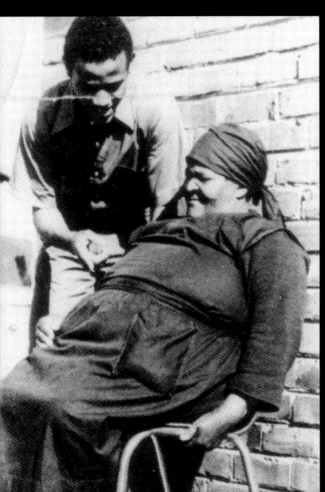

the hospitality of a meal to such unexpected guests. And I think this was fairly common knowledge in our neighbourhood for there were those who seemed to know when to pitch up just as Mother was dishing up. Then she would be in her element.

I loved her dearly. My father often drank a lot and sometimes would assault my mother. I would fume, getting really angry with him. I know that had I been physically stronger I would have fought him.

Leah, my wife, called my mother 'the comforter of the afflicted' because she always took the side of whomever was the worst off in an argument. I have told audiences that I remember my mother physically – short and stumpy, with a large nose. Then I would add that I hope I can remember her spiritually – to emulate her generosity and compassion and concern for the weak. When I have been asked who the greatest influence in my life has been on me I have without hesitation replied: 'my mother'.

Thank you God for women, for our mothers. Thank you for my mother."

Gogo, our mother, left us there in Ventersdorp and went to work [as a maid] in Krugersdorp. She could not find work in Ventersdorp. We had a lovely time with my dad. On Sundays we used to go down to the river to have a bath. We moved, with my brother, to where my mother was working. [She was a 'live-in' domestic worker for a white family. She occupied an outside room on their property in an area zoned for residence for white families although, by law, they should not have been living there.] We left our father in Ventersdorp. They allowed me to stay with my mother but my brother had no place to stay. He stayed in the township in Roodepoort with my grand-aunt. It was so difficult for him; he wanted to be with us all the time.

Boy was a delicate child. My brother used to have a lot of friends. In those days we used to mix. Boys and girls played together, not doing all these silly things that are being done today. And my brother would come back: "Oh, I'm sick. My head aches." This, that. "My tooth, my what, my what-what." Gogo loved him so much. She'd never say anything that was not right to her boy. My mother didn't like it when he was apart from her. She would rather I'd gone down to Roodepoort and stayed there and my brother stayed with my mother. It went on and on and on until my mother asked the father there in charge: "Where have you seen a mother staying that side and the children separated from the mother?". So he gave my brother a place to stay with us. We were very happy.

There was a school not very far away. My brother was very brilliant, very clever. He just went through all his classes. He sat for his standard-six examinations. As he was a brilliant person, we were expecting very good results. But what happened? We were so disappointed. My brother failed. He cried. We were all sad.

My father had a friend, Mr Madibane, who had a school. My father went to that friend of his and told him that "such and such a thing has happened to my son". Mr Madibane said, "Bring him." When he got there he did everything very well.

We were so close! It was even more when we were both attending school at Madibane. But my brother liked studying and reading. I was not interested in that. I liked playing. When we were still very small we used to fight ... and Gogo used to take my brother's side. She was just interested that her boy was all right.

As poor as we were at home, we loved one another. It was a beautiful, loving family. We grew up so well because Gogo was so loving. My father was also, but he liked drinking a lot. Despite us being poor, we never

slept hungry. My parents loved giving to people. My father would go on an empty stomach rather than a person coming into the house being hungry; he'd give that person his plate. My brother takes after them in that. He shares. I'm not praising him because he's my brother. He's very good, very, very good. He's a kind man, very kind. But when he gets cross, he gets cross. He used to be cross with [our father] Mkhulu. When Mkhulu used to fight with Gogo he used to be so cross and answer back!

Then he got sick. By then he was staying in Sophiatown with my uncle, because we didn't have money for him to move in. He went to stay with Father Huddleston. He got sick and Father Huddleston had to take him to Coronation Hospital. Father Huddleston came to the house to report. We were so shocked when we saw a white man coming into a black man's house during those times. Father Huddleston said, "I came to tell you that Desmond is in hospital." Gogo was so so worried. The following morning Gogo went to the hospital and we found him there. He didn't look seriously ill but he was very sick.

They had to transfer him to Rietfontein Hospital. That's in a dangerous place. Today you cannot walk there, being a woman. Gogo used to go. The bus used to stop very far away and she had to walk right down through a little forest to get to my brother. But she got there. Every month Gogo went to check Boy. I also sometimes went with her. Boy stayed a long time in hospital. He was writing and doing all these things at the school. He sat for his junior certificate and he got very, very good marks. So he went on to his matric. He was so good he went to Bantu Normal College. He passed there and got a post at Madibane. He stayed there for a year. Then he came to teach in Munsieville.

One day I was with Ntemi [his wife, Nomalizo Leah Tutu] and there were people who were busy in the rubbish bins looking for food. When we got to the house Ntemi told Boy. He asked her, "Did you give them something?" She answered, "No, I had nothing." He said, "You know, when one says, 'I'm hungry,' I know what hunger means." He told me, "My sister, the way we were poor at home, I don't want my children to grow up the way I've grown up. I don't ever want them to live in other people's houses. I want to give them a better life." And he has given them a better life. God has provided that and God has given him all that. He said another thing: "If my children are working, I don't want them to give me their money. I don't want their money, that's theirs."

was five years older than my brother. He was born in Klerksdorp. That's where my father was head of a school called an amalgamated school. That's where we lived.

My mother took in washing from the white town. We used to collect the washing in town and then she would do it at home. If my aunts were there, they would help. That's what she did for most of the time.

My brother and I were very close to each other except that there were times we didn't agree. He was very stubborn from childhood. He was really very stubborn. A story I will never forget was from one winter's day. We were very cold that morning. Mum used to sew pyjamas, for us. She would buy material, flannelette material, and make us pyjamas and night-dresses. On this day we were alone. I don't know where my mum had gone. I think my dad was at school. It was very cold. There was a plantation next to where we lived and we used to get our firewood from there. That morning I gathered the wood and brought it home. We made a fire outside. The flames went up. Boy was just stubborn. He kept saying, "It's cold. I'm getting next to the fire. I'm getting next to the fire." When he was close to the fire, it caught his pyjamas and whoosh! It was just flames all over. I tried to dampen the flames, but I didn't know any first aid then. Instead of rolling him down, I patted the flames on him and so he got hurt and burnt. The burns were quite serious. He had to go to hospital. When he was in hospital we used to visit him daily. He made such a noise in the hospital. He didn't want to stay there. Whenever we visited him we would hear him crying, telling the sisters that he wanted to go home. I don't know how long he was in the hospital. They managed to help him with the burns. I think after a week or two weeks he was discharged to go home. But that scar, that scar remains to this day. It's there because he was stubborn and he has been stubborn ever since.

We used to hold hands together when going to school. When he was attending school at Madibane High we would be together every morning running for the train. There was a local train at the end of the location and we would run to that train every day. Every morning we would leave at such and such a time to get that train. Otherwise there was no other transport for him to get to school and me to get to work. He would be on the same train with me. He would get off at Westbury and then go to the school that he attended. I was already working by then. When we travelled together in the morning, it was when I was going to the

school where I was teaching in Crown Mines.

He used to visit me a lot when we lived in Standerton. After my husband died, whenever I needed help, he would come. I was already a Seventh Day Adventist by then. When I went out to church affairs, church meetings, or when it was holiday, every holiday he spent in Standerton. I would leave him to look after the business. I owned a general dealership.

We two were very attached to church affairs. I used to go to the AME [African Methodist Episcopal] Church. Our younger sister Gugu and he followed me to every church I went. I was about ten years old then. We grew very religious the two of us. And then, when I went to St Peter's for my secondary education, I joined the Anglican Church. When I came back home I found him still very attached to church affairs. I said to the whole family, "Let us join". We used to go to the Methodist Church here but, when I came back from St Peter's I said we should change. I said to them, "We are now becoming Anglicans." So it was after that time that we all were Anglicans.

He was very much attached to our mother, Gogo. They were very much attached to each other. Before he was bishop and other things he and Mazi [Nomalizo Leah Tutu] lived in a garage. They rented a garage. I was staying in Wattville then so we used to visit each other. But each time he moved from a place to another, Gogo was always the first to visit. She wouldn't visit us first. But if Boy moved from place to place, Gogo would be the first to visit. They were very much attached to each other and they looked alike, especially the nose. Really Boy took after my mother's nose. He even inherited her attitude and everything. My mother was somebody who didn't like it when people quarrelled and had disputes. They gave her a name that she was a reconciler. We called her our mediator. Whenever there was a problem in the family, Leah would say, "Oh, there comes the mediator!"

Mkhulu, our father, was a great storyteller; he would tell us stories. He would say, "Experience is the greatest teacher, but you pay heavy school fees." He liked that. Mkhulu used to drink a lot. There are some things that were not pleasing when he had taken a lot of drinks. Mkhulu was very fond of having family meetings, especially when he had taken a lot of drink. But some of the things my brother didn't agree with. That's why they didn't go very well. But mostly what made them not to agree was just that Mkhulu just liked his drink. When he had taken a lot of drink, he would just be careless in talking and he wouldn't be nice to Gogo.

kindergarten classes in a room that had no desks, only benches. Tutu's main achievement during the family's sojourn in Ventersdorp was that he learned Afrikaans in the predominantly Afrikaner *dorp* (town), a vital tool in his later life as he tangled with leaders of the apartheid regime.

The Tutu family was never poor by black South African standards, but money was always scarce. When Desmond was ten years old, Matse left for Johannesburg to supplement their income by taking a job as a cook in an institution for the blind. That began a peripatetic phase in Desmond's young life as ZZ kept shifting to new jobs trying to get closer to Matse. They moved half a dozen times before he finally landed the position of headmaster at St Paul's Anglican School in Munsieville. The family established their permanent home there, and Desmond began commuting to high school in Johannesburg's Western Native Township, where he eventually matriculated.

The only problem was that the commute was long – Desmond had to take a taxi, then a train and walk the final stretch, returning the same way – which meant the family soon found they could not afford the fares. Happily, they were able to get him into a hostel for boys run by an Anglican order called the Community of the Resurrection in its Sophiatown mission. And so began a relationship that was to transform Tutu's life when later he left teaching to become a priest.

The Community of the Resurrection is a small Anglican monastic order founded in the industrial north of England in 1892 by a handful of churchmen who felt the church had become too aloof and cut off from the lives of working-class people toiling in the mills and collieries of that region. The monks, who take vows of poverty, chastity and obedience, live together as a community at the House of the Resurrection in Mirfield, Yorkshire, where they follow a strict daily routine of prayer, Bible readings, meditation and worship, but are committed at the same time to vigorous social and political involvement on behalf of the struggling community among whom they live.

Nowhere has the Community of the Resurrection had a greater impact than in South Africa, thanks to the founders of its Sophiatown mission: Father Raymond Raynes and Father Trevor Huddleston. The latter particularly had an enormous influence on Desmond Tutu and, in fact, became his role model. Tutu still recalls the first time he saw the tall priest in a big black hat and flowing white cassock. Desmond was walking with his mother in the street when Huddleston walked by and doffed his hat. "You could have knocked me down with a feather …" Tutu recounted years later. "He doffed his hat to my mother. Now that seemed a perfectly normal thing I suppose for him, but for me, it was almost mind-boggling, that a white man could doff his hat to my mother, a black woman, really a nonentity in South Africa's terms."[3]

Huddleston was a larger-than-life figure in Sophiatown of the 1950s, and Sophiatown itself was a larger-than-life community in South Africa. It was a slum really; it was poor, overcrowded, dirty and violent, but it had a vitality drawn from a polyglot community living on the edge: writers, artists, musicians, tricksters and gangsters, all struggling to survive and be creative in the process. Lewis Nkosi, one of its rising literary stars at the time, likened it to Elizabethan England: "the cacophonous, swaggering world …" he wrote, "which gave us the closest parallel to our own mode of existence; the cloak and dagger stories of Shakespeare, the marvellously gay and dangerous times of change in Great Britain, came closest to reflecting our condition."[4]

It couldn't last, of course. In the eyes of apartheid's obsessive social engineers, this raucous mixed-race community in the heart of what was supposed to be "white" Johannesburg was an abomination. It had to go. And so in one of the crudest crimes of the whole apartheid era, the bulldozers were called out and Sophiatown with its 70,000 inhabitants was erased, to be replaced by a dreary lower-middle-class white suburb obscenely named Triomf – a triumph for apartheid.

But, while it lasted, Huddleston was a dominant figure there, always with crowds of children swarming around him. He loved children, and Tutu especially. When Desmond, in the midst of his high school years, was diagnosed with tuberculosis and sent to a sanatorium near Alexandra township on the far side of the city, Huddleston visited him regularly, bringing him books and often a car-full of playmates. The bond between them grew.

Huddleston, who described himself as an Anglican socialist, had been deeply influenced while a student at Oxford by the Great Depression and the sight of hunger marches from the

We were both close to the same person who spoke about the Lord: Archbishop Trevor Huddleston. Huddleston got me my first trumpet. He always asked, "Have you ever met Desmond? He is a wonderful, wonderful man. I hope you do cross paths with him." Desmond went to the seminary, St Peter's, where I went to boarding school.

I don't think that one person can give another person the kind of gift that Archbishop Tutu has, but I think that Huddleston saw somebody similar to him. He saw somebody who had the potential to be a fighter for right and for good. He saw somebody who, like him, believed so much in faith and who was totally against injustice. I think Huddleston might have just said, "If you believe in this, then go all the way." Which Archbishop Tutu did. And I think, maybe Trevor Huddleston's bravery in the face of a fascist, violent government was an inspiration. He showed that the government might act like lions, but, in the face of truth, they become lambs.

I first met Archbishop Tutu in New York through Charmaine Modjadji, who is a dear cousin. At the time, Arch was doing one of his first consciousness-raising tours of the United States, and I met him in New York. Very few people really knew who he was. It was in the early eighties. He was just as focused then as he became later. We didn't talk much then. We only really started talking when I came back home. I came back home in 1990. So it was about seven years after I had met him.

My first impression of him was that he was very quiet. I had known of his work. I knew what he was doing at home. I have always been very impressed with Arch. I admired his bravery in the face of the very draconian and very violent apartheid government. He always stood and stated his beliefs very clearly. He really believes in standing for the right thing. He doesn't care who it is; when he feels that they are insulting humanity, he just says it like it is and he's fearless. He's as fearless about it with our present government as he was during apartheid. He doesn't bat an eye to say what he means, and he means what he says. And he sticks to it. When he is confronted he calls for a meeting and he faces up to the people. He is one of the few people that I know who always proves that the truth conquers all.

The first time we had a real encounter we were at Mandela's eighty-fifth birthday party. It was at the Convention Centre. We were both in the men's room. We were standing next to each other taking a leak, and he turned around and said, "Ah! There you are, you must come and play at Leah's seventieth birthday."

So I said, "But uncle, I won't be here. I will be on tour."

"No, you must cancel the tour. You must play. It's imperative that you play."

"I can't. And then even if I had to play, you will have to at least pay the band."

"Pay the band? You must be crazy!"

So we laughed about it and he said, "We will talk." But I wasn't there. I was on tour.

....

DOMINIC WHITNALL

I was professed here in January of 1948 and in October of '48 I was sent to Sophiatown to live with Trevor [Huddleston], Matthew and Vaughn [members of the Community of Resurrection]. One of the very first jobs Trevor gave me to do was to visit the TB hospital nearby – I'm not quite sure where it was – and to find out if there were any boys or patients that would like us to come and see them. I found a black boy – I guess twelve years old. I went armed with some comics, and I gave him some of the comics and he told me that his name was Desmond. I said, "I will come again soon and bring you some more," to which he replied, "No, Father, bring me proper books."

"IF YOU COULD SAY ANYBODY SINGLE-HANDEDLY MADE APARTHEID A WORLD ISSUE, THEN THAT PERSON WAS TREVOR HUDDLESTON."

DESMOND TUTU

TUTU: THE AUTHORISED PORTRAIT

coalfields and docklands of Great Britain. He arrived in South Africa at the outbreak of World War II, when he was just thirty years old, to run the Community of the Resurrection's mission. That meant he was already entrenched there when the Afrikaner National Party won the 1948 election and began its ruthless implementation of the apartheid programme. Given his background, Huddleston was appalled and enraged. He quickly became one of the earliest and most articulate publicisers, through both his preachings and his writings, of the pain and hardships being inflicted on the black South African population. His book, *Naught for Your Comfort*, published in 1956, became a classic of anti-apartheid literature alongside Alan Paton's *Cry the Beloved Country*.

As Tutu was later to contend: "If you could say anybody single-handedly made apartheid a world issue, then that person was Trevor Huddleston."[5] But you could equally say that if anyone had a transformational impact on Tutu, that, too, was Huddleston – which means that the tall priest's work of making apartheid a world issue continued long after he was recalled to Mirfield in 1956.

Despite the long break in his schooling caused by his time in the tuberculosis sanatorium, Tutu matriculated comfortably with a university entrance pass. Then at teachers' training college in Pretoria he again flourished academically, completing the three-year teacher training course with ease and winning the college's debating prize. It was during this time that Tutu first met Mandela, when the tall and charismatic young lawyer adjudicated a debating contest between the college and the Jan H. Hofmeyr School for Social Work. Tutu was not to meet the founding father of the new South Africa again for nearly half a century, until that dazzling day of 11 February 1990 when Mandela walked out of prison after twenty-seven years and spent his first night of freedom with his then wife, Winnie, at Bishopscourt, the official residence of Archbishop Desmond Tutu of Cape Town.

Tutu took his first job as a teacher at his old school in Western Native Township while continuing to study by correspondence for a degree through the University of South Africa. That done, he moved to the bigger Krugersdorp High School where his old English teacher was headmaster.

It was during this time that Tutu married Nomalizo Leah Shenxane, who was also born in Krugersdorp, had studied for a time at ZZ's Munsieville school, and was also studying to be a teacher. He and Leah established one of the great political partnerships that has characterised South

Africa's liberation struggle heroes, along with the likes of Walter and Albertina Sisulu, Oliver and Adelaide Tambo, and, though it collapsed sadly in its final years, Nelson and Winnie Mandela.

The Tutus' first child was born a year after they were married, a son whom they named Trevor in honour of Huddleston. Sixteen months later they had a daughter, Thandeka, then in 1960 another daughter, Naomi. Finally, the last-born, Mpho, who was to follow in her father's footsteps and become an ordained Anglican priest, arrived. By then the family was in England. The major turning point in Desmond Tutu's life had taken place.

My first impression of him was that he was the stuck-up headmaster's son. When I first saw him it was early days. I was in my teens. That was Krugersdorp, where his father was the headmaster of the elementary school I went to. Elementary school in those days was longer than it is now. What would be called middle school now, was then part of elementary school. I was about thirteen or fourteen and he was two years older. The first time I saw him, his father was in our classroom and he had come to collect pocket money. I knew he was the headmaster's son who had been ill. He was in high school in a different place than where we lived.

I was great friends with his younger sister. I was in and out of his home long before I ever had visions of dating him. That didn't change my impression of him as the headmaster's stuck-up son.

He had been very ill with tuberculosis. He had been recovering and the family was really dancing around him. They sort of nursed him, or guarded him, as one does a sore tooth. But I liked him. He seemed a nice guy to have around. He was very thoughtful. He was very gentlemanly. I think his parents were very fond of me, too.

When I was in high school, I thought he looked smashing! I don't know whether he looked smashing because he was the headmaster's son or whether it was really a crush. There was always an attraction about headmasters' sons at that stage.

We started dating when I was at teacher training college. It was my last year of training. In the meantime, my friend, his younger sister, had dropped [out] and got married. I continued to visit her from college. I don't remember seeing her brother there. But then, one day, just out of the blue, there he was. He said something, I don't remember what, but just some comment. It was the first conversation we had in all those years. I think he asked about how I was faring in college, or something unimportant like that. That was when I started talking with him as equals and eventually we started dating. We dated for about two years.

The strange thing about his proposal ... I can't really, in all fairness, say that he proposed, because of how he put it. He said, "You know my parents want me to get married." I thought, "Well!" The conversation went on thereafter to other topics. And then later, when I'd gone back to college, I wrote to him and said, "Well, I think I will assist you in being obedient to your parents."

His "non-proposal" was very close to my writing the final exams of the teacher-training course that I

was taking. I was very aware of the impression I would make on our parents about my schooling. He said that he would like us to start family negotiations about our marriage in December when I got home. But I said, "You know what my mother would say if I failed? She would say, 'I'm not surprised that you failed. How could you pass exams when you were looking at being married?'" So I said he shouldn't start anything like that before my results came out. When the results came out, I had passed very well. We agreed that negotiations could start. That was after Christmas.

We were married in July. By then both his sisters were married and in their own homes. I went to live with his parents. In those days this was a done thing. You got married and went to live with your in-laws. The Xhosas have a word for it: *uyakotisa* which means you are a new *umakoti* [bride]. And *ukukotisa* [the act of being a newly-wed in the home of her husband] in true African tradition is when you want to impress your in-laws with what a good wife you are going to be to their son. You wake up early, you make them tea ... and I did absolutely nothing of the sort. It was winter when we married. It was cold. His father used to knock at our door early and say, "Hoo, don't get up, it's freezing outside! What would you have, coffee, tea or cocoa?" Desmond used to have cocoa and I would have tea. His father would bring us cocoa and tea in bed. In our African tradition that was not the done thing. It surprised my mother quite a bit how spoiled I was at my in-laws' home.

His parents loved him. They spoiled him. It was always, "Boy this" and "Boy that". He was very spoiled by his mother. His mother thought the world of him and he of her. He didn't get on that well with his father. His father sometimes drank quite a bit and he hated that. He hated when his father was soused. His father was so friendly when he was soused. He was very loving while under the influence. But Desmond didn't like it at all. He didn't want his father to drink.

We married in July and it was after Christmas when we actually moved into our own place. It was three rooms: a bedroom, a kitchen and a dining-room. But we had a sofa in the dining-room, which we used as a guest bed. There was sort of a shower with cold water which we never used as a shower; instead we used it as storage. There was no bathroom really to speak of. We used to warm water on the coal stove and have a bath in this big metal tub that we put in the centre of the room. That was the bathroom.

Desmond never cooked like my father-in-law used

to do. He was only good in cleaning. He would clean. He would wash up. Actually, I think he is one of the few African men of his age who used to wash nappies. I'm still surprised when I hear young women talking about men that won't do this and won't do that. I think he was far ahead of his time as far as helping in the house is concerned. We used to work together. He is a very tidy man, tidier than I am. He hates messes. He would get up and dust. He would get up and sweep. We just shared baby caring. From the beginning he was more of a parent than I have been. I'm very short-tempered and my children would never call out for me. It was always "Daddy, Daddy". At night, when the blankets had fallen off anybody's back, it would always be "Daddy, Daddy, my blankets have fallen off". Never "Mummy" – they knew better.

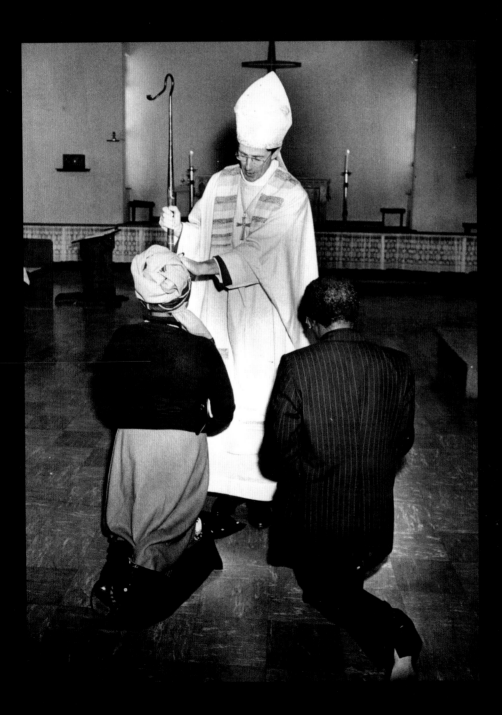

Left: Desmond and Leah are blessed by the bishop of Johannesburg, Timothy Bavin, on their twenty-fifth wedding anniversary, July 1980.

Following page: The Tutus walking in Soweto, Johannesburg, circa 1986.

CHAPTER THREE

....

A MAN OF ALMOST UNIQUE VALUE

It was on April Fool's Day 1953 that the apartheid govern-ment implemented its Bantu Education Act and ordered the churches to hand over all mission schools to government control. Minister of Education Hendrik Verwoerd made it clear that the move was aimed at equipping black people to serve their own communities and to not aspire to the "green pastures of European society" which would be closed to them.[1] This presented the churches with a huge moral dilemma: Were they to collaborate with this shameful scheme, or should they have nothing to do with it, close their schools and leave thousands of black children without education? After much soul-searching, the Anglican Church decided on closure.

Left: The final days of Sophiatown, November 1959. The forced removals and destruction began on 9 February 1955, and the township was replaced by Triomf (Triumph), a white suburb representing the Verwoerdian policy of the 1950s.

The Tutus at the time were teaching in government schools and enjoying their work, but it was not long before they began to feel the heavy-handed effects of the government's determination to impose its apartheid doctrine on the education system. Teachers were required to become active agents in preparing the black community for its assigned role in the separatist dispensation. Discriminatory pay scales were introduced and teachers who were not considered ideologically trustworthy were bypassed for promotion. By the end of the school year, the Tutus decided they could no longer be a part of it.

These were dark years in South Africa as the apartheid regime moved to counter a rising tide of black protests. A nationwide Defiance Campaign, which began in 1952 culminated three years later with the African National Congress (ANC) calling a massive Congress of the People. Anti-apartheid groups of all races attended and drafted the Freedom Charter demanding a non-racial democracy in which all races would participate equally. The meeting – at which Huddleston was awarded the ANC's highest honour, the Isitwalandwe medal, for his crusading work against apartheid – lasted two days before it was broken up by a large detachment of police who arrived with Sten guns, seized the platform, confiscated documents and announced that they believed treason was being plotted.

Pursuing that pretext, the regime ordered a massive crackdown the following year. Even as the bulldozers moved in to begin flattening Sophiatown, the flamboyant minister of justice of the time, Charles Robberts Swart, a one-time Hollywood extra, sent squads of police on dawn raids throughout the country to search the homes of almost everyone perceived as being a radical, including some of the most prominent political names of the day, among them Chief Albert Luthuli, then leader of the ANC, Nelson Mandela, Oliver Tambo and Walter Sisulu. After an initial weeding out, 156 of them were flown to Johannes-burg to stand trial on allegations of treason. The trial itself was a fiasco. The prosecution's case fell apart piecemeal as it dragged on for more than five years before the last thirty-three were acquitted.

It was against this highly charged backdrop that the Tutus quit their jobs and Tutu decided to train for the priest-hood. He still felt no great sense of calling, but it was a job and he needed one. It turned out not to be as easy as he thought it would. Despite a letter of recommendation from Huddleston, he was not immediately accepted as a candidate and had to wait until the intake of 1957.

It was a difficult time. There were obviously money problems, since both Desmond and Leah had lost their incomes. Desmond's stipend as a trainee priest was well below even his meagre teacher's salary, while Leah, too, had to change jobs. She decided to train as a nurse, which involved going to a mission hospital in the remote, small

Above: A deserted
Ikageng School in
Alexandra, Johannesburg.
Under the Bantu
Education Act of 1953,
black education fell
under the control of the
Department of Native
Affairs, headed by
Minister of Native Affairs
Hendrik Verwoerd.

"There is no place for him [the Bantu] in the European community above the level of certain forms of labour ... What is the use of teaching the Bantu child mathematics when it cannot use it in practice? That is quite absurd. Education must train people in accordance with their opportunities in life, according to the sphere in which they live."

Hendrik Verwoerd, minister of native affairs, 1954.

"We should not give the Natives any academic education. If we do, who is going to do the manual labour in the community?"

town of Jane Furse, some two hundred and fifty kilometres north of Johannesburg, while Desmond moved into a men-only residence at St Peter's Theological College, a small but intense institution run by monks of the Community of the Resurrection in Rosettenville on the south-western fringes of Johannesburg. Their two children at that time, Trevor and Thandeka, went to stay with their grandparents in Munsieville.

It was a rigorous experience for the married father of two. From the status of being a teacher in charge of a class, he was a student once again, in a spartan institution where he and his fellow students were expected to help run the place by sweeping the floors, cleaning the toilets, washing the dishes and weeding the garden. More importantly, the students had to follow the same rigorous spiritual routine observed by the monks themselves: up at 6:30 a.m., Holy Eucharist at 7:00 a.m., followed by silent meditation and then other strictly set times for prayer, recitation of texts, theological lectures and other religious rituals and services throughout the day. Lights went out at 9:00 p.m. followed by silence until after meditation the next day. It came as a shock at first, but he quickly adapted and then became absorbed by it to the point where, to this day, it is an absolutely essential framework for his daily life.

The financial difficulties worsened when ZZ became ill and was put on half pay and Leah became pregnant again and had to stop working. Yet Tutu shone in his theological studies, winning the archbishop's essay prize in competition with students of all races from other theological colleges. His final report, upon completion of the three-year course for the degree of licentiate in theology, described him as "exceptionally conscientious" and concluded with the prescient assessment that "his outstanding intellectual gifts, combined with well-tried moral integrity, mark him out as a man likely to be of almost unique value to the Church of the future in South Africa".[2]

Tutu was ordained as a deacon on 18 December 1960, just four days after the ANC leader Chief Albert Luthuli accepted the Nobel Peace Prize in Oslo. He was appointed an assistant curate

was a year ahead of Desmond at St Peter's. After seminary I went to Orlando. The parish was next to where this Soccer City stadium now stands. Then, it was just a playground with a tin shack and nothing else. We still managed to link up, because, in their final year, Desmond's class was allowed to come out to Orlando for practical training. So we would be going around in our white cassocks in the township. Sometimes it was quite funny, because I remember there was a whole group of us going down a main road and a young man in a taxi just wound down his window, and shouted, "*Abafundisi Zaphel'inkhukhu!*", meaning, "Here come the priests and there go the chickens!" The myth was that when priests appeared in a home, chicken dinners would be served.

Then, of course, he was ordained and he went to the East Rand. There was a kind of break there. And then, soon after the Sharpeville massacre in 1960, I left. I went to Francistown, which was the Botswana protectorate.

I was one of the angry young men, whereas Desmond was the model of restraint. You never really knew he had a political side to him at that time. I'm sure he had views. After all, we know why he gave up teaching. He had views, but he was quite, quite restrained about it. I know he rebuked me once because white friends of his invited me to their home and I wouldn't go. I wouldn't go because their friends wouldn't shake hands with me. It was a woman wearing her gloves and she wouldn't shake hands with me. I said, "I'm not going there." And Desmond said, "Oh you are supercilious!"

I think that one simply has to add that when you've been cocooned in the oasis of St Peter's, where you have seen an alternative South Africa, and then you go to the townships after ordination and see exactly what apartheid does to people, you boil, you boil. And I think that is probably what happened to me.

So then I went to Francistown for three years,

I stayed there and quietly went on with my work. I really went into voluntary exile. Then history came to me, and all these refugees started arriving from South Africa.

Then in '63 I came to England. And here we made contact once again, when he was in Golders Green. I was in the East End of London, in Poplar working in a parish. He was now at King's College.

Both Desmond and Nomalizo have, in many ways, been quite special in my life. They had, and still have that quality of being quite unassuming. He didn't have a chip on his shoulder like the rest of us. He was blessed with a command of English and a sense of humour. When we were treated as curiosities, he really knew how to deal with that side of things without getting furious. And so from time to time I would go down to Golders Green and see them and they were both very gracious. After all, he was there to study, not to receive South African visitors. They were very, very gracious about it, which was very lovely.

Years later, when he was appointed dean of Johannesburg, Nomalizo was in a great turmoil. They lived in Grove Park and I went out there and we chatted. It was a very difficult time. Well, look here; imagine that you come from South Africa where you're not allowed to own anything, and here they were virtually setting up home in Grove Park. They had bought the house. The prospect of turning back to South Africa – well, you can understand the turmoil. It means the security of the children goes overboard, the security of tenure of the home goes overboard, they were going into the unknown. They didn't even know whether their ministry would be accepted in Johannesburg. So, in any case, when he was offered the job it was unsettling, it was very unsettling. I was torn; I sympathised with her but I realised, and have always believed, that there was potential in him. Remember, he was one of the first crop of graduates coming into the priesthood amongst Africans. So one, in a way, looked up to him. One asked questions – very fundamental questions:

people? If this bishop [Timothy Bavin] is brave enough to appoint him, what does it say? Do we thwart that because of these other considerations? So I was really, really torn for him and for our church at home. It was important that we had people that we could see as role models to stand up. That generation of graduates in South Africa was a special breed at a certain time. The rest of us, who were not educated, were nonentities and here was someone who had the humility of his learning. He was just calmly getting on, quietly getting on with what he had to do. So I thought, "Well, he should go, he should go."

of people of colour, to know that, despite the lies we had been told about our inferiority, there were people who were capable. And he was there to prove it. Do you disqualify him simply because of his pigmentation? No. He must go. But we knew full well it was not going to be easy. After all, even our relationship within the church was difficult when we rubbed shoulders with some of our counterparts on the other side. Remember also that when we were in seminary we were sent to the wealthy, white, northern suburbs to take services for domestic servants on a Sunday afternoon. Some of those parishes didn't even allow us to use the church.

NOMALIZO LEAH TUTU

went back to work after Trevor was born. Trevor stayed with my mother-in-law because she was still very close; so did Thandi. Thandi was born in 1957. Desmond started at St Peter's College in 1958. He had decided to leave teaching. That was because of the introduction of Bantu Education. The law was passed in 1953 but there was not any change until the rules were imple- mented in late 1958–59. That's when he decided he was not going to go on teaching.

I remember that his father was fiercely opposed to him leaving teaching. He had visions of his son growing up in this family tradition of teaching. His father was a teacher. His elder sister was a teacher. Although Desmond's grandfather was a minister of the church, his father didn't think much of Desmond deciding to take up ministry.

I didn't really see it coming but he was always very much in church circles. He liked staying with the monks of the Community of the Resurrection

schooling. I think he was attracted to their way of life. I remember, once when we were dating and we had quarrelled, he said, "You know what? If you don't marry me I think I will join the CR [Community of the Resurrection]." He just liked church. He never missed service. He was a server and he was the deacon. I didn't really see it coming as a profession, as him going into it the way he did but, when it did happen, I was very supportive. His family thought he was making a mistake. They thought he was far better off when he was a teacher. I think they had visions of him being headmaster or inspector of schools or going up in that line. I think it was a bit of a disappointment, to my father-in-law particularly, that he would want to move off teaching. I supported him when it became quite clear that he was really serious. And, obviously, when he left off teaching, it was miserable. I thought, "I can't stay either. I'm leaving." I left off teaching and went to train as a nurse whilst he was at college training to be a

I met Desmond when he was a student at St Peter's College. I was the vice-principal. He was the senior student. In those days, the senior students organised the students in various ways. They assigned certain chores. They arranged visiting. I remember Martin Jarrett-Kerr saying, "It's remarkable how this college runs itself." It didn't run itself; it was run by some very competent senior students and Desmond was one of them. I think he came for two years and it must have been 1956–57. I taught the gospels and some elementary Greek but the principal, who was Godfrey Pawson, recognised that Desmond had special gifts and gave him a lot of private tuition. He took Desmond away from my gospel lectures and had sessions with him on his own. He taught him quite a lot. Godfrey was one of our real theologians. He was first class.

Desmond was a very outgoing, lovable person. He worked very hard, he prayed very hard, he did his best everywhere. I think he got up at four o'clock in the morning to pray and to work.

He often referred to his impression of prayer. He went into the commemorative chapel and found one of the fathers praying. He was impressed that the brothers took prayer seriously. Somehow he was impressed that people spent quite long times in prayer. I like to think that he caught this bug of the importance of prayer in a big way. He has been very faithful to it. He's always kept it up, I think, spending quite long times in prayer.

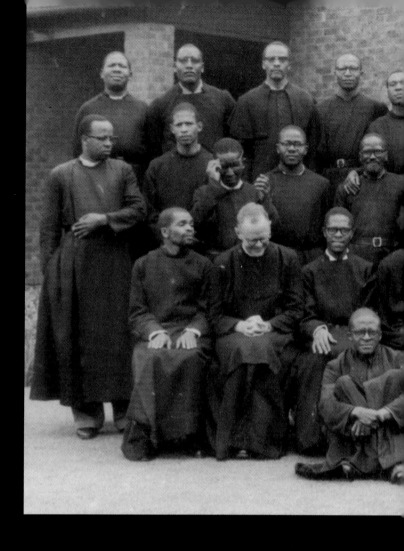

Above: Priests at St Peter's Theological College, Rosettenville, Johannesburg, 1958. Tutu is sitting on the ground on the left.

at a parish in the East Rand town of Benoni, where the future Nobel laureate and primate of his church throughout southern Africa was reunited with his family and housed in a converted garage with double doors, a tin roof and a bucket latrine.

It was appalling accommodation, but symptomatic of a degree of racial discrimination that prevailed within the Anglican Church even as its leaders railed against the injustices of the apartheid regime – a measure of hypocrisy that Tutu was to fight against and ultimately redress as he rose to positions of greater authority within the church.

Things improved within a year as Tutu was transferred to another parish near Johannesburg where the family had a proper house across the road from the church. But plans were already in the pipeline for another transformational move in the lives of this remarkable young man and his family. The principal of St Peter's Theological College, Aelred Stubbs, who was presumably the one who had detected Tutu's potentially "unique value to the Church", decided his former pupil could best realise that potential by becoming a theology teacher.[3] He wrote to the dean of King's College London, asking him to admit Desmond Tutu for graduate study at what is one of the most venerable seminaries in Britain, founded in 1829 by King George IV and the Duke of Wellington, who was then prime minister. Tutu was accepted, and the devoted monks of the Community of the Resurrection set about making funding and travel arrangements for their star student.

After months of haggling to get the South African government to give him a passport, Tutu

flew to London in August 1962. It was his first venture abroad and he went alone, leaving his family behind until he could find accommodation in London. So began the most transformative phase of his life. The combined experience of living outside South Africa – free of the blinkering effects of apartheid where familiarity can cloud your vision – and four years of total immersion in profound theological study and contemplation awakened the deep well of spirituality latent within him and, at the same time, sharpened his awareness of the inherent evil of apartheid. This fired up the lukewarm ex-teacher into a passionate religious and political activist, transforming him into what his biographer, John Allen, has called a "rabble-rouser for peace".[4]

Meanwhile, even as Tutu left the country, South Africa was itself undergoing a fateful transformation. The vicious cycle of intensifying repression and resistance that characterised the 1950s reached a climax as the decade ended. A radical element under the leadership of Robert Sobukwe had split from the ANC in November 1958 to follow the more "Africanist" philosophy of Kwame Nkrumah, who had led Ghana to independence the previous year – itself a portentous event that prompted British Prime Minister Harold Macmillan to warn the South African government in a famous speech to its Parliament in Cape Town that a "wind of change" was blowing down Africa.[5] Hendrik Verwoerd, the former education minister who by now was prime minister, joined issue with Macmillan. As the primary architect of the apartheid ideology, Verwoerd responded by asserting that the white South Africans, who regarded themselves as an indigenous

people on the African continent with no metropolitan homeland to return to, had an equal right to stay and would respond to the African challenge by establishing separate homelands for each of the indigenous tribes where they could develop their own "nationalities" according to their own cultures and abilities. White South Africa, which just happened to possess 87 per cent of the territory and nearly all its natural resources, had to be separate and sovereign.

Barely had Macmillan uttered his warning words than the first gust of the wind he spoke about hit South Africa in the form of a violent clash that was to change the course of the country's history. To demonstrate his movement's new level of militancy, Sobukwe, who rejected the ANC's "multiracialism" on the grounds that Africans should first liberate themselves psychologically, launched a mass campaign against the hated pass laws. These specified that only Africans in permanent employment could stay in South Africa's so-called "white" cities and were subject to instant arrest if they could not present their passbooks on demand. Sobukwe called on all Africans to defy these laws by presenting themselves for arrest at police stations throughout the country. His idea was to fill the jails, then call for a national strike to paralyse the economy and so force the government to abandon the pass laws. Playing catch-up, the ANC quickly did likewise, turning it into a mass all-party campaign.

The launch day for the anti-pass campaign, 21 March 1960, dawned bright and clear, a crisp autumn day in what is the loveliest time of year in South Africa. Sobukwe set out from his home in Soweto to walk the eight kilometres to the Orlando police station in the company of a group of colleagues. They were duly arrested and charged. Meanwhile, some eighty kilometres to the south, another group began gathering at the police station in a smaller black township called Sharpeville. There they milled around and waited. The police station was surrounded by a security fence with a small contingent of police inside and three Saracen armoured cars on standby. The police appeared nervous in the face of the swelling crowd and made no move to arrest anyone. As the hours ticked by and the crowd grew ever larger, the tension rose. Suddenly there was a commotion near the fence and, with no warning, the machine-guns mounted on the three Saracens opened fire, raking back and forth as the panicked crowd turned and fled. The shooting lasted only two or three minutes, but, by the time it stopped, sixty-nine people lay dead, mostly shot in the back as they had turned to run, and one hundred and eighty were wounded.

Sharpeville has gone down in South African history as the day the strategy of non-violent resistance to apartheid died. It was also a turning point in international attitudes towards the apartheid state. The massacre produced an outburst of horror and condemnation the likes of which South Africa had not experienced before. The Johannesburg stock market crashed, property prices plummeted as thousands of whites emigrated, and a new sense of rage swept through the black community.

The switch from non-violence was not immediate. The ANC and the Pan Africanist Congress (PAC) tried briefly to continue their protest campaigns but they found it increasingly difficult. Nine days after Sharpeville, another critical confrontation took place which alarmed the government and hardened its determination to dig in. With a spontaneity that took even the vigilant security police by surprise, a crowd of some thirty thousand black people emerged from the sprawling townships on the sandy flatlands outside Cape Town and began marching in procession along the broad De Waal Drive motorway which snakes along the lower slopes of Table Mountain towards the city. At the head of this vast column was a young man dressed like a schoolboy in short pants and no socks, leading them in a silent and orderly procession. His name was Philip Kgosana, only twenty-three years old, who for just a single day was to play one of the most remarkable roles in the history of the anti-apartheid struggle before disappearing from it again forever.

As the white citizens of Cape Town quaked at the sight, Kgosana led his formidable procession into the heart of the city towards the Houses of Parliament. Inside that imposing red-brick and white-pillared establishment the legislators and their all-white aides and staffers panicked, all reaching for their telephones at once so that the parliamentary switchboard jammed and none could make contact with the world outside their citadel. It was, in the words of *New York Times* correspondent Joseph Lelyveld, "an hour in which the Bastille might have been stormed in South Africa and wasn't".[6]

It wasn't, because young Kgosana ordered his army of followers to stop – and then to sit down. They obeyed the youngster with total discipline. In ordering them to stop, he was obeying his leader, Sobukwe, who had instructed his followers to avoid violence. Any violent confrontation, he said, would provoke retaliation and that would alienate the black masses from his objective, which was to fill the jails. "We are not leading corpses to the new Africa," was Sobukwe's injunction.[7] So Kgosana halted the march when he saw a helicopter hovering above him and armoured cars with police and army units surrounding the Houses of Parliament.

He stepped forward to speak with the police commander in charge of the defending units. The youngster demanded to see the minister of justice so that he could present a protest against the pass laws on behalf of his followers. The police commander told Kgosana the minister was busy having lunch but offered the young man a "gentleman's agreement" that he would arrange a meeting later in the day if Kgosana would first send his people home. Naively, but mindful of his leader's injunction to avoid violence, Kgosana agreed. Then followed another astonishing display of discipline and authority as the youngster turned back to face the massive crowd of adults and told them to stand up, turn around and go home. They did.

Kgosana returned to Parliament that afternoon. But he did not see the minister. In a characteristic act of perfidy, he was arrested instead and charged with "incitement". But this one-day boy wonder of South Africa's resistance struggle didn't go to jail. He skipped bail and disappeared into exile, not to be seen or heard of again until his unnoticed return four decades later to a transformed homeland where he now lives quietly as an old man and an unsung hero.

The government moved swiftly to crush the resistance. It declared a state of emergency and, eight days after Kgosana's great march, declared both the ANC and the PAC to be "unlawful organisations". That meant not only that the two main black political movements were outlawed but that for anyone to further any of their aims or objectives was now a criminal offence. In a

"THERE CAN BE NO FUTURE WITHOUT FORGIVENESS."

DESMOND TUTU

single stroke, all of black nationalism was criminalised. The movements became unmentionable in the press and, as factors in the South African public debate, they ceased to exist – except as demonised images that the government could use to frighten white voters into supporting ever tougher security legislation.

Another wave of mass detentions followed. The ANC leader and newly anointed Nobel laureate, Chief Albert Luthuli, was banished to the remote district of Groutville, in northern Natal province, where he died in a freakish accident, knocked down by a train as he crossed the tracks. Sobukwe was sentenced to three years' imprisonment for organising the campaign against the pass laws, then interned in solitary confinement on Robben Island for another six years before being allowed to live under house arrest in Kimberley until his death in 1978.

The ANC made one last forlorn attempt to keep functioning under these crippling circumstances. The leadership sent Oliver Tambo abroad to lobby international support and made Nelson Mandela leader of a National Action Council to organise continuing protest activity. Working underground, Mandela wrote to Verwoerd, the prime minister, calling on him to establish a new union of all South Africans and warning that if his government did not agree to this before going ahead with its plans to declare the country a republic under a new whites-only constitution, there would be a three-day stoppage of work nationwide.

Verwoerd did not deign to reply. Instead he mobilised the military, threw a cordon of steel around every black township and warned that any who went on strike would be fired and endorsed out of the urban areas – meaning they and their families would starve. Not surprisingly, the strike flopped and Mandela called it off after two days.

It was at that point that the ANC came to the conclusion their strategy of non-violence was futile. If they could not organise legally, and naked force was to be used to crush every peaceful demonstration, how could they ever get anywhere? In July 1961, Mandela and a handful of others who had managed to evade detention met secretly and decided to form their military arm, Umkhonto we Sizwe. Its first action took place on 16 December 1961 – the day Afrikaners celebrated their victory over the Zulu kingdom at the Battle of Blood River in 1838 – when saboteurs blew up electricity installations and government offices in Johannesburg and Port Elizabeth.

It was in that forbidding atmosphere that Tutu left South Africa to begin the next transformational phase of his life. As his plane took off, a deeply oppressive political silence settled over the black community he was leaving, and it was to continue for the rest of the decade.

CHAPTER FOUR

....

HOW CAN YOU LOVE GOD AND
HATE YOUR BROTHER?

It was during South Africa's "silent sixties" that the experience of life in faraway Britain began the transformation of the newly ordained priest theologically and politically into the activist he eventually became back in South Africa and that enabled him effectively to assume the role of leadership of his reawakened people through the stormy seventies and eighties that followed.

Until then, not even Sharpeville had stirred the depths of his passion. He and his fellow students at the theological college were in a state of shock, a kind of disbelief that such a thing could have happened. "But even then," he confessed years later, "I can't say that I was madly political and angry." He also accepted the situation of partial segregation in the church. "I didn't think that I ought to go and work in a white parish."[1]

The change came in phases. It began with the sheer physical impact of being transported out of the land of apartheid for the first time in his life. From the moment of touchdown at Heathrow Airport, the difference was palpable: no separate channels for whites and non-whites; no separate queues and counters; and, above all, no being accosted by police officers. Tutu waxes nostalgic when he speaks of the British police, especially the legendary London "bobbies". For generations, black South Africans had grown up to regard the police as the quintessence of racist violence: compulsively aggressive, crude and wilfully vindictive. They not only symbolised the apartheid system, they exuded its viciousness with every expression and gesture in their everyday contact with black people. Nor was it only the white police who did this. Often black police, who numbered nearly half the force, were even worse as they sought to ingratiate themselves with their white overlords.

For the Tutus, therefore, contact with the tall, studiously courteous London bobbies was a novelty to be savoured. So much so, says Tutu, "that we became the ones who did the accosting. We would stop a police officer and ask for directions, even when we knew where we were going, just for the novelty of having a police officer, a white police officer, speak to us courteously, addressing us as 'sir' and 'madam'."[2]

The sense of liberation that sprang from being able to live for four years without carrying that hated passbook, of being able to dine in any restaurant, attend any theatre, stay in any hotel, live in any suburb and board any bus or any train, was life-changing.

The Tutus lived in Golders Green, a predominantly white middle-class suburb in north-east London, where they were given the curate's flat behind the local Anglican church. The flat was small by English standards, but for the Tutus it was unprecedented luxury – particularly compared with the converted garage in Benoni. Among other firsts, it was there that Tutu preached to a white congregation for the first time – and everyone responded warmly to him, both in church and in his parish work of meeting with the sick, the lonely and the bereaved.

The Tutus were taken in hand by the small but highly efficient network of the Community of the Resurrection, who introduced them to a wide circle of friends and new experiences. One friend in particular, Martin Kenyon, a gregarious man, took Desmond to such inner sanctums of English life as The Travellers Club in Pall Mall and the members' stand at Lord's cricket ground, to concerts at the Albert Hall and to some aristocratic homes in the English countryside.

It is the smaller things, too, that still stand out sharply in Tutu's memory. He likes to tell the story of the day he was standing in line at his bank when a man, obviously in a desperate hurry, pushed in front of him to be

JOYCE PILISO-SEROKE

I met Desmond in 1963 in London, the day after his youngest daughter Mpho was born. I was attending a meeting and we had spare time on a Sunday, so I went to see the Tutus with Edith Hlatshwayo – she knew them. She said to me, "Come on, just come with me and let's go and see my friends from South Africa." I said, "Well, fine," and we went there.

And, gosh, I was suddenly involved in the excitement. Mpho had been born the day before and now we were there. For me it was something so wonderful and so strange because I wasn't used to home births done by midwives. I always knew that if you were going to have a baby you would go to hospital. So I was so enthralled and delighted to hear Nomalizo [Leah] say, "No, I got the baby here. And it was yesterday."

Just when we were talking and looking at the baby, I remember Nomalizo said to Edith and me, "Oh, Desmond has gone shopping for food but he will be back in a minute." For me that was strange – the man does the grocery shopping for the house? When he came, I was charmed by this man who just chuckled and greeted us as if he had known me from the dawn of time.

There were so many firsts for me there. The crowning glory of this day was when Desmond said, "What will you people have? I'm preparing lunch now." And I said, "A man preparing lunch?" You must remember I was working with the Young Women's Christian Association at the time and we were starting these women empowerment programmes. We were battling with this inequality between men and women – the manner in which women were degraded and regarded as second-class citizens. And so I said to myself, "Wow! Here is a man who is going to cook for us." In Xhosa we say he would *lungiselela umdlezane*, which means he would "care for the mother of a new-born". In our culture it's done by an aunt or another married female relative. In this case it was Desmond who was looking to the needs of Nomalizo and all that. It was a fascinating day for me. At the end of the day, I was exhausted because there were so many firsts for me: things that really stretched my mind to say, "Indeed, this is what we should fight for, for women! I have seen it happen. I have seen it here."

I often visited Desmond and Nomalizo in their home. He was somebody who would leave his guests to go and pray at a specific time. That, for me, was very poignant. I began to really respect the man because, even with the social call like that, he would say to his guests, "I will see you guys later." Then Nomalizo would be very, very careful to say we must observe the quiet time and not be loud.

At his daughter Nontombi's fiftieth birthday celebration in church, you know, after the children had been blessed and the adults decided to go forward, I just had that feeling of jump and go also and be blessed by Desmond. I just regarded Desmond as my friend's husband, a friend of mine. I knew he was an archbishop and he is a man of God but, for me, that day I just saw him as a man of God and I just wanted him to bless me. It was not for a special reason or maybe, "Bless me because I am unhappy" or "because I'm thankful for this operation the way it went". I just wanted him to touch me, and I feel that Desmond, who is a man of God, has touched me.

served. "I'm sorry, sir," the teller, a middle-aged woman, chided the intruder, "but that gentleman is next" – pointing to Tutu. "For most people, that was just a simple act of courtesy on her part but for me it was a bombshell experience," Tutu recalls today. "I went back to the bank afterwards and spoke to the woman. I told her: 'From now on you are my pin-up; you don't know what you did for me.' She had forgotten all about the incident, so natural was it for her, but for me, here we are forty-eight years later and it is still something that resonates."[3]

This is not to say there was no racism in Britain at the time. Indeed there was. The arch-conservative MP, Enoch Powell, was raising a storm over "coloured" immigration from the former colonies as Britain began dismantling its empire. In language redolent of the apartheid firebrands back home, Powell made his name with a notorious "Rivers of Blood" prediction of the consequences that would flow from this black influx into white Britain. "As I look ahead," he thundered, in an allusion to Virgil's *Aeneid*, "I am filled with foreboding. Like the Roman, I seem to see 'the River Tiber foaming with much blood'."[4] Such rhetoric drew applause as well as votes from a sizeable section of the British population. Notices proclaiming "No Coloureds" sprouted on the walls of boarding houses and bed-and-breakfast establishments.

But the Tutus were not touched personally by this racism, although they were aware of it. Tutu thinks they may have been insulated from it because they were living in a church community. Also, of course, it bore no real comparison with South Africa for it was not legalised. It was simply part of the political noise of a particularly boisterous decade.

Far more important, in terms of the influences on Desmond Tutu, was the fact that the sixties was indeed a tumultuous, exciting decade in Britain: a decade of social and cultural revolution throughout the Western world, in fact, but especially in Britain. Not only were empires being dismantled and new nations being founded – thirty-two in Africa alone – but social norms were being turned upside down in everything from the arts to fashion to human relationships. The "Swinging Sixties" the decade was called, because of the fall of a whole range of social taboos, especially relating to sexism and racism. It was the decade of The Beatles and The Rolling Stones, of Carnaby Street, the miniskirt and women's liberation, of hippies and Woodstock and psychedelia, of the Vietnam War and peace marches and flower children – and of a man landing on the moon.

This counterculture of questioning all established mores reached into every sector of life, including theology. So it was that as Tutu entered King's College an explosive new book by Bishop John Robinson of Woolwich, called *Honest to God*, hit the headlines. In the book Bishop Robinson argued that secular man required a secular theology – that God's continuing revelation to humanity was brought about in culture at large, not merely within the confines of "religion" or "church". A review of Robinson's book in the *Observer* newspaper carried the startling headline "Our Image of God Must Go".[5]

This was also the decade of the Second Vatican Council, convened by Pope John XXIII, because, he said, it was time to open the windows of the Catholic Church and let in some fresh air. The Pope invited other Christian denominations to send observers and all the main Protestant and Eastern Orthodox churches did so. Thus began a major new phase of theological liberalism and ecumenism as the Catholic Church engaged for four years in serious dialogue not only with those other Christian denominations but, in time, with non-Christian religions as well.

Meanwhile, the Anglican Church itself was headed by perhaps the most liberal primate it has ever had, in Michael Ramsey, who was appointed archbishop of Canterbury in May 1961 and served throughout the decade. He had a respect for honest agnosticism and atheism and believed they might not be barriers to salvation. He had respect for members of other faiths as well, and once made a barefoot pilgrimage to Mohandas Gandhi's grave.

All these factors combined to produce an atmosphere of liberal open-mindedness that infused the venerable precincts of King's College. It influenced the style of teaching among Tutu's theological lecturers, who included some of the most distinguished names in Anglican scholarship. "They never confused authoritativeness with authoritarianism," Tutu says. "They seemed to have an allergy against dogmatism. They would never say to us, 'This is the answer'. That wasn't their style. They would come into the room, throw a range of things at you, then give you a reading active in my local church in London as Sunday School teacher and choir member, I had never heard of the name Tutu until a new young curate arrived in 1963 at St Alban's, Golders Green, with his wife Leah and children Trevor, Theresa and Naomi. I was thirteen at the time. Mpho was born in Golders Green. I think she was the first baby born in the curacy at the church.

There was very little notice given that the family was coming and we had to run around and quickly sort out the tiny apartment that was to be their home. We thought it very cramped but, for the newly arrived Tutus, it appeared to be paradise. The rooms were filled by a generous congregation with every necessity that a family could possibly need. We were so delighted to welcome this new family to our church. My mother Sylvia was churchwarden and regularly arranged the flowers at church. Desmond would talk with her as she carried out her duties and she was entranced by his personality from the moment she met him. She told me: "That man will go far." She just adored him.

And, among the many very special memories of long and continuing friendship with my family, one occasion in particular reminds me very much of Desmond's unique spiritual gifts. Sylvia died in 2009 at the age of eighty-nine. Through me, Desmond had always kept in touch with her. She remembered him so well from his time at St Alban's. As her health deteriorated, she was eventually moved to a hospice. I had to go to India on a business trip. I emailed him as I boarded my plane, "Here's her number. She's in a hospice because she's really not at all well." Because I was away at the time, my niece was sitting with her grandmother at the hospice. She told me that the nurse came in and said, "I've got Archbishop Tutu on the phone." Too frail to take the call herself, my niece held the phone to my mother's ear. My niece said my mother's face was transfixed. Sylvia smiled and simply listened as she was unable to speak. I understand that she managed to whisper goodbye, and that was

the end of the phone call. Very shortly afterwards, my mother died peacefully. When I asked Desmond, "How did you know to call her on that particular day?" he replied, "Sally, God's good, that's it." And so one of my greatest joys is that her last few moments were filled with words from the one spiritual person that she had really adored, ever since their first meeting so many years ago.

As an impressionable teenager, who had never travelled outside my own country, I found it quite magical that Desmond had come to Golders Green from a part of the world that seemed then to be an awful distance away. He represented a fulfilment of all that we sang about in Sunday school. In those days we still used to chant, "Over the sea there are little brown children, mothers and babies and fathers too." And here they were! South Africa was, for most of us, just a very distant country where we knew things weren't quite the same as they were with us – and not as they should be. And of course Desmond and Leah took huge delight in being treated as the wonderful people that they were. Desmond would notoriously and unnecessarily regularly ask a policeman the way just because he so liked to hear a police officer call him "Sir."

I had four brothers and they all got to know Trevor. As I was thirteen, I was allowed to babysit as did some of my girlfriends. We were all active in the Girl Guides and we also sang in the church choir. Back in the 1960s, the church provided our entire social life, so the Tutu family's arrival simply added a new dimension. For Desmond, it was the very first time he'd been in a ministry with a totally white congregation. He told me, more recently, that for him it was an opportune experience and equipped him well for the later challenges he was to face on his and the family's return to apartheid South Africa.

The Tutus were and remain a family that I have loved from the moment I met them as a young girl. Desmond's presence and preaching provided a start to my own personal spiritual journey. He broadened my mind and that of our younger congregation as he opened our eyes to a wider world. Golders Green had a large Jewish community and with Desmond's influence we were not only becoming more internationally aware, but we were also led to have greater tolerance of other faiths. We youngsters were very proud of him being amongst us. To be fair, some of the older ladies in the congregation sometimes found it quite difficult to penetrate his then still marked South African accent. Of course what they all remembered, what everybody remembers, is his chuckle and good humour cutting through every social and spiritual barrier. Whatever accent he may have had, his infectious laughter was invaluable as a means of communication.

His preaching and his whole approach to explaining the scriptures were highly educational. I'd been brought up in an age when you received a stamp that you stuck in a special book on each occasion when you attended Sunday school. You listened to biblical stories that had no real and meaningful context or relevant application to you. Desmond put scripture into context. He possessed that wonderful ability of being able to communicate in a manner that brings exemplary theological understanding. If you sat at his feet, as my mother literally used to do, you could readily understand his teaching on the meaning of life, the scriptures and God. In fact, I have tried in my own theological studies and discourses through essays and sermons to emulate in some way Desmond's exceptional gift of bringing the Bible into relevance to the real world. Right from the start of his ministry in Golders Green, he talked so convincingly and well about the meaning of each piece of scripture. His communication skills are exceptional. Back in the 1960s, we were well used to sitting and listening to a very lengthy sermon that you could just about follow for ten minutes before wishing that the service could be over. He transformed worship at our church. Looking back, I see that he had this wonderful mix of sound theological teaching that he could relate to positive

action. He was a natural communicator: a rare gift. We are still very short today of priests who can actually communicate the Christian message in a way that is found compelling.

I realised how important the Community of the Resurrection [CR] was to his early life. I went with him on a return visit to Mirfield. It's a great seminary and there are wonderful people there. I learnt to sit still in contemplation, thought and prayer for hours on end and not talk – wonderful. My husband David was to drive him back down to Golders Green for an evening celebratory service. As we set off, after a brief prayer, Desmond said, "Right, I'm going to have a conversation right now. I'm going to get the hotline going." And he talks to God. I learned much about my own spiritual discipline from him. He told me that the CR did train him in a discipline of daily worship that he's always kept up. That is terribly important today. Anything can happen at any time. Get your spiritual life in order and you then know that you've got something that is always with you. Everything else really doesn't matter.

He won't be with us forever. I think we need to do more than just to encapsulate in print some of his wonderful work – I know he is not keen on celebrating his achievements. However, we must capture his wonderful pervasiveness to modern theological and political thought. To me, he's probably of greater stature than any other religious person that I can think of, yet he has great modesty and an innate humility. In his years of preaching, he has done so much. Words that Desmond has spoken to me are always highly memorable. He's a great educator. I think we all probably underrate his immense influence. I've heard him give so many talks and sermons to different audiences. Sometimes you may hear the same little stories and anecdotes. But the messages vary – he's so expert at crafting for the time and the place. That's unique. He has been and remains one of our greatest and best Christian communicators.

TREVOR THAMSANQA TUTU

I think my first memory is of him teaching my sister Thandeka and me to sing the Lord's Prayer. We were living in Munsieville. I can still remember us sitting in the alcove right next to the coal stove. It being summertime, the stove wasn't lit. That's a very, very happy memory. Even though we must have been near poverty, I didn't know how poor we were. I was perfectly happy because I was with my parents. My parents looked after me. I had friends. We all had enough to eat.

I didn't really grow up in South Africa at all. I had sporadic times in South Africa; I mainly grew up in England. When we lived in England, even in the middle of his studies, in the middle of his exams, he always managed to take us to the park solely to play cricket but maybe to play soccer as well. He always found time to play games with me and to ride the bicycle: all the normal fatherly things. Certainly he knew how little time we had even then. He made sure that what we did have of it we used to the utmost.

My parents' style of discipline relied, pretty much, on a self-correcting mechanism. They set down their expectations and we just tried to live up to those. You more or less punish yourself for not achieving that. It's actually much, much more difficult than having an external invigilator or whatever it is, knowing what you have to do to achieve and being left to your own devices to achieve it. I mean, that's a far, far tougher road to walk than it is with the constant threat of punishment or with rewards for good behaviour. I can remember being caught smoking when I hadn't been given permission to smoke. My dad said that I must stop for a month and he didn't check or anything else but I did actually maintain that smoking ban. But he expected me to. That is worse than knowing that you'll be checked every morning or evening for cigarettes or cigarette odour.

It almost seems as though my first home was in England, really, when I was five. Through all my childhood I never thought we lived in extreme poverty. But now ... in comparison, clearly we did. I don't think I really felt poor though, probably because everybody was more or less at the same economic level. I never felt deprived, materially deprived, you know. And definitely never emotionally deprived. And so, we just never thought we were poor.

I think that the first memory I have of my dad being very angry at me as a child was in Bletchingley. We lived in an apartment. It was a small apartment and we lived over the parish caretakers' house. They were an elderly couple. One of the things my brother and I used to like to do was to jump off the bed and onto the floor. We would make a whole lot of noise, because it was a wooden floor. My dad told me to stop doing that because, obviously, if you are jumping onto a wooden floor, the people living below you are hearing thuds all the time. I think he was also trying to study at the time. I guess the walls were pretty thin. But as a child you don't think about those things. It's only as you get older that you make all the connections. At the time I didn't make the connection. So I continued jumping. I think my brother stopped or he did something else. I continued and my dad got so angry that he gave me two or three slaps on the bottom. That was the first and, I think, the last time. The only person who used to give the children spankings was my mum. I was not the child who got spanked very much anyway, by either parent. So for it to be done to me was a shocker. For it to be done by my dad to me was, like, truly traumatic. That was not his modus operandi. I don't remember him ever smacking me again. So I guess maybe that's why it's imprinted on my mind, because it was the first and only time that it ever happened.

His way of disciplining was just to look at you over his glasses. There's a look and you know. If that doesn't shut you up or calm you down or whatever, then nothing will. I think I've seen it a few times in my adulthood and it's not the look you particularly want. He doesn't shout at you. He doesn't scream at you. It's the disappointment in you. He looks over his glasses at you and his eyes go wide. He's so shocked that you would actually misbehave.

My mum, though, she was the disciplinarian, and she's called the wicked witch, you know – she used to complain about that. He made her the wicked witch. He got to be the fun guy. She used to tell us that at night all of the kids without fail – not one of us called Mummy. If one of us had a bad dream, wanted water or whatever, we always called Daddy. She would not be a happy camper if you called her. Daddy would come and pick you up. If you wanted water, he would bring you water or whatever you needed. He would soothe you and put you back to sleep. He certainly wouldn't take you to his bedroom. My mum was not having that disturb her sleep.

He's always put my mum first, you know. As much as you know the children are special, she had a unique place that nobody could circumvent.

Looking back, my dad was not the typical male. He would give me baths and he took on a lot of responsibility for taking care of us. I didn't like him giving me baths. His right hand is partially paralysed because of polio he had when he was a child, and so he doesn't feel how hard he is holding you. I didn't want him to give me baths. I remember saying, "He washes you rough." So I wanted my mum to do it. His role as a caregiver was normal for us but, when you look back, that wasn't particularly normal in our society. It's more acceptable now but he's always been just a little off the curve. I just think it's part of his nature and, probably, my mum was like, "Hey, I'm not doing this alone." So it was partially his nature and, probably, a lot hers.

Right: Desmond and
Leah with their children.
From left:
Trevor Thamsanqa,
Thandeka Theresa,
Nontombi Naomi
and Mpho Andrea,
England, circa 1964.

assignment that provided yet another aspect of what you were studying, and leave you to make up your mind which likely answer satisfied all the evidence you had in front of you."[6]

Tutu found this hugely liberating compared with the didactic style of teaching he had known in South Africa. It stimulated his fertile mind, opening new doors of thought, reflection and perception, which then evolved within him during all those hours of daily prayer and his week-long retreats into isolation. He threw himself into his studies with an intensity that delighted his lecturers, who wrote glowing reports back to his sponsors in South Africa.

It was at King's College that the priest began deepening into the seriously thoughtful and profoundly devout theologian he became. Many South Africans, including some of his admirers, believe to this day that Tutu was primarily a political activist who used his pulpit as a platform. The opposite is the truth. It was the depth of his spirituality that drove him to political activism. He was not a politician with a strategy but a churchman with a mission – a mission he believed had been given to him by God "to work for the realisation of something of his kingdom in this country".[7]

The liberal teaching at King's College added a further dimension to Tutu's development into a devout Anglo-Catholic, which has at the core of its faith the doctrine of the incarnation, of God coming into the world as a human being in the form of Jesus Christ – a dictum that shapes the most fundamental features of Tutu's philosophy of life. "God didn't come as an angel," Tutu explains. "He could have come in so many forms, but he chose to be a human being – a God who could know hunger, who could feel tired, a God who takes seriously the fact that we are body and soul. That sacramentalism makes you realise that the material, the so-called secular, is important for God."[8]

This forms the basis of Tutu's humanitarianism. "Because God became a human being," he says, "it means human beings are not just important – they are to be revered, they are very close to

Above: Leah and the children visit friends in Lydbury, England, 1965.

being worshipped because we are all created in the image of God and therefore each one of us is a God-carrier. And so to ill-treat a human being is not just a criminal act, it is of religious concern, because it is blasphemy."[9]

So this is also the basis of Tutu's activism; people of his faith, he says, are driven to act by their encounter with God in those intimate moments of prayer, in the Eucharist and in retreats. "It is anything but an escapist kind of faith," he insists. "An encounter with God is an encounter with someone who says, 'If you love me then the way to express that is by loving your neighbour, because how can you say you have seen God, that you love God, and yet you hate your brother or your sister?'"[10]

Tutu did well academically, scoring near the top of his group in the final examinations for his bachelor of divinity degree, then plunged immediately into a third year for his master of theology degree. At this point, to widen his experience, he asked to be moved to a new parish in a working-class part of London. Instead he was shifted to the upper-class village of Bletchingley, in Surrey, where he encountered the full spectrum of the British class system ranging from aristocratic families to farm workers. It was not what Tutu had wanted but it turned out to be one of the highlights of the family's stay in Britain as the entire community took them into their hearts – to the point where the whole village turned out for a farewell party when the time came for the Tutus to return to South Africa. The warmth with which they were received in the two parishes where Tutu served, and the wide range of friends they made during their four years in Britain, probably immunised Tutu permanently against any anti-white sentiment back in the racially polarised society to which he now had to return.

But perhaps the greatest benefit of all is that it was in Britain that Tutu developed the confidence, the self-assertiveness, to disagree openly and vigorously with whites: to shake off remember riding the train with my father in England. He would pick me up from nursery school and I remember being on the underground with him. Part of that daily ritual was getting ice cream. I would invariably end up with most of the ice cream all over my face. There was something about the day when I finally was able to eat ice cream without getting it all over my face. That was a big thing. Each time we would come home, my mum would say something about the ice cream around my face. In my mind it seems to have been a daily occurrence but, then again, I was three or four years old, so I could have been making up this wonderful thing that, when I was picked up from nursery school, I got ice cream every day. Somehow I don't think that it was very likely that I got ice cream every day. But in my mind, I did.

The family was divided by the move to England. My dad went first; my mother and siblings followed. I was three when I rejoined them, so I have no memory of that time; all I have are the stories I have been told. My family in South Africa said that the family friend with whom I travelled, Rev. Norman Montjane, is also short and has glasses. In my confusion, I thought that he was my father. We travelled to England together and, subsequently, I started calling him my father from the aeroplane. By the time I got to England, Trevor and Thandi were speaking a lot in English or at least throwing in English words. I understood no English whatsoever. I had been living with my grandparents. My dad's dad was somebody who swore a lot. Apparently I arrived with much of his mouth. The first time that my daddy said to me, "You know that we don't use that kind of language in this house", I packed my bag and was ready to head back to South Africa. I said, "I am going back because Daddy says that I can't talk in his house."

Trevor, Thandi and I went to boarding school in Swaziland. When we were home on holidays we used to go to soccer games. The thing that stood out for me at that time was that my parents seemed to be forever hosting somebody; they were entertaining at home. There would be students from Fort Hare over at the house: people like Barney Pityana who is now the vice-chancellor of UNISA [University of South Africa] and

was the first head of the Human Rights Commission. We had those students who were involved in questioning on the Fort Hare campus, and seminary students: Reuben Philip, who is bishop now, and Mervyn Castle, who is bishop in Cape Town. All of these people would be in the house and there would be these discussions that I didn't really understand, but there was also a lot of fun. There was a lot of laughing and dancing. It sounded like this was a place that was a kind of refuge for many young people. It was also a place where people could relax. You could have a political discussion and then you could have dancing going on. That was who my parents were to that community.

When it came to discipline, my mum was the volatile one. She was the one who would go off in a minute. She would yell and threaten all kinds of things. My dad was always the one who wanted to sit down and talk about what you had done and why they were disappointed and what could be done differently. I think I preferred the yelling and screaming because I knew that it would be over really quickly. So when my mum was the one who was disciplining, you knew that it was hard but it would be over. Once she had finished yelling, you could go back to being your normal self. With my dad you were going to be held to what you had said in the conversation, whatever you had agreed to try and do. You were going to be held to thinking about why you did that and why they felt that way about what you had done. You had to see the impact of your action on them or on others, the people whom you might have hurt. Very often that was harder, to have to face things and deal with them.

Schoolwork, that was my failing. I was very social, doing stuff and playing a lot of sport. Homework and schoolwork weren't the reasons I went to school. There were a lot of discussions about my responsibilities in terms of academics, particularly when we were at boarding school. He talked about how people had given for us to have that opportunity; so there was the responsibility, not just to yourself, but to those who had given and also to those who were hoping to receive from those who had given to you. If you mess it up then the givers might not be willing to try with the next person.

MPHO A. TUTU

I was born in England. We returned to South Africa when I was about three years old. South Africa was so different. A few years ago, I was with my father in the Eastern Cape. As we went past this park in East London, my dad said, "You wanted to go and play in there and I had to tell you no. And you said 'Why?' I had to tell you that it wasn't for children like you."

The three-year-old Mpho was looking into the playground. I couldn't see the difference between the children who were playing there and the children who were "like me". He had the challenge of having to explain apartheid to a three-year-old. I think that it was confusing to me. I couldn't see the difference between those children and me. They were just children playing in the park. They were children like the friends I had had in England. I couldn't figure out what it was about them that was so different.

I don't know how he explained it to me. There's no bitterness attached to the memory in me. As I think about it, and as I think about the people who I have come to call friends over the course of my life, I would have to say that whatever it was that he said or however it was that he explained it to me, I didn't walk away with having written off a race of people for the stupidity of some.

We had a parish meeting to say that he was going to join the parish as a curate with his wife Leah and their four children. The Lamberts said the house opposite us in the High Street would be available. The women of the village got together and furnished the house, got it all ready for their arrival. There was a great deal of rejoicing and excitement at the fact that they were coming and, knowing how they had had to put up with so much rejection, under apartheid, in their own country, we wanted to make them feel as welcome as possible. When they were delivered to Bletchingley, I just remember this young couple getting out of the cars with Trevor, Theresa, Naomi and Mpho, who was only three. We greeted them as warmly as we could.

There had been a great deal of difficulty getting them out of South Africa. Apartheid was in full swing. Other people, not me, were involved in making representations to the National Party government to allow them to leave South Africa. I had gone out to South Africa on a business trip with my husband, Philip. I had been able to visit Soweto when Father Trevor Huddleston was there. It was very difficult to get into Soweto in those days, but two ladies, Black Sash people, arranged it. And so I went to Soweto, and I saw exactly what the conditions were like. The permission had been given for Desmond to come to England, because he was going to do his thesis at King's College London. We didn't see much of him at the parish during the day; he went up to London to King's.

Of course he took part in the services. I, in particular, had a lot of contact with him. In order to go to Eucharist at a peaceful time, not necessarily on a Sunday, I went to Warwick Wold. There was a little tiny tin-roof church in the valley. It was within the parish and Desmond was immediately given the task of taking that service at seven in the morning, in the dark. I used to go because it was a place that I could pray peacefully without all the demands of my family and household. It was where my great-uncle Archie Bell used to serve. He used to say his favourite remark of "Four, and myself, five", which

very much amused Desmond in those early days. I also remember the atmosphere in that small church. Even with very few people in attendance, Desmond gave all of himself to each thing he did. This was something that was perhaps unusual for us in England.

It's difficult to explain, but the reverence and the quiet sacredness of the way he celebrated the Eucharist was something that struck me immediately. Well of course we had absolutely no idea of what he would become, but he had a presence. It's very difficult to describe, especially now that I have seen so much of him. This was really early days but, even so, he had a quality and a presence about him that was his own. I know that he was trained by the Mirfield monks. From my point of view, as I was brought up as a high church Anglo-Catholic, Mirfield training was the best in the world really.

Everything he did, he did with all of himself. They very often came to meals with us because we gave dinner parties in those days. We always involved them. We wanted them to meet the widest possible collection of people. It wasn't just on social occasions. Often we had family meals and that's why they got to know my boys so well. But Desmond, whatever he was doing, he gave all of himself to it. He had this particular presence is all I can really say to describe it. He was great fun. He taught Ricky to do the click in the Xhosa language when he was going to Botswana to do voluntary service overseas [VSO]. All my three boys did VSO when they left Eton. Ricky went to Botswana and Michael went to India and Kim went to South America. But Ricky set off at age eighteen, and with no knowledge of Africa at all. Desmond was great. He was so funny getting him to practise the Xhosa click until he got it right. I still can't do it, but he could.

The other thing that was lovely for my family and me was that we were in Bletchingley House. It was a big house and had a large garden, and it was opposite where they lived in Bletchingley. Right from the beginning, we said, "Please come anytime. Don't even telephone or ring up. Just use the garden as your space with the children. I was very lucky. I had three Spanish people to look after me. My cook, who couldn't read or write or speak English, adored Leah and her children, and Desmond of course. Whenever she saw them in the garden, she would call out and she would have cookies and orange juice for the children. Very often I was in and so Leah would come and talk. I just had the most profound admiration for this young woman who had been brought up in Soweto and lived under apartheid, just to see her adapt to this country and to take in the warmth and the welcoming that was offered, and not to bear any resentment because of all that she had suffered.

When they went back to South Africa from Bletchingley, I went and visited them at the seminary in Alice. A member of the congregation here had given a small amount of money, about two thousand pounds, to build a house for Desmond in the seminary when he was appointed there. Leah gave a supper party for some of the young seminarians. It was a lovely evening. We had a memorable evening because those young men were going out into the townships still in the middle of apartheid with enormous courage. I remember that evening particularly because Leah, who had been in my house where I had people waiting on everybody, said to me, "The tradition here is that we feed the men before we eat ourselves." So I said fine, and helped. It was a great privilege to be there in the very early days.

Both Desmond and Leah have always stayed in touch. I mean not only the Christmas cards, but we've written to each other. I've always written; I can't now because of the blindness. Whatever was happening in the family, we wrote and Desmond always replied. He has always kept in really strong personal touch with us. We are very, very blessed to have that.

Much later on, I came to Cassandra [Goad]'s wedding at South Park and I was on my own. I think attending a wedding on your own is rather a boring thing to do but I wouldn't have missed it for anything. During the reception, I found that I was getting

exhausted from too many people, so I came back and went into St Mark's Chapel. I was aware that somebody was there but I couldn't see them, so I had about fifteen or twenty minutes, and then the other figure got up and it was Desmond. I was in wedding garments, as one was. We hugged each other on the doorstep and he said, "Susan, your perfume has distracted my prayers." The caterers were scurrying backwards and forwards but I just whipped my hat off and knelt down where I was and asked for his blessing. It was an automatic response for me. It was a feeling that this was someone very, very special whose blessing was very special. And, of course, it's so lovely, as he always blesses in his language.

The other occasion that I want to describe is after Desmond had left Bletchingley. They had come back to England after their time in Alice. He came over and took a weekend retreat for those of us who had been at Bletchingley when he was there. There were about twelve or fourteen of us. I went into the chapel to prepare things for the next session. There was a rather splendid carved wooden chair in which Desmond sat and gave the addresses. He was kneeling in front of it with his hands locked, and he was – I can only describe it as – wrestling in prayer. I just stayed for a few moments when I saw what was happening and then I left the chapel. I was running the thing so I saw him in the evenings to see whether he was all right and to find out what he needed for the next day. That evening he said, "This is between ourselves but I have been asked to take up the appointment as dean of Johannesburg, and Leah is not really very keen to go back." I think there was a chance that he could have stayed out of South Africa. But I saw him really wrestling in prayer with this enormous decision that he was trying to make. Whenever I hear in the Bible of the wrestling with God in prayer, I think of that moment. And then of course, the next minute, he was sitting on the chair giving the next address. But I felt very privileged to have been part of that wrestling.

Above: London,
March 1975.

the self-doubt, the crippling sense of inferiority, the Uncle Tomism that life as a second-class citizen can induce in an oppressed community. This still angers Tutu today as he reflects on the entrenched habits of interracial relationships that induce it. He recalls an adult black working man who habitually removed his cap while speaking to his white employer on the telephone. More insidious still is the racism embedded in everyday language: people speak of having a black day, being in a black mood, of an unpopular relative being the black sheep of the family; while in children's stories witches wear black, angels wear white, even the devil is invariably black. Moreover, the very identity of black people during the apartheid years was expressed in negative terms as non-Europeans, non-whites – ultimately, he notes, nonentities. So it was a psychologically stronger and more assertive Desmond Tutu who returned to South Africa. Not surprisingly, he and his whole family found it hard.

Trainee diplomats are warned before their first foreign posting that the culture shock of having to adapt to life in a foreign society is mild compared with what they will experience on returning home. It is the surprise of feeling disorientated by what you thought was familiar that is so unsettling when you return. So it was too with the Tutus. They thought they knew all about apartheid but, after four years of freedom from it, re-encountering its harsh realities hit them like a thunderclap. Desmond recalls how, shortly before leaving Europe, the family had dined out in one of the finer restaurants in Paris. Days later they found themselves in the significantly more modest South African port city of East London where, of course, there was no restaurant of any kind in which black people could have a meal. The Tutus had, perforce, to buy fish and chips wrapped in newspaper and eat them in their parked car.

The church's purpose in sending Tutu to England was to have a highly qualified black teacher join its team of lecturers training "non-European" candidates for the ordained ministry. But when Tutu returned, he was to find that his old seminary, St Peter's, had moved from Johannesburg. The wretched Bantu Education Act had wrought more damage, disrupting the long-established training system run by the various denominations. The government had taken over the universities and colleges that the churches had used for nearly a century, tribalising them in accordance with its apartheid ideology, which in turn resulted in some of their finest lecturers leaving in protest. The churches were determined to have nothing to do with the despised system so, after intense debate, the four main denominations – Anglican, Congregationalist, Methodist and Presbyterian – decided to pool their resources and establish their own independent seminary run on a federal basis, with each denomination having its own college, principal and staff, but all operating under a central administration. Each principal took it in turn to be head of the whole institution for a two-year period

The Federal Seminary – or Fedsem, as it was commonly called – was built in a hill-girt valley near the small Eastern Cape town of Alice. The site was chosen because, despite its remote rural setting, Alice and its environs had long been the main centre of black education in southern Africa. Not only was it home to Lovedale College, but adjoining it was Fort Hare university, which produced many of the key figures of the African National Congress, notably Nelson Mandela, Oliver Tambo and Govan Mbeki, as well as the Pan Africanist Congress founder Robert Sobukwe and the Inkatha Freedom Party's Mangosuthu Buthelezi. All of this made the apartheid government determined to gain control of this hotbed of African nationalism and bend it to its cause of tribal separation and subjugation.

But now Fedsem was there, an independent anachronism, multiracial and ecumenical in the midst of this grotesque attempt at human segregation. The Anglican Church decided that the Community of the Resurrection should continue to run its division of the seminary, and so the white monks who had taught Tutu moved there from Johannesburg, bringing the name of

TUTU: THE AUTHORISED PORTRAIT

"WE WOULD STOP A LONDON 'BOBBIE' AND ASK FOR DIRECTIONS EVEN WHEN WE KNEW WHERE WE WERE GOING, JUST FOR THE NOVELTY OF HAVING A POLICE OFFICER, A WHITE POLICE OFFICER, SPEAK TO US COURTEOUSLY, ADDRESSING US AS 'SIR' AND 'MADAM'."

DESMOND TUTU

St Peter's with them. Tutu now joined them as the only black lecturer on the Anglican staff. Leah got a job as an assistant in the library. But it was a tough transition for the family; aside from all the offensive trappings of apartheid, it was unthinkable after their four years in British schools that the children should be subjected to the appalling Bantu Education system, so the three eldest were sent to boarding schools in Swaziland, some one thousand kilometres away. Little Mpho, born in England, joined a campus group of other four-year-olds, but she had her own challenges reconciling her identity with apartheid. Tutu recalls that she once described herself to a friend as a "non-white European".[11]

Nevertheless, it was an enriching time, both for Tutu and for the students at Fedsem and Fort Hare. In another ironic twist, Tutu found himself serving as the Anglican chaplain at what he called the "the travesty next door", for even Fort Hare students could not escape the discriminating practices of the Bantu Education Department.[12] The disgruntled Fort Hare students found Tutu to be a breath of fresh air, with many of them escaping to the friendlier Fedsem campus during downtime, while the Tutus themselves hosted coffee evenings on Sundays, to which Fort Hare and Fedsem students came for lively political discussions.

Looking back, Tutu feels today that he was still a fairly orthodox Anglican preacher and teacher in the English tradition during his three years at Fedsem, and that he was still "fairly apolitical".[13] But the evidence points to this being a transitional time when he encountered the start of new developments that were to influence him profoundly later on. Central to Tutu's theology is the notion that theology itself is evolutionary. "Theology is not the same thing as religion or faith," he explains. "Theology is always temporary, transient; there is no final theology. We are always evolving, always growing in our understanding of things."[14]

So here he was, at the beginning of a new growth phase, about to encounter the nascent political concept of Black Consciousness, and to experience his first personal encounter with police violence – which in turn led to his first moment of political activism.

South Africa's silent sixties were drawing to a close and a new ferment was beginning to arise among the black youth, foreshadowing the stormy seventies and eighties that lay ahead. The Black Consciousness Movement first manifested itself at a conference of the multiracial University Christian Movement in the Eastern Cape town of Stutterheim, near Alice. The white students essentially supported the aims of the black students but the latter were becoming frustrated because they were outnumbered and had come from poorer schools, with the result that the whites took most of the leading positions in the organisation and the blacks felt they had no say in policy formulation. The blacks felt, too, that the whites could never adequately understand their situation. So they pulled out of the conference to form their own "black caucus" to discuss their problems. Thus was born the Black Consciousness Movement.

The new movement posed obvious problems for Tutu. He had many white friends, in Britain and South Africa, and the whole object of his mission in life was to bring black and white, all of God's children, together in harmonious unity. Yet Tutu also sympathised with the aims of these young black students and could see the logic of the strategy they decided to pursue – especially as Stephen Biko, the movement's leader, defined it.

"All in all the black man has become a shell," Biko wrote in his seminal book, *I Write What I Like*, "a shadow of a man, completely defeated, drowning in his own misery, a slave, an ox bearing the yoke of oppression with sheepish timidity. This is the first truth, bitter as it may seem, that we have to acknowledge before we can start on any programme designed to change the status quo. It becomes more necessary to see the truth as it is if you realise that the only vehicle for change [is] these people who have lost their personality. The first step, therefore, is to make the black man come to himself; to pump back life into his empty shell; to infuse him with pride and dignity, to remind him of his complicity in the crime of allowing himself to be misused and therefore letting evil reign supreme in the country of his birth. This is what we mean by an inward-looking process. This is the definition of Black Consciousness."[15]

The rapid growth of this new radicalism among the students gave rise to seething tensions on the Fort Hare campus, particularly after the arrival of a new, ultra-conservative rector,

Above: With Leah at the Diocese of New West Minster's youth synod, Vancouver, 3 May 1977.

J. M. de Wet. Soon after returning from the mid-year break, the students launched a series of strikes to protest against what they called "racist education" and to demand more competent academic staff. There was no representative student body to engage the university administration on these issues, but a group of students that included Barney Pityana, a rising star within the Black Consciousness Movement, asked to see the new rector to press their demands. De Wet's response was inflammatory. Instead of listening to their grievances, he ordered that the protests stop immediately and that political slogans that had been painted on walls be erased, failing which he would take disciplinary action.

Enraged at being treated so derisively, the entire student body embarked on a sit-down strike on the lawn in front of the university's administration block. They sat there peacefully for several days – then one morning a loudspeaker announcement informed them that all students had been expelled and were to leave the campus by 2:00 p.m. Silently they remained where they were, until suddenly a convoy of armoured cars roared onto the campus, disgorging a body of police armed with guns, tear gas and dogs, who quickly surrounded the students. As the police pointed their guns at the students and the snarling dogs lunged at them, injuring some, there was a brief stand-off. The students began singing freedom songs, enraging the police still further. As the tension rose, nobody knew what was going to happen. Then Tutu, dressed in his cassock, came hurrying across from the seminary with chaplains from its other denominations. The police tried to stop them, but Tutu burst his way past them to join the students on the lawn, where he knelt, blessed them and prayed with them. Nonplussed, the police held back, and the moment passed.

was born at the end of the 1920s, which makes me just on two years older than the subject of our conversation. He never forgets my birthday. I regularly forget his. We met when he was thirty and I was thirty-two – I think that could be right – in 1962. I had a letter from Father Aelred Stubbs, who was the leading member of the Community of the Resurrection [CR] in Johannesburg's Sophiatown. He asked that I look out for this young student whom he was posting off to King's College London to study for a bachelor of divinity.

I know Desmond was set up as a part-time assistant in Golders Green, and provided in return with a flat for his family who would come soon. We met, and I can't remember a thing about it. We must have gone off in the car talking a hundred miles an hour. I introduced him to a variety of this and that, including my rather pompous old male establishment, The Travellers Club, where he came with me quite soon after his arrival. He remembers eating grouse, newly shot – no doubt on some grand hill in Scotland – and spitting out the pellets with which the grouse had been killed.

You have to remember that was nearly fifty years ago. Things were very different in London. It was very unusual to be seen with somebody of a different colour on the streets. One had to take great care as to where one took a black person to eat in London. My club was always friendly to people from overseas, it being called The Travellers Club. I wouldn't have taken him to the Carlton Club or the Junior Carlton or other places. It would not have been frowned upon, but they would have somehow looked askance.

I know from my visitors' book that Leah, Thandi and Trevor arrived – I think on a boat train – at Victoria Station on 30 November 1962. Naomi arrived later, by air. She had whooping cough and had to be held back by her grandparents. Mpho was born on 30 November 1963, exactly a year to the day after Leah, Trevor and Thandi had arrived in this country. We scooped them up in my car and they came back to my flat. From then on we became firm friends. It wasn't very long before they met bits of my family and my friends in London of whom I had a great many.

My very marvellous bosses, the trustees of the Overseas Student Trust, agreed with my idea that, having met a lot of students in this country, I should go to where the students came from. So I spent two months or more visiting twelve countries of the Commonwealth in Africa: staying in hostels, visiting, staying with people, visiting relations of students here. I had a delightful Sunday lunch with the Tutu parents. Desmond's father

wrote to him to say that this chap 'Mr Martin', as he called me, had come to lunch. He said that it had been all right and that Mr Martin had washed the dishes for his mother. This was considered rather unusual. I'm not sure they'd ever entertained a white man to lunch but if they had, they'd probably never had him washing up.

We saw a lot of each other. I saw a lot of the family as a whole. I used to go to the house. It was a second family home for me. I would have eaten Sunday lunch there more often than I would anywhere else in London at the time. It was quite normal. There was no effort ever with them. The Tutu family were very close to being my best friends in London; perhaps they were. I had visits to Africa later, after the Tutus' return to Africa after 1966. I represented their family at the degree-giving in the Albert Hall. He was disappointed that he was vying for first but he didn't quite get it. I remember that occasion. I don't know whether we celebrated afterwards – I hope we did. One has to keep remembering that Desmond Tutu was completely unknown, except as a student at King's who made great friends. Of course he was unusual in the sense that he was always going to be an unusual person, but he wasn't recognised in the streets. I think he was pretty poor. There was always a question whether he had enough money. It's quite funny to watch the boot being on the other foot now. I am now the regular recipient beneficiary of his largesse, whereas at that time …

If one thinks of Desmond Tutu, it is the peak contrast between the man who is always the life and soul of the party, and somebody who can be totally still and an example to us all in the capacity to reflect and meditate. He can be a ball of energy dancing in church leading so that you can't fail to do whatever, because it's the right thing to be doing at that time – it just seems natural. He has an extraordinary gift for leading and yet everybody joining in. I wouldn't say "following", but they are doing what they wouldn't normally do. They are behaving out of character and glad they are doing it. They are not embarrassed – with very few exceptions would say – by what they are doing, which wouldn't be something that they normally did.

At home or driving in the car any distance, it was silence and repose and snoozing and praying. His inviolable rule about waking early, praying and saying his office was something that he learnt at the feet of the Mirfield fathers of the CR. It has stood him in very good stead since then. I think it's been a huge notable thing and it's very much shown in the well-organised life, in relation to other people, that he has portrayed.

archbishop was newly installed at Bishopscourt. He'd been there a matter of months. This man said to me it was an extraordinary experience for the clergy. They had expected a man of his gifts, but they thought that of course he wouldn't be able to do what English-origin archbishops did, which was to be concerned about their flock. On the contrary, they were more aware of the way in which Desmond Tutu was able to ensure, through a well-organised office obviously, but with his own initiative, leadership and insistence and enthusiasm,

of the clergy were remembered. People's birthdays were remembered. The births of their children were remembered. The deaths of their mothers were remembered. All these were remembered in very particular concrete ways. I have been a beneficiary of this every single birthday. I have received a telegram. I have received a large bunch of flowers. Lately I have received huge cornucopias of fruit that I can hardly get through but I am able to share with my friends and neighbours.

CHRIS GREEN

I first came to know about Desmond as a fresher student in my first few days up at King's. I was with a little group, and we were all finding our way around the corridors in King's. We were wondering where the next lecture room was going to be, and I heard some laughter. I saw this wonderful, happy man on the other side of the corridor in another little group. I don't know what they were laughing about; I can't remember that, but I thought, "there is somebody who is full of something, full of joy for sure." We said hello, and that was when I first got to know him. I didn't know anything about him at all until that first meeting. It was great that it began with a laugh, because he's so good at sharing his laughter and it is a very powerful weapon!

With somebody like Desmond, what you see at a first encounter forms an instant and unforgettable impression. With Desmond that impression, which is so immediate, is of someone who is full of the joys of life, but who also has great depths. The more I got to know about where he'd come from, the more I learnt about the difficulties that he'd faced – even in becoming a priest – the more I appreciated the substance of this remarkable man. I was fascinated by the fact that becoming a priest hadn't been his first choice. I think he wanted to be a doctor if I remember rightly. It seemed all the more remarkable that he was now so sure of his vocation.

He was massively compelling. I was almost straight out of school and so Desmond was somewhat older than me, probably ten years or so. He was already ordained and considerably more mature, but in so many ways he still seemed very young. I think it was the fact that somebody could be so alive and so warm

and so happy and so certain about everything, and yet have come from such an extraordinarily difficult and challenging background with so much unhappiness in it that was striking. It seemed nothing short of a miracle that he could be who he was.

I had a private school education in the UK. It is quite closeted. Most of my school contemporaries took up a profession or joined the family business. With my kind of background, I was not as aware of the world as some might be at the age of eighteen. I hadn't been exposed to looking at the world from anything other than a typically traditional British point of view. Desmond prompted me to look more carefully at what was happening in the world and especially in his native South Africa, and the more I looked, the more appalled I became at the way people were treating each other. He probably doesn't have any idea at all what impact he had on me at the time, and probably on so many of my fellow students. It was knowing Desmond that encouraged me to become an active anti-apartheid campaigner.

On the occasions I have re-engaged with Desmond over the years – at the time of the "Thirty Years On" King's College London theological faculty reunion in 1995 (when Desmond officially opened the student bar and nightclub Tutu's); over dinner with him and Leah with old friends David and Jennie Johnstone and at a more recent magnificent Royal Geographical Society lecture Desmond gave – I have continued to be moved by his fabulous gifts of communication, humour, humility and compassion. Desmond has the unique ability to move most of us to tears – tears of joy and tears of compassion. I hardly need add that he is simply magical

TUTU: THE AUTHORISED PORTRAIT

That was the day Desmond Tutu the political activist was born. He had acted impulsively, driven by the passion of compassion. That compassion was itself the product of his ever-deepening spirituality, his belief that humanity is sacred and that every individual is a God-carrier to be cherished. Not for one second did any political strategy or agenda play a role in what Tutu did that day. And so it has been ever since.

The students were allowed to pack their belongings before being put into buses, driven to various railways stations and sent home. They had to apply for readmission to the university, and those whom the authorities deemed to have been "political agitators" were denied readmission. But it was an indelible moment for everyone who had witnessed Tutu's action. Barney Pityana, who later became a priest himself, and later vice-chancellor of the University of South Africa in the post-apartheid era, still recalls it as a turning point in his own life. "It was a deeply moving experience," he told author Shirley du Boulay years later. "The students flocked around him in relief and excitement, asking for his blessing. I knew then what I wanted to do. That was my first real experience of what it means to be a priest."[16]

Tutu was deeply affected too. Friends recall how shocked he was, almost disbelieving, at the brutality of the police; how he wept openly at the Eucharist service the next day, tears streaming down his face as he passed the chalice. But he was to witness that savagery many more times and shed many more tears in the years ahead.

Before then, however, there were also to be more experiences to broaden his faith still further. To the dismay of his mentors who had nurtured him thus far and earmarked him as a future principal of Fedsem, Tutu decided to leave the seminary after three years and accept a job as a lecturer in the theology department at the University of Botswana, Lesotho and Swaziland, based at Roma in Lesotho, the independent country entirely surrounded by South Africa. The salary was significantly higher than it had been at Fedsem, which occasioned some accusations of avarice, but in fact a more compelling reason for the Tutus was that the move brought them much closer to two of their children, Trevor and Thandeka, at boarding school in Swaziland, while the other two, Naomi and Mpho, could join their parents at a school on the university campus. Thus, all could still evade the horrors of Bantu Education without being so painfully split as a family.

The move was fortuitous in another respect as well. A year after the Tutus left Fedsem, the Fort Hare administration, obviously annoyed by what it saw as the contagious influence of the

The story of our meeting is a story I'm always a little bit reluctant to tell. During my gap year I was working on a farm in Hertfordshire before I went to university to read agriculture. I came home one weekend and my mother said, "We've got a new curate at the church." I said, "That's good." There had been a gap between curates.

And she said, "Well, he's arrived. He arrived a couple of weeks ago with his family. I think you'll like him. He's very jolly. He's black, you know."

And then I met Desmond in church that weekend or the weekend after. There was an age gap of fourteen or fifteen years but I think because he was also a student and we were both at London university there was a bond. By then I think Desmond had got to know my mother. She used to go to the early morning service and we just made friends.

Desmond has sometimes introduced me as somebody who was a server at St Alban's church all those years ago. I think probably one of my earliest recollections of Desmond would be of going into the church, maybe five or ten minutes before the service started, and seeing Desmond kneeling in the front pew facing the altar just so quietly, and then getting up quietly two or three minutes before the service, going into the vestry, putting on another robe, and then the service starting. I think it was that quietness but then breaking out into huge jollity at some point: meeting somebody, greeting somebody.

His ability to be with somebody when things are rough, to cry with them when they're crying and to laugh with them when they're laughing and to be able

to do that with almost anybody is marvellous. It makes somebody feel special. I've become more conscious of Desmond saying it over the years, because I've heard him say it more often, but he must have said it to me very early on. He said, "But you're special." And if you're growing up, at almost any age, but particularly when you're growing up, you're probably quite vulnerable to thinking, "I'm not very good at this" or "I'm embarrassed" or "I don't know what direction I'm going in" or whatever. If somebody says to you, "You're special. You're special in God's eyes. You're a very special person. God loves you," that is incredibly supportive and moving.

I wouldn't have been interested in Africa if I hadn't had some exposure to people who came from Africa. In terms of South Africa I remember saying to Desmond, "When you preach in church you give us a lot in a sermon, lots of things to think about, but you don't talk about South Africa." He said, "Well, of course the situation in South Africa is terrible, but I don't want to preach about it when I'm here as a parish priest. But if you want to join me I'm actually going down to meet a group one evening next week. Come with me if you like. I am going to tell them a little bit about what life is like in South Africa for black people." So I went. And that was quite different. The people in the audience were much more politically aware than I ever was, certainly at that time. They were asking a lot of political questions that opened my eyes a little bit more.

When I went back to college, I was offered the chance to go to Cuba, and for the first time I saw poverty.

little seminary next door, made an offer to buy the campus, claiming it needed the space for expansion. The churches refused, but three years later the government simply expropriated the property and gave the seminary one month's notice to leave.

Lesotho also had the unique advantage of being an island free of apartheid within itself, but also intimately in touch with what was happening in South Africa. The proximity brought its own internal problems, of course, with South Africa being able to exert enough pressure to ensure that a government headed by the acquiescent Chief Leabua Jonathan ran the show rather than the more radical Basutoland Congress Party and, at the same, time infiltrating enough informers to keep the sizeable political refugee population there under constant surveillance. Still, it was a good listening post that enabled Tutu to follow and become increasingly interested in the emergence of the concept of "black theology" in South Africa in the slipstream of the by now fast-growing Black Consciousness Movement.

The other consequence of Tutu's sojourn in Lesotho was that his growing reputation as the subcontinent's major black theologian drew him more and more into ecumenical work throughout the region. This brought him to the attention of the World Council of Churches, so that after

-two. I came back from Cuba and found the contrast of coming back to the affluence of London more daunting than seeing Cuba. My mother had saved up, without me having any idea of this, and bought me a new sports car. She said to me, "I've got a surprise for you. I want you to come along with me tomorrow morning." We went along to this garage where this brand-new, pale blue Triumph Spitfire was unveiled. And I said, "Mother, it's lovely but ..."

She said, "It's for you darling."

I said, "I don't need a car like that." I had an old banger and it broke down. "I don't need a new car." I just couldn't believe the contrast to where I had just come back from. So I went home. I did not accept this present. I was not happy. My mother was very sad and confused as to why I hadn't been really excited about this new car. And I then talked to Desmond the next day and he said, "Malcolm, don't you think you're being ungracious? Don't you see how much this means to your mother? Sometimes you've got to realise it's better to receive than to give. Enjoy the car. Share it." (Something he's often said.) "Share it with your friends. Enjoy it. Let your mother enjoy it. But go with it." That was such a surprise. There are many times Desmond's surprised me.

Many years later when I was working in London, I still had itchy feet to work in Africa. I saw a job advertised with a large company called BICC as finance director for their South African operation. I went to the first interview and it went well. I went back for the be based near Johannesburg on very good conditions. We would have gone there for two or three years. The family was happy to go and I was offered the job. I went home and talked it through with Helene, my wife, and decided that I just couldn't accept it. It just couldn't be right to go and work in apartheid South Africa at the height of apartheid – this was sometime in the eighties. I let it go and carried on where I was. There were some regrets but I felt that it was the right decision.

Some months later I was with Desmond and told this story to him. He said, "Malcolm, why didn't you ring us up and talk about it?" I said, "Perhaps I should have done but I thought you wouldn't want me to take it. I thought I knew what you would say."

"You may have missed a chance there. Of course it's difficult working in South Africa. Of course we've got huge problems but you might have done the job. In fact, I'm sure you would have done the job better than perhaps the person who has taken the job on. You would have had more sensitivity to the issues. You would have been much better at looking for talent that's emerging that could be helped through and promoted in the company. You would have understood the issues and reflected them in how you'd taken on the job."

"Desmond, I never believed you would say that!"

"Next time, phone up. It's only the cost of a phone call, Malcolm."

He did surprise me. I think this is one of his great strengths.

only eighteen months in Lesotho he found himself confronted with an offer to join that august body's Theological Education Fund (TEF) as its associate regional director for Africa. It was an exciting offer that would require him to travel constantly around sub-Saharan Africa helping to fund and generally improve theological training institutions throughout that vast region. Not least of the job's attractions was that the TEF was based in London, which meant the family would relocate there with all the advantages they had enjoyed while Tutu was studying at King's College.

So the Tutus returned to Britain early in 1972 to begin what Tutu himself describes as one of the most formative phases of his life. The TEF was headquartered in South London and had a simple but highly efficient structure. It was headed by a Taiwanese exile, Dr Shoki Coe, with four associate directors each assigned to covering a particular region of the world: Latin America, South-east Asia, the Pacific and sub-Saharan Africa. Coe himself dealt with North-east Asia. Each of the associate directors came from the region to which he was assigned and all were from different Christian denominations, which gave the group a broad racial and ecumenical spread that Tutu found hugely stimulating.

"THIS GOD DID NOT JUST TALK ... HE SHOWED HIMSELF TO BE A DOING GOD. PERHAPS WE MIGHT ADD ANOTHER POINT ABOUT GOD – HE TAKES SIDES. HE IS NOT A NEUTRAL GOD. HE TOOK THE SIDE OF THE SLAVES, THE OPPRESSED, THE VICTIMS. HE IS STILL THE SAME EVEN TODAY; HE SIDES WITH THE POOR, THE HUNGRY, THE OPPRESSED AND THE VICTIMS OF INJUSTICE."

DESMOND TUTU

The job involved a great deal of travelling. Over the next three years, Tutu criss-crossed his parish of twenty-five different countries, at a time when they were going through great, and often traumatic, changes. Nearly all were newly born, having just emerged from colonial pasts, and struggling to establish their national identities from the hodgepodge of different ethnic, linguistic and religious groups that fell within the arbitrarily drawn boundaries they had inherited. It was a time of hope and excitement, but also of military coups and wars and the nefarious interference of Cold War rivalries. Thus Tutu found himself in Uganda at the time of the murderous Idi Amin, in the Democratic Zaire (later to become the Democratic Republic of Congo) during the early takeover and dictatorship of Mobutu Sese Seko, in Nigeria in the painful aftermath of the Biafran war, in Rhodesia (later to become Zimbabwe) during Ian Smith's unilaterally declared independence, but also in Kenya, Tanzania and Botswana during the promising years of their founding presidents: Jomo Kenyatta, Julius Nyerere and Sir Seretse Khama. He also became aware of the encounter between Christianity and Islam, which ran in a broad band right across the continent from its west coast to the Horn, slicing through such national giants as Nigeria and Sudan, and posing both the prospect of healthy interfaith dialogue and frightful conflicts. In the course of these travels, Tutu met all the key political and religious leaders of the day, engaged in endless discussions with them, and wrote copiously about everything he saw and learnt: emerging from it all with a greatly sharpened political mind and a keen understanding of the daunting challenges facing Africa.

But it was in the further development of his theological thinking that Tutu underwent the most profound change during those three years. The transforming factor here, he explains, was that the TEF was mandated to work within the framework of what it called "contextual theology" – in other words to examine the needs of theological training within the contexts of the different societies being surveyed by the five regional directors. Inevitably this led, in the course of their intense mutual discussions, to a growing awareness in Tutu's mind that theology itself was moulded by the particular social contexts in which it arose, that all denominations and faiths were shaped by the different historical, sociological and cultural contexts in which they had arisen.

Typically, Tutu explains this profound concept by way of a joke: "You know the story of the drunk who accosts a pedestrian and asks him: 'I shay, which is the other side of the shtreet?' The nonplussed pedestrian says, 'It's over there of course', pointing across the road. 'That's strange,' the drunk says, 'when I was that side they said it was this side'."[17]

"So you see," Tutu concludes with a characteristic chuckle, "the other side of the street depends on where you are. Contextual theology attempts to make sense of a particular community; to make sense for a particular Christian community who lived in a particular context. Therefore, by definition, you can't have a universal theology, because the contexts differ. The kinds of questions a community asked, and for which you would have to provide answers, depended very much on who they were and where they worked."[18]

The transformational effect of this realisation was to lead eventually to Tutu embracing the validity of all faiths in their particular contexts. But for the moment its impact was confined to broadening his thinking within Christian theology. Tutu had been trained as a fairly orthodox priest in the Anglo-Catholic tradition, and that remained – and still is – the bedrock of his faith. But theology and faith are not the same thing. So now, with the influences of the Black Consciousness Movement and black theology still fresh in his mind from his experiences at Fedsem and in Lesotho, Tutu began asking himself some difficult questions.

If there could be no universal theology, that must mean that Western theology had no universal validity, which in turn must mean that the people of Africa – and of everywhere else, for that matter – had no need for white missionaries to bring them the word of God in order to save their souls. Africans had their own spiritual awareness of God that had evolved in the context of their own circumstances and spiritual needs. African spirituality therefore had its own theological validity.

Moreover, Tutu felt the universalist attitude of the white missionaries had induced a form of schizophrenia among African Christians. The missionaries felt Africans had to become Westernised before they could become Christians. "They had to deny their African-ness before they could become genuine Christians …" he says. "Virtually all things African were condemned

TUTU: THE AUTHORISED PORTRAIT

as pagan and had to be destroyed ..."[19] This left African Christians with split personalities: on the face of it they accepted what the missionaries were saying, but deep down they clung to their traditional thoughts and rituals.

A second major shift in Tutu's theological evolution came through his encounter with the TEF's associate director for Latin America, Aharon Sapsezian, a Brazilian citizen of Armenian extraction. Sapsezian introduced Tutu to the concept of liberation theology – essentially a movement which holds that Christianity is obligated to champion the cause of the poor and the downtrodden – which was sweeping like a populist movement through Latin America at that time, and it had an immediate and visceral appeal to Tutu's humanistic instincts.

Liberation theology is based mainly on the contention that the life and teachings of Jesus Christ commit Christians to become socially active on behalf of the poor. But Tutu, who concentrated on Old Testament theology at King's and during his teaching career at Fedsem and Roma, adds an interesting new dimension from that background. He notes that the book of Genesis was written at a painful time in Jewish history, during the Babylonian exile when the Jews were being ill-treated and exploited as slaves, a time when they must have thought God did not care about them and perhaps did not even exist. But then God came to their rescue and led them into the Promised Land.

"This God did not just talk – He acted," Tutu once explained. "He showed Himself to be a doing God. Perhaps we might add another point about God: He takes sides. He is not a neutral God. He took the side of the slaves, the oppressed, the victims. He is still the same even today; he sides with the poor, the hungry, the oppressed and the victims of injustice."[20] But typically, Tutu then added a note of caution. God might be on the side of the oppressed black people of South Africa, he told the young deacons, but that was not because they are inherently better or more deserving than are their white oppressors, but simply because they were being oppressed. God loves all of humanity, all are made in his image, but, when there is oppression or poverty or suffering, he sides with the disadvantaged and intervenes to liberate them.

In another exposition of this theme, this time in a paper presented at a conference in the United States, Tutu described black liberation theology as "a clarion call for man to align himself with the God who is the God of the Exodus, God the liberator, who leads his people, all his people, out of all kinds of bondage – political, economic, cultural, the bondage of sin and disease – into the glorious liberty of the son of God."[21]

And then, again the cautionary addendum. White oppression was not the only bondage from which blacks needed to be liberated, he warned in an obvious reference to his years of experience travelling around Africa. "When the white oppressor is removed, far too often he is succeeded by his black counterpart."[22]

Consequently, Tutu was able to reconcile his support for Black Consciousness and black liberation theology with his own profound belief in non-racialism. That is the frame of reference that gave shape and purpose to his leadership of the liberation struggle for the next decade and a half after his return to South Africa to become the first black dean of Johannesburg in 1975. It was then that he began speaking out with increasing forcefulness about the iniquities of apartheid.

Left: Dean of
Johannesburg,
10 March 1976.

CHAPTER FIVE

....

I DO NOT FEAR THEM

"I WILL DEMONSTRATE THAT APARTHEID, SEPARATE DEVELOPMENT OR WHATEVER IT IS CALLED, IS EVIL, TOTALLY AND WITHOUT REMAINDER, THAT IT IS UN-CHRISTIAN AND UNBIBLICAL. IF ANYONE WERE TO SHOW ME OTHERWISE, I WOULD BURN MY BIBLE AND CEASE TO BE A CHRISTIAN."

....

DESMOND TUTU

My most vivid memory of Desmond Tutu in action during those struggle years was in September 1982 when, as a correspondent for several foreign newspapers, I watched this diminutive figure, clad by now in a purple bishop's cassock, stab a finger towards five stony-faced white commissioners sitting before him in an austere government office and declare: "You whites brought us the Bible; now we blacks are taking it seriously. We are involved with God to set us free from all that enslaves us and makes us less than what he intended us to be."[1]

Throwing his arms wide in a gesture like a benediction, Tutu boomed at them: "I will demonstrate that apartheid, separate development or whatever it is called, is evil, totally and without remainder, that it is un-Christian and unbiblical." Then lowering his voice almost to a whisper he added: "If anyone were to show me otherwise, I would burn my Bible and cease to be a Christian."[2]

It was not just the sermon of his life, it was an act of courageous defiance in defence of everything he believed in and represented. For Tutu was effectively on trial. He had returned from London to become dean of Johannesburg. Within a year he was elected bishop of Lesotho; then he was seconded to take over as general secretary of the South African Council of Churches (SACC), which he propelled swiftly to

Left: Bishop of Johannesburg, 29 September 1977.

the forefront of the crusade against apartheid. Now the government of Prime Minister P. W. Botha was trying to crack down on the SACC. Botha had appointed the commission to investigate the SACC's interpretation of its Christian mission, as well as its foreign connections and financial records, and report to the government on whether it was a subversive organisation.

The problem facing the council was that most of its funds came from churches in Europe and the United States, and much of them had been used to defend political prisoners, help their families and educate their children. These were people the government regarded as subversive elements and terrorists so, to protect them, the council did not record all names in its financial records. That meant it was vulnerable to disclosures that Botha hoped he could use against it.

To that end, Botha's appointed commission, headed by Justice C. J. Eloff, resulted in a year-long hearing – a sort of open-ended trial with no specific charges or even allegations – accompanied by nearly two years of continuous investigation with state-appointed chartered accountants and police investigators examining every aspect of the SACC's finances and going through more than twenty thousand documents. It was a disruptive intrusion into the council's work, and also stirred up conflicts within the staff and among member churches, some of whom felt Tutu had brought trouble upon the council and into their lives with his political statements.

The greatest danger, though, came when the security police testified at the hearings. They contended that the SACC was representing the views of its foreign funders rather than its local church members, and that it was giving credibility to the African National Congress (ANC) – which in itself constituted a crime under South Africa's security legislation. The police asked the commission to recommend that the government declare the SACC an "affected organisation", which would mean that its foreign funding would be cut and that government-sponsored people would be placed in its finance department. That would have effectively put the council out of action. So Tutu was fighting here for the very life of his organisation.

But instead of putting up a defence, Tutu used the occasion to counter-attack not only the government but the theological justification for apartheid provided by the South African branch of the Dutch Reformed Church (DRC) – a church historically so close to the ruling Afrikaner establishment that it was mockingly referred to as "the National Party at prayer". From the mid-1930s, a group of young politicised DRC theologians, along with other Afrikaner intellectuals who formed an elitist society called the Broederbond (Band of Brothers), became intimately involved in formulating the apartheid policy, the purpose of which, as one of its leading lights described, was "to ensure a fatherland for the white man in South Africa that for ages to come can serve as a home for posterity".[3] The DRC endorsed the group's analysis, and the policy was then formally adopted by the National Party when it came to power in 1948.

The basis of the theological justification for apartheid was extrapolated from a doctrine developed by a Dutch Calvinist theologian and politician, Abraham Kuyper, who founded the Free University of Amsterdam and became prime minister of the Netherlands in the early twentieth century. Kuyper's big political issue was the right to teach religion in schools, which the government was refusing on the grounds that public education should remain neutral on religious matters.

TUTU: THE AUTHORISED PORTRAIT

"I WANT THE GOVERNMENT TO KNOW NOW AND ALWAYS THAT I DO NOT FEAR THEM. THEY ARE TRYING TO DEFEND THE UTTERLY INDEFENSIBLE, AND THEY WILL FAIL. THEY WILL FAIL BECAUSE THEY ARE RANGING THEMSELVES ON THE SIDE OF EVIL AND INJUSTICE AGAINST THE CHURCH OF GOD. LIKE OTHERS WHO HAVE DONE THAT IN THE PAST – THE NEROS, THE HITLERS, THE IDI AMINS OF THIS WORLD – THEY WILL END UP AS THE FLOTSAM AND JETSAM OF HISTORY."

DESMOND TUTU

was the religion correspondent for the *Star* from 1976 through to 1982. The first time that I remember meeting him was when he was a guest speaker at the SACC [South African Council of Churches] national conference, probably in July of 1976. It was memorable, because the conference was held within a month or six weeks of the Soweto uprising and passions were running very high at the conference. Desmond Tutu was a guest speaker and managed at the same time to bring a measure of calm to the conference, but also to engage the burning issues seriously. He was a powerful communicator.

That impression was reinforced a couple of months later in November of 1976 at the Anglican Provincial Synod. He came to the synod as bishop of Lesotho. He reached out to everybody, no matter who they were or what side of the political divide they were on. He was quite clearly on the side of liberation and on the side of people who were suffering, but he had a very power-ful effect on everyone. He moved the synod to a new place in its debate on the Soweto uprising and brought everybody together.

From what I saw then, and at ensuing national conferences of the SACC, I wrote later that he was destined to be one of the country's great church lead-ers. I think I reached that conclusion after his second SACC national conference as general secretary, so he had been there just over a year.

In the 1960s to the early 1970s, there was a whole generation of church leaders who were sent abroad on TEF [Theological Education Fund] grants for further training abroad. Significant among them were people from the multiracial churches. They came back and in that period from the late 1960s to the early 1980s, when the leadership of the multiracial churches changed from majority white leadership to majority black lead-ership or substantial black leadership, many of those leaders had been recipients of TEF grants. There were a lot of strong, powerful leaders: Sigqibo Dwane of the Order of Ethiopia, Khoza Mgojo of the Methodist Church, Stanley Mogoba, also of the Methodist Church. What distinguished Desmond Tutu from them? Why did he become prominent? Why didn't they become as prominent, especially internationally?

For me, there are a number of reasons: Tutu is an extraordinarily powerful communicator and he can reach out to all sides. There is a sense of humanity that he conveys and displays, and a sense of human solidarity that he evokes in people. He communicates in lots of different ways. He can read an audience. I don't

think he does it consciously; I think he does it intuitively. With audiences he is accustomed to, often societies he is accustomed to operating in, when speaking he will drop in jokes and allusions. He picks up on what they respond to and what they don't respond to, and is guided by that. He reads audiences well and he knows audiences well. That's one way he communicates powerfully.

Another one is that he has the gift of the sound bite. Again, I think it's intuitive. He's not a person who sits and plots things out in advance. I think he's a person who operates from the gut. I remember hearing it best from a friend who was a South African newspaper correspondent in Washington. After the Nobel Prize was announced but before it was awarded, the Arch went to see Reagan. When he came out of the White House and the press asked, "Well, what's your take on this?" he responded, "Constructive engagement gives democracy a bad name." And it was the perfect sound bite. It worked with the media.

He has always been one of the most accessible and open public figures for journalists to work with. With the Arch, what you see is what you get. There aren't contradictions. There is a deeply private part of him that I suspect only Leah and maybe his children know. He has hidden private depths but that's to the degree that he's a very self-contained person who is at ease within his own skin.

His power of communication is, of course, rooted in spirituality. His spirituality is natural and normal and is the central part of his life. In one way or another, the first four hours of the day were spent in silence, probably two hours in the middle of the day and an hour at the end of the day at least, so you're talking about six or seven hours of the day in silence. When I was a staff member, even if we were travelling, he kept the silent times. If you were arguing with people who were scheduling him, you would say, "Who do you want? Who did you invite? Did you invite the ebullient, warm, communicative Tutu who wows the crowds? If that's who you invited and if you want that, then you have to recognise that the warmth and the ebullience and the reaching out to crowds, that loving to be loved and enjoying the crowd and reading of the crowd and the sharing of the emotion and the sense of inclusive humanity, that's one side of a coin. The other side of the coin is hours and hours a day in silence. And if you schedule him to run around morning, noon and night, you are not going get the Tutu you want. He can't do the ebullient without the hours of silence."

I learnt in working with him that you need physical stamina to keep up with him. He maintains an extraordinary pace. To work with him successfully you need to be able to keep up that pace. I remember my first overseas trip with him was in commencement season 1988. We were four and a half weeks into a five-week trip and we were in Atlanta. We were taking an early morning walk. He had stopped jogging by then because of suspected thrombosis but he did a fast walk. At the end of the walk, he said, "I'm feeling a bit tired today." I burst out, "Father, I'm twenty years younger than you and I'm exhausted! I want to go home!"

In his relations with staff, he doesn't ask of you what he isn't giving himself. And it's an all-embracing kind of relationship. I think it's partly in his nature, but it's also part of his vocation to the priesthood. There isn't a distinction between a personal life and a business life, as it were.

One of the memorable experiences working for him that I recall was sitting in the Oval Office and being told, "Just take notes. Just take notes." I didn't think we were ever going to do anything with the notes but we needed to look serious and I needed to look professional. The White House people all had their note takers so I needed to take notes. That was Clinton and Gore in 1993. He was the first South African they saw after Clinton took office.

The most memorable experience was not one event, but a series of events. We were in Khartoum under al-Bashir. He wasn't there himself at the time; he was on a visit to somewhere in the Middle East. Then we were in Addis Ababa under Mengistu. We were in Panama the year before Noriega was overthrown. And lastly we were in Kinshasa under Mobutu. In all four places, I heard Tutu preaching in services or speaking publicly to big audiences using the same language about human rights and liberation as he used in South Africa. He was, ostensibly, talking about South Africa. He would say, "Well, in South Africa we have restrictions on press freedom. We have detention without trial. We have this happening and that happening." And then sometimes he would say, "I'm talking about South Africa." The audience would roar with laughter, because they knew he was talking about their own situations. He was preaching human rights and liberation in a wide range of oppressive situations and getting the same instinctive, warm, celebratory response from his audiences.

Of course there were other memorable times: seeing him present Mandela to the Grand Parade on the day he was elected president, being in Parliament when he was elected president, and the day Mandela was released. That day we had been in Johannesburg. Mazwi Tisani picked us up from the airport. He said that the ANC [African National Congress] had asked if Madiba [Nelson Mandela] could stay overnight at Bishopscourt, and they'd said yes.

We got to the city hall and waited in the Mayor's Parlour while the crowd outside got more and more restive as the afternoon went on. Mandela had come to town and they tried to get into the city hall, but they couldn't get him through the crowds, so they had to take him away again. It was getting really chaotic, and then a bunch of people broke into the city hall. They saw the Arch and said they wanted to see Nelson Mandela. They didn't believe he had been freed. They said that the Boers were lying; they were tricking us. So the Arch said, "I will get you to see Mandela." He led them through the city hall like the Pied Piper. He took them out through the back door and, of course, someone shut it behind them as we left and made sure they couldn't get back in again. Then we walked them up to District Six, outside St Mark's Church.

Initially about three thousand people were gathered there. As we waited, slowly people drifted away. Eventually there were a few hundred people left but they were the really hard-core angry youth. One boy shouted that the Arch was De Klerk's impimpi and picked up a rock. It was touch and go. It was frightening. The Arch and the Muslim clergy who were there agreed to take them back down to the Grand Parade. The youngsters were so close on our heels, you know there were a couple of times the youngsters actually trod on my heel and pulled off my shoe as we went back down. When we got back to the city hall we went to the back entrance out of which we had taken these people. The ANC had a whole line of marshals to block off the street. They saw us coming and they all linked arms as we came. They parted to let the Arch and the clergy and me through, and then they closed ranks to stop these other guys from getting through.

It was getting very desperate. It was getting very late. Then somebody got hold of Madiba. David Turnley took a lovely picture of the Mayor's Parlour with Gordon Oliver, the mayor, in the background and a whole bunch of people. The Arch is on the phone to Madiba saying, "You've got to come here! You've got to come. The city is going to get burned down if you don't come." And so he turned up at about seven o'clock.

Above: A linocut by John Ndevasia Muafangejo in celebration of Tutu's enthronement as archbishop of Cape Town, 1986.

Right: Bishop of Johannesburg, 30 November 1979

To further his campaign, Kuyper developed what he called the doctrine of *soevereiniteit in eigen kring* (the divine right to sovereignty in one's own sphere). According to Kuyper, the sovereignty of God takes two forms: the mechanical sphere of state authority, which citizens are bound to obey; and the organic sphere of various "social circles", such as family life, corporate associations (including schools and universities) and communal life, which form part of what Kuyper called the "ordinances of creation", meaning they developed naturally or organically, "like the stem and branches of a plant", as part of God's will when he created the universe.[4] They are therefore immutable. No government has the right to impose its laws on those social spheres, which do not owe their existence to it, but directly to God.

The point the Afrikaner theologians fastened on to was that Kuyper contended that nations were also part of "the ordinances of creation", as God had prevented the building of the Tower of Babel so as to divide humanity into separate nations and states. That meant, they argued, that the right to have your own nation was God-given and therefore immutable. Thus apartheid was justified not only to give Afrikaners their own white state in South Africa, but it meant they were also under a divine obligation to enable the various black nations or ethnic groups to develop their own separate nation states as well – the so-called bantustans.

This, Tutu attacked frontally in his testimony to the Eloff Commission, thus waging what I called at the time "a theological civil war" as a powerful additional front in the total liberation struggle. His testimony to the commission was a virtuoso performance. For three hours Tutu sat there, bouncing and twisting in a Carver chair, his hands shaping the outlines of his ideas with vivid gestures. It was like a mime show with voice accompaniment; when he spoke of the resurrection of the body, his arms folded around his own body in a hug. The voice was the other instrument in this concert performance. Sometimes it would be deep, playing with the cadences of his African accent, and sometimes it would break into a high-pitched chuckle as he would hit on a pertinent new insight. It would be sombre, joyful, impatient, humorous, reflective, switching rapidly between all of them. And, all the while, the white commissioners watched, expressionless.

The first eleven chapters of Genesis, Tutu told the commissioners, showed that unity and wholeness were God's will for all of his creation. The story of the Garden of Eden was a poetic presentation of God's intention for the universe: a world of peace, prosperity, fellowship, justice, wholeness, compassion, love and joy. But this primal unity was disrupted by sin. Thus Genesis ended with the shattering story of the Tower of Babel, where human community and fellowship became impossible. "It is a perverse exegesis," Tutu added pointedly, "that would hold that the story of the Tower of Babel is a justification for racial separation, a divine sanction for the diversity of nations. It is to declare that the divine punishment for sin has become the divine intention of mankind."[5]

I was present in the executive meeting of the South African Council of Churches [SACC] when they were discussing the invitation to have the Arch serve as general secretary. At the time I was director of Mission and Evangelism. He was then-bishop of Lesotho, so that must have been 1986–87.

After he was appointed he came into the office. He called the heads of department in to speak with him one by one. It was a very general and easy conversation. It was unthreatening. He was listening. I remember the ease of the meeting. This was going to be our new boss. He would direct our work and he could make it easy or difficult, we didn't know. We weren't fearful at all but we didn't know. It was a gentle approach, almost like a tutor or mentor, just talking. I forget the content but it was reassuring.

Overall he is probably the best person I've worked under. He left it to us and we had a sense of accomplishment, a sense of freedom. We would take initiative. We had him all the time backing us and, if necessary, directing us.

One didn't barge into his office. He had two secretaries, and one had to make an appointment. We saw him, of course, at prayers. His insistence on early morning prayers was a feature of our work, and we had daily contact with him there. But his management style wasn't a day-to-day supervision. It's the same now in the office at Mpilo Ministries: he leaves it to us. We are comfortable with taking initiative. You learn, I think pretty soon where you need to check direction with him, not in making long speeches or presenting long papers, but you check and he guides. He is a very, very good person to work for.

When he came to the council, it was a very tense time on a number of levels. Nationally, it was soon after [the Soweto student uprising of] 1976 and there was lots of talk of what could happen next, whether in corridors or in prayers or executive meetings. Internally, it was also tense with our anger at what we perceived as gross injustice. We were incensed as staff that, whereas the archbishop's predecessor had been given carte blanche in spending, the then finance committee was making it very plain that it was they who would control the spending. It seemed to us that our general secretary (the archbishop) had hardly any say at all and that the satellite organisation that the finance committee had created to handle the money was only there to stop the general secretary, a black man, from dealing with the finances. It was sad. He very soon appointed an able accountant, Matt Stevenson,

to be his finance person, and at the end of the day, the SACC, under the general secretary, controlled its own finances.

When the Nobel Peace Prize was announced, it was an extremely exciting time. The days were heady. The Arch was in the United States when the announcement was made. When he came back to South Africa, we had a chapel celebration with the council staff. He made a speech to the effect that it wasn't he who had won the Nobel Peace Prize. The prize was awarded to him as a representative of the people. Coming then, at that time, it was very moving to hear it. We felt ten feet tall. When he expanded that into an invitation to most of the senior staff to attend the ceremony with him in Norway it was a landmark in our lives. I don't think we knew the extent of the impact of the award internationally. It soon became apparent that it had brought about an international turnabout, with churches and with governments understanding more clearly his role and the popularity of our cause. Reagan met with him soon after that. But for us at the time it was just a huge and exciting thing. Very soon after the Nobel award he was elected bishop of Johannesburg. He didn't really come back to the council and we were devastated.

He had the knack – he has the knack – of making you feel that you have a part to play. All of us felt that. For instance, during the days of the Eloff Commission we would all be involved in talking through the issues, talking sometimes together at the same time. He listened and reacted and we felt we were doing this with him. That is his gift. I believe he had the same style in Bishopscourt. I think it must come from his faith and value system. He believes in the worth of people and he practised it then as now. He has a very firm understanding of the divine purpose in each individual. For us who worked for him then, those were good days.

He asked me to come to work in his Milnerton office in 2003. Fairly soon after he asked me to accompany him on his travels. Madiba [Nelson Mandela] had discovered that he was travelling without an aide then and said to him that he shouldn't travel alone.

There was stress in the job, naturally. Travel always brings its stress. There was the need to think ahead and to plan and to interact with the organisers at each event. He is a good traveller, and in the air would either be sleeping or reading or praying. While we travelled there was no rehashing of the day past, or the need to thrash the details of the day ahead. You weren't required to talk, and so you could relax entirely during a long flight.

LIBERTY IS NOT TREASON

He was always a stickler for time. If his prayer time ended at twelve and you were to meet with him, then you would wait outside his door until it was exactly twelve o'clock before knocking. If there was a crisis and you happened to barge in on his devotions because of it, he would sign you politely to please be quiet, or to leave a note, but he wouldn't speak to you.

He always practised at home what he said in public. Increasingly I saw the focus of his teaching sharpening: that you can be God's instrument for peace, and if you can see the other as a brother, as a child of God, you won't be hostile, because you don't fight the people you care for. His success in moving the crowds is not because this is something new. People just need the reminder. He gives it to them in a fun-filled way; they recognise and like the truth. That is his success.

Above: Tutu speaks out against detention without trial at a meeting in Khotso House in April 1985. The building was a landmark for anti-apartheid activities, housing the South African Council of Churches, Black Sash, United Democratic Front and Detainees' Parents Support Committee. The police firebombed the building in 1988.

The entire story of the Bible thereafter, Tutu contended, was of God's mission to restore the harmony, the unity, the fellowship and the spirit of community that were there in the beginning. For that reason, God sent his son to effect reconciliation and atonement. "So Jesus came to restore human community and brotherhood … Apartheid quite deliberately denies and repudiates this central act of Jesus, and says we are made for separateness, for disunity, for enmity, for alienation, all of which we have shown to be the fruits of sin."[6] Therefore, apartheid itself was clearly a sin. "The only separation the Bible knows is between believers on the one hand and unbelievers on the other. Any other kind of separation, division, disunity is of the devil. It is evil and from sin."[7]

Moreover, Tutu told the commissioners, the story of Exodus was a paradigm not for the liberation of a chosen people, but for all who were oppressed. Thus it was the oppressed and underprivileged everywhere who were the chosen, who were the children of Israel. Because of this, the church council believed Christians were enjoined to take sides in the struggles of the oppressed. It did not accept the notion that religion should be separated from politics. "Our God is not a God who sanctifies the status quo … He cares that children starve in resettlement camps. He cares that people die mysteriously in detention. He is concerned that people are condemned to a twilight existence as non-persons by banning them without giving them the right of reply to charges brought against them."[8]

This was how the members of the SACC interpreted their Christian mission. Was it subversive? Was it revolutionary? Yes indeed. "The God of Exodus is subversive of all situations of injustice," Tutu declared. "And the Bible is the most revolutionary, the most radical book there is. If any book should be banned by those who rule unjustly and as tyrants, it is the Bible."[9]

Tutu ended with a ringing declaration of his determination to carry on with his Christian mission regardless of what action the government might take against himself or the council: "I want the government to know now and always that I do not fear them," he said. "They are trying to defend the utterly indefensible, and they will fail. They will fail because they are ranging themselves on the side of evil and injustice against the Church of God. Like others who have done that in the past – the Neros, the Hitlers, the Idi Amins of this world – they will end up as the flotsam and jetsam of history."[10]

The commissioners stared stonily ahead of them as Tutu finished. The blacks in the public benches burst into applause. Tutu leaned back, closed the leather-bound Bible he had been brandishing throughout his testimony and mopped his brow.

Seldom can a more courageous declaration of defiance and commitment have been made so publicly in what was then a police state equipped with a battery of laws empowering it to take draconian action without trial or public explanation against any individual or institution it deemed to be subversive of its own definition of the public interest.

As it turned out, the hearing was a triumph for the SACC and for Tutu personally. As Tutu later put it to his deputy, Dan Vaughan: "It was our finest hour in what were potentially the council's darkest days."[11] In fact, it turned the situation around completely, boosting the SACC's image in the world, reuniting it internally and rooting it more emphatically in the activist role defined so vividly by Tutu, and, in doing so, strengthening the religious thrust to the overall

"YOU KNOW THE OLD STORY OF HOW, WHEN THE MISSIONARIES CAME TO AFRICA, WE HAD THE LAND AND THEY HAD THE BIBLE. THEN THEY SAID, 'LET US PRAY', AND WE DUTIFULLY SHUT OUR EYES, AND WHEN WE SAID 'AMEN' AT THE END AND OPENED OUR EYES, WHY, THEY HAD THE LAND AND WE HAD THE BIBLE. THAT SEEMS TO HAVE BEEN A BAD BARGAIN. BUT WE ARE FOREVER INDEBTED TO THOSE INDOMITABLE MEN AND WOMEN FROM ACROSS THE SEAS WHO BROUGHT US THE GLORIOUS GOSPEL OF GOD'S LOVE FOR US AND WHO HELPED TO EDUCATE US IN THEIR SCHOOLS AND COLLEGES AND WHO HELPED TO IMPROVE OUR HEALTH WITH THE CLINICS AND HOSPITALS AND HEALTH CARE THEY PROVIDED. WE ARE FOREVER GRATEFUL TO THEM."

DESMOND TUTU

liberation struggle – while for the Botha administration, all the consequences were negative. It lost face internationally as all the major churches sent top-level observers to the hearings, where they endorsed Tutu's outline of the SACC's Christian mission. Worst of all, although Eloff's 450-page report contained some criticisms of the SACC, it recommended no action against the council.

The only negative for the SACC was that the inquiry led to the prosecution of Tutu's predecessor as general secretary, John Rees, whose concealment of details to protect anti-apartheid activists and their families, known colloquially as "struggle accounting", resulted in a conviction for fraud – but a sympathetic judge imposed a fine and a suspended prison sentence. It was a painful issue for those close to Rees, and led to the resignation of the SACC's president, the Reverend Peter Storey, who had stood strongly by Tutu throughout the ordeal and had himself delivered a powerful presentation to the hearing. But the council itself emerged strengthened and Tutu's role in the struggle was soon to be enhanced.

It had not been an easy road for the church council to travel. Storey, who worked alongside Tutu for five years – first as vice-president, then as president of the council – recalls that many of the leaders of the twenty-six member churches had difficulty coping with Tutu. The bishop was not a strategist; he operated on the basis of instinct and inspiration in what was a highly volatile political situation. This meant his statements and actions often went way beyond the official positions agreed upon by the council's national committee, causing waves of conflict with both the government and the churches' own congregations.

Even as the SACC was launching its counter-attack before the Eloff Commission, the religious assault on apartheid was widening on another front, striking, as Tutu had done, at the very foundations of its theological underpinning – only this time from within the DRC community itself. The issue had first arisen there in 1960, when the World Council of Churches convened a meeting of its South African members in the Johannesburg suburb of Cottesloe to try to find a way to unite in Christian witness against racism. It was a meeting that sowed the seeds of doubt in the

minds of some Afrikaner intellectuals that were gradually to germinate over time and eventually play a significant role in the historic decision by the National Party government to abandon the policy and settle for a negotiated transition to a non-racial democracy.

The debates at Cottesloe were the most intense and soul-searching that had been held in South Africa at that time. The delegates worked hard to maintain unity and, through discussion and compromise, managed to bring the DRC with them in issuing a consultation statement that rejected church apartheid as un-Christian. "No one who believes in Jesus Christ may be excluded from any church on the grounds of his colour or race," it declared.[12] The Nederduitsch Hervormde Kerk, the most conservative of three Afrikaner churches, whose constitution had a clause officially excluding blacks from membership, refused to accept this. But the DRC, the main Afrikaner Church, did so, despite its own segregated structure and its own historic role in evolving the theological justification for apartheid and co-authoring the political policy.

But the government, led then by Prime Minister Verwoerd, one of the key architects of apartheid, was outraged. It put huge pressure on the DRC and forced them to backtrack. This posed an acute moral crisis for the church's Cottesloe delegates, foremost among whom was the Reverend C. F. Beyers Naudé, moderator of the biggest provincial synod and a rising star in the Afrikaner nationalist establishment; his father had been one of the six founders of the Broederbond, and he was himself being spoken of as a possible future prime minister.

As a consequence, the most potent Afrikaner rebel of the apartheid era, Naudé had several young DRC admirers, and together they formed an ecumenical body called the Christian Institute, aimed at declaring what in theological language is known as a "status confessionis", a moment when the church is faced with a challenge so great that it must declare its faith anew. The counteraction was swift and savage. The DRC ordered Naudé to choose between his ministry and his institute and, when before a packed congregation in his prestigious church in Johannesburg, he chose the institute, declaring boldly that "We must obey God rather than men", it defrocked him.[13]

Above: With Allan Boesak, Cape Town, February 1985. An inspiring orator, Boesak suggested a united front of churches, student bodies, trade unions, civic associations and sports bodies in a speech in January 1983, a proposal which led to the formation of the United Democratic Front.

I first came to hear about Desmond Tutu because of his leadership in the anti-apartheid movement. I always admired the way he was able to be both a clergyman and a politician. That can be very difficult. I, together with, I hope, most South Africans, admired his tremendous courage and his faith.

I was a newly appointed judge in about 1982. John Rees, who was then the secretary-general of the South African Council of Churches [SACC], was charged with financial fraud committed against the church council. It was the only case in South African history where an offence such as fraud was charged against the wishes of the victim. The charge arose from a complaint that Rees made. He found that one of his employees, an African employee, had been stealing money. Rees reported it to the police.

At that time there was a huge vendetta against the SACC. They were really a thorn in the flesh of the apartheid government in the 1980s. When the police went to investigate the theft by this employee, they found evidence that Rees himself had been defrauding the council of hundreds of thousands of rand. They found he had opened about forty bank accounts in different names. Some were in his wife's name, some in his name and some in false names. The police reported that to the council. The council said, "Look, it's our business. We'll look after Mr Rees, we don't want you to investigate it." For political reasons the govern- ment insisted and Rees was charged. As a result of the charge, Rees was obliged to resign as the general secretary of the SACC. Desmond Tutu was appointed in his place. I was then on the Transvaal Supreme Court and the senior judges decided it would be a good idea for a Jewish judge to be in this trial. Then there wouldn't

Above: Tutu with the Reverend Peter Storey, former Methodist bishop of South Africa.

was appointed for that reason.

One of the charges, as I recall, was that the largest single cheque that Rees fraudulently issued was signed two weeks after he ceased to be secretary-general of the SACC and when Bishop Tutu was already in office. Rees signed a cheque as secretary for some tens of thousands of rand. I remember that, when he gave evidence, that fact infuriated the bishop. He saw that as a breach of trust, and that it reflected on him because Rees had already handed over authority to him.

In any event, the first time I was physically present in a room with Desmond was when the state called him as the first state witness. He went into the witness box and he looked at me and said, "My lord, before I take the oath I want to say something." Then I thought, "Oh my God, he is going to refuse to give evidence and I'm going to have to send him to prison for contempt of court!" I tell you, I was shivering with anxiety.

His statement was simply to the effect – I'm paraphrasing – that he was not there to give evidence because he wanted to, he was under subpoena, and he said, "Now I'm prepared to take the oath." He did take the oath and he gave evidence and implicated John Rees. His evidence was really not seriously challenged and was absolutely supported by all the evidence. In any event, Rees couldn't really explain what he had been doing. What Rees was doing was secretly funding freedom fighters without the consent or knowledge of the SACC. It was fraud, but he didn't enrich himself from it. Still, I found him guilty of fraud.

PETER STOREY

Here he is, he goes to Denmark to raise funds for the SACC [South African Council of Churches], which is a perfectly normal, harmless exercise. Then suddenly in the middle of a television interview he makes this call for Denmark to boycott South African coal. All hell breaks loose at home. Desmond is still in Denmark, so we call a church leaders' meeting because we're getting flak left, right and centre. I chaired the meeting, and some members say, "Look, the SACC has never made a decision on the sanctions issue; the churches are divided on it, so what is this man doing standing up and making this sort of bold statement? He's not representing us accurately."

That's a fair case, but then there's another voice in the meeting, which says, "Read your Bible; prophets don't necessarily wait for a vote before they say, 'Thus saith the Lord'." So we had to decide whether we wanted some kind of civil servant – a bureaucrat – when in fact what we had was a prophet.

What we needed to do was to say, "We're going to support this prophet. We may not always agree with what he's saying, but we know why he is saying it, and we need to hear what God is saying to us through him." That was the voice that carried the day. We said, "It's going to be hard and sometimes it's going to be very

uncomfortable and we reserve the right to challenge him, but we've got to set him free to be what God is calling him to be at this time."

There were times when I would wake up in the morning and say, "Oh hell, Desmond, what have you done today?" But that was life with Desmond. He had an unerring sense of what needed to be said at a particular time. What gave me confidence was that I knew there was no political motive. There is not a shred of political ambition in Desmond Tutu. He was accused of it regularly of course, but there wasn't any. This was a man driven by his theology and his passion for God's justice.

Another periodic irritation was that a crisis would erupt and Desmond would be out of communication on a retreat. It was pretty annoying. I would have to carry the can and field what was coming in, and where the hell is Desmond? Oh, he's praying. Great! But then on his return from these retreats there would be a marked clarity about an issue that we had maybe been wrestling with for weeks. There was always a sharper definition to his thinking after those retreats, so that's why you honoured those times of retreat, knowing they were times when his resolve was being strengthened and his thinking sharpened.

The government later banned both him and his institute, and Naudé was treated as an ethnic traitor and outcast. But he kept on asserting his considerable behind-the-scenes influence, particularly among the black and mixed-race "coloured" branches of the DRC.

It was there that a major new rebellion now erupted. In 1981, the Reverend Allan Boesak, who had been chaplain at the "coloured" University of the Western Cape, took the lead in forming an Alliance of Black Reformed Churches in southern Africa under a charter that denounced apartheid as a sin and declared that "the moral and theological justification of it is a travesty of the Gospel, a betrayal of the Reformed tradition, and a heresy".[14] The major battle of the theological civil war had begun, with the medieval-sounding concept of heresy as the central issue.

A year later, just as the Eloff Commission was beginning its hearings, Boesak took the heresy issue before a conference of the World Alliance of Reformed Churches in Ottawa, Canada, and in a powerful speech urged it to declare the apartheid theology developed by the DRC in South Africa to be a "pseudo-gospel" that challenged the authority of the true gospel, and should therefore be declared a heresy.[15] The world alliance accepted Boesak's indictment and issued the declaration. It suspended the membership of the DRC and the Nederduitsch Hervormde Kerk, saying they could be readmitted when they rejected apartheid, began working to dismantle it and gave concrete support to those who had suffered under it. The world alliance went on to elect Boesak its president. It was a thunderous victory for the anti-apartheid crusaders, and Boesak returned to South Africa to join with Tutu in a partnership that was to develop into a major force as the decade advanced.

Two years later, in 1984, there was another major boost when the Nobel Committee announced that Tutu had been awarded the Nobel Peace Prize. Not only was this an encouraging gesture of international solidarity for black South Africans in their struggle for equality, it also raised Tutu's status and amplified his message calling on the major world powers to impose sanctions and other pressures on the apartheid regime. As I wrote at the time: "Overnight this hitherto amorphous struggle has acquired a figure of international prestige as its visible leader, who will

```
ZCZC TD0861 GXI086  ON199
UINY CO NOOO 068
OSLO 68/66 16 1346


BISHOP DESMOND TUTU
C/O GENERAL THEOLOGICAL
SEMINARY 175 9THAVE
NEWYORKNY(10011)


THE NORWEGIAN NOBEL COMMITTEE HAS THE HOUNOR TO INFORM YOU
THAT THE NOBEL PEACE PRIZE FOR 1984 HAS BEEN AWARDED TO YOU
STOP THE PRIZE AMOUNT IS 1650000 SWEDISH KRONOR STOP
YOU ARE INVITED TO COME TO OSLO AND RECEIVE


COL 175 9THAVE (10011) 1984 1650000


ON199 BISHOP DESMOND TUTU P2/16


THE PRIZE ON THE 10TH OF DECEMBER 1984 STOP LETTER FOLLOWS
     EGIL AARVIK - JAKOB SVERDRUP
```

"UNLESS WE WORK ASSIDUOUSLY SO THAT ALL OF GOD'S CHILDREN, OUR BROTHERS AND SISTERS, MEMBERS OF OUR ONE HUMAN FAMILY, ALL WILL ENJOY BASIC HUMAN RIGHTS, THE RIGHT TO A FULFILLED LIFE, THE RIGHT OF MOVEMENT, OF WORK, THE FREEDOM TO BE FULLY HUMAN, WITH A HUMANITY MEASURED BY NOTHING LESS THAN THE HUMANITY OF JESUS CHRIST HIMSELF, THEN WE ARE ON THE ROAD INEXORABLY TO SELF-DESTRUCTION, WE ARE NOT FAR FROM GLOBAL SUICIDE; AND YET IT COULD BE SO DIFFERENT.

WHEN WILL WE LEARN THAT HUMAN BEINGS ARE OF INFINITE VALUE BECAUSE THEY HAVE BEEN CREATED IN THE IMAGE OF GOD, AND THAT IT IS A BLASPHEMY TO TREAT THEM AS IF THEY WERE LESS THAN THIS AND TO DO SO ULTIMATELY RECOILS ON THOSE WHO DO THIS? IN DEHUMANISING OTHERS, THEY ARE THEMSELVES DEHUMANISED. PERHAPS OPPRESSION DEHUMANISES THE OPPRESSOR AS MUCH AS, IF NOT MORE THAN, THE OPPRESSED. THEY NEED EACH OTHER TO BECOME TRULY FREE, TO BECOME HUMAN. WE CAN BE HUMAN ONLY IN FELLOWSHIP, IN COMMUNITY, IN *KOINONIA*, IN PEACE."

enjoy a measure of immunity from government action and be able to speak to the world from a platform of unimpeachable respectability." Tutu himself put it more vividly: "One day no one was listening. The next, I was an oracle."[16]

There were scenes of jubilation as a crowd of singing, cheering black supporters gathered at Johannesburg airport to greet their returning hero – while the government viewed Tutu's award with a hostile indifference and most white South Africans continued to scowl at the man they regarded as an objectionable political priest being egged on by meddlesome foreigners. In a brief interview at the airport, Tutu dedicated his award to "the little people of this country whose noses are rubbed in the dust every day".[17] He then drove to the SACC headquarters, where he expanded on that theme in an address to clerical colleagues that moved some to tears.

"This award is for you," he said, "you mothers who sit at railway stations trying to eke out an existence selling potatoes, selling mealies [maize], selling pigs' trotters, whatever. This award is for you and I am proud to accept it on your behalf." Referring to thousands of black migrant workers who left their families in tribal bantustans to work in dangerous conditions deep underground in South Africa's mines, Tutu went on: "This award is for you, you fathers who sit in single-sex hostels, separated from your wives and children for eleven months of the year. I am proud to accept it for you."[18] Next he dedicated his award to black families that had been forcibly removed from their ancestral lands because these were located in regions now zoned for white occupation, and to black shack dwellers, engaged in a grim struggle with the white administration which repeatedly demolished their illegal shanties that they erected near the "white" cities in the hope of getting jobs to feed their families. And finally: "It is for you who, down through the ages, have said that you seek to change this evil system peacefully, for you who have marched against the pass laws peacefully and who, unarmed, have been shot, mowed down and killed. With this award, the world is saying that you have been peace-loving to a fault."[19]

A year later, Tutu was elected bishop of Johannesburg, and the following year, at the height of a new wave of black unrest that saw the government crack down with yet another state of emergency, he was elected archbishop of Cape Town, primate of the Anglican Church throughout

SOUTH AFRICAN BROADCASTING CORPORATION

Broadcasting Centre, c/o Annet Road & Canary Street, Johannesburg 2001
P.O. Box 8606, Johannesburg 2000.   Telephone 714-3921

Comment: "The Nobel Peace Prize"   **Date:**

The exuberant reaction of South Africa's enemies to the awarding of the Nobel Peace Prize to Bishop Desmond Tutu throws suspicion on this event. And it raises the question of whether the will of Alfred Nobel is being correctly interpreted by the Peace Prize Committee in Oslo, Norway.

Nobel, the famous Swedish chemist, inventor of dynamite and pioneer of the explosives industry, was a quiet man who was only too aware of the potential destructive power of his inventions and products. In his 1897 will, he set out very clearly the qualifications for the Peace Prize. This award, he specified, should be made to the person or institution elected to have made the greatest contribution in the previous year to the promotion of the international brotherhood of man -- and then the qualification -- in the prevention of armed conflict or the arranging of peace negotiations. What he had in mind, therefore, was the promotion of understanding between nations and the prevention of war.

The Peace Prize Committee, it was reported from Oslo in 1982, evidently did not always adhere to this criterion -- for example, in selecting Mother Theresa for this award. That she was deserving of international recognition no one can deny. The question is whether this should have been given by way of the Peace Prize. Regarding last year's awarding of the Peace Prize to Polish trade union leader Lech Walesa, one commentator declared that he was more deserving of a prize for resistance, as he always chose resistance above peace, no matter what the cost.

It is difficult to escape the impression that the Peace Prize has degenerated into an international political instrument. And this is probably best illustrated by the reaction of Norwegian Prime Minister Kaare Willoch, who said yesterday that awarding the prize to Bishop Tutu would bring increased pressure from the international community to bear on South Africa to abandon its apartheid policy.

The fact that in 1960 the award was made to Albert Luthuli, a former president of the African National Congress -- a fully-fledged terrorist organisation - bears testimony thereto that the methods employed by the recipient in his struggle against this country, are also not much of a consideration ... as long as he is a symbol of radical opposition to South Africa.

2/......

THIS AWARD IS FOR YOU, YOU MOTHERS WHO SIT AT RAILWAY STATIONS TRYING TO EKE OUT AN EXISTENCE SELLING POTATOES, SELLING MEALIES [MAIZE], SELLING PIGS' TROTTERS, WHATEVER. THIS AWARD IS FOR YOU AND I AM PROUD TO ACCEPT IT ON YOUR BEHALF."

"THIS AWARD IS FOR YOU, YOU FATHERS WHO SIT IN SINGLE-SEX HOSTELS, SEPARATED FROM YOUR WIVES AND CHILDREN FOR ELEVEN MONTHS OF THE YEAR. I AM PROUD TO ACCEPT IT FOR YOU."

"IT IS FOR YOU WHO, DOWN THROUGH THE AGES, HAVE SAID THAT YOU SEEK TO CHANGE THIS EVIL SYSTEM PEACEFULLY, FOR YOU WHO HAVE MARCHED AGAINST THE PASS LAWS PEACEFULLY AND WHO, UNARMED, HAVE BEEN SHOT, MOWED DOWN AND KILLED. WITH THIS AWARD, THE WORLD IS SAYING THAT YOU HAVE BEEN PEACE-LOVING

southern Africa. Coming on top of the Nobel Prize, that not only thrust Tutu into the highest position ever attained by a black South African, but also made him the most widely acclaimed South African of any colour since the wartime Prime Minister Jan Christiaan Smuts, who had been a member of Churchill's War Cabinet and later drafted the preamble to the Charter of the United Nations.

Ironically, it also made Tutu the official but illegal occupant of one of the stateliest homes in the country, Bishopscourt, in one of Cape Town's most gracious white suburbs of the same name, not far from the official residence of President P. W. Botha. A further irony was that the grand old place had originally been built as the official residence of the governor of the first white settlers in South Africa, the Dutch East India Company's Jan van Riebeeck, in 1652. Now, as a sign of the changing times, it was taken over by its first indigenous occupant.

The enthronement itself, in Cape Town's Gothic cathedral of St George the Martyr, on 7 September 1986, was both a splendid liturgical ceremony and a day-long act of political defiance in the face of the most stringent of the four states of emergency the apartheid regime had imposed since Sharpeville. The emergency regulations, which came on top of a barrage of other security laws, prohibited political meetings and speeches, restricted funerals, banned certain indoor gatherings, imposed curfews and ordered journalists, especially television camera crews, to leave any spot proclaimed by a police officer to be an "unrest area". Penalties included indefinite detention without trial, which frequently meant interrogation under torture. But on this early southern spring day Tutu's enthronement turned into an exhilarating celebration of the emergence of a man now universally recognised as the voice of black South Africa's resistance to apartheid.

The cathedral ceremony was a wonderful syncretism of the high-church liturgy of medieval England with Ntsikana's "Great Hymn" and other African praise songs and chants. The day began with a trumpet fanfare and a procession of one hundred and fifty prelates from all parts of the world – including the archbishop of Canterbury, Dr Robert Runcie – in colourful copes and mitres.

Solemn though it was, the enthronement ceremony had the atmosphere of a gala performance. A crowd of 1,340 people of all creeds and colours packed the cathedral to the walls and, in their enthusiasm, broke into applause several times during Tutu's sermon. At the end, the big congregation gave him a standing ovation. The sermon itself, called a "charge" in the Anglican tradition, was characteristically a blend of profound religious faith, political indignation, wit and personal warmth. Tutu's theme, taken from the Book of Ezekiel, was that the essence of religion was not ritual, but to pursue justice and champion the oppressed. "It is madness to suppose that you can worship Jesus in the sacrament and Jesus on the throne of glory when you are sweating him in the bodies and souls of his children," Tutu said.[20]

The Christian Church was like a family, a single communion whose members were supposed to treat one another with understanding and compassion, he told the mixed congregation. "You can't choose your family. We have them as they have us. Your brother may be a murderer or worse, but he remains forever your brother. Can you imagine what would happen in this land if we accepted that theological fact about ourselves? Whether I like it or not, whether he likes it or not, P. W. Botha is my brother, and I must desire and pray for the best in him."[21]

Then, in a prescient moment when his vision seemed to leap five years into the future, the new archbishop spoke of his recent meeting with President Botha, and how he had responded to the Great Crocodile's demand that he cease calling for sanctions against South Africa. "I told him," Tutu said, "if you were to lift the state of emergency, remove the troops from our townships, release political prisoners and all detainees, unban our political organisations and then sit down with the authentic representatives of every section of our community to negotiate a new constitution for one undivided South Africa, then for what it is worth, I would say to the world: 'Put your sanctions plans on hold'."[22]

On 2 February 1990, that is exactly what Botha's successor, President F. W. de Klerk, did. But back then, as Botha faced Tutu across a table in his executive office, he remained as obdurate and dismissive as ever.

My husband, Robert Powell, was an Episcopal priest and he was Africa secretary for the National Council of Churches. Desmond was working in London for the Theological Education Fund. Somehow or another they intersected. I don't know how exactly they met. That was long before he was the bishop or at the SACC [South African Council of Churches] or anything like that. They became good friends and good colleagues. He and Robert shared a sense of humour. They both shared a commitment to working against apartheid and against injustices in the world and on behalf of African people, but they also had this sense of humour they enjoyed in each other. I have always enjoyed Desmond's sense of humour. Anybody who has ever heard him laugh will never forget his laugh. It's a very unique laugh, it's a very joy-filled laugh and it's a laugh that comes easily. He likes life and he likes people. He gets energy from that and he laughs. I've always enjoyed that about him.

When Desmond went to the SACC, Robert was more involved with him professionally. Robert was very instrumental in finding financial support from churches in the US, and other kinds of support too. I got to know Leah at that time too. I really enjoyed both of them. I enjoyed Desmond but I also enjoyed Leah. I was very clear that people didn't really appreciate the force that she was in that partnership. It was always clear to me that it was a partnership. She was just as actively involved in working against apartheid in her own way, not only being supportive to Desmond, which she was, but also in her own sphere working with domestic workers.

As the years went on, I would occasionally visit South Africa during the bad old times. It was always difficult from the very moment that you decided you were going. The price of getting a visa was dehumanising. First of all, I had to lie and say that I was staying at that big high-rise hotel, the Carlton, on my visa application. I never was; I would always stay with the Tutus. Then I was always made an honorary white person. There was a particular number and letter that you got on your visa that said that. That was really dehumanising to me. I've always been happy in my own skin.

I was working for the governor of New York State. That was one of the reasons that I ended up getting an unlimited entry visa. It was pretty unheard of at the time. Bob couldn't go to South Africa; they wouldn't give him a visa. The government of South Africa wouldn't give Desmond permission to travel when Robert died in 1981. They wouldn't give him permission to travel to come to the funeral, so Leah came.

When Robert was still alive, I remember us having a conversation in which he was very clear that he felt that (a) Desmond should receive the Nobel Peace Prize and (b) there was a possibility to make a way for that to happen for him, because it doesn't just fall out of the sky – much as we might like to think it does, it doesn't. So in the late seventies he began to think who were the people Desmond needed to meet and where were the places that we needed to make sure that Desmond got an opportunity to speak so that we could begin to make sure that the story of the SACC and Desmond Tutu got told? The first place that we looked was Riverside Church in New York City. I was a member of Riverside and I was on the board of deacons. I remember going to Bill Coffin [William Sloane Coffin], the senior minister there, and saying: "We have this friend. He's head of the South African Council of Churches, and we really think that he should come and preach at Riverside." I remember having to convince Bill Coffin that Desmond was worthy and that he was a good enough speaker. Nobody knew of Desmond at that point. Of course he did come and he was great, and that was one of the first times that I think he got a larger American audience. And people outside of this very small, tiny little anti-apartheid movement began to know who he was and what the work of the SACC was. There were other people and other places that Robert really worked to make sure that Desmond met and went.

When the Nobel Peace Prize actually came Desmond called me up and said, "I really want you to try and come to Oslo, because I recognise the role that Robert played in all of this." It was one of those times in your life you never forget. How many people go to the Nobel Peace Prize dinners and award ceremonies? A lot of South Africans were there. Desmond had made sure that a lot of people who normally would never get a travel document came. Some of them had never been on an aeroplane, even in South Africa. One of them had never had a suit, so we had to get him a suit. A lot of very common, ordinary people came.

Franklin Williams was the head of the Phelps Stokes Fund, of which Desmond was a trustee. Franklin was one of the first African American ambassadors. He was very committed to Africa and he had approached Desmond with the idea that the Phelps Stokes Fund should create a privately funded scholarship for refugees from South Africa and Namibia. Those were young people who had fled after the 1976 Soweto uprisings. Desmond asked me to be the first director of the Bishop Desmond Tutu Southern African Refugee

and travelling with him a lot.

Working for him was exhausting most of the time. I was, of course, a lot younger than I am now, and eighteen-hour days were not unusual for us. He's an extraordinarily high-energy person – even now, I think he's much more high energy than most eighty-year-olds. I quickly learned that you'd better not schedule him at certain times of the day. Whether you schedule him or not, he was going to have his prayer time. Rather than put yourself in a predicament and have to undo what you had done, you're better off just protecting those times from the beginning.

We prayed in some very strange places. Praying on aeroplanes is easy. There are some other places that are not so easy. How did he find a place of quiet in the midst of all the chaos going all around him? He has the ability to do that. I began to understand that it was through the prayer time that he got the strength and the courage and the wisdom to know which battles to fight. He gathered the strength to stand up to some very difficult situations in the government and in his own community, some life-threatening situations.

Sometimes it was frustrating. When Desmond makes up his mind, he makes up his mind, and there's not a lot you can do to change his mind. So sometimes that would be frustrating. I remember the first time he spoke out on behalf of the Palestinians. We were in New York. I remember saying to him when he arrived, "I'm not telling you don't do this, but I just want you to understand the firestorm that you're about to step into." This was 1985 or something like that. He was way ahead of his time. He sat there and listened to me and he did what I knew he was going to do: he said what he thought. He thought that the Palestinians were living under apartheid. Now, I'm very involved in the World Council of Churches, and we were saying the Palestinians were living under apartheid. In that case, I really wasn't trying to dissuade him. I just wanted him to know what he was getting into.

I've been very blessed in my life to meet some extraordinary people and work with some extraordinary people. I worked with Desmond Tutu. I worked with Vernon Jordan when I was at the National Urban League. I was married to Robert Powell who was an incredible person. There've been a lot of people in my life who have been important in my own development, in my own journey. Desmond was really at the top of the list. I thank God for that. Each one of them has taught me certain things about who I am and who God is, and so I'm just grateful.

TREVOR THAMSANQA TUTU

I was actually grown up by the time my father became "Desmond Tutu", if you want to put it like that. He won the Nobel Prize in 1984. I was married and I think I already had a daughter by then. It isn't like growing up as Mick Jagger's son, when he's always been a Rolling Stone, you know. It was quite a significant part of my life when he was just an ordinary Joe and, as I said, I was already grown up by the time he became Bishop Tutu or became a Nobel laureate or became the bishop of Johannesburg and archbishop of Cape Town.

I think he became more himself. If you ask people like Martin Kenyon or Malcolm Alexander or the people in Bletchingley, you know, Ron and Frankie Brownrigg, they would say that, in fact, all that has happened is that it's more him than it was before. The huge, plucky sense of humour was always there. The love of life and caring for people was always there. His love for his parishioners and his love for his junior priests has always been there. He's always cared deeply about people, particularly about ordinary people, and particularly for the downtrodden and unappreciated. That has always been his life. All that happened is that he got bigger and bigger as he found more and more important platforms from which to express that love and appreciation. You know, I can actually truly say, all these things haven't changed him, only made him noticeable to more people. I mean, the people who have loved him since he was training for priest-hood or since he was a teacher just out of education college, that's how far back his friendships stretch. The pomp and ceremony – I'm not saying that he dislikes it, because that isn't true, but I'm saying it hasn't changed him. He hasn't become the great "I AM". He expects no more respect than he would if he were a rector of Holy Cross in Soweto. That is all that he expects and all he thinks he deserves.

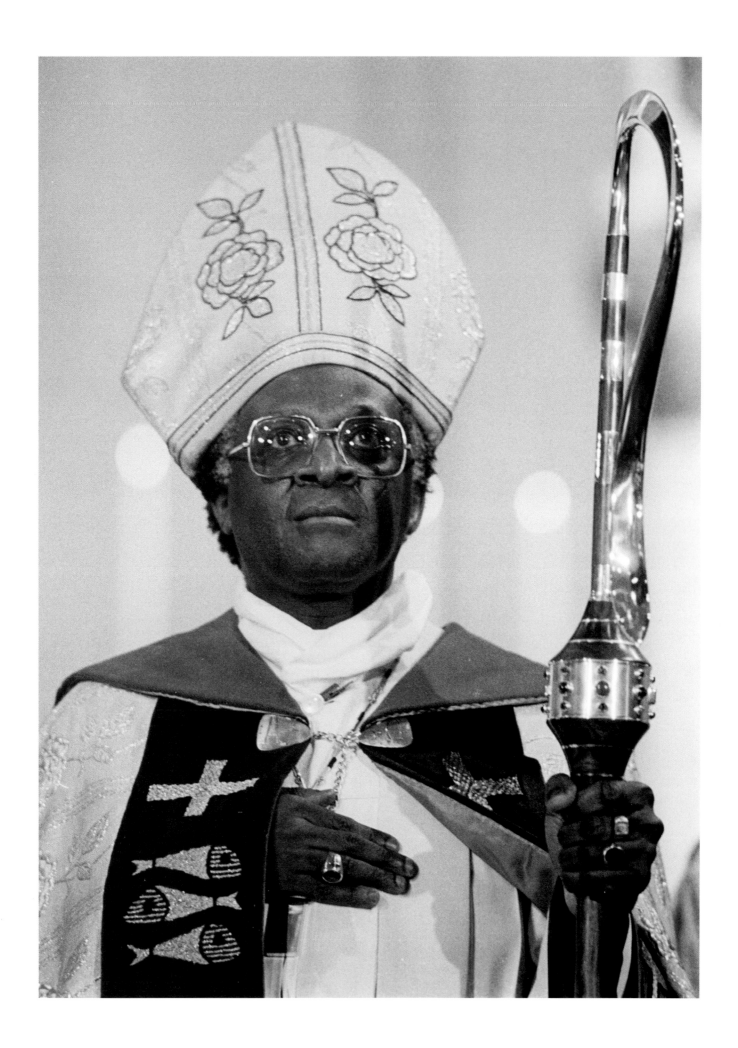

TUTU: THE AUTHORISED PORTRAIT

The day ended with a ceremony attended by ten thousand people at the Goodwood Showgrounds on the outskirts of the city. It took the form of a mass Eucharist service and had something of the atmosphere of a big sports event, with a great cheer going up from the crowd as the robed bishops marched like a team on to the field from the changing rooms under the grandstand. Political demonstrations erupted throughout the day, with young black activists jogging around the field chanting slogans and raising their fists in the black power salute – all in open defiance of the emergency prohibitions. A crowd of youths mobbed Winnie Mandela, the wife of the imprisoned Nelson Mandela, as she arrived at the stadium. She brought a message from her husband in nearby Pollsmoor Prison congratulating Tutu and describing him as the pride of the nation. All this was in open defiance not only of the emergency regulations but of the special restrictions imposed on Mrs Mandela herself. She had been banned and banished to a small town in Orange Free State province, which meant she was prohibited from meeting with more than one other person at a time, forbidden to write or utter political statements, and allowed to visit her husband in Pollsmoor only under the strictest of conditions. All this she now brazenly violated by attending what had effectively become a political rally and delivering a politically loaded message from her imprisoned husband. But the security police did nothing – a telling indication of Tutu's enhanced international image and his untouchability – at least on this special day.

That enhanced international image now thrust Tutu into the upper echelons of influential global figures. Important doors opened for him and he found himself visiting presidents and prime ministers and prelates around the world, where he was able to press home his message of sanctions and diplomatic pressure to force change in South Africa. He was in demand everywhere as a public speaker and his vivid personality ensured him growing media attention. He visited Canada, where he met with Conservative Prime Minister Brian Mulroney, was invited to France together with Mother Teresa and other Nobel laureates, addressed the United Nations Security Council and was given a standing ovation by the US House Subcommittee on Africa. He also met President Ronald Reagan and Britain's Margaret Thatcher, but didn't get on with either of them. There were reciprocal visits too. Early in 1985, Senator Edward Kennedy made a high-profile tour of South Africa, following in the footsteps of a historic trip by his brother, Robert, in 1966 that gave South African liberals a huge boost, and which Robert himself described as a highlight of his career. Ted Kennedy visited Soweto among other hot spots in what was a tense country at the time, and spent the night at the Tutus' township home on Vilakazi Street where he was welcomed by a group of

I DO NOT FEAR THEM

Left: Bishop of Johannesburg, 1986.

Below, left: Tutu is hugged by Leah after his ordination in Johannesburg.

Below, right: Tutu walks hand in hand with Leah, who is carrying a newspaper with the headline "Tutu Chosen as Archbishop", April 1986.

five hundred people with candles, and the wonderful Imilonji KaNtu choir.

Tutu became a hit in the United States particularly, where his preaching style struck a chord with white and black Christians alike, and his crusading passion evoked nostalgic memories of Dr Martin Luther King Jr and the whole civil rights campaign of the 1960s. John Allen, who was Tutu's press secretary at the time, quotes Hays Rockwell – rector of the prosperous 2,400-member St James's Episcopal Church on Madison Avenue, New York – to explain how Tutu's special appeal to American audiences stemmed from his ability to rise above traditional divides: "He's Anglo-Catholic ... but he would never make that his primary way of addressing the church. He is able to proclaim the gospel with such energy because he believes in the evangelical mandate – not as an ideological thing, but because that's what his faith requires of him. He reaches into individual lives in a way that's transformative ... Very few evangelical preachers are as profoundly intellectual as he is, though he would scorn that word. His faith is beautifully informed by his learning, his knowledge."[23]

An African American priest from Harlem, Fred Williams, offered a more colourful explanation: "He's a crossover artist. Black preaching of an evangelical style scares the bejesus out of most white mainline Protestants. They don't think they're supposed to experience emotion. Desmond appeals to that emotional level without scaring them to death, because his humanity comes across in a wave and they hear the emotion. It's sort of like making love without screaming."[24]

Bush voices 'shadow' of doubt over Tutu in US

The broad base of support Tutu was able to build up in the United States proved vital in producing a turnaround in American policy towards South Africa. Fearing that a black takeover of power in South Africa would open the door to a Soviet-backed regime being established there, the Reagan administration opted for a policy it called "constructive engagement", aimed at trying to persuade the apartheid regime to introduce gradual reforms. But Tutu's widely publicised speeches attacking

Above: With President Reagan at the White House, December 1984.
Right: Tutu's notes for his meeting with President Reagan, December 1984.

"YOU WOULD NOT COLLABORATE WITH NAZIS AND COMMUNISTS. NOT CASTING ANY ASPERSIONS ON [THE] INTEGRITY OF ANYONE NOR THEIR CHRISTIANITY BUT COLLABORATION IN MY VIEW [IS] EQUALLY EVIL, IMMORAL AND UN-CHRISTIAN."

DESMOND TUTU

1 Thanks for invitation and meeting.

2 Agreed that apartheid evil, immoral and un-Christian and to be changed, dismantled peacefully – our commitment.

3 Agreed to try persuasion, carrot – this has been tried for 4 years.

4 We differ about efficacy of so-called constructive engagement. Now I speak from within as a victim consequently hope my criticism is not dubbed rubbish.

5 We believe it has worsened our situations as blacks. Constitution – politics of exclusion. Use of army – opp Catholics – violence of authorities, detentions, population removals, bans KTC squatters, denationalisation. My own nationality undeterminable at present turned into aliens. Namibia.

6 One side reciprocity, 2 way traffic. In my view it has not produced positive results – Nkomati – non aggression. Has made them more intransigent and consequently = collaboration. Poland, Latin America perceived inconsistencies. Is it that blacks dispensable? What would have been reaction if it was whites over 200 killed; 24 or 6000 sacked.

You would not collaborate with Nazis and Communists.

Not casting any aspersions on integrity of anyone nor their Christianity but collaboration in my view equally evil, immoral and un-Christian. Danger to whites, handing blacks over on platter to Communists; hurrying violent outbreak; giving bad name to democracy.

1 End of violence and use of army, not just Labour leaders but also election boycott.

2 Release or charge all detainees immediately.

3 Lift all banishment orders esp Winnie Mandela – or charge.

4 Stop immediately all population removals especially imminent removal of Kira Ngema people and stop denationalisation of blacks.

5 Reinstate sacked workers who participated in 2 day lock out, but especially 6000.

6 General Amnesty for all political prisoners as a prelude to National Convention of all authentic leaders and representation of all sections of our community.

1 Meeting at invitation of President Reagan – a full, frank and friendly meeting.

2 Agreed Apartheid evil, immoral and un-Christian.

3 Agreed to dismantle peacefully.

This page: Tutu speaks
at the Cathedral Church
of St John the Divine
in New York, 1986.

this approach began to gain traction in Congress, including with many Republicans. He then brought his campaign to a head with a speech on Capitol Hill, shortly after Reagan's comfortable re-election, in which he didn't mince his words, denouncing constructive engagement as "an abomination and an unmitigated disaster", then adding, "In my view, the Reagan administration's support and collaboration with it is equally immoral, evil and totally un-Christian."[25]

That speech began the build-up to the passage through Congress of the Comprehensive Anti-Apartheid Act of 1986. President Reagan vetoed the act but, with his own Republican Party turning overwhelmingly against him, Congress overrode the veto and the act became law. It was a turning point in the struggle against apartheid, opening the way as it did for US sanctions and disinvestment from South Africa. For Tutu it was a personal triumph.

remember seeing the archbishop on CNN. Larry King was interviewing him. Larry King asked him a question and I am sure he wasn't prepared when the Reverend Desmond Tutu answered. It caught him by surprise. Larry King was saying, "You know if we don't come over there to South Africa and do this and do that, you know, the communists, the Russians will come and they will."

I remember Desmond Tutu saying, "Well, let me get this thing straight. You're saying that someone is going to steal my car so why not you? Uh-oh! The Russians are going to steal my land and take advantage of the people, steal our resources, so why not you?"

I thought, "Oh my God, that's perfect!" because it had clarity. It had no malice, it had no sting. It just had so much sweetness, so much strength. That's what really warmed my heart. And I was really happy that someone had enough love, courage, light and clarity to respond to a question in a way that really set Larry King and America in place.

I grew up with the Black Panthers, you know. Them and Harry Belafonte and Martin Luther King and Malcolm X. I grew up with all that and I'm a child of that, but I've never heard someone speak, since Martin Luther King, with this kind of voice of all-inclusiveness, this kindness. It isn't black or white. This is like unconditional love, a love supreme.

I met him later. He came to our house with Mrs Tutu. He did a speech at the Marin Center and we gave a dinner for him at our house. I was in seventh heaven. I played him my song "Victory Is Won". He gave me that song. It was something he said in an

the brutality, and the enemy had his knee on our throat, suffocating the life from us, we were looking up – his knee on our throat, his feet on our throat. We looked up to the enemy and said, 'Join us in our celebration. You already lost, we already won.'" And so I heard "Victory Is Won". I immediately heard a song and I was, like, "Oh my God. I've got to write this thing down. If I don't write it down, it's gonna go away." So, I should pay royalties to him because he gave me that song!

When I hear the name Desmond Tutu, I hear that laughter that he has like a child. But the qualities that stand out are forgiveness and compassion. It takes a lot of strength to forgive. Most people say, "Well, I will forgive but I won't forget." That's like a present with nothing inside. A beautiful present, wrapped up and everything, and you open it up – there's nothing in it. The greatest gift is total forgiveness. Like Jesus Christ, you don't keep count. Love doesn't keep count. What I learned from him is that love doesn't keep track of how many times this or how many times that. It's like the sun. The sun will never say to the earth, "You owe me." It's just: "You want more? I got more." The more I give you, the more I have.

I was there in South Africa and I got to see this footage of him in the middle of this hurricane of crazy people: people with violence and anger. He was inside just like a conductor. He was dismantling that anger and rage. I was like, "Oh my God. He's a combination of compassion, forgiveness and really straight-up ferocious lion," 'cause you have to have a certain kind of courage to do this, you know? So that's how I see the qualities of who he is for me: he is forgiveness

CHAPTER SIX

....

FAITH AND REVOLUTION

"I AM WRITING TO YOU, SIR, BECAUSE I HAVE A GROWING NIGHTMARISH FEAR THAT UNLESS SOMETHING DRASTIC IS DONE VERY SOON THEN BLOODSHED AND VIOLENCE ARE GOING TO HAPPEN IN SOUTH AFRICA ALMOST INEVITABLY. A PEOPLE CAN TAKE ONLY SO MUCH AND NO MORE ... I AM FRIGHTENED, DREADFULLY FRIGHTENED, THAT WE MAY SOON REACH A POINT OF NO RETURN, WHEN EVENTS WILL GENERATE A MOMENTUM OF THEIR OWN, WHEN NOTHING WILL STOP THEIR REACHING BLOODY DENOUEMENT WHICH IS 'TOO GHASTLY TO CONTEMPLATE', TO QUOTE YOUR OWN WORDS, SIR."

DESMOND TUTU

Left: Tutu calls for the release of Nelson Mandela and the unbanning of the African National Congress and other political parties at a United Democratic Front rally at the University of the Western Cape, June 1989.

By now the feisty "Arch" was moving steadily beyond rhetoric and appeals for foreign pressure and becoming more directly involved in political activism on the seething home front as well. Peter Storey believes Tutu became fully awakened politically only by the violent police action in Soweto on 16 June 1976. Tutu, then only a year back from London and on the point of leaving again for Lesotho, nonetheless sensed that trouble was brewing in the big township and wrote a prophetic letter to Prime Minister Vorster. "I am writing to you, Sir, because I have a growing nightmarish fear that unless something drastic is done very soon then bloodshed and violence are going to happen in South Africa almost inevitably. A people can take only so much and no more ... I am frightened, dreadfully frightened, that we may soon reach a point of no return, when events

will generate a momentum of their own, when nothing will stop their reaching bloody denouement which is 'too ghastly to contemplate', to quote your words, Sir."[1]

In a cursory reply, Vorster dismissed Tutu's warning as "political propaganda".[2] This meant Tutu was doubly traumatised when the violence did indeed break out. "I think he was still trying to get a grasp of what was happening in our country," Storey recalls. "He came into the SACC [South African Council of Churches] offices and he was in tears. He said the police were driving up and down shooting people. He couldn't believe it. He knew things were bad, but he actually couldn't believe it."[3]

If that was Tutu's moment of political awakening, more was to come. A year later the Black Consciousness leader, Steve Biko, was savagely tortured and beaten to death by his interrogators – the twentieth activist to die in detention over the previous eighteen months, but in a manner more diabolical than any other in the ugly history of apartheid.

Biko had been banned in 1973 and confined to the

magisterial district of King William's Town, his home town in the Eastern Cape. In August 1977, he slipped away to attend a clandestine meeting, rumoured to have been with a representative of the African National Congress (ANC) to discuss collaboration, but he was arrested at a roadblock and taken to security-police headquarters in Port Elizabeth. The authorities tried desperately to cover up what happened to him in detention, the minister of justice, James Kruger, even falsely intimating to Parliament that he had died of a hunger strike. Eventually, the Johannesburg *Rand Daily Mail* revealed that he had died of brain damage.

Years later, after South Africa's political transition, more of the truth emerged during the Truth and Reconciliation Commission hearings chaired by Archbishop Tutu. It became clear that Biko's white interrogators became enraged at the proud young black man's refusal to be intimidated by their bullying tactics. He stood up to them. A fight ensued during which Biko suffered a massive blow to the head and sank into a coma. Assuming he was faking, his interrogators chained him, naked and spread-eagled in a crucifix position, to an iron grille. Later, they left him lying naked and in leg irons on urine-soaked blankets in his cell for forty-eight hours. When he still did not respond to their questioning, they sent him to state doctors who examined him cursorily before recommending he be hospitalised, at which point Biko's interrogators bundled him into the back of a Land Rover, still naked and manacled, and sent him on a 1,200-kilometre drive through the night to a prison hospital in Pretoria, where he arrived with no medical papers and was left lying unattended on a trolley in a corridor where he died on 12 September 1977. He was just thirty years old.

News of Biko's death sent a wave of fury through the black community, aggravated by another crass statement by Minister Kruger that Biko's death "leaves me cold". The funeral was set for 25 September in King William's Town and Tutu, then still bishop of Lesotho, was asked to deliver the graveside eulogy.

It was one of the most highly charged and emotional funerals in South African history, a combination of a religious ceremony and a frenzied protest rally, with angry young supporters doing the aggressive toyi-toyi war dance and pumping their fists in the air to cries of "*amandla!*" (power). Some fifteen thousand mourners attended, but thousands more were prevented from reaching King William's Town from all the major centres as police with FN rifles and mounted machine-guns stopped them at dozens of roadblocks. Leah Tutu and a group of her friends were among those stopped, assaulted by police and prevented from attending the funeral.

In his eulogy, an emotional Tutu drew a parallel between Biko's death and the crucifixion of Jesus. After the crucifixion, he said, it seemed as though the powers of evil had triumphed over faith. But with Christ's resurrection, life had triumphed over death. "We, too, like the disciples of Jesus, have been stunned by the death of another man in his thirties. A young man completely dedicated to the pursuit of justice and righteousness, of peace and reconciliation."[4]

But then, true to his own innate belief that Black Consciousness was not incompatible with racial reconciliation and non-racialism, Tutu had the courage to urge the seething, angry crowd to realise that injustice in South Africa had dehumanised whites as well as blacks. He went so far as to ask the crowd to pray for white South African leaders and policemen, because they needed to regain their humanity, as did their victims. "Steve knew and believed fervently," he added, "that being pro-black was not the same thing as being anti-white."[5] For the government, he had a message too: "Please, please, for God's sake listen to us while there is just a possibility of reasonably peaceful change."[6]

Five months later, Tutu was caught up in another tense scene, this time at the funeral of Robert Sobukwe, the Pan Africanist Congress (PAC) leader, who had been held in prison and under house arrest ever since the Sharpeville massacre seventeen years earlier. Many of Biko's young Black Consciousness supporters, who felt they had much in common with Sobukwe's Africanist philosophy, attended the ceremony at his birthplace in the Eastern Cape town of Graaff-Reinet. It was they who were at the forefront of an outburst of anger when the Zulu bantusan leader, Chief Mangosuthu Buthelezi, who had been a fellow student at Fort Hare university with Sobukwe, joined the crowd of mourners.

"IN 1976, OUT OF A GROWING CONCERN AND DEEPENING APPREHENSION ABOUT THE MOOD IN SOWETO, ONE OF INCREASING ANGER AND BITTERNESS AND FRUSTRATION, I WROTE AN OPEN LETTER TO THE THEN PRIME MINISTER MR B. J. VORSTER. IN IT I WAS WARNING HIM THAT UNLESS SOMETHING WAS DONE AND DONE URGENTLY TO REMOVE THE CAUSES OF BLACK ANGER THEN I WAS FEARFUL OF WHAT WAS LIKELY TO ERUPT BECAUSE BLACK PEOPLE WERE GROWING INCREASINGLY RESTIVE UNDER THE OPPRESSIVE YOKE OF APARTHEID AND FOR YOUNG PEOPLE IT WAS REPRESENTED IN THE INSENSITIVE DETERMINATION TO ENFORCE AFRIKAANS AS A MEDIUM OF INSTRUCTION ON THEM IN THEIR INFERIOR SCHOOLS IN A SYSTEM OF EDUCATION THAT HAD BEEN DESIGNED BY ITS AUTHOR DR VERWOERD FOR INFERIORITY. MY LETTER WAS DISMISSED CONTEMPTUOUSLY BY MR VORSTER AS A PROPAGANDA PLOY SOMEHOW ENGINEERED BY THE PROGRESSIVE FEDERAL PARTY. HE DID NOT EVEN THINK I COULD AS A BLACK PERSON HAVE THE INTELLIGENCE TO KNOW THE GRIEVANCES OF MY OWN PEOPLE NOR THE ABILITY IF I DID TO COMPOSE A LETTER TO EXPRESS THOSE GRIEVANCES."

DESMOND TUTU

Biko had expressed his contempt for blacks he considered were collaborating with the apartheid system, especially those who headed the tribal bantustan regimes. Buthelezi was a particular target. The Zulu prince had been a member of the ANC Youth League at Fort Hare and had continued to express support for the movement. He became chief minister of the KwaZulu "homeland" in 1976, and the government recognised it as a self-governing territory, but Buthelezi refused to accept independence, which he saw as a way to obstruct fulfilment of the policy.

But for Biko, it was precisely Buthelezi's record as a critic of apartheid that made his decision doubly objectionable. It lent credibility to the policy, Biko said, while for white South Africans "a man like Buthelezi ... solves so many conscience problems".[7] For the young Africanists, therefore, Buthelezi's appearance at Sobukwe's funeral was an abomination. They jeered and hissed at him and as the atmosphere grew ominous, with the crowd beginning to swarm towards Buthelezi, Tutu hastened to the Zulu chief's side and persuaded him to leave for his own safety. In the haste to escort him to safety, one of the chief's bodyguards fired a shot and wounded three mourners. The entire experience left the proud Zulu prince humiliated and bitter. It was a wound that never healed, and foreshadowed violent clashes between Buthelezi's followers and the liberated ANC – which absorbed most of the Black Consciousness Movement's following after Biko's death – that marred, and at one point nearly derailed, the process of political transition in the 1990s.

But back in the late seventies, deep within the white Afrikaner community, subtle changes were taking place. Even the most faithful supporters of the apartheid policy began to realise that its central objective – to reverse the flow of black urbanisation at least to an extent where it could give some semblance of legitimacy to the concept of establishing separate black states – was a pipe dream. More and more black workers were surging into the cities as the economy expanded. Moreover, the policy was flying in the face of the needs of an emerging new Afrikaner entrepreneurial and technocratic class.

In earlier years, the Afrikaners had been people of the land, rough pioneer farmers who had penetrated the interior in a series of conquests over the black African tribes. But the Anglo-Boer War, fought from 1899 to 1902 and in which the British ultimately prevailed, left the Boer economies devastated. Their farms, which had been used as staging posts by Boer guerrilla fighters, were ravaged, forcing many of the farmers and their families into the towns and cities as "poor white" unskilled labourers to scratch a living – in competition with equally unskilled black workers.

That was where apartheid had its roots, and the founding of the Afrikaner National Party as well. After the party came to power in 1948, the Afrikaner regime took care of its own. Starting with a large number of parastatal corporations, then extending into the private sector, a substantial Afrikaner entrepreneurial and technocratic business class emerged. Afrikaner banks and businesses were established and by 1973, 30 per cent of South Africa's rich gold-mining industry was in Afrikaner hands. Gradually this new Afrikaner business class made common cause with their English-speaking counterparts against the old pre-industrial practices. Suddenly the option of sending all the black workers back to their bantustans and of the black urban townships "withering away", as the apartheid ideologists had predicted, not only looked increasingly improbable, but was also completely antithetical to their own business interests.

As the economy became more sophisticated, these entrepreneurs not only needed more black labour, they needed more skilled and stable black labour. So something had to bend, and that meant, firstly, allowing blacks to acquire the same skills as those that white workers had and, secondly, bowing to pressure for them to be able to join trade unions. And once black people had trade unions, they had a foothold in political power. They could organise, strike and bring the economy to a standstill – which is exactly what eventually happened.

Then there were the Afrikaner intellectuals. Through the 1960s, such a tumultuous decade everywhere, a group of young Afrikaans writers rebelled against the traditional genre of Afrikaans literature about sturdy men and pure maidens braving the hardships of drought on the farm and the inevitable journey to the sinful city. The Sestigers (Sixtiers), as they called themselves, travelled to Europe, particularly Paris, to study and begin experimenting with existential themes in their writing. By the 1970s, the contrived precocity of their early work matured into more searching themes about the mind and values of Afrikanerdom itself. Because these new writers were now the deans of Afrikaans culture, the impact of the challenging, rebellious literature they produced when they returned home was considerable.

Finally, and most important of all, the theological challenges presented by Tutu, Boesak and others were beginning to cause a ferment in the Afrikaans churches – at the very foundation of the theological justification for apartheid. And so, in all these sectors of the Afrikaner nationalist movement, fissures began to appear. Pride in their Afrikaner history and heritage was still there, but these modern men and women of the world were pained by the stigma they bore when they went travelling abroad. Distinct factions began to appear in the movement, which the Afrikaans news media quickly dubbed the *verligtes* (the enlightened ones) and the *verkramptes* (the cramped ones). The verligtes called for change, while the verkramptes warned of the perils of yielding to pressure.

Then in early 1983, Botha attempted to ease the mounting pressures on the country by introducing some piecemeal reforms to the apartheid policy without relinquishing white minority control. He scrapped what he called "outdated" and "unnecessary" apartheid statutes, such as the outlawing of mixed marriages and sex across the colour line, to present a new image of reformism to the world.

It almost succeeded. The Western powers, ever eager to read the South African situation optimistically, were deceived for a time into believing that Botha really was dismantling apartheid. But, on closer examination, when Botha unveiled constitutional changes he intended making, it became clear what he had in mind was not reform but rather a reformulation of apartheid. He set out his plan to establish a Tricameral Parliament in which the mixed-race "coloured" and Indian minorities would have separate chambers to legislate for their "own affairs", while the existing, much larger, whites-only House of Assembly would deal with both "white issues" and the nation's "general affairs". The huge black majority, meanwhile, would get nothing beyond the right to vote in their remote tribal bantustans, and the municipal councils would run their separate black townships in so-called "white" South Africa. But even these urban councils were not autonomous. The legislation enabled the white minister to remove members, appoint others, or dismiss the whole council and appoint a new one. It meant that the black councils had to implement government policy rather than be responsive to their own electorates. "Neo-apartheid" the *Economist* called it, in a perceptive article by its then political editor, Simon Jenkins.[8]

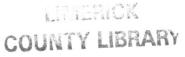

Previous page: Youths
following a funeral
in Duduza township,
Transvaal, July 1985
(see image page 6).

Most white South Africans saw Botha's "reforms" as a generous concession, a bold, even courageous breaching of the political colour bar which the government had been prepared to take even though it meant splitting Afrikaner nationalism. Pieter Koornhof, who was in charge of black African affairs under the euphemistic title of minister of cooperation and development, likened this new bill to Britain's Great Reform Act of 1832, and invoked the name of William Wilberforce to stress its liberatory potential. Even some white liberals, though critical of its inadequacy, felt that the change was "at least a step in the right direction".

The reforms were an initial victory for the verligtes, while causing the hardliners among the verkramptes to break away to form the Conservative Party under the leadership of a former DRC pastor turned politician, Andries Treurnicht. It was the second such breakaway by right-wingers in just over a decade, the earlier one forming the Herstigte (Reconstituted) National Party. Both remained minority groups, but their defection reflected the increasing fragility of what had once been a monolithic ethno-nationalist movement.

At a referendum on 2 November 1983, two-thirds of the white electorate approved the new constitution. But when the elections were held ten months later, four-fifths of the "coloured" and Indian "beneficiaries" rejected it in a massive boycott. Seldom had the gulf between white and black political perceptions been so vividly illustrated. As a black journalist, Ameen Akhalwaya, observed wryly at the time: "If you are being oppressed, the view from below is quite different from the view at the top."[9]

But the real importance of Botha's neo-apartheid move was that it triggered the first organised black response to the regime's actions since the banning of the ANC and PAC twenty-three years earlier. No sooner had Botha spelled out his intentions, early in 1983, than the Reverend Allan Boesak, in an impromptu remark during a speech in Johannesburg, suggested that a united front of churches, civic associations, trade unions, student organisations and sports bodies should be formed to oppose the constitutional proposals. Seven months later the United Democratic Front (UDF), encompassing 565 affiliate bodies, was formed at a meeting in Cape Town's "coloured" township of Mitchell's Plain. The front was organised on a federal basis, with each organisation retaining its individual identity, and an umbrella committee was tasked with reaching consensus decisions on strategy. The meeting appointed three presidents, all veteran members of the ANC of the 1950s, including Albertina Sisulu, wife of Mandela's lifelong *consigliere*, Walter Sisulu, who was imprisoned with him in Pollsmoor. It also named Tutu and Boesak as patrons of the organisation.

From then on, Tutu was drawn into the vortex of the liberation struggle as the UDF spearheaded the most intense and longest insurrection yet. It employed a variety of strategies: consumer and rent boycotts, school boycotts, strikes, huge funeral rallies, protest marches, and a mix of street confrontation and occasional negotiation. Tutu was involved particularly as chief preacher and speaker at the funeral rallies, and in organising and leading the mass protest marches. He was also the chief spokesman throughout for the black liberation cause.

The UDF's initial focus was on organising a nationwide boycott of the black-township council elections. It was spectacularly successful. There was a 5 per cent poll in Soweto, 11 per cent in the Port Elizabeth townships, 15 per cent in the Vaal Triangle, south of Johannesburg, and 19 per cent in Durban. This galvanised interest in the UDF and, by the end of the year, the number of its affiliates rose to seven hundred, representing three million people. Black politics was fully activated for the first time since the banning of the ANC and PAC. Rallies were held everywhere, the old freedom songs rang out again, as well as the chants and slogans of the 1950s and 1960s.

For a year, the UDF ran its campaign against the reform package, addressing mass rallies and recruiting supporters all over the country. It

Right, above: Tutu and Professor Jakes Gerwel are caught in a volley of tear gas shot at them by riot police as they leave St Mary's Church, Guguletu, on 23 August 1989 after addressing students. The action was denied by police until this image appeared the next morning.

Right, below: Rival groups battle for turf at Crossroads settlement in Cape Town, June 1986. The government had enlisted, paid and armed vigilantes nicknamed *witdoeke* after the white scarves they wore.

Above: A Duduza township resident lies dead while members of a special police squad take a smoke break after an all-night "clean-up". Photographs such as this led to the government emergency regulations making it an offence to photograph police in an "unrest area or situation". Below: A mother says goodbye to her son as he prepares to flee their home to escape right-wing vigilantes in Leandra township, Transvaal, April 1986. Right: After being overcome by tear gas, a woman is helped by fellow mourners at a funeral for eight people shot by police in New Brighton, Port Elizabeth, April 1986.

Above: A mass funeral in Alexandra township, Johannesburg, 1986. Alexandra was established in 1912 and, like Sophiatown, was a freehold township. Situated on the edge of the wealthy Johannesburg northern suburbs, "Alex" organised a formidable opposition to apartheid in the 1980s. In February 1986, Alex erupted into what became known as the "Six-day War". Mass funerals, night vigils and stadium rallies were commonplace and, on two occasions, Tutu tried to calm angry crowds who were ready to turn against him.

ALLISTER SPARKS

For a white person, getting to one of the funeral rallies was almost like making an international border crossing. First you had to pass through a cordon of riot police at the outskirts of the township, with their guns and Hippos and camouflage uniforms. Sometimes an officer would ask you to produce a press identity card like a passport before letting you pass. You would then cross a stretch of no-man's-land until a young UDF [United Democratic Front] marshal wearing an armband would approach and direct you to where you should sit in the stadium. Inside the stadium, you would enter the other South Africa, black South Africa, the one that the vast majority of white South Africans never saw:

another country — warm, spontaneous, volatile and very different from the orderly, uptight one you had just left.

The funeral might have been scheduled for 10:00 a.m., but you arrived knowing it would start late and go on all day. The coffins would be there – five, ten, twenty of them set out in a row on the field, in front of a platform where the speakers sat. They were mostly of dark wood but, if there were children – and there always seemed to be – they would be in small, white coffins. There would be banners too, in the colours of the various trade unions: the yellow and black of the UDF, and the green, black and gold of the still-outlawed African National Congress.

was the most vigorous and sustained campaign black South Africans had ever been able to run. Come August 1984, the UDF's dramatic success with its boycott of the "coloured" and Indian parliamentary elections, coming on top of its crippling of the black council elections, effectively stripped the new constitutional system of any legitimacy. Nevertheless, the government stubbornly went ahead and installed the new parliamentarians in their seats – one of them on the strength of a paltry 154 votes – but in the black community there was a sense of triumph and expectation.

Five days later, a massive nationwide revolt began. It started, fortuitously, in Sharpeville – thrusting that modest township in the Vaal Triangle into world headlines for the second time. The explosion was the result of a build-up of grievances that stemmed from the municipal election that had taken place there the previous year, but was symptomatic of what was happening country-wide. The election had been heavily boycotted, so it was an unpopular township council that had taken office. Its unpopularity soared even higher when one of its first acts was to increase rents by 10 per cent – the sixth increase in six years in a poor community with 40 per cent unemployment. That done, the fourteen councillors added greed to grievance by privatising the municipal beer halls and agreeing by unanimous vote to divide the township's liquor stores equally among them-selves and their families – in the process granting themselves 100 per cent council loans repayable over twenty years. They also agreed to issue no new liquor retail licences while these council loans were outstanding – so preserving a monopoly for themselves.

It was a nice deal, and while the struggling township dwellers faced their rent increases the councillors built themselves fancy mansions with two-car garages and bathrooms decorated with Italian tiles – which stood out provocatively among everyone else's little "matchbox" houses and mud-daub shanties, some with their tin roofs held down with heavy rocks.

As anger built up over the rents, an Anglican priest, Father Geoffrey Moselane, decided to call his congregation together to discuss the issue. It turned into a general meeting of township dwellers, at which it was decided to march to the council offices to tell the despised councillors the residents were not prepared to pay the increased rents. Hearing of the plans, the councillors accused Moselane of stirring up trouble in the Vaal Triangle townships and that night his house was stoned.

Sunday night, 2 September, tensions were running high in Sharpeville, and indeed in town-ships nationally. Some rioting had broken out in nearby areas in the excited aftermath of the "coloured" and Indian elections. There was anger in the air and the police were jumpy. A police officer spotted a shadowy figure in the dark and fired a shot. Reuben Twala, the popular captain of a local soccer team, fell dead. It was the spark that set fire to the nation.

That night, enraged students roamed the streets of Sharpeville crying vengeance. "Twala is dead, we are going to get them!" they yelled. They converged on the fancy homes of the councillors, chanting slogans and yelling to them to come out. Sam Dlamini, the deputy mayor, was the first to die as he came out of his front door to be cut down with handmade machetes. His mutilated body was flung into a car and set ablaze. Someone filled a tyre with petrol, lit it and rolled it down Dlamini's hallway. It hit a wall at the end, splashing the blazing petrol into an eruption of fire. Two more councillors died that night, one of them incinerated along with his guard in his fancy home.

Meanwhile, Father Moselane and his group, now numbering close to five thousand and unaware of what had happened during the night, set out early in the morning on their march to the council offices bearing a memorandum of protest – only to find a large contingent of police blocking their way. The township was on fire, three councillors were dead, the rest had fled for their lives, and now here was a mob marching on the council offices. The police panicked and opened fire with shotguns, rubber bullets and tear-gas canisters. From there on it was chaos. For two days, angry youths stoned the police, burned automobiles and torched every council building in sight, while the police in turn opened fire on anything that moved. Thirty people were killed.

With the whole country a tinderbox of tension, rioting flared across the land – from the Vaal Triangle to the East Rand to the squatter camps of Cape Town, the townships of the Eastern Cape and Durban and back to Soweto – ultimately even into the countryside and the small towns of South Africa. The insurrection raged for three years, resulting in more than three thousand

Previous page: Tutu mediates between mothers of children who had been randomly arrested and the police, Soweto, Johannesburg, 28 August 1985.

Following page: On 21 March 1985, commemorative services observing the twenty-fifth anniversary of the Sharpeville massacre were held throughout South Africa. As a group of people gathered in Langa township, near Uitenhage in the Eastern Cape, the police opened fire, killing and wounding people without provocation. Tutu was one of the presiding priests at a mass funeral for twenty-eight victims attended by eighty thousand people on 18 April 1985.

deaths, thirty thousand detentions and much damage to property and the national economy. The government had to mobilise the army and declare two states of emergency to bring it under control – and then only partially.

With both the black council and the tricameral elections over, the main thrust of the insurrection became an attempt to drive out the black township administrations the government had established and replace them with the UDF's own organisational structures. The call to make the black townships "ungovernable" became the battle cry of the uprising. Hordes of young comrades, the shock troops of the uprising, descended on the homes and offices of the terrified black councillors and officials, and literally drove them out of the townships. They either fled or resigned in scores of townships. The UDF then set up its own area and township committees in the vacuum left behind, and so provided an alternative government that effectively took control of the townships.

Black police were targeted too, and frequently forced to barricade themselves inside their compounds. The comrades and the UDF committees organised their own crime-prevention controls. Some established what they called "people's courts" which meted out rough justice to anyone deemed to be assisting the white administration. Residents stopped paying rents to the government agencies; instead the street committees would go door to door collecting fees, recruiting supporters for their campaigns, deciding when strikes and boycotts should be called, and organising funerals for the victims of the ongoing clashes between comrades and the police across the country.

These huge funeral gatherings became the rallying points of the whole insurrection. With the emergency regulations prohibiting all other forms of political activity, they became the only opportunities for black people to express their frustrations. So tens of thousands turned up at the funerals, usually held in some big sports stadium. For all the grief that attended them, these were heart-swelling events at which the spirit of the people seemed to rise to a crescendo of collective support. They were blatantly political events at which orthodox religious rituals featured hardly at all, yet they were spiritually powerful. It was here that Desmond Tutu reached the peak of

Tutu's magic fails to move the masses

Jon Qwelane

ON TUESDAY afternoon Bishop Desmond Tutu's magic subdued the heated emotions of 35 000 people gathered inside the Alexandra football stadium.

He elicited from them an agreement to disperse and return quietly home while he and other senior churchmen travelled to Cape Town to see senior Government officials.

On Friday afternoon an even bigger crowd of 40 000 turned up to hear him report on the talks — and his magic failed to move the masses.

By the time the delegation of churchmen left the stadium, tempers were such that a gang of youths blocked Bishop Tutu's path before he reached his car and demanded to know from him where they were supposed to sleep because "the police ha-

rass us and raid our homes every night".

The Bishop stopped to talk to the youths, who were clearly unhappy with the state of things. He appealed to them to be calm and take what he and other churchmen said "because we are your leaders and your parents".

The youths made it clear to the Bishop that whatever assurances the police and Government spokesmen gave him, they were not worth a tittle.

"They say those things to you but as soon as you leave they come down hard on us. There they are right now, waiting for you to leave so they can start," said one gum-chewing boy of about 18 years old, pointing down the road.

Bishop Tutu, whom crowds had earlier refused to allow out of the stadium because they were apparently dissatisfied with the report brought back from Cape Town, told the youths whatever they did must not provoke the police or spark off a fresh wave of violence.

But the youths were adamant and told him: "As soon as you leave here we will deal with the police in our own way because they are merciless."

Earlier, during his main address to the huge crowd, he had pleaded with them not to mak hemselves "canno. sodder" by doin' ything to give

"WE ARE YOUR LEADERS" . . . But for once angry youths didn't listen

the security forces cause to shoot.

"As your leaders and parents we cannot stand by and watch people pointing guns at you and shooting you. It is important to remember that we are dealing with people who have guns. So we need to have other strategies which will not make us cannon fodder," he said, appealing for more peaceful methods.

The crowds applauded when he said: "We are on the winning side. Our cause is just, and we will succeed against the evil system of

apartheid."

He said churchmen had even told overseas bankers to stop lending money to the South African Government as part of the effort to help end apartheid "but they did not listen to us".

Impatient bands of youths immediately behind the truck on which he stood were incredulous when Bishop Tutu said black people would be free.

"When will we be free?" they chorused.

When he 'd he and his delega... n had secured rances that

residents would not be harassed, some elderly people joined the youths and said Bishop Tutu had allowed himself to be lied to by the police.

"They are harassing us right now. We don't sleep at home," said the youths.

"The police are lying. They conduct night raids and take our children away. Many of them no longer sleep at home," protested the parents.

The Bishop continued, telling how they were unable to meet President Botha but instead

met the Deputy Minister of Law and Order and of Defence, Mr Adrian Vlok.

He said apologies were made on behalf of President Botha, who could not alter his schedule because the appointment had been made at short notice.

Bishop Tutu told the gathering that he and his colleagues had done all they could to convey the urgency of the situation in Alexandra and other black areas to the authorities.

"They did not give us what we want. We want apartheid, injustice and oppression to end. They said they would look into the question of detentions, and we told them it was not safe for children to go to school because the security people were still in the township.

"We told them we wanted the soldiers out of our townships and the lifting of the emergency. We told them about the coming funerals and they mentioned the existence of a law barring mass burials, but we replied there was no way they could tell people how to go about burying their dead.

"The promise is that there will be a mass funeral, and detainees might be released by then. We did deliver your message and grievances to the Government," he told the crowd, which was evidently unhappy about the report.

TUTU: THE AUTHORISED PORTRAIT

his role as an activist. The sight of this figure in his clerical robes – dwarfed by the vast crowds, but defiant as he stood there behind the rows of coffins set out on the field, his powerful oratory both soothing and uplifting the distressed and angry throngs – became a symbolic tableau of the liberation struggle itself.

As the people arrived, the singing would begin, thousands of voices coming together in surging African harmonies, with every now and then a solo female voice rising above the mass with a piercing ululation. The row of coffins, the pained faces of bereaved relatives, the harsh slogan shouting, the angry speeches and the aggressive toyi-toyi dancing of the comrades as they jogged around the field chanting a call-and-response theme, all merged under the hot African sun into an evocative blend of faith and revolution. It found its ultimate expression in the haunting beauty and terrible words of a hymn of praise to the guerrillas that was sung as the coffins were borne away to the graveyard. "Hamba kahle Umkhonto" (Go Well Umkhonto), the crowd would sing with the lilt almost of a lullaby:

> *Go, Go well, Umkhonto*
> *Umkhonto, Umkhonto we Sizwe*
> *We, the people of Umkhonto*
> *Are ready to kill the Boers.*

Sunday after Sunday these events took place, each ending almost invariably in a clash as the young comrades left the field singing their revolutionary songs and taunting the police who were waiting for them in their armoured personnel vehicles, nicknamed Hippos because of their lumbering, top-heavy appearance. It was always an unequal clash between the heavily armed police and the youngsters hurling stones and sometimes petrol bombs, which invariably left more bodies for another funeral rally the following Sunday. And so the cycle repeated itself, each clash producing more bodies for another funeral and another clash and yet more bodies. The comrades seemed oblivious to the inevitability of the casualties they suffered. "These young people frighten me,"

Left, above: A pall-bearer battles on through tear gas at a funeral for fifty victims killed by witdoeke vigilantes at Crossroads township, Cape Town, May 1986.

Left, below: A Casspir with armed police at a student march, September 1986.

This page: Police reload after firing at funeral mourners in Duduza township, near Johannesburg, 1985.

Tutu often said. "They think their lives are not worth living, so they might as well die for the sake of liberation."

Tutu would try in advance to draw the young men away from this repetitive duel of death, and sometimes he would succeed. His funeral oration would usually begin with a passionate identification with the grief of the bereaved. Then he would try to boost the morale of the activists, assuring them their cause was righteous and their eventual victory assured, for God was on the side of the weak and the downtrodden. Finally he would break into a call-and-response theme of his own. "Do you truly believe you will be free?" he would cry out. "Yes" would come a desultory response from a few in the crowd. Cupping his hand to his ear he would say, "I can't hear you. Louder please." This time the response would be stronger, but Tutu would call again and again for an ever louder response until he had the whole crowd chanting rhythmically: "We will be free! Black and white together!" Well then, he would challenge them, if they were so confident they were going to be free they should go home peacefully rather than pick a suicidal fight with the police outside. Sometimes it worked.

In spite of the reckless courage of the young comrades, over time the forces of repression gradually gained the upper hand. But it was an ugly business that put the authorities in a quandary. While the police went about their business with ever-increasing relish, this posed a problem for the state, which was anxious to present a reformist image to the world. Television footage of the beatings and the shootings was turning apartheid into an international moral issue, fanning the appeals for sanctions that Tutu had made earlier, and was still repeating with increasing urgency, to avoid what he warned was the threat of a racial bloodbath.

The reformists in the cabinet, led by foreign minister Roelof Botha, universally known by his nickname "Pik", and the constitutional affairs minister, Chris Heunis, kept hoping the reforms would begin to mollify the discontent, and that the "coloured" and Indian MPs would begin to win some recognition, but, as the trouble intensified, the security forces became increasingly restive. In a desperate bid to keep their advantage against the growing pressure of the security chiefs, the cabinet reformists tried to persuade Botha to make a clear statement of intent that would convince the major Western powers – particularly the United States, Britain and West Germany, South Africa's major trading partners then fortuitously led by the friendly conservative trio of Ronald Reagan, Margaret Thatcher and Helmut Kohl – that real reform was on the way.

Just how bold this statement was supposed to be remains unclear but what is clear is that the reformists oversold it. Pik Botha flew to Vienna for a meeting with senior diplomats from the three Western countries at which he told them to expect a dramatic statement from President Botha at the Natal provincial congress of the National Party on 15 August 1985. The news quickly leaked. Reagan's national security adviser, Robert McFarlane, who had been among those briefed by Pik Botha, returned home and, in his eagerness to justify the administration's controversial "constructive engagement" policy, doubtless added his own embellishment to what the foreign minister had told him. Startling headlines began hitting the American news-stands. *Time* magazine announced that President Botha was about to make "the most important statement since Dutch settlers landed at the Cape of Good Hope three hundred years ago".[10] *Newsweek* wrote that South Africa may be going to announce "a giant step" away from apartheid that would include power-sharing with black Africans, scrapping the bantustans, granting common citizenship to everyone and inviting black leaders to a national convention to write a new constitution.[11] Back home, newspapers splashed headlines telling the public to stand by for a "Rubicon speech" by the president that would change the face of the nation forever.

The only problem was that Botha had no intention of doing any such thing. He was furious, believing his reformist ministers had conspired to push him far beyond where he intended to go. During the National Party congress in Durban on 15 August, with the largest corps of foreign reporters and television crews ever to have gathered in South Africa, Botha delivered not only a king-sized damp squib, but a boomerang. His bulging eyes blazing with anger, he put on a display of finger-wagging belligerence that exceeded even his own reputation as the Great Crocodile. "They think I'm weak, that I can be pushed around," he thundered, "but I'm no jellyfish." No

Above: Tutu consoles the family of Diliza Matshoba, a United Democratic Front and South African Council of Churches activist, who was killed in a suspicious car accident, June 1986.

indeed. Heedless of the consequences, the iron man of Afrikanerdom seized the occasion with the global spotlight on him to make it clear to all of the world that he was not going to be pushed around by foreign pressures, internal unrest or anything else on God's earth.

The reaction was swift and painful. For some years, the South African government had experienced difficulty in raising foreign loans, thanks largely to Tutu's sanctions campaign abroad. To get much-needed foreign capital, the regime had been forced to raise high-interest, short-term loans. It meant that two-thirds of the country's US$16.5 billion foreign debt was made up of these short-term loans. It was an accident waiting to happen – and Botha's big let-down speech was what made it happen. For Chase Manhattan Bank, already under pressure to withdraw from South Africa, it was the last straw. Chase called in its loans. Within days, other American banks followed; then, like lemmings on the run, British, German and Swiss banks did likewise. By month's end, South Africa was facing demands for the repayment of US$13 billion by December. It simply didn't have the money. As the rand currency crashed 35 per cent in thirteen days, the government froze the debt and imposed strict foreign exchange controls which included introducing a two-tier exchange rate for the rand: one rate for the currency internally and another lower rate for it externally. Eventually, a Swiss banker was engaged to negotiate a rescheduling of the repayments, but the net result was that South Africa was turned into a siege economy, desperately short of foreign exchange to fund development and subject to chronic inflation.

From there on, it was all downhill for the apartheid regime. There was still a way to go, but Botha's "Rubicon speech", as it has become sarcastically labelled, is recognised today as a turning point in the decline and fall of its despised system.

For a time, the reformists benefited from the debacle. As the economic backlash worsened, the security chiefs went into retreat and the verligtes tried to revive the image of reform and win back the approval of the benign trio in the West. President Botha made a more reformist sounding

speech when he opened Parliament in February 1986, and even lifted the state of emergency in September.

But it was short-lived. As the insurrection continued, tensions increased between the reformists and the security chiefs. Then came another unforeseen event to precipitate a new crisis. At a biennial summit meeting of Commonwealth heads of government in Nassau, Bahamas, Britain's Margaret Thatcher came under pressure to agree to the association of former British colonies imposing collective sanctions against the apartheid state. South Africa had itself been a member of the Commonwealth years before, but had withdrawn when newly independent black states, led by Kwame Nkrumah's Ghana, objected to its continued membership when it had to reapply on declaring itself a republic in 1961. To avoid another crisis arising in this club of nations at the Bahamas conference, Thatcher, who was strongly opposed to sanctions, proposed a stalling compromise: before taking a decision, the Commonwealth should send a group of eminent figures to assess the prospects for change in South Africa, and see whether it could initiate a dialogue between Pretoria and the country's black leaders.

And so, in March 1986, a strange group known as the Commonwealth Eminent Persons Group (EPG) arrived in South Africa, headed jointly by former Australian Prime Minister Malcolm Fraser and General Olusegun Obasanjo of Nigeria. After the first proximity talks between the ANC and the government, it soon became clear that there was a widespread desire among ordinary people for a settlement and, on the face of it, enough potential common ground to get negotiations going. On that basis, the EPG prepared what it called "a possible negotiating concept" which required the government to make an unambiguous declaration of its reformist intentions and take a series of "confidence-building measures" to demonstrate its good faith – including the release of Nelson Mandela and other political prisoners; unbanning the ANC and the PAC; withdrawing the army from the townships; and allowing free assembly and political activity. For its part, the ANC should suspend its guerrilla struggle and enter into negotiations.[12]

The ANC was skeptical at first, but gradually warmed to the idea and signalled that it might respond positively, but first wanted to hear the government's response. Nelson Mandela, visited in prison, indicated his approval but said he would need to communicate with his colleagues in Lusaka before making it official. Pik Botha was eager and sent an envoy to London for further talks and to invite the EPG back to South Africa. But although they returned for a week in May 1986 to hear the responses from both sides, the operation was aborted when South African commandos launched pre-dawn raids on ANC bases in the Zimbabwe capital of Harare and the Botswana capital of Gaborone, while the air force had bombed a base in Lusaka.

The security chiefs were delighted. Emulating Verwoerd, they had been trying for some time to persuade Botha that introducing reforms under outside pressure was tantamount to blackmail and would lead to increased pressure rather than alleviate it. Botha had in any event greatly increased their influence. Like the majority of Afrikaners, Botha believed all African politics was essentially tribal and that a pan-tribal and partly multiracial organisation like the ANC had little authentic support inside the country; that it was essentially a puppet of Moscow intent on capturing South Africa's rich mineral resources for the communist empire. He contended too, that the Soviet Union was waging a "total onslaught" at all levels – political, economic, psychological, through education and religion, indeed every aspect of life – to undermine South Africa's will to resist.[13] South Africa therefore needed a "total strategy" to counter this onslaught at every level.[14]

To this end, Botha reorganised his administration, drawing all his security and intelligence sources and several sectors of civil society into a powerful National Security Management System (NSMS) with himself as chairman and his security chiefs as the main strategists. Since virtually every aspect of life, in terms of this analysis, was a potential security issue, the NSMS could intervene anywhere.

So began the most vicious assault yet on the black resistance movement. Botha declared a new and much tougher state of emergency. He gave the minister of police, Adriaan Vlok, the power to prevent individuals or organisations from taking part in "any activities or acts whatsoever", a number of UDF affiliates were banned and its president, Albertina Sisulu, placed under restriction,

Left: Tutu weeps at the funeral of Diliza Matshoba, June 1986.

Following page: P. W. Botha at a government rally to show army strength, 1985.

while all trade unions were prohibited from taking part in politics – effectively putting the UDF out of action.[15]

A year after the state of emergency was declared, ninety-seven townships were under military occupation, thirty thousand people were detained, including eight thousand children, some aged only nine or ten years old, and three thousand women – more than in all the twenty-five years since the Sharpeville massacre. By the end of 1987, the rebellion was effectively crushed.

But although the resistance movement was disrupted organisationally, its legitimacy in the black community remained intact. Its strikes and consumer boycotts still drew strong support and another round of black municipal elections in 1988 was again heavily boycotted. Most important of all, the churches moved onto centre stage once more to give the resistance some coherence and purpose. Soon after the government had issued its banning orders, the SACC convened a meeting of church leaders who decided they should pick up where the UDF had left off. On 29 February, a group of twenty-five religious leaders and some one hundred other clergy met in Cape Town's St George's Cathedral where Frank Chikane, now in Tutu's old job as general secretary of the SACC, read a petition addressed to the president and members of Parliament, and proposed that they march to the legislature and present it there.

They were aware that such a march was prohibited under the new emergency regulations but decided to go ahead anyway. So they set out in full clerical regalia, marching in rows with arms linked towards the gracious Victorian building next door. Tutu, Chikane, Peter Storey, the Catholic Archbishop of Cape Town Stephen Naidoo and the president of the World Alliance of Reformed Churches Allan Boesak were in the front row. A line of uniformed police stretching across the street blocked their way. An officer with a megaphone warned them that their action was illegal and ordered them to disperse. Instead the churchmen knelt on the sidewalk, as though in prayer.

The police promptly arrested the leaders and marched them away, then turned a water cannon on the rest, sending them tumbling down the street in chaotic disorder. Several were injured.

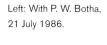

A week later, the church leaders met again with educationists, sports administrators and women's organisations to form a Committee for the Defence of Democracy. It was banned by the government. The leaders organised a protest rally, but that too was banned. Finally, Tutu, Boesak and Naidoo organised a service in St George's Cathedral to replace the rally. Thousands turned up, packing the big cathedral to the walls, into the chancellery and even crowding around the pulpit. Tutu and Boesak both delivered powerful sermons, Boesak telling the regime bluntly that "Your days are over!" and Tutu amplifying that by saying, "You have already lost! We are inviting you to come and join the winning side. Your cause is unjust. You are defending what is fundamentally indefensible, because it is evil. It is evil without question. It is immoral. It is immoral without question. It is un-Christian. Therefore you will bite the dust! And you will bite the dust comprehensively."[16]

Days later, Tutu received a reply from Botha to the petition they had tried to deliver to Parliament, in which the president accused Tutu of joining a revolutionary campaign led by the ANC and the South African Communist Party (SACP) to establish an atheistic, Marxist dictatorship. "The question must be posed," Botha wrote, "whether you are acting on behalf of the kingdom of God or the kingdom promised by the ANC and the SACP? If it is the latter, say so, but do not then hide behind the structures and the cloth of the Christian Church, because Christianity and Marxism are irreconcilable opposites."

Tutu replied that his position derived from the Bible and the teachings of the church, adding with biting sarcasm that "the Bible and the Church predate Marxism and the ANC by several centuries ... Our marching orders come from Christ himself and not from any human being." As a Christian leader, he said, he rejected communism and Marxism as atheistic and materialistic, then ended with a question of his own for Botha: "I work for God's Kingdom. For whose Kingdom with your apartheid policy do you work? I pray for you, as I do for your ministerial colleagues, every day by name. God bless you."[18]

Chikane followed up by convening a conference of churches to campaign for the release of political prisoners. Soon afterwards, Tutu himself appealed from St George's pulpit for a boycott of the impending new round of black municipal elections in blatant defiance of the emergency regulations. Seeing this boldness on the part of the church leaders encouraged more ordinary people to come out in support of renewed civil disobedience. Members of the disrupted UDF formed a new organisation called the Mass Democratic Movement, which launched a national campaign of civil disobedience and called for a boycott of another round of tricameral parliamentary elections. Thousands of people responded.

PERSONAL

Tuynhuys
Cape Town

Archbishop Desmond Tutu
Anglican Archbishop of Cape Town
Bishopscourt
CLAREMONT
7700

16 March 1988

Dear Archbishop Tutu

I hereby wish to acknowledge receipt of your letter of 1 March 1988 with the attached petition dated 29 February 1988.

Before I comment on your petition, I wish to ask whether it is your considered opinion that the so-called march on Parliament was really necessary, and worthy of the cause and message of Christ and the churches represented by those who were involved, knowing that the actions were illegal?

You know that you and others who were with you on that day, have on more than one occasion been well received at Tuynhuys and the Union Buildings – sometimes in a blaze of publicity but sometimes also unknown to others in order to maintain a measure of confidentiality that is apparently necessary at times to protect some of those who have discussions with the Government. The truth of the assertion in your petition that you have "virtually no other effective and peaceful means" of "witnessing effectively", therefore stands under serious doubt.

Furthermore, in your petition you referred to trade unions; and you are no doubt aware of the fact that only last week I extended an invitation to various important trade unions in our country, to have talks with me and members of the Government in Tuynhuys. Some of the very people you referred to, were among those who did not turn up for the meeting, some even without having the courtesy of replying to the invitation.

I am sure you will agree that the whole basis of your action is therefore seriously in question, and that it was to a large degree planned as a calculated public relations exercise.

But it goes much further than that, as you know so well. To illustrate the point, I wish to quote from a recent broadcast by the ANC's propaganda radio, Radio Freedom:

"The church must now be developed into a fierce battleground against the regime … we must organise our forces for a physical confrontation with the forces of the apartheid regime."

The question inevitably arises whether it is possible to come to any other conclusion than that actions such as the march to Parliament may be seen as part of the campaign referred to in the ANC propaganda broadcast? But there is also a wider element involved, as illustrated by Sechaba of September 1985 where it was stated that:

"Members of the ANC fully understand why both the ANC and SACP are two hands in the same body, why they are two pillars of our revolution."

You are no doubt aware that the expressed intention of the planned revolution by the ANC/SACP allicance is to ultimately transform South Africa into an atheistic marxist state, where freedom of faith and worship will surely be among the first casualties.

If you disagree with this, you should state so clearly and publicly, because it also directly relates to your petition, and in particular the statement that: "victory against evil in this world is guaranteed by our Lord".

What is clearly at issue here, is your understanding of evil: is atheistic marxism the evil, or does your view of evil include the struggle on behalf of Christianity, the Christian faith, and freedom of faith and worship, against the forces of godlessness and marxism?

6 4 1 5 5

M.54

|PERSONAL|

Archbishop Desmond Tutu
Anglican Archbishop of Cape Town
Bishopscourt
CLAREMONT
7700

Tuynhuys
Cape Town

16 March 1988

Dear Archbishop Tutu

I hereby wish to acknowledge receipt of your letter of 1 March 1988 with the attached petition dated 29 February 1988.

Before I comment on your petition, I wish to ask whether it is your considered opinion that the so-called march on Parliament was really necessary, and worthy of the cause and message of Christ and the churches represented by those who were involved, knowing that the actions were illegal?

You know that you and others who were with you on that day, have on more than one occasion been well received at Tuynhuys and the Union Buildings - sometimes in a blaze of publicity but sometimes also unknown to others in order to maintain a measure of confidentiality that is apparently necessary at times to protect some of those who have discussions with the Government. The truth of the assertion in your petition that you have "virtually no other effective and peaceful means" of "witnessing effectively", therefore stands under serious doubt.

Furthermore, in your petition you referred to trade unions; and you are no doubt aware of the fact that only last week I extended an invitation to various important trade unions in our country, to have talks with me and members of the Government in Tuynhuys. Some of the very people you referred to, were among those who did not turn up for the meeting, some even without having the courtesy of replying to the invitation.

In the petition you used phrases such as the following: "people's organisations", "democratic activity", the "struggle for justice and peace", and "the real struggle for democracy".

In this regard I wish to quote again from the already mentioned broadcast by Radio Freedom:

"In the name of justice we must take up the fight: we must participate in such means of struggle; the democratic movement must be given a voice in all churches; church services must be services that further the democratic call; the church must be for liberation."

You owe all Christians an explanation of your exact standpoint, for we are all adults, and the time for bluffing and games is long past. The question must be posed whether you are acting on behalf of the kingdom of God, or the kingdom promised by the ANC and the SACP? If it is the latter, say so, but do not then hide behind the structures and the cloth of the Christian church, because Christianity and marxism are irreconcilable opposites.[17]

In your petition you urged the Government to take a number of immediate steps. In reply to that, I urge those who support this petition to reply to the following questions:

* does the phrase: "the transfer of power to all the people of our country" as used in your petition have the same meaning as the same phrase used by the ANC and the SACP, that is for the ultimate creation of a marxist regime in South Africa?

* are you and those who co-signed the petition in favour of the establishment of a marxist dictatorship in South Africa under the rule of the ANC and the SACP, and to the detriment of the church?

* do you believe it to be in line with your interpretation of the church's "prophetic mission" and so-called "liberation theology" to which you subscribe, to further the cause of the ANC and the SACP, and thus marxism and atheism?

In conclusion I wish to ask you whether it is not true that the Christian church knows no other power than love and faith, and no other message than the true message of Christ; and if it brings its spiritual power into secular power-play, and the message of Christ into disrepute, then it becomes a secular instead of a sacred spiritual subject, thereby relinquishing its claim to be church?

If you accept this statement as true, you should establish whether you were acting in the name of God and the church, or whether it was in your individual capacities as members of society embracing secularism, thereby doing a disservice to the very churches which you claim to have represented.

Yours sincerely

P W BOTHA
STATE PRESIDENT

I am sure you will agree that the whole basis of your action is therefore seriously in question, and that it was to a large degree planned as a calculated public relations exercise.

But it goes much further than that, as you know so well. To illustrate the point, I wish to quote from a recent broadcast by the ANC's propaganda radio, Radio Freedom:

"The church must now be developed into a fierce battle-ground against the regime. ... We must organise our forces for a physical confrontation with the forces of the apart-heid regime."

The question inevitably arises whether it is possible to come to any other conclusion than that actions such as the march to Parliament may be seen as part of the campaign referred to in the ANC propaganda broadcast? But there is also a wider element involved, as illustrated by Sechaba of September 1985 where it was stated that:

"Members of the ANC fully understand why both the ANC and SACP are two hands in the same body, why they are two pillars of our revolution."

You are no doubt aware that the expressed intention of the planned revolution by the ANC/SACP alliance is to ultimately transform South Africa into an atheistic marxist state, where freedom of faith and worship will surely be among the first casualties.

If you disagree with this, you should state so clearly and publicly, because it also directly relates to your petition, and in particular the statement that: "victory against evil in this world is guaranteed by our Lord".

What is clearly at issue here, is your understanding of evil: is atheistic marxism the evil, or does your view of evil include the struggle on behalf of Christianity, the Christian faith, and freedom of faith and worship, against the forces of godlessness and marxism?

In the petition you used phrases such as the following: "people's organisations", "democratic activity", the "struggle for justice and peace", and "the real struggle for democracy".

In this regard I wish to quote again from the already mentioned broadcast by Radio Freedom :

"In the name of justice we must take up the fight: we must participate in such means of struggle; the democratic movement must be given a voice in all churches; church services must be services that further the democratic call; the church must be for liberation."

You owe all Christians an explanation of your exact standpoint, for we are all adults, and the time for bluffing and games is long past. The question must be posed whether you are acting on behalf of the kingdom of God, or the kingdom promised by the ANC and the SACP? If it is the latter, say so, but do not then hide behind the structures and the cloth of the Christian church, because Christianity and marxism are irreconcilable opposites.

In your petition you urged the Government to take a number of immediate steps. In reply to that, I urge those who support this petition to reply to the following questions:

* does the phrase: "the transfer of power to all the people of our country" as used in your petition have the same meaning as the same phrase used by the ANC and the SACP, that is for the ultimate creation of a marxist regime in South Africa?

* are you and those who co-signed the petition in favour of the establishment of a marxist dictatorship in South Africa under the rule of the ANC and the SACP, and to the detriment of the church?

* do you believe it to be in line with your interpretation of the church's "prophetic mission" and so-called "liberation theology" to which you subscribe, to further the cause of the ANC and the SACP, and thus marxism and atheism?

In conclusion I wish to ask you whether it is not true that the Christian church knows no other power than love and faith, and no other message than the true message of Christ; and if it brings its spiritual power into secular power-play, and the message of Christ into disrepute, then it becomes a secular instead of a sacred spiritual subject, thereby relinquishing its claim to be church?

If you accept this statement as true, you should establish whether you were acting in the name of God and the church, or whether it was in your individual capacities as members of society embracing secularism, thereby doing a disservice to the very churches which you claim to have represented.

Yours sincerely

P W BOTHA
STATE PRESIDENT

Letter to Tutu from P. W. Botha, dated 16 March 1988, in response to a march to Parliament on 1 March 1988.

Gradually it began to dawn on the more thoughtful securocrats, as this new power elite became known, that their testicular thesis was wrong: hearts and minds were not responding to the use of intimidation, the black masses clearly were interested in political participation and, while it might be possible to put them down with brute force for a time, they would always bounce back. Some, especially in the intelligence services, began to realise that, after the most determined repressive action ever undertaken in their country, they had failed to crush the legitimacy of the liberation movement or win legitimacy for their own system. At the same time, it was clear that the liberation movement did not have the ability to achieve the revolutionary overthrow of the white regime. The conflict was in a state of violent equilibrium, or stalemate. Some began to realise the only way out of that situation was going to be through negotiations, so they began to establish more and more secret contacts with Nelson Mandela in prison and some ANC leaders in exile. But the main stumbling block remained the Great Crocodile. He, too, realised what was becoming obvious and authorised these clandestine contacts, but he couldn't bring himself to cross that Rubicon. So the stalemate continued.

Then fate intervened, as it had done so often in these final stages of the old regime. Botha suffered a mild stroke at the age of seventy-three. It was not incapacitating, as the fact that he lived to the age of ninety subsequently indicated, but Botha decided, presumably on medical advice, to lessen the load on himself by telling his cabinet members he was resigning from the leadership of the ruling National Party, but would remain president of the country.

This necessitated the election of a new party leader. Botha hoped it would be his finance minister, Barend du Plessis, a relatively young man whom he doubtless believed he could control. But by now party members were tired of the crabby old Crocodile and resentful of his down-grading of the party with the new militarised structure of the administration. Though the verligtes did not feel strong enough to elect one of their own to the job, they settled for a centrist, Frederik Willem de Klerk, the minister of education and a trained lawyer, whom they knew to be a strong party man who would shift the locus of power back to the political establishment.

De Klerk, sensing that the party and indeed the county were desperate for a change of national leadership, moved quickly to seize the advantage of his powerful new position. Two months later, the cabinet confronted Botha to tell him the division of power was unsatisfactory and they wanted De Klerk to take over as president. The angry old man went on national television to growl out his resignation while protesting that he was in fact still fit enough to carry on. De Klerk was duly sworn in as president in September 1989.

Few analysts believed the switch from P. W. to F. W. would mean much in the way of political change. De Klerk was leader of the largest and most conservative provincial branch of the party, and there was nothing in his record to suggest he might do anything radical.

Tutu, expecting little from the change, threw his weight behind new efforts to step up the pressure, both at home and abroad. He sent appeals for tougher diplomatic action to an array of world leaders, including Margaret Thatcher, West German Chancellor Helmut Kohl and US Secretary of State James Baker, while on the home front he backed the right of activists to defy the government's emergency laws in launching a national campaign of civil disobedience to protest against a general election called for 6 August. But, within four months, all the experts, including Tutu, were to be taken by surprise.

CHAPTER SEVEN

....

WE CAN'T ARGUE WITH GOD

When President de Klerk stepped up to the podium in the South African Parliament at 11:15 a.m. on the morning of 2 February 1990, everyone expected him to make a reformist statement of some kind: probably an expansion of the neo-apartheid project of his predecessor to include the black South Africans in some way. There was nothing in De Klerk's long conservative record to suggest he might go further than that. He had just run a notably conservative election campaign, thundering from platform to platform that "We don't talk to terrorists!" Not even his opening line prepared his audience for what was to come: "The general election on 6 September 1989 placed our country irrevocably on the road of drastic change." These masters of double-talk had used such language before.

But, thirty-five minutes later, De Klerk had indeed set the country on the road to dramatic change. In that time the new president – short, balding, polished but without much charisma, head cocked to one side like a sparrow, and bobbing on his right foot as he spoke – turned three and a half centuries of South African history on its head. In quick succession, but with no inflections of drama in his voice, he announced that his government was unbanning the African National Congress (ANC), the Pan Africanist Congress (PAC), the South African Communist Party (SACP) and all other black political organisations with immediate effect, that it was releasing all political prisoners, including Nelson Mandela who would be freed at a date still to be announced (it turned out to be nine days later, on 11 February) and that his government would enter into negotiations for a new national constitution with all parties and all black leaders.

I was one of about two hundred journalists assembled in a briefing room adjoining Parliament half an hour before De Klerk

Left: With F. W. de Klerk in Cape Town, 22 January 1993.

delivered his speech. The doors were locked and we were handed copies of the text and told we could not leave until the president had finished speaking. A hush settled over the room, changing into a rising buzz as we read the text before watching De Klerk on closed-circuit television. I recall my own astonishment as I flipped through the pages. "My God, he's done it all," I murmured to my *Washington Post* colleague, David Ottaway. "It's all over. There'll be no stopping the ANC when it can organise and mobilise its people."

My first thought was – and still is – that De Klerk didn't appreciate the full import of what he was doing. As unfolding events were to show, in those few minutes he unleashed forces that within four years were to sweep away the old South Africa and establish an altogether new country with a new constitution, a new flag, a new national anthem, a new ethos – and within a decade even render extinct the once invincible National Party itself. At a stroke, De Klerk demolished the long-held Afrikaner vision of a white South Africa that would be their *volkstaat* (nation), without which they believed they could not survive as a national entity. In future they would have to take their chances as a minority group in a country run by "the other" in which, after three and a half centuries, their national identity might fade and eventually disappear.

It amounted to one of the most astonishing self-transformations of a country and its society in modern times, for which De Klerk and Nelson Mandela were jointly awarded the Nobel Peace Prize, thus joining Desmond Tutu and an earlier ANC leader, Chief Albert Luthuli, and bringing to four the number of South Africans to earn that acme of all international honours because of their role in the long and painful struggle to end apartheid.

What made this man with a reputation of being one of the most conservative leaders of the National Party, this scion of a family that had been among the founding fathers of apartheid, do such a thing? It was, after all, the only time in modern history that an undefeated and still powerful ruling nationalist party has negotiated itself out of power.

The answer, I think, is twofold. Firstly, I believe De Klerk – a far more intelligent man than the crabby old Crocodile – realised that a situation of deadlock, or violent equilibrium, had arisen between the two sides. The security forces could repress the black resistance but not crush it, while, for their part, the resistance could hurt the government but not overthrow it. Oliver Tambo, the exiled ANC leader, was never going to ride triumphantly into Pretoria atop a Russian tank, but nor was he ever going to hoist a flag in surrender. Which meant the only way out of the deadlock was through a negotiated political settlement, failing which the country would gradually be reduced to an economic wasteland, which would be in no one's interest. Secondly, I think De Klerk believed that if he acted boldly – took a quantum leap to get ahead of the game, gain the moral high ground to win international support for his action, while at the same time throwing the unprepared resistance movement off balance – he would be able to control the transition process to his advantage and secure a settlement that fell short of majority rule.

The United States Assistant Secretary of State for African affairs, Chester Crocker, who was involved with the South African issue during the Reagan administration, has said the transition took place because a constellation of factors came together at the same time to make it possible. That is a fair analysis. What was also important is that those factors were both internal and external, forming a pincer movement that left the obdurate white government no room to wriggle away.

Archbishop Tutu was instrumental in applying both arms of that pincer movement. His long advocacy of foreign diplomatic pressure and sanctions built up the external arm, while his activism in the anti-apartheid struggle at home built up the internal arm. And the two interacted: the brutal police action to repress the resistance at home resulted in television footage that appalled foreign audiences, which pushed their governments into toughening the economic sanctions and stepping up the diplomatic pressure.

At the same time, Tutu's constant assaults on the immorality of apartheid, his exposure of its essentially un-Christian foundations and its violation of all that the deeply religious Afrikaners professed to stand for steadily stirred the consciences and undermined the political self-confidence of influential figures in the ruling establishment. Doubts arose, questions began being raised, and steadily the once-monolithic edifice of Afrikaner nationalism began to show cracks.

Economic sanctions and disinvestment, together with the effects of the racial unrest, had plunged South Africa into the deepest financial crisis in its history. Business confidence was at an all-time low, foreign exchange reserves were down to a few weeks of imports and, from all quarters, the murmurings were going up that "we can't go on like this". All of which added considerably to the pressures on De Klerk to act. On the diplomatic front, meanwhile, the interplay of different policies towards South Africa brought some creative strategies into play. As public pressures for tougher action built up in Britain, Prime Minister Margaret Thatcher, who at that point still remained the solitary opponent of sanctions among South Africa's major trading partners, was able to play a classic good-cop-bad-cop strategy, urging De Klerk to introduce reforms that would enable her to resist those pressures. Her ambassador in Pretoria, Sir Robin Renwick, believes this had a significant influence on the new South African president.

But the most important external influence was undoubtedly the fact that Mikhail Gorbachev's reforms in the Soviet Union were beginning to unravel the communist empire. In August 1989, Hungary had opened its border to Austria. One month later, thirteen thousand East Germans escaped to the west through that border crossing. In October, Erich Honecker, the East German leader, quit his job and, on 9 November, the Berlin Wall came down – just as De Klerk was preparing to go to his holiday home on the Cape coast, where he began drafting his historic speech. All this had eased Pretoria's phobia that the ANC was really a Soviet proxy and that opening the door to it would be an act of suicidal folly.

It was also evident that under Gorbachev the Soviet Union was pulling back from its earlier expansionist policies. Vladimir Shubin, who headed the Africa Section of the Soviet Communist

could put my experience of Archbishop Tutu and my interactions with him into a number of phases: In the first phase I hadn't met him; I'd only read about him and I'd formed a picture in my mind, not of a turbulent priest, but of somebody very active and a leading figure. He was growing in importance with regard to the debate that was taking place in South Africa about our future. Then the second phase was during my presidency. The third phase was during his chairmanship of the TRC [Truth and Reconciliation Commission] and the fourth phase is post-TRC and when both of us are retired from public life.

In the second phase, when I was president, I regularly had meetings with church leaders and I met him in that capacity. However, on more than one occasion, he asked to see me on a one-on-one basis. One meeting I recall clearly. A few people who were in prison went on a hunger strike. They were falling more and more into ill health. They were on their way to dying. They had certain demands. He asked to see me and he came to ask me to do something about this, to prevent them from dying. I recall that I said, "Before we discuss the substance of this, can I, as a fellow Christian, just ask you, what is your advice as a minister of religion? As I understand the Bible, it's a sin to commit suicide." I remember him shifting a bit uncomfortably in his chair. I said, "If you promise to put strong religious and moral pressure on them not to do so, then I will talk about what I can do to facilitate your position." I think he left my office reasonably satisfied that within the framework of what was possible I would be helpful. In the end their deaths were averted.

I developed tremendous respect for his fearlessness. It wasn't fearlessness of a wild kind. It was fearlessness anchored in his deep faith in God. I believe also that if you really believe in God, then you know that life is in God's hands. He showed that kind of anchored fearlessness to speak the truth, and I have developed a tremendous respect for him. He was an exception to the rule in this sense: while he was highly critical of government and of past policies, he was also not afraid to criticise the ANC [African National Congress] and the liberation movements when they overstepped the bounds: when they became guilty of unacceptable things like gross violations of human rights within their own organisations. With regard to black-on-black violence, with regard to the "necklacing" episode in our history and with regard to the strife in KwaZulu-Natal, he always came out for the truth, and pointed out the guilt of all those who were guilty. He didn't just favour one side and criticise the other side. That respect for him never left, and I maintain it to this day.

The final phase in which we now find ourselves has us continuing to work together, along with Nelson Mandela, in the fight against AIDS – when we put pressure on the Mbeki government with regard to their ill-founded neglect of the AIDS problem – as well as other initiatives. The three of us are often called upon, as the living [South African] Nobel Peace Prize laureates, to associate and be active in civil society. Nowadays he calls me *boetie*, which means "little brother" in my language, Afrikaans. I'm not so much younger than he is, but he has an attitude as if I am almost a younger brother. I cherish that warmth that I get from him.

MPHO A. TUTU

I have a vivid memory from my childhood about visiting a beach. We were living in Alice. We drove with a white family to the beach. The parents were colleagues of my father's. We dropped them off at the sparsely populated miles of sandy beach and continued to the beach designated for black people. It was a small, stony place. There was nowhere to lay a towel and not enough sand for a sand castle. Even so, that rocky outcropping was crowded with black people wanting to enjoy the ocean.

Years later I watched my four-year-old demolish the language barrier to play in the sand with a little Afrikaner girl. I wondered what all the fuss had been about.

Above: Tutu leads a march to a "whites only" beach in March 1989 as part of the Mass Democratic Movement's civil disobedience campaign, which culminated on the eve of the elections in September 1989.

Party's International Department, has revealed that as far back as February 1986 Gorbachev emphasised at the twenty-sixth congress of the Communist Party of the Soviet Union (CPSU) that all regional conflicts should be settled politically, a statement he said produced an atmosphere at the congress different from any that had gone before. A few months later, at a dinner in honour of the Angolan president, José Eduardo dos Santos, Gorbachev spoke of his belief that "there exists a reasonable and realistic alternative to bloodshed, tension and confrontation in southern Africa".[1]

While these developments were taking place on the diplomatic front, a series of secret contacts between influential white South Africans – including high-level government officials – and ANC leaders had been quietly under way for several years. Paradoxically, these contacts began while P. W. Botha was still at the helm, and he even approved some at the official level, but he could never summon the will to act on the positive reports he was receiving about them, and was so nervous about the risk of leaks tarnishing his macho image that he did not keep his cabinet properly informed about them. Not even De Klerk knew as he took over. The result was that the new president learned of them only when the officials involved came to report to him after he took office. "Who authorised you to talk to the ANC?" De Klerk demanded angrily. While the convergence of this extraordinary constellation of factors made it easier for De Klerk to contemplate a bolder step towards reform, escalating events on the home front were making it imperative that he do so.

As it turned out, September 1989 was a critical month, when all these factors, external and internal, came together and in which Tutu's role reached its apex. For six weeks leading up to the next tricameral election on 6 September, the Mass Democratic Movement had waged a new campaign of civil disobedience, with Tutu and other church leaders heading a series of demonstrations in open defiance of the ban on public protests.

A climax to this campaign was planned for 3 September, the Sunday before the election, when the campaign leaders planned simultaneous marches on Parliament from three different points in Cape Town. In a state of panic, the police launched attacks on these marchers with a degree of violence they had not shown before in full view of a populous city centre. At the entrance to St George's Cathedral, they arrested the leaders, then lashed their followers and even some bystanders, including tourists, with whips and batons in full view of white shoppers and foreign television cameras. The violent assault culminated in the security forces bringing a water cannon mounted on a truck and opening up on the gathered crowd with a jet of purple-dyed water, staining their skin and clothing.

At the height of this melée, one bold protester clambered aboard the truck and, to loud cheers from the crowd, turned the water cannon on public buildings in the city centre, including the Cape Town headquarters of the National Party. The infuriated police retaliated by firing tear gas into the crowd, and by hunting down and beating purple-stained protesters trying to escape. It was a crude scene that caused widespread outrage and more adverse television coverage, but even more humiliating for the authorities were slogans which appeared on walls all over the city the following morning proclaiming that "The Purple Shall Govern" – a neat play on the ANC slogan, "The People Shall Govern".

So anxious were the police to stop demonstrations against the election, that they banned a university choir from singing in St George's Cathedral the following evening. They also banned a service in a nearby Methodist church, and backed an armoured personnel carrier against the church door, trapping scores of people inside. When Tutu arrived to protest, he and others with him were arrested and kept in police cells for several hours. Election day itself saw more violence in which twenty demonstrators were killed by police gunfire. When Tutu heard this, he broke down in tears, went to his chapel where he spent several hours praying, spent the evening alone and slept fitfully.

The next morning there occurred one of those extraordinary moments that have periodically marked Tutu's career and left his closest associates awestruck. Tutu awoke from his restless sleep with a clarity of mind he says he had not experienced since being moved to write his warning letter to Prime Minister Vorster on the eve of the Soweto uprising in 1976. He knew, with absolute certainty, that he had to organise another march right away. He consulted no one else. When some protested that he should do so, Tutu's response was terse. "God told me," he said, "and I'm afraid we can't argue with God." As he explained in an interview years later: "It looks as if you are arrogant and presumptuous, yes, but the trouble is that I knew I was not my own master. At least *I* believed that."[2]

After some cajoling, Tutu reluctantly agreed to delay the march by two days to give his colleagues some time to organise. It was a rush, but the response turned out to be spectacular. The white citizens of Cape Town, appalled by what they had seen, responded in droves. The newly elected mayor, Gordon Oliver, announced that he would join the march, resulting in newspapers labelling it "the mayor's march". White opposition parliamentarians declared their intention to take part. The heads of some multinational corporations announced their support. A police

lieutenant, Gregory Rockman, swayed public opinion further by issuing a press statement saying he had been sickened by the actions of his colleagues who he said had behaved like "wild dogs".[3] Tutu wrote letters to thirteen heads of governments and received pledges of support from several, including Margaret Thatcher and George H. W. Bush.

As support for the march ballooned in an unprecedented way, anxiety gripped the administration. The security chiefs favoured stopping the march, fearing that, if it were allowed, things could get out of hand; others feared that any attempt to stop something that had already gained such momentum would be catastrophic.

As the anxiety mounted, a prominent Dutch Reformed Church (DRC) minister, Johan Heynes, flew to Cape Town to urge Tutu to accompany him to see De Klerk to ask his permission for the march. Tutu refused. The minister of police Adriaan Vlok called on Tutu who was in a meeting with church leaders to ask him to limit the number of marchers and to seek permission from a magistrate. Tutu refused that too. Then, in a typical moment of levity, Tutu put Vlok on speakerphone and, to the delight of a crowd outside, told the minister: "I really don't mind if your policemen line the route so long as they put their hands in their pockets and whistle as we go by."

In the end it was left to De Klerk to make the decision. It was just days before his inauguration as president, but he was already acting in the role. His decision was crisp and to the point. He allowed the march. "The door to the new South Africa is open," he said. "It is not necessary to batter it down."[4]

Left: At a rally in Soweto, Johannesburg, 1990.

Right: Tutu and companions carry a cross, 31 May 1988.

What followed was a spectacle not seen in South Africa since young Philip Kgosana's mass march on Parliament twenty-nine years earlier. An estimated thirty thousand people of all races, including bishops and parliamentarians, workers and businessmen and women, students and children in their school uniforms, marched in a huge column 1.5 kilometres long, through the downtown area of the city, past the railway station to the Grand Parade, an open square in front of the city hall where five months later Mandela would address another great crowd on the day of his release. Tutu, Allan Boesak, Peter Storey, Mayor Oliver, Sheikh Nazeem Mohamed of the Muslim Judicial Council and leaders of the United Democratic Front (UDF) led the march, with UDF and ANC banners being waved as they marched, and crowds of workers leaning out of office windows to cheer them on. There were no police in sight: UDF marshals with "coloured" armbands directed the march and controlled the traffic. They were in charge.

Tutu halted the great crowd in front of the city hall, called on everyone to raise their hands in the air, then to the delight of the crowd delivered a triumphant address to De Klerk. "Mr De Klerk," he cried over a loudspeaker system, "please come here. We are inviting you, Mr De Klerk. We invite you, Mr Vlok. We invite all the cabinet. We say, come, come here, can you see

Above: Press conference
at the Cape Town
City Hall after the first
"March for Peace", to
Parliament to protest
about deaths and
injuries, 13 September
1989. From left to right:
Catholic Bishop, Allan
Boesak, Adv. Dullah
Omar and Tutu.

the people of this country? Come and see what this country is going to become. This country is a rainbow country! This country is Technicolour! You can come and see the new South Africa!"[5]

It was a crucial moment in the whole anti-apartheid campaign. The Cape Town marchers had smashed the ban on peaceful protests, after which a series of such marches took place all over the country. As De Klerk himself admitted in his autobiography: "We were faced with the fact that it would be impossible to avoid a gathering of thousands of people committed to the march. The choice, therefore, was between breaking up the illegal march with all the attendant risks of violence and negative publicity, or of allowing the march to continue subject to conditions that could help to avoid violence and ensure good order."[6]

More significantly, De Klerk added that the key factor that tipped the scales in making his decision was "my strong conviction that the prohibition of peaceful protests and demonstrations could not continue. Such an approach would be irreconcilable with the democratic transformation process that I was determined to launch."[7]

The door to the new South Africa was open and Tutu had led the final assault on it. The following month De Klerk released Walter Sisulu and five other ANC lifers who had been imprisoned with Mandela. Delirious excitement engulfed Soweto as the six men held a press conference in the packed Holy Cross Anglican Church. When an eager questioner asked Sisulu whether their release meant a black government would soon take power, Sisulu gave a cautious reply: "We believe that in our lifetime there will be a government that includes black people. We are not seeking a black government as such. We are seeking a democratic system in which a black man can be president and a white man can be president. There is no question of judging people on the basis of colour."[8] But more important even than what Sisulu said, was the fact that this banned senior member of the banned ANC was speaking publicly and the media were reporting what he said, while crowds were waving ANC banners and shouting its slogans without being arrested. It meant that the ANC was effectively already unbanned and politically active.

Next, De Klerk held a two-hour meeting with Tutu, Boesak and Frank Chikane to discuss the steps that would be needed to begin negotiations. Tutu remarked afterwards what a pleasant difference it had been from his last finger-wagging confrontation with Botha. "We were listened to …" he said.[9]

On the night of 13 December, De Klerk met secretly with Nelson Mandela for the first time, when the ANC icon was smuggled into Tuynhuys, the official presidential residence. "He was taller than I anticipated," the stocky De Klerk wrote later, "slightly stooped by his seventy-two years. The first impressions that he conveyed were of dignity, courtesy and self-confidence. He also had the ability to radiate unusual warmth – when he so chose. He was every inch a Tembu patriarch and bore the mantle of authority with the ease of those who are not troubled by self-doubt. His heritage, his training, his volatile political career, the hard lessons of self-control

Above: Tutu with African National Congress leader Walter Sisulu after his release from prison, October 1989.

Previous page: With Winnie Mandela at a rally outside Parliament in Cape Town calling for the release of Nelson Mandela, 2 February 1990. Unbeknownst to the crowd, the same day President F. W. de Klerk was to announce the unbanning of black political organisations and the release of Nelson Mandela and other political prisoners.

Following page: In the garden of Bishopscourt the day after Mandela's release, before meeting the world's press, 12 February 1990. From left: Tutu, Nelson Mandela, Winnie Mandela, Walter Sisulu, Albertina Sisulu.

and fortitude that he had learned in prison had all prepared him for this moment of history."[10] According to De Klerk, the conversation was cautious, with both men tiptoeing around their differences over group rights versus majority rule, but agreeing "that it would be possible for us to do business together".[11]

Then, on 2 February 1990, De Klerk made his blockbuster speech in Parliament, leading to Mandela's release nine days later. The release, watched by billions around the world, was a breathtaking event – but also a chaotic one. Mandela walked out of the prison gates with the stiff gait of an elderly man, a beaming Winnie beside him. He looked slightly bemused at the wildly cheering crowd waiting for him. Getting him through the traffic and the crowds to the Grand Parade in Cape Town sixty kilometres away was a nightmare. He arrived late, by which time it was dusk and the crowd was boisterous. Some rioting and looting had taken place, and Tutu had to play a risky role trying to bring some rowdy youths to order.

When it came time for Mandela to speak, he discovered that in the confusion of leaving the prison he had left his reading glasses behind – so he had to borrow Winnie's. The result was that his speech, written for him by a committee, was somewhat turgid and his delivery hesitant as he struggled to see the text in the fading light and as the borrowed spectacles kept slipping down his nose. It was a carefully composed address, not a grand Dr Martin Luther King Jr oration, aimed primarily at countering any lingering suspicions about his talks with the government and any possible attempts by the government to use his release to sow dissention in the liberation movement. In words intended more for the doubters in distant Lusaka than the great mass audience before him, Mandela gave an assurance that he was "a loyal and disciplined member of the African National Congress" and that he had "at no time entered into negotiations about the future of our country, except to insist on a meeting between the ANC and the government".[12] Nothing stirring in that. But no matter. The icon was free and there was national hysteria in the air.

After such a frazzling day, Mandela and his wife spent that night in the comforting company of the Tutus at Bishopscourt. The next morning, Mandela gave his first press conference on the spacious lawns of "the Arch's" residence. Then he flew to Johannesburg, to the throbbing, feverish crowds of Soweto. If ever there had been any doubts about the magnetism of his image and the grassroots strength of the ANC's popularity, they were dispelled there in an instant. All those theories the amateur Afrikaner anthropologists had nurtured about the ANC being a proxy of Moscow, and that real African politics was rooted in tribalism, and therefore the bantustans, were blown to smithereens. To their consternation, it must have been obvious that the game was over before it had even begun.

Like Gorbachev, De Klerk was soon to find that once you let the genie of popular democracy out of the bottle there is no squeezing it back in. He had unleashed a process that swiftly generated its own momentum and led to majority rule within four years. But in one respect De Klerk differed from Gorbachev: he stayed with the changes and did not try to freeze the process. He came to recognise that you cannot reform an oppressive system, that if you start to relax it you have to go the whole hog. You can't have *perestroika*, or neo-apartheid, only abolition. De Klerk accepted that as it became evident. His own process of personal change kept pace with events as they unfolded, which is what saved him – and South Africa – while for Desmond Tutu the wheel of fortune took another turn, bringing to a close his role as interim leader of the black resistance and opening a new chapter in his remarkable career as a key player in the transformation of his country.

Above: Tutu celebrates with wife Leah and son Trevor outside Mandela's house in Soweto, Johannesburg, at the news of his release, 1990.
Below: Tutu celebrates the news of Mandela's release, 1990.

CHAPTER EIGHT

....

WE ARE UNSTOPPABLE

Nothing became Desmond Tutu in his role as interim leader of the anti-apartheid struggle more than the manner of his leaving it. It was a gracious retreat, unaccompanied by any public announcement. The moment Nelson Mandela was released, Tutu slipped quietly into the background and took no further part in active politics, so giving the lie to the many who had regarded him as an ambitious politician in clerical clothing. As he had always said, his was a holding operation: the real leaders were in prison and in exile. Now they were home again and he could revert to his true calling as a religious leader whose faith had driven him to play that interim political role in the interests of humanity, of God's children suffering under oppression.

But that did not mean he fell silent. Nor did he remain inactive. It was simply that his role changed. Mandela's release by no means brought an end to the struggle. In fact, the transitional phase between the unbanning of the black political parties and the advent of the new South Africa was the most turbulent part of the whole process. It was a classic instance of the Italian philosopher Antonio Gramsci's observation that "the crisis consists precisely in the fact that the old is dying and the new cannot be born; in this interregnum a great variety of morbid symptoms appear".[1]

The morbid symptoms in this case came from two sources: a violent power struggle between Chief Mangosuthu Buthelezi's Inkatha Freedom Party (IFP) and the African National Congress (ANC) for political dominance among the Zulu people of Natal province, and an equally violent attempt by right-wing Afrikaner extremists and rogue elements of the security forces to derail the negotiating process. There was an element, too, of these factions converging in an unholy alliance.

This multilayered civil warfare played itself out against a backdrop of intense negotiations involving delegates from twenty-six political parties to establish a process of transition to a new South Africa, and then to craft a constitution to define its structure and ethos. The negotiations lasted almost exactly two years, with periodic interruptions as the violence intruded upon them, but, in doing so, paradoxically also spurred on their progress by raising the alarming threat of failure.

Tutu played no part in the negotiations. But he did play an important new role as a peacemaker and sometime mediator during the critical moments of breakdown, particularly in repeated efforts to intercede in the conflict between Buthelezi and the ANC. The Zulu chief was a devout Anglican and, though he had often disagreed with Tutu during his interim leadership years, Buthelezi always acknowledged Tutu as "my archbishop".[2] Tutu used this connection to make frequent trips to Buthelezi's seat of power at Ulundi, capital of the KwaZulu bantustan.

In the drawn-out talks about talks between Mandela's release in February 1990 and the actual start of the negotiations shortly before Christmas 1991, a compromise to meet De Klerk's commitment to power-sharing and the ANC's to majority rule was reached by dividing the negotiations into two stages. The first stage would be a multiparty convention, which the National Party wanted because it could form a coalition with the bantustan parties, to draft an interim constitution. The second stage would be the holding of "one person, one vote" elections under this interim constitution for a constituent assembly that would draft the final constitution for the new South Africa – which the ANC wanted because it would have a numerical advantage after the election. The Convention for a Democratic South Africa, commonly referred to by its acronym CODESA, took place in the World Trade Centre, a cavernous exhibition hall alongside a highway

Left: Tutu and Nelson Mandela on their way to meet Chief Buthelezi of the Inkatha Freedom Party, June 1993.

near Johannesburg airport. The convention was divided into five working groups to cover different issues, and a deadline of 15 May was set for the working groups to report to a plenary session. But the negotiations ended up in deadlock, and the ANC's chief negotiator, Cyril Ramaphosa, walked out of the group saying it was pointless continuing because the National Party members were inflexible. That was CODESA's first collapse.

By now the expectant masses were growing restive. The groups were meeting behind closed doors and there was little information about what was going on there. The ANC's regional branches felt excluded from the process, and some of the more romantic militants who had been lukewarm about the negotiations from the start, because they felt their revolution had been snatched away from them, became suspicious that their leaders were giving away too much. A call for a demonstration

Above: The year 1990 was witness to the beginning of the worst black-on-black violence in the country. Here, Tutu manages to calm an angry crowd in Sebokeng township, near Vanderbijlpark.

of mass action went up, especially from the Congress of South African Trade Unions, whose members felt they knew more about the techniques of negotiation than the ANC did.

Pressure for a more activist campaign increased as violence erupted in Natal province between supporters of Buthelezi's IFP and those of the ANC. Inkatha had long been the dominant movement among the Zulu tribe which has its roots in that province, but with the legalising of the ANC, young Zulus in particular began identifying with the more glamorous liberation movement, and turf battles began erupting between the two. Soon these spread into the black townships of the Witwatersrand, the industrial heartland of South Africa centred on Johannesburg. The first eruption was in Sebokeng, a black township sixty kilometres south of Johannesburg, starting a cycle of violence that raged up and down the urban belt of the Witwatersrand. There were attacks on minibus taxis, drive-by shootings in township streets, random bombings, machine-gun attacks on bars and nightclubs and, worst of all, attacks in packed commuter trains with armed men rampaging through the cars stabbing and shooting passengers and flinging some from the moving trains.

No arrests followed these terrible attacks, causing people in the black communities to conclude, although there was no clear evidence, that there was a "third force" within the military-security apparatus colluding with Buthelezi's followers in these attacks.

With pressure on him to take more militant action, Mandela convened a special ANC strategy committee meeting in which they decided to launch a campaign of rolling mass action. It was to consist of a continuous series of strikes, work stoppages, consumer boycotts and street demonstrations.

But before the ANC campaign could get under way, an even worse crisis occurred. On the night of 17 June, a posse of armed Zulus made their way from a migrant workers' hostel near the black township of Boipatong, a few kilometres south of Johannesburg, and in an orgy of violence

massacred thirty-eight people in their homes, including a nine-month-old baby, a child of four and a pregnant woman. Again the survivors claimed police had escorted their attackers. No conclusive evidence was found, but it was significant that tapes from the police central control room were found to have been tampered with and weapons found in the hostel were never checked for fingerprints. The wrath of the black community reached new heights.

On the Saturday following the attack, De Klerk came face-to-face with this wrath when he paid a visit to Boipatong as an intended gesture of sympathy. A mob swarmed around the president's silver BMW, shouting abuse at him and waving posters with the words: "To Hell With De Klerk and Your Inkatha Murderers" and "We Want Police Protection, Not Murderers". As the official convoy sped away to safety, several armoured personnel carriers edged their way deeper into the township, where another violent drama unfolded.

I followed the vehicles to an open patch of ground that looked like a makeshift soccer pitch, where the crowd was beginning to reassemble. Someone in the crowd told me the police had shot a young man there and were trying to prevent the crowd from retrieving his body for burial; the

Above: At Phola Park, East Rand, 30 April 1992.

have never known him as "Arch". I wasn't part of that grouping that was close and intimate and loving, speaking about "the Arch" or "with the Arch". I think I do call him "Desmond" when I meet him, but we don't use first-name terms. We are so close to each other we don't even need a first-name description. When we meet we just connect to each other. It can be a hug or embrace; the conversation just picks up immediately and it's not prefixed by anything. Maybe he wouldn't know whether to call me "Judge". It would be in a slightly humourous way. It would be respectful, but not ultra respectful. That's part of the friendship between us.

I think the connection is actually a very strong one. It is a strong one of opposites that are not so opposite. Desmond Tutu is a very spiritual person. His vocation, his place in life, is spiritual. It's churchly. Prayer and the sense of God are enormously important to him, yet he's got a very shrewd sense of the material world and the world of people and society and the way it functions. He manages to connect the two in a rather marvellous way. It's almost uncannily effective, whether it's the humour, the jokes, the points of reference or the kind of language. There are moments when he is very much the ecclesiastical person totally embodied in the spiritual vocation, but he reaches out to a broad public.

I would describe myself as a totally secular person who grew up in a completely secular home. I'm thoroughly embodied in a secular existence and appear to have a deeply spiritual nature. There are two people with whom I have connected most powerfully: one is Desmond Tutu; the other is Oliver Tambo [OR]. OR frequently thought of giving up politics to become a full-time minister in the Anglican Church. In a sense, OR was a marvellous rehearsal for meeting Desmond. I was less astonished at the sense of connection that I had. I admired his capacity to work in this world, but responded to the clarity and integrity and honesty of his vision and his way of dealing with people. There was

also a sense of fun, a sense of slight irreverence that we both shared. Desmond has a marvellous sense of fun and of occasion.

Just after Chris Hani was assassinated, there was a gathering to honour him at St George's Cathedral. I remember going there. We all had a sense of dread. It was impossible. We could hardly believe what had happened and the sense of ill portent for the country. There was a car burning at the Grand Parade or somewhere, and dark smoke was curling up into the sky. There was that feeling of murder. The cathedral was crammed, and there was a sense of utter gloom, heaviness and anger, and that burning smoke. We were destabilised and anxious. We hadn't got rid of the old; it was still there, but it was on its way out. We hadn't established the new. It was a very in-between kind of a period. I don't remember the sequence really well, the moment at which Archbishop Desmond Tutu spoke, but he came forward and opened his arms and in a strong voice he said, "We are the rainbow people of God!" I think that was the first time he used that phrase publicly. He was saying it almost as a commander, a commander of faith, a commander of belief to rally people: not in denunciation but in affirmation. It was intensely powerful, very profound, very needed.

For me, one of the lasting features of that statement was that the word "rainbow" was sometimes used as a sort of wishy-washy, softy, "everybody is nice and happy" statement. Sometimes people say Archbishop Tutu said that to indicate he is a nice, happy kind of a person who smiles at all the difficulties in life as if they will simply go away. It wasn't said in that context at all. It was a powerful, strong affirmation of solidarity and of courage, and it had the resonance and strength that we used to get from shouting, "*Amandla*! [Power!] *Mayibuye*! [It must be returned!]" It had that meaning, but it was presented without a clenched fist. It was said with a forcefulness that was absolutely apposite for the moment. We all came out of that occasion feeling bolder and united in a way that we hadn't before.

An experience that bewildered me a bit was at Grahamstown during the Grahamstown festival; I think it was 2004. I'm not sure what the dominant theme of the march was but we marched through the streets, ending up at the cathedral. At the cathedral, people picked up branches, twigs with leaves, and they waved them over each other. It was a form of blessing. The archbishop picked up one, and he gave the branch to me and he asked me to bless him. It was artful, it was moving, it was confusing – bewildering for me, because I'm not a religious person but I seem to have a lot of religiosity in me. I did it out of respect for his wish, and I felt honoured and moved by it as a gesture from him. I felt uncomfortable, because as a kid I had to struggle against any religion. I am a Jew by history, by culture, by all sort of definitions. It has quite a lot of meaning for me. But I wasn't religious, and I felt to pretend to a belief that I didn't have would be disrespectful to me, but also disrespectful to God if God exists. That's quite tough for an eleven- or twelve-year-old weighing up those things. So these things shaped me; they weren't just incidental. Here I was at a cathedral, being asked to participate in a religious-type activity. I was moved and disconcerted and honoured, very much honoured. I suppose you can't really have a hierarchy of spirituality. You can have a hierarchy of leadership but, on any account, the archbishop would have been kind of at the top. And here is this totally secular person who's only got one hand – it's not even my strong right arm, but my weak left arm – waving the branch over him.

He gave me the award from the Institute for Justice and Reconciliation, with which he's been very closely associated. I said, "I feel a lot of sadness this evening because we are saying goodbye to Desmond Tutu." The audience stood up and cheered him. It was very, very powerful and really was his occasion and rightly

So. I said that, in a way, he's giving up something. He's giving up fame, public life, being significant, important, being listened to. We must respect him for giving it up and not pester him. We must let go. That was the point: he's letting go of that, the public life, and we must let go of Desmond Tutu. The evening pleased me very much because everybody there was able to show their love and appreciation and respect and the feeling of the illumination that he brings. Some people you admire because they come up with a sharp insight and they make a major intellectual contribution; others are just brilliant conversationalists and they use language in a marvellous kind of way. With Desmond it is a sense of goodness and rightness and fairness and then decency: not as moral commandments, but as a life lived and the way to be. Desmond doesn't allow Satan, the devil, the enemy, or the wicked to dominate. He isn't in a constant diatribe against evil and wickedness; he is affirming of the goodness and positive qualities of life. It doesn't stop him from denouncing indignity, unfairness and injustice, but the denunciation isn't done in that bitter, sharp, personalised, angry way. There would be indignation rather than anger, critique rather than denunciation. Maybe because I have mainly known him in the post-apartheid period, I'm more aware of that side. Maybe I responded more to the power of goodness, of warmth, of joy, of love, of appreciation of searching for the good in people. Finding the good is a greater denunciation, because it's denouncing by example, by its own virtue, by its vitality, rather than the slashing language and the vituperation. He does not look to people to cast out the evil in themselves, but rather to discover the goodness in themselves.

I was very taken by a comment he made in his farewell, his last farewell, when he retired from his retirement. He said that he often wondered what it was like to be tall. It's lovely to be tall. It's sometimes inconvenient. You bang your head sometimes.

Above: A political cartoon by Jonathan Shapiro (aka Zapiro) entitled "The Rainbow Nation Overrun with Xenophobic Violence", *Mail & Guardian*, 22 May 2008. Shapiro is an iconic South African political cartoonist whose work came to prominence during the 1980s.

police wanted to take it away themselves. A cordon of about thirty police in camouflage uniforms and armed with heavy-gauge shotguns strained to keep the crowd back. As the crowd swelled with newcomers, it became increasingly agitated. Suddenly a shot rang out; no order had been given but it seemed someone in the police line had stumbled and fired his gun accidentally. The rest took it to mean an order had been given, and the whole line opened fire on the crowd at point-blank range. I hit the ground at the feet of one of the policemen as he fired repeatedly over me into the fleeing mob.

When the shooting stopped, there was an eerie silence. I lifted my head and saw a field of carnage. Bodies lay in a tangled pile about twenty metres from me, with more strewn haphazardly across the field. There were groans and screams from the shocked people who had fled to their houses some hundred metres away. One of the policemen rose to his feet and yelled in Afrikaans: "Who told you to shoot? I told you not to shoot without orders!" He was clearly the officer in charge and was in a high state of agitation. I walked among the fallen people, trying to count them and offering what little help I could. I counted twenty bodies with gaping wounds. The police made no attempt to help. Suddenly a shot rang out from the houses, with the angry hiss of a bullet passing nearby. Someone in the township was opening up a retaliatory fire. The police officer barked an order and his men sprinted for their armoured vehicles and scrambled in. They started their motors and sped out of the township.

Two days later, a wave of popular anger hit Mandela at a rally in another township near Boipatong. He encountered heckling, perhaps for the first time in his life, and angry voices shouting things like "You are like lambs while the government is killing us".[3] Clearly Mandela had to respond to this public fury. He issued a statement listing fourteen demands that he said

Above: Joined by other
church leaders, Tutu visits
victims of a massacre
of forty-six residents
of Boipatong, outside
of Johannesburg, by
Inkatha hostel dwellers,
18 June 1992.

the government would have to meet before the ANC would agree to resume negotiations. The government refused the demands. So for the next three months the two sides waged what Cyril Ramaphosa called "a war of memoranda".[4]

In that time, as the militants gained the upper hand within the ANC, the strategists among them decided to target the nominally independent bantustans. The ANC was galled by the fact that they were unable to organise there, and Mandela sent a memorandum to De Klerk demanding that he intervene to permit free political activity there. The president refused on the spurious grounds that these territories were "independent" and he could not interfere. Angered by this, the strategists decided to target the Ciskei homeland, a piece of territory allocated to a segment of the amaXhosa tribe which was particularly irksome to the ANC because it lay in the heart of their Eastern Cape stronghold.

Members of the militant group travelled to the Eastern Cape and pronounced it ripe for popular insurrection. Opinion polls showed the bantustan's military ruler, Oupa Gqozo, to have negligible support. Ronnie Kasrils, a member of the ANC's armed wing and leader of the reconnaissance group, devised a strategy to lead a march of protesters from the nearby King William's Town, which lay technically inside white South Africa, and then cut across the unmarked border to occupy the Ciskei capital of Bisho with a people's assembly until Gqozo agreed to resign.

When Gqozo got wind of this he sought an urgent court order to prohibit the march, to which the ANC replied that since it didn't recognise the Ciskei's independence it wouldn't recognise any order from its courts. A bizarre court hearing resulted in a compromise ruling, allowing the march but ordering that it should not go beyond the homeland's Independence Stadium on the very edge of the unmarked border. In other words, the marchers couldn't enter the Ciskei.

But Kasrils had surveyed the area and spotted a gap in the stadium fence. He planned to lead the marchers into the stadium, then dash through the gap, across a highway and into the capital. Next morning a huge crowd of some eight thousand gathered in King William's Town and began their march, singing, dancing and chanting ANC slogans. At the same time, several hundred Ciskei soldiers, with white officers seconded from South Africa's military intelligence, took up position around the stadium. Kasrils led the marchers into the stadium as planned, then sprinted for the gap with a section of the crowd following him – at which point the Ciskei soldiers opened fire in two long fusillades with automatic weapons and grenades. Kasrils and the other ANC leaders survived but twenty-eight marchers were killed and more than two hundred wounded. It was another outrage, but this time not only the regime was held blameworthy, the ANC was deemed to have acted recklessly as well.

Chastened by what had happened, Mandela issued a statement saying he had compressed his fourteen demands to three and, if De Klerk would agree to address them, he would be able to go back to his people and say: "Look he has met them. Let us meet him."[5] De Klerk responded with an invitation to Mandela to meet with him, which duly took place, and the two sides signed a Memorandum of Understanding in which they agreed to resume the interrupted talks.

That became the pattern of crisis-driven negotiations. Time and again the talks came close to breakdown but, as they did so, the key negotiators for the two main parties – Roelf Meyer, the Minister of Constitutional Development and Cyril Ramaphosa for the ANC – would get together and cobble a compromise. It was as though each side had to stare into the abyss to recognise their mutual dependency. Both came to realise they were bonded together in the negotiating process; neither could retreat. The government could not re-ban the ANC and return

RICHARD GOLDSTONE

He invited us, on a number of occasions, to Bishopscourt. I remember a very lovely evening at a party for the archbishop of Canterbury. I remember very clearly saying to the archbishop – he and I were alone – I said, "You know, one of the great things about Archbishop Tutu is the way he changed direction with the release of Nelson Mandela. Until that time he had a very high political profile. Archbishop Tutu, like me and probably like most people, quite enjoys publicity. But from the minute Madiba [Nelson Mandela] was released from prison he set aside his political activity. That took tremendous character and discipline." As I said it, Desmond came out and the archbishop repeated to him what I had said. It's true; I think it took tremendous self-discipline to withdraw at the time that he was an international hero. He withdrew from the political scene in South Africa during the transition and I have always greatly admired him for that.

He spoke out on moral issues but it was as archbishop and it wasn't as a political leader. One can't divorce the politics from these huge, huge issues but there is a moral dimension to them. I admired his

Mandela to prison, nor could the ANC return to exile and resume its guerrilla war. So there developed what became known as the "Roelf and Cyril channel" as the two chief negotiators attempted to anticipate sticking points and work out compromises.

But while this new level of understanding between the government and the ANC speeded up the negotiations when they resumed, it provoked fresh problems with Buthelezi who suddenly found his party cut out of the action. Buthelezi had taken offence from the very start when the conference refused what on the face of it was an outrageous demand that while other political parties were allowed one delegation each, he wanted three: one for his IFP, another for his KwaZulu bantustan and a third to represent the king of the Zulus, Goodwill Zwelithini. Feeling snubbed, the prickly Buthelezi walked away from the negotiations, leaving the IFP delegation to be headed by its chairman, Frank Mdlalose.

In his pique, Buthelezi retaliated by forming an alliance – against all his own deeply held principles – with the far-rightist white Conservative Party and the leaders of two of the bantustans,

Ciskei and Bophuthatswana, whom he had always despised. The alliance was called the Concerned South Africans Group (COSAG). It was to pose a grave new threat to the whole transition process, and threw Desmond Tutu into action once more with frequent attempts at intercession. Ultimately Tutu's shuttle diplomacy was to play a role in saving the day by helping to bring the difficult Buthelezi back to earth, but not before the process went to the brink several more times.

The new crises came mainly from the right. The first and most devastating occurred on the Saturday before Easter, 10 April 1993, when Chris Hani, leader of the South African Communist Party (SACP) and the most charismatic of the young black leaders, pulled into the driveway of his home in suburban Boksburg, east of Johannesburg. As he stepped from his car, a man in a red car parked across the road leaned out the window and fired two shots from a nine-millimetre Z88 army-issue pistol, and Hani slumped to the ground. Casually, the man walked across the road, fired two more shots into the body, returned to his car and drove away.

Hani's neighbour, a white Afrikaner woman named Retha Harmse, heard the shots and saw the red car pull off. She memorised the car's registration number and telephoned the police. Fifteen minutes later the police stopped the car and arrested a thirty-eight-year-old Polish immigrant, Janusz Waluś. The smoking gun was literally still in his car.

Hani's assassination ignited an inferno of rage in the black community, where Hani was regarded as a struggle hero, particularly among the radical youth. Now he was dead, murdered by a white racist who was soon revealed to have close links to the Conservative Party through his collaborator in the crime, Clive Derby-Lewis, a leading party member.

For nine days the country hung on the edge of disaster as the fury raged, rising in its frenzy to the day of the funeral. It was a week during which the long-feared apocalyptic South African bloodbath might well have erupted – but didn't. The fact that it didn't was due primarily to two men: Nelson Mandela and Archbishop Desmond Tutu.

President De Klerk himself was helpless in this national emergency. There was no way the exiting apartheid leader could pacify the outraged black community. Realising this, De Klerk wisely handed the national platform to Mandela. At the height of the fury, Mandela went on national television to issue a moving appeal to blacks and whites to close ranks and prevent their emotions from destroying their joint future. "A white man, full of prejudice and hate, came to our country and committed a deed so foul that our whole nation now teeters on the brink of disaster," Mandela said. "A white woman, of Afrikaner origin, risked her life so that we may know, and bring to justice, this assassin."[6] He sounded presidential, and from then on effectively assumed the mantle of national leadership that would be formally bestowed on him a year later.

Next it was Tutu's turn. He conducted the funeral at which more than a hundred thousand agitated people packed into the country's largest sports stadium outside Soweto, and twenty

courage but also his astuteness in speaking out on those issues which really had a clearly moral content. I believe that as a religious leader he had not only a right but the duty to speak out on those issues. His huge national and international moral stature had made it so important.

I was impressed by his modesty, his openness and his tremendous friendship. I never dreamt I would end up calling him by his first name. Very soon after we were together at cricket and I was calling him "Father Desmond", he said, "No, Desmond". It's been Desmond ever since.

Our correspondence more recently has been in two areas: the one was through Human Rights Watch, over human rights in Chad. The other, more important contact has been in the aftermath of the report on the Gaza war "Operation Cast Lead". Of course the archbishop had led the previous fact-finding mission into Lebanon, so he was very much involved in the whole area. But when the attacks started – they were vicious personal attacks on me – I received a wonderful email from him telling me that I will be vindicated.

"WE WANT TO MAKE A
DEMAND TODAY, WE
DEMAND DEMOCRACY
AND FREEDOM ... NOW!
... WE DEMAND A DATE
FOR THE DEMOCRATIC
ELECTION ... NOW! WE ARE
THE RAINBOW PEOPLE
OF GOD! ... WE ARE
MARCHING TO FREEDOM!
... BLACK AND WHITE
TOGETHER! ... WE ARE
UNSTOPPABLE! ... BECAUSE
GOD IS ON OUR SIDE!"

DESMOND TUTU

Above: Funeral of Chris
Hani, 20 April 1993.

thousand followed the coffin to the cemetery in Boksburg fifty kilometres away. The early morning saw some running battles between students and the police outside the stadium; a few cars and houses were set on fire, some windscreens were smashed, and one youth in a demented moment unleashed a burst of AK47 gunfire at a police helicopter circling overhead.

But silence fell when Tutu arrived and gestured to the massive crowd to stand in respectful silence as the coffin was carried into the stadium. Then, in his familiar call-and-response style, he led them through what was part praise chant and part funeral oration, declaring that just as the resurrection had followed the crucifixion, so too could Hani's death lead to victory. "We want to make a demand today," he cried, calling on the crowd to repeat after him: "We demand democracy and freedom ... Now! ... We demand a date for the democratic election ... Now!" Skilfully he worked up the crowd's emotions, identifying with their anguish, then gradually led them to a soft landing by calling on all to raise their hands in the air and sway from side to side as they chanted after him: "We are the rainbow people of God! ... We are marching to freedom! ... Black and white together! ... We are unstoppable! ... Because God is on our side!"[7]

There was more trouble at the cemetery and, by the end of the day, six people had been killed and fourteen injured. But, given the incendiary nature of the day it was little short of a miracle that the casualties were so few. At the World Trade Centre, Ramaphosa announced that the ANC-led alliance had decided to speed up the negotiations, not delay them, because of the assassination. Joe Slovo, chairman of the SACP and a close friend of Hani, added his own sense of urgency. "Any suggestion of calling off the negotiations would be playing into the hands of the murderers, whose purpose is to stop them," he said.[8] So the crisis-driven process continued.

Six weeks later, as delegates to the negotiating council gathered for their morning session on 25 June, a raucous mob of some three thousand Afrikaner extremists made their way towards the World Trade Centre. There were farmers in sun-hats with women and children in tow, and young men in khaki carrying placards calling for an Afrikaner *volkstaat* and banners with the swastika-like insignia of the Afrikaner Weerstandsbeweging, the Afrikaner Resistance Movement

commonly known by its initials AWB. Some wore the black uniforms of the AWB's Ystergarde, or Iron Guard, with SS-type shoulder flashes and cap badges. Many had holstered pistols on their hips, long hunting knives in their belts, and shotguns and rifles sheathed in bags. They also carried picnic hampers, cooler bags and barbecue equipment.

As they approached the building, a yellow armoured vehicle edged its way through the crowd and crashed through the plate-glass frontage into the foyer. The mob surged in behind it, yelling as they went: "Where are they? We want them." They raced up the stairways and down corridors, searching for the delegates and bellowing threats that they wanted to shoot them. They emptied the delegates' bar, poured fruit juice on the carpets and urinated on the desks. The leader of the AWB, Eugene Terre'Blanche, revelling in the occasion, marched triumphantly into the foyer accompanied by members of his Ystergarde and delivered a fiery address, saying this was their finest hour; they had shown the world the Afrikaners were a tough lot, determined to fight for their rights and prevent De Klerk from selling out their birthright. Eventually the intruders withdrew to light their barbecue fires on a stretch of ground beside the exhibition centre, open their picnic hampers and quaff gallons of beer.

There were crises provoked by left-wing extremists as well. Five members of the armed wing of the Pan Africanist Congress (PAC), which had boycotted the negotiations, burst into a Cape Town church firing automatic weapons and throwing grenades into the white congregation, killing twelve people and wounding fifty-six. Soon afterwards, another group of black youths murdered an American Fulbright scholar, Amy Biehl, when she gave three black friends a lift home to Cape Town's Guguletu township on 26 August 1993. Still the negotiations forged ahead until the last clause of the new constitution was adopted just before dawn on 18 November.

But there was one more crisis to be weathered before the founding election of the new democracy could be held. In a violent last-ditch effort to establish a power base from which to fight for their separate state, the right-wing extremists under General Constand Viljoen, the recently retired chief of the South African Defence Force whom the extremists had elected to

"THE MOMENT FOR WHICH I HAD WAITED SO LONG CAME AND I FOLDED MY BALLOT PAPER AND CAST MY VOTE. WOW! I SHOUTED, YIPPEE! IT WAS GIDDY STUFF. IT WAS LIKE FALLING IN LOVE, THE SKY LOOKED BLUE AND MORE BEAUTIFUL.
I SAW THE PEOPLE IN A NEW LIGHT. THEY WERE BEAUTIFUL. THEY WERE TRANSFIGURED. I TOO WAS TRANSFIGURED.
IT WAS DREAMLIKE."

DESMOND TUTU

Opposite: Tutu
introduces Nelson
Mandela to the crowd
at City Hall, Cape Town,
after he is elected state
president, May 1994.

head a new Afrikaner Volksfront (Afrikaner People's Front), planned to lead a volunteer group of Citizen Force reservists to seize control of the Bophuthatswana bantustan in the north-west of the country. The idea was for the volunteers to link up with the bantustan's white-officered army and occupy the capital, Mmabatho, in the belief that the regular South African army would take no action against their popular former commander. It would in effect be a military coup that would give the right-wingers an impregnable base from which to negotiate the secession of an Afrikaner state from the new majority-ruled South Africa.

It could well have worked – except that its most enthusiastic supporters, the AWB, ironically screwed up the plan. Eugene Terre'Blanche's racist Rambos, eager to spearhead so heroic an adventure, drove into the homeland while the volunteer unit was still assembling outside. They drove in a cavalcade of private cars, firing indiscriminately at black people in the streets of Mmabatho as they roared through, killing several. In the chaos and fury this provoked, the Bophuthatswana army mutinied and refused to open its armoury to the volunteers as prearranged, leaving Viljoen's men unarmed and out of action.

Meanwhile, the AWB cavalcade, their derring-do sortie done, turned for home with their lead cars bursting through a police roadblock on the way. The last car in the convoy was an old, light blue Mercedes-Benz, and a bearded man in the passenger's seat was firing through the window at the police manning the roadblock. There was a burst of gunfire from the soldiers, and the car slewed to a halt at the roadside. As the shooting continued, the passenger's door opened and the bearded man slumped into the dust with blood pumping from his neck. His two companions, Alwyn Wolfaardt and Fanie Uys, crawled out and squatted beside his body, their hands in the air. For twenty minutes, Wolfaardt and Uys, both bleeding, lay slumped in the dirt pleading for help while a gathering crowd taunted them. A young black policeman walked up to Uys and screamed at him: "Who do you think you are? What are you doing in my country? I can take your life in a second, do you know that?" When a reporter tried to calm him, the policeman snapped back: "We want to shoot these dogs. They have killed women. They are animals, not people."[9]

Minutes later they were indeed shot like dogs. While television cameras rolled, another frenzied policeman stepped up to Uys, pointed his assault rifle at him and fired a single shot into his body. The policeman then walked over to Wolfaardt and shot him in the back of the head. That night the grisly scene was broadcast on the six o'clock television news. As I wrote at the time, for the men's families and for white rightists everywhere, the impact was enormous. The image of the execution, in all its awfulness, had blown away an ancient myth that had underpinned generations of colonialism and racial domination – the myth that the white race, with its superior arms and training, could always and everywhere command indigenous people of colour. Now everyone had seen on their television screens that black people, too, had lethal weapons, and that to go to war against them was not a hunting expedition. The bubble of adventure, the heroic re-enactment of historic Boer myths, was punctured in a day of blood and humiliation.

All that remained now was to coax Buthelezi into participating. His Inkatha party was too significant to exclude. Tutu had been working ceaselessly trying to persuade him, even to the extent of arranging a nine-hour meeting between him and Mandela, but the disgruntled chief remained recalcitrant. Then a miracle happened. A little-known Kenyan academic, Washington Okumu, who was working for an evangelical organisation in Natal and had befriended Buthelezi, called on him and persuaded him to participate. Hearing the news, Tutu was ecstatic. "I'm over the moon …" he cried. "It's just like a dream; we are not going to cease giving thanks to God that we have a God of surprises, a God who performs miracles all the time."[10]

The way was clear at last for all parties to participate in the historic election that completed the remarkable transformation of apartheid South Africa by its own people into a non-racial democracy. A process that was consummated by the inauguration of Nelson Mandela as the first president of the new South Africa on 10 May 1994 at a glittering ceremony for which Archbishop Desmond Tutu planned the religious component as a multi-faith event with readings and prayers by Christian, Hindu, Jewish and Muslim leaders: appropriately, a rainbow of faiths for the "rainbow nation of God".

CHAPTER NINE

....

THERE ARE THINGS THAT
WENT WRONG

The young woman in a vivid orange-red dress began to sob as she told the story of that terrible night when she and her friend waited hour after hour in a rising fever of anxiety, wondering why their husbands had not returned home after a day-long meeting with fellow activists. Then suddenly Nomonde Calata broke off, threw herself backwards and unleashed a wail of anguish that came from the very depths of her soul. It was a sound that chilled the audience in the East London City Hall; it chilled the whole nation as it was broadcast repeatedly to all corners of the land over the next days and weeks by the national broadcaster's radio and television networks. It was, wrote Antjie Krog, the Afrikaans poet, author and broadcaster, "the signature tune, the definitive moment, the ultimate sound" that was beyond words, beyond language, of what South Africa's Truth and Reconciliation Commission (TRC) was about. "That sound … that sound … it will haunt me for ever and ever."[1]

It was 16 December 1995, a public holiday, South Africa's Day of Reconciliation, that had been chosen to start the commission's hearings into the atrocities committed during the struggle against apartheid between 1960 and 1994, covering the most violent period of that conflict. Nomonde Calata was one of the first witnesses on the first day of those hearings which were to last nearly three years under the chairmanship and guiding hand of Archbishop Desmond Tutu.

It was, by Tutu's own admission, the most challenging job of his long and illustrious career. From before the commission was established until long after its five-volume report was presented to President Mandela in 1998, it was buffeted by the winds of controversy from all points of the political compass. Some on the left felt the process was a cop-out that allowed many who had committed atrocities to get away literally with murder, while

Left: Cartoon by Jonathan Shapiro.

others on the right accused it of being an Afrikaner witch-hunt; yet others objected that it was the foot soldiers who caught the flak, while their commanders who handed down the orders got away scot-free.

It was buffeted from within as well. The seventeen commissioners who had to run the show were drawn from all elements of society and were seldom in agreement, leaving it to Tutu and his deputy, Alex Boraine, a former president of the Methodist Church in South Africa and a businessman and liberal parliamentarian, to maintain the peace and keep the commission on course. To make matters still tougher for Tutu, he was diagnosed with prostate cancer in January 1997, which enforced his absence for several weeks then and a critical two months later in the year while he underwent radiation treatment in the United States. The cancer affected him psychologically as well. As Boraine wrote later: "I think Tutu's illness affected him very deeply but in a strange way enabled him to guide and direct the work of the commission with even greater sensitivity."[2]

But Tutu's main contribution to the TRC process was that he gave it a clear ethical framework in which to operate. This was the twenty-first such commission established in the post-World War II world to probe a nation's own human rights violations, but it was by far the most textured, sophisticated and purposeful. Tutu gave it a clear objective, which was not only to establish the truth of what had happened during those years of vicious racial violence but to lay the basis for the start of an ongoing process of national reconciliation. That concept is hard enough to define, let alone be clear about whether or not it was achieved. Its success or failure remains a matter of conjecture, but I and most other journalists who were close to the process – such as Antjie Krog and Max du Preez who covered it throughout the three years for national radio and television respectively – have no doubt about its achievements. Nor do they doubt

that this was primarily because of Tutu's leadership. "No one else could have done it," Du Preez told me years later. "Tutu was essential to the whole process."[3]

What Tutu did was to take what was essentially a political deal that emerged from the negotiations – a compromise between those who wanted a Nüremburg trial and those who wanted a blanket amnesty – and embed it in a theological framework, an essentially Christian ethic, calling for repentance and reconciliation of all God's children in his rainbow nation. It was a call in harmony too, with the African concept of ubuntu which idealises the interdependence of the whole community, so that an injustice to one diminishes all. Without that, the TRC could easily have become no more than a retributive political exercise to settle scores with the oppressor, whereas Tutu's aim was to make it a process of restorative justice to start a process of reconciliation leading to national unity. This was particularly important in such a strongly Christian country where faith and politics were so closely enmeshed.

The TRC structure comprised three specialist committees. One dealt with human rights violations, and Tutu himself presided over it, regarding it as by far the most important, because that was where the survivors and the victims' families could tell their harrowing stories, both as a cathartic exercise and to re-establish their human dignity before the whole country. Another dealt with amnesty applications, where the perpetrators of those violations could seek condonation if they told the whole truth and could prove that they had acted as part of, or on instructions from, a political organisation involved in the struggle over apartheid. These hearings were presided over by three judges in a committee which operated independently within the TRC and whose findings were final and had the force of law. The third, and sadly the least successful, was a committee to consider reparations for victims.

The archbishop's commission thus became a travelling confessional that moved around the country hearing thirty-one thousand cases of human rights abuses in three years and in the end presented President Mandela with a report of a million words. Unlike truth commissions in countries such as Chile, Argentina and El Salvador, which sat behind closed doors and kept their reports secret, South Africa's TRC was open to the public. Hearings were in community halls in cities and small towns – often in the black townships where the atrocities were committed and the victims lived – and were packed with spectators. More than that, they were broadcast nationwide on radio and television in all eleven official languages, and extensively reported in

"TO KNOW HIM IS TO LOVE HIM.
YOU CANNOT SPEND TIME
IN THE PRESENCE OF
DESMOND TUTU WITHOUT
BEING PROFOUNDLY
CHALLENGED IN TERMS
OF YOUR OWN LIFE
AND PURPOSE."

ALEX BORAINE

the newspapers. And so this remarkable process of confession and catharsis, of victims and torturers, widows and assassins, confronting one another and talking through their guilt and pain reached all communities across the land. Nobody could justifiably claim afterwards, as so often happens with national atrocities, that they didn't know what went on under apartheid. They could see for themselves as an interrogator demonstrated before the cameras how he had tortured a victim to extract information, or described in grisly detail how he had hacked someone to death.

The most gripping hearings were those where the survivors and the families of victims told their emotional stories of the agonies they had suffered; they told those stories directly to Desmond Tutu, the chairman, there in his purple robes, questioning, encouraging, supporting them through the painful process of recalling the most harrowing moments of their lives, and then quietly, gently asking them at the end whether they could bring themselves to forgive and be reconciled with their persecutors. A remarkable number did. These were incredibly intimate moments, making for high human drama. Television viewers grew accustomed to seeing the emotional archbishop sink his own head into his hands and weep openly as he shared the pain of the victims breaking down before him.

It was before this committee that the hearings began in the packed East London City Hall on 15 April 1996. The opening day was charged with excitement and emotion as the first witness, Nohle Mohape, was able for the first time to tell the story of how her husband, Mapetla, had been killed in detention twenty years earlier. But the next day was even more moving, for it was then that Nomonde Calata relived that terrible night of waiting, young and pregnant with her second child, waiting and waiting for her beloved husband, Fort, to return from the meeting; it was when she relived the pain that unleashed that wail of excruciating grief and loss that defined for Antjie Krog the whole process of remembering this country's painful history, in being thrown back, as she puts it, "into a time before language".[4]

Nomonde's story was that of the murder of the "Cradock Four". Cradock is a modest country town not far from Alice in the Eastern Cape province where African nationalism first arose, where Tutu taught at the Fedsem, and which in those days was the heart of black radicalism. The bearer of that tradition in Cradock's black township of Lingelihle was the bright young headmaster of Sam Xhallie Secondary School, Matthew Goniwe, who with his close friend and fellow teacher, Fort Calata, had formed the Cradock Residents Association (CRADORA) which began campaigning for improvements to the wretched conditions in the township. As the rebellion burgeoned, CRADORA's influence spread to neighbouring towns, and Goniwe became first a regional and then a national figure. Worried about his fast-growing influence, the government transferred him to another school in a distant town, but a mass meeting of Lingelihle residents demanded that Goniwe refuse the transfer, which he did at the cost of his job. So the young man became a full-time political activist and a major problem for the apartheid regime.

I met Goniwe in November 1984. I had gone to Cradock to report on the remarkable phenomenon of a rural revolution that had effectively paralysed a chain of country towns. I was immediately fascinated by the young man, by his charm, his intelligence and particularly his broad Jimmy Carter smile. When I left to make a brief tour of Lingelihle, I was promptly arrested and taken to the police station for questioning. What was I doing there? What was my interest in Goniwe? What did I know about him? It was a sharp introduction to the hazards of the environment in which he and Fort were operating. We became friends and I telephoned him frequently after that for updates on what was happening in his region.

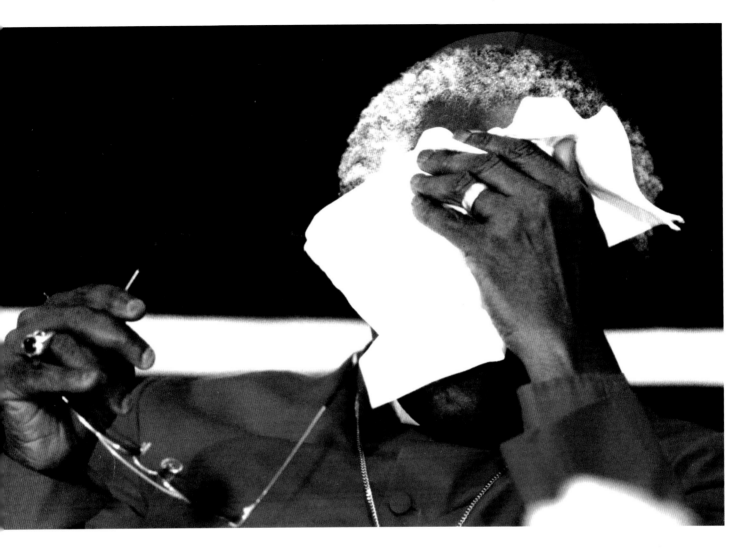

I drove back to Cradock the following May with my wife and young son to introduce them to Goniwe, who I had decided was a young man who was going to play a major role in the unfolding drama of our country. The next day I gave him a lift to Port Elizabeth where he was to attend a regional meeting of the United Democratic Front (UDF). We chatted animatedly as we drove along the lonely country road. As I dropped him off, we bade each other farewell. "Please take care, Matthew," I enjoined him. "I don't like that road. It's too lonely."

A month later he was dead: he, Fort Calata, another Cradora colleague, Sparrow Mkhonto, and a friend, Sicelo Mhlawuli. While Nomonde and Goniwe's wife Nyameka waited anxiously for them to return from another meeting in Port Elizabeth, they were waylaid by a security police death squad at a spot along that lonely road and murdered. Their bodies were found four days later, mutilated and dumped in separate spots fourteen kilometres apart. Mhlawuli had been stabbed more than thirty times, his throat had been slit and his right hand was missing (the killers had cut it off and kept it preserved in a bottle in their security police office to terrify other political prisoners during interrogation). The other victims had also been stabbed, and Mkhonto, the first to be found, had been shot in the head. All the bodies had been burned to prevent identification.

The killings caused a national outcry and the Cradock Four were canonised as instant martyrs. Sixty thousand people attended the funeral in Lingelihle, where Allan Boesak didn't mince his words in his funeral oration. "The people know and I know who murdered them," Boesak declared to thunderous applause. "I say to you it was the death squads of the South African Police."[5] So indeed it turned out to be when the amnesty hearings began.

Eight security officers who formed the hit squad applied for amnesty. Only two succeeded. The amnesty committee refused the others for failing to make full and truthful disclosures. One

JOYCE PILISO-SEROKE

For me, a very important and meaningful time was when I worked for the Truth and Reconciliation Commission [TRC]. I was not a commissioner, but I was a member of the Human Rights Committee of the TRC. We were responsible for arranging the hearings where people could come and share their experiences. They were very sad and traumatic experiences: police brutality and losing loved ones and so on. Desmond, as chairperson, was not just there to listen to these people, he was also emotionally involved.

The first hearings were traumatic because we didn't expect that we would listen to such tragic stories, you know. When you plan things, you are just there. When you are an administrator, it's just technical – you want to have the mikes [microphones] in order and so on. But that first hearing, it made the members of my committee realise what trauma the statement takers, the people who went out to look for these victims, had experienced. They were the ones who did the first interviews. They brought them written out for us. What was stressed to the statement takers was: "You mustn't show these people that you are emotional as well." But when, at some stage during the hearings, Desmond just put his head down and wept quietly, I just felt that it was something that we had wanted to do ourselves but we had been suppressing. I thought he was noble. He was the chairperson and a man of God who should be strong to listen, yet it hit hard at him. He was associating with these people.

After that I said, "Well, who are we to prescribe rules to say when you interview you must not be emotional, you must try to be in rapport with this person. How can you be in rapport with that person if you don't feel what she feels?" What we needed were not just the listening powers and a listening capacity and knowing how to ask the questions, we realised that we also needed to be human. We needed to be emotional but strong enough to say, "I understand what you went through and this is how I feel about the whole thing. I'm one with you."

As we went on with the hearings, we found that the stories of the women were not coming through. The women would come to the commission. They would talk about what happened to their husbands, to their sons and to their children. But we knew that some of them also went through these brutal experiences. That was why we decided that we should have a special women's hearing. Women would be given the chance to really talk about what happened to them rather than to their loved ones. I remember Desmond saying, "Oh, does it mean now we won't want to have male commissioners there?" We said, "No, it would be all the more important that the men also listen to these stories of women being raped in the prisons, women looking at the dehumanisation of their husbands, and women who had lost their children, who didn't even know where those children were."

IF YOUR MOTHER WAS **TORTURED** FATHER **MURDERED** AND CHILDREN **ABDUCTED** WOULD YOU BE **SILENT**

LET'S SPEAK OUT TO EACH OTHER. BY TELLING THE TRUTH. BY TELLING OUR STORIES OF THE PAST, SO THAT WE CAN WALK THE ROAD TO RECONCILIATION TOGETHER.

truth reconciliation commission

TRUTH. THE ROAD TO RECONCILIATION.

I had an opportunity to sit in delegations of the churches. I was present for a conversation with Mr De Klerk and others. In his usual way, when we had gone through all the formalities, Bishop Tutu says, "Tell me, why would you continue with the system of repression? Why would you continue to destroy us and destroy our dignity? Why would you continue to witness so much human suffering? What is it? You and we are also people made in God's image." And he went on, as Desmond would, in his own style. It was half a sermon, half a message. We were all silent, and at the end Mr De Klerk says to Bishop Tutu, "If that is your approach to our discussions I'm going to answer you in an honest way. We are afraid of the revenge from the black community and the black people. We don't know what they will do to avenge all these things that we have done."

Desmond is a real believer, in a genuine way, in the notion of reconciliation. He really believes in it. It's not just a statement because he is a theologian. He really believes that by forgiving other people we are able to live and have peace within ourselves. To live with the hurt of the old, to live with the remembering and the bitterness of the old, will make us unable to have the kind of peace that we all need as human beings. Apartheid had brought too much pain to too many families, to too many individuals, to too many people, and so we need as people to live in a reconciled way, in a reconciled community, not only with Christ but also with other people in our lives.

This is the person who finally led the Truth Commission. I had the privilege of being on a panel chosen by Mr Mandela to select the people who would be the members of the commission. I do wish we could have recorded these things but when we were

doing the interviews of the panellists it was very private. We had a very strict way of managing our information. Every time we completed the process of interviewing a candidate, we would not discuss that candidate. Each of us would simply rate a candidate. We would write the information on a piece of paper. Then we would vote. Afterwards we would destroy our notes. But I can now talk about the session with Desmond.

There were many of us on the panel. We were very diverse. Sometimes candidates would get votes and we were surprised at how they had scored. We never knew who had voted for whom. This time, when we were scoring the points we realised that Bishop Desmond Tutu had the highest rating from all of us. There were some people in our group who were of course more conservative. Historically they wouldn't have approved of a person like him because he was known to be an activist and a radical. Everybody was surprised that all of us had given the same scores, all high scores, 100 per cent – interesting. One of our panellists was a conservative person who had belonged to the apartheid government party. That was all he had known and supported all his life. At the end of our work he said, "People must be surprised at the way that I voted. You can all guess that I also gave my vote to this candidate, Bishop Desmond Tutu. As we were interviewing him, I felt the whole time he was talking to me. I listened, and the more I listened to him when he spoke of forgiveness and he spoke of reconciliation and the challenges of it, I was healed. That is why I couldn't do otherwise. I had to vote for him. I didn't vote for him because he was articulate, I voted because it became for me a personal conversion."

THE TRUTH HURTS BUT SILENCE KILLS

LET'S SPEAK OUT TO EACH OTHER. BY TELLING THE TRUTH. BY TELLING OUR STORIES OF THE PAST, SO THAT WE CAN WALK THE ROAD TO RECONCILIATION TOGETHER.

truth & reconciliation commission

TRUTH. THE ROAD TO RECONCILIATION.

of those who succeeded, Eric Taylor, told the committee he knew he had done wrong and hoped for forgiveness. He spoke of how difficult he found it to face his four-year-old daughter and other members of his family since everyone knew what he had done. But tearfully Nyameka Goniwe said she could not forgive him because she didn't believe he had told the full story. For her part, Nomonde Calata spoke at a conference much later of how her thoughts had turned to the unborn child she was carrying when her husband was killed, and who by now was a teenager. "She keeps asking questions," Nomonde said. "'Who was my father?' It is hard to explain to her. At times she comes and says, 'Can't you draw a picture for me? Can't you say something that he said?' That is very, very hard."[6]

Bit by bit, in town after town around the country, the truth came out about at least some of apartheid's worst atrocities. Television viewers saw a burly security-police torturer, Captain Jeffrey Benzien, squat on the back of a black prisoner, Tony Yengeni, lying face down on the floor, and demonstrate how he had pulled a wet bag over his face to suffocate him to the edge of death. Others described how they had "tubed" political prisoners, pulling a strip of rubber tubing over the prisoner's nose and mouth and sometimes keeping it there too long so that the victim died. When the victims suddenly voided their bladders, one torturer explained, "then you knew they had gone to another place".

Captain Dirk Coetzee, former commander of a death squad based on a farm outside Pretoria called Vlakplaas, explained in ghoulish detail how to burn a human body to destroy evidence of an assassination. The case study he presented to the amnesty committee involved a young activist named Sizwe Kondile. The assassins stopped at a river bank at dusk, sat in a circle on the ground and poured themselves some brandy. Unobtrusively they spiked Kondile's drink with drops provided by a special military chemical warfare unit. "Four drops for not too big a person," Coetzee explained, adding bizarrely that more could be fatal. "We gave Kondile his spiked drink. After twenty minutes he sat down uneasily ... then he fell over backwards. Then Major Nic van Rensburg said, 'Well chaps, let's get on with the job.' Two of the younger constables with the jeep dragged some dense Bushveld wood and tyres and made a fire. A man, tall and with blond hair, took his Makarov pistol with a silencer and shot Kondile on top of his head. His body gave a short jerk.

"The burning of a body on an open fire takes seven hours. Whilst that happened we were drinking and *braaing* [barbecuing] next to the fire. I tell you this not to hurt the family, but to show you the callousness with which we did things in those days. The fleshier parts of the body take longer ... that's why we frequently had to turn the buttocks and thighs of Kondile. By the morning we raked through the ashes to see that no piece of bone or teeth was left. Then we all went our own ways."[7]

It was Almond Nofomela, a thirty-two-year-old *askari* killer of special notoriety, who blew the whistle on Vlakplaas, flushed into the open the single most shocking death-squad base of the apartheid era and brought a string of applicants, starting with Coetzee, hurrying to the amnesty committee. Nofomela's moment of decision came while he was on Death Row in Pretoria for shooting a white farmer in a fit of fury when the man insulted him racially. Here he was, assassinating members of his own race on behalf of the white regime and this man had the effrontery to call him a "Kaffir" (South Africa's most derogatory slang for a black person). Bang! Given his record at Vlakplaas, Nofomela expected the senior security-police officers to protect him. But when one of them visited him on 19 October 1985 to tell him he would have to "take the pain" at dawn the following day for killing a white man, he decided he had better act swiftly to save himself.[8] He telephoned Lawyers for Human Rights in Johannesburg to tell them he wanted to make a statement. With literally hours to go before taking the drop, Nofomela swore an affidavit to lawyer Shanks Mabitsela that blew the lid off the Vlakplaas death squad, naming Dirk Coetzee as the commander. That saved Nofomela's life. He was granted a stay of execution as an important state witness, then indemnity and finally amnesty.

His testimony, followed by Coetzee's, gave a gory account of the death of civil rights lawyer Griffiths Mxenge. Coetzee ordered the assassination on the instruction of security-police Brigadier Jan van den Hoven, while Nofomela led the Vlakplaas team that carried it out.

THE HOLE TRUTH

NP SUBMISSION

NP

TRC

SOWETAN 23-8-96
ZAPIRO

F. W. DE KLERK

During the Truth and Reconciliation Commission [TRC],
we developed serious stresses and strains within our
relationship. I supported his appointment as chairman
and, looking back, I am still glad that he was the chairman of the TRC. However, I think he needed a more
objective panel on the TRC. The commission that he
was given was too one-sided. The legal advisers
around him were, to my mind, too prejudiced. This led
to an overemphasis on the wrongs, the indisputable

Above: Cartoon by
Jonathan Shapiro,
The Sowetan,
23 August 1996.

Right: Cartoon by
Jonathan Shapiro,
Mail & Guardian,
19 September 1996.

Nofomela recounted how his four-man team waylaid Mxenge one rainy night as he crossed a sports stadium on his way home. David Tshikalange was the first to strike, stabbing him in the chest and twisting his *okapi* knife to maximise damage. The knife stuck there behind Mxenge's ribs and Tshikalange couldn't withdraw it. Mxenge himself grasped the handle, jerked the knife out of his chest and fought back, slashing furiously at his attackers. It was an heroic effort but he was hopelessly outnumbered. Nofomela eventually struck Mxenge on the head with the wheel spanner, knocking him to the ground where all four attackers fell upon him in a stabbing frenzy. They inflicted forty-two stab wounds, penetrating his lungs, heart and liver. They slashed his throat open, nearly cut off his ears and, finally, ripped open his stomach and tore out his intestines.

Coetzee meanwhile was cruising around Durban in his car, stopping off periodically to have another drink, while waiting for the rendezvous time to meet up with his team. When they arrived, some wearing Mxenge's clothes and Nofomela his silver watch, they reported the success of their mission, then went to a bar where they told the tale of their struggle with Mxenge while they laughed and downed brandies in a spirit of celebration. Not surprisingly, as members of the Mxenge family listened to the crass callousness of this testimony, told in the emotionless tones of these professional killers, they felt unable to express forgiveness. But ironically it was precisely the comprehensiveness of their confessions that won the killers their amnesty. As the amnesty provisions required, they told the full truth in all its awful detail.

Four years after Mxenge's death, his lawyer wife Victoria was also assassinated, by another death squad. As for Coetzee, he admitted to having been involved in twenty-three serious crimes, including six murders, "in the line of duty" as a member of the South African security police.

Coetzee was succeeded as commander of Vlakplaas by an even more notorious killer, police Colonel Eugene de Kock. Aged forty-four by the time he appeared in court on multiple charges of murder (this was before the formation of the TRC), De Kock had been in the killing business all his adult life, and his unique talent for violence had earned him the nickname "Prime Evil" among his colleagues. His special unit, which was tasked with undertaking covert operations against "enemies of the state", meaning supporters of the African National Congress (ANC), killed scores of people: De Kock told the court he didn't really know how many. Senior police officers around the country would telephone him and give him the names of individuals they wanted "taken out". Some of the killings were wantonly savage. Once De Kock cleaved a victim's head

Left: Tutu holds his
head as he listens to
a testimony during a
Truth and Reconciliation
Commission hearing,
Johannesburg,
3 December 1997.

open with a garden spade. On another occasion, in a fit of rage, he attacked one of his *askaris* with a billiard cue which he smashed over the man's head, then beat and kicked him to death.

The members of De Kock's unit usually disposed of their victims' bodies by wrapping them around a stick of dynamite and blowing them to smithereens. They mailed poisons and booby-trapped bombs hidden in pens, manuscripts, tape recorders, radios and letters to exiles living in Swaziland, Tanzania, Mozambique, Angola and Zambia. They were responsible for blowing up Khotso House, the South African Council of Churches (SACC) headquarters in Johannesburg, as well as bombing the ANC's headquarters in London. De Kock admitted, too, to having been involved in the murder of the Cradock Four. Moreover, they were formally commended for their work. De Kock became one of the most highly decorated officers in the South African Police Force.

But none of his superiors came to his aid when the moment of reckoning arrived. At his trial on eighty-nine charges, including murder and other crimes of violence, the apartheid regime's prize hit man found himself abandoned. He was sentenced to a total of two hundred and twelve years' imprisonment. Boiling with anger, he then applied to the TRC for amnesty and, when his hearing began, he set about pointing accusing fingers at his superiors, from the former commissioner of police, General Johan Coetzee, to presidents P. W. Botha and F. W. de Klerk, whom he accused of selling out the uniformed police who had been required to do their dirty work for them.

"The security forces didn't want to fight," De Kock told the amnesty committee, "but we were urged to do so by the politicians in their quest for patriotism and with their talk of confronting the forces of evil and darkness. I can't believe they had so much influence on us and then, at the first sign of problems, they fled."[9] But he added that the way in which peace had finally been reached was admirable – and mercifully so. Nonetheless, the committee refused to grant De Kock amnesty. He had appeared with eight other former police officers and the amnesty committee found they had given different accounts of the reasons for the killings.

When De Klerk stated publicly in 2007 that he had a "clear conscience" about all that had happened during his term of office, De Kock said in a radio interview from prison that the former president and Nobel laureate's hands were "soaked in blood", that he had ordered political killings and other crimes during the conflict.[10] At the time of this writing, De Kock is still in prison.

> "Week after week, voice after voice, account after account, it is like travelling on a rainy night behind a huge truck – images of devastation breaking in sheets on the windscreen."
>
> Antjie Krog

The cascade of horror at the TRC hearings was traumatising for all involved in the process. Even the hard-nosed reporters covering it had to be given psychological counselling. "We listened to stories of betrayal, of informers, of dirty tricks, of cover-ups, beatings, stabbings, shootings, electric shocks, the burning of bodies," wrote Alex Boraine. "It was like a huge sewer spilling out its filth and stench."[11] And Antjie Krog again: "Week after week, voice after voice, account after account, it is like travelling on a rainy night behind a huge truck – images of devastation breaking in sheets on the windscreen."[12]

Through all this trauma and all the recurring conflicts between different elements of the TRC staff, Desmond Tutu was the central pillar of stability, the compass, as Krog called him, the one who kept them all on course and who found the language to articulate their common objective and keep the public informed. It was an immense strain on him, especially when he had to undergo the radiation therapy, but he meticulously took his two or three hours of quiet time each day to pray and meditate and find new strength.

But Tutu also had his emotionally testing times. None more so than when he had to preside over a human rights hearing into the activities of the Mandela United Football Club, not so much a soccer team as a gang of tough youths based at Winnie Mandela's home and operating under her matriarchal authority as a private vigilante gang to enforce her disciplinary will on the society around her, and especially to inflict harsh punishments on anyone suspected of being a police informer. It was a strange and still unexplained annus horribilis in Mrs Mandela's life, that year before her husband's release, when she seemed to lose control of herself. Neither Mandela in prison nor the ANC president Oliver Tambo in Lusaka could reason with her, while the United Democratic front (UDF) leaders at home publicly distanced themselves from her.

When some Soweto parents testified before the TRC that their children had disappeared after being taken to the Mandela home, she was subpoenaed to attend a hearing behind closed doors. Belligerently she demanded a public hearing to clear her name but, since she didn't ask for amnesty, she was under no compulsion to tell the truth. This was the awkward hearing over which Tutu had to preside as more than two hundred journalists from sixteen countries converged on South Africa to cover what instantly became known as "The Winnie Mandela Hearing".

For Tutu the hearing was doubly difficult, for he was a long-time friend and admirer of the Mandelas, and Winnie particularly, having lived right across the road from their home in Soweto's Vilakazi Street. He had been Winnie's pastor and supporter during her years of grass widow-hood, and had visited her periodically to conduct Holy Communion alone with her when she was banned and restricted to the remote little country town of Brandfort. Now he was cast almost in the role of a judge at her hearing.

The hearing centred on the Mandela United Football Club's kidnapping of four young boys from a Methodist manse where Winnie Mandela claimed they were being sexually abused by the resident white minister. The boys were taken to the Mandela house, where Mrs Mandela claimed one of them, a fourteen-year-old youngster named Stompie Seipei, with a reputation as a wildly daring political activist, was an impimpi, a police informer. The football club, led by a thuggish older individual, Jerry Richardson, beat Seipei to a pulp over days. Richardson later confessed to having murdered Seipei. He took the barely conscious youngster to a remote spot one night, made him lie on his back beside a stream and stabbed him to death with a pair of garden shears. His

Above: Tutu during a Truth and Reconciliation Commission hearing.

"I SPEAK TO YOU AS SOMEONE WHO LOVES YOU VERY DEEPLY, I WANT YOU TO STAND UP AND SAY, 'THERE ARE THINGS THAT WENT WRONG.' THERE ARE PEOPLE OUT THERE WHO WANT TO EMBRACE YOU. I STILL EMBRACE YOU BECAUSE I LOVE YOU. I LOVE YOU VERY DEEPLY. THERE ARE MANY OUT THERE WHO WOULD HAVE WANTED TO DO SO. IF YOU WERE ABLE TO BRING YOURSELF TO BE ABLE TO SAY, 'SOMETHING WENT WRONG,' AND SAY, 'I'M SORRY, I'M SORRY FOR MY PART IN WHAT WENT WRONG'. I BEG YOU ... I BEG YOU ... I BEG YOU PLEASE. YOU ARE A GREAT PERSON. AND YOU DON'T KNOW HOW YOUR GREATNESS WOULD BE ENHANCED IF YOU WERE TO SAY, 'I'M SORRY ... THINGS WENT WRONG. FORGIVE ME.'"

DESMOND TUTU

decomposed body was not discovered until five days later. Richardson was eventually sentenced to life imprisonment for the murder, but the question remained as to whether Winnie had any hand in the murder. Had she ordered Richardson, who was obsessed with her, called her "Mommy" and said he would do anything for her, to kill the boy?

There was no evidence to indicate that and this was not a trial anyway, not even an amnesty hearing. But what Tutu considered essential was to persuade this iconic struggle figure to express her regrets and, in the interests of national reconciliation, to say she was sorry for what had happened. But Winnie, now divorced from the president and going by the surname of Madikizela-Mandela, denied all the allegations against her, brushing them aside as "ludicrous" and "ridiculous".[13] But Tutu persisted, stressing that it was important to demonstrate that the new South Africa was morally different from the old, that its people needed to stand up and be counted for goodness, truth and compassion.

"I speak to you as someone who loves you very deeply," he implored her. "I want you to stand up and say, 'There are things that went wrong'. There are people out there who want to embrace you. I still embrace you because I love you. I love you very deeply. There are many out there who

Above: Winnie Madikizela-Mandela conferring with her lawyers Ismael Semenya (right) and Moses Mavundla during her appearance at a Truth and Reconciliation Commission hearing, Johannesburg, December 1997. Witnesses have accused Madikizela-Mandela of involvement in the murder of Stompie Seipei, a fourteen-year-old activist who died in 1989.

TUTU: THE AUTHORISED PORTRAIT

would have wanted to do so if you were able to bring yourself to be able to say, 'Something went wrong', and say, 'I'm sorry, I'm sorry for my part in what went wrong'. I beg you ... I beg you ... I beg you, please. You are a great person. And you don't know how your greatness would be enhanced if you were to say, 'I'm sorry ... things went wrong. Forgive me'."[14]

There was a breathless silence as the two looked directly at each other. Then, in a soft monotone, speaking as if by rote, Madikizela-Mandela responded: "I am saying it is true. Things went horribly wrong and we were aware that there were factors that led to that. For that, I am deeply sorry."[15]

It was hardly the most spontaneous or heartfelt apology, and many in the audience were outraged. They felt it was a piece of stagecraft, that she hadn't meant what she said. But Tutu had achieved something. He had at least persuaded, cajoled this proud and wilful person to bend her knee publicly to the national process of truth-telling and accountability. She had not even asked for amnesty to begin with, she had demanded the hearing to vindicate herself in public, but for the first time in her life she had admitted before the whole nation that things for which she was responsible had gone horribly wrong.

So what did it amount to, this long and searing national inquisition? Did it achieve its key objectives of establishing the truth of what had happened and of achieving national reconciliation? Certainly it achieved the former. Even though only a small proportion of those involved in atrocities appeared before the TRC, and the political leaders responsible for the whole wicked system evaded accountability, the facts that were publicly admitted – of systematic torturing, of state-sponsored death squads, official lies and cover-ups and the systematic corruption of the justice system – were sufficient to remove any question of doubt or denial. It means that future generations of South Africans can be taught a national history that is based on fact and not on some mythologised or sanitised version of the past.

Whether the TRC was equally successful in bringing about national reconciliation is harder to answer. There were certainly some individual cases of forgiveness and reconciliation that were remarkable and uplifting, but whether there was the same kind of cathartic relief at group or national level is open to question.

Tutu himself, in his foreword to the five thick volumes of the TRC report, which he handed to President Mandela on 29 October 1998, admitted that the work had limitations but urged that it be seen as the beginning, not the end, of a process of national reconciliation. He spoke of ubuntu, saying that members of the South African family, composed of Afrikaner, English, "coloured", Indian and black, were all valued equally and it was now up to them all "to close the chapter on our past and to strive together for this beautiful and blessed land as the rainbow people of God".[16]

Towards the end of the commission's hearings a Dutch Reformed Church minister, the Reverend Ockie Raubenheimer, invited Tutu to preach in his suburban Pretoria church. It was a significant invitation, not only because of the Afrikaner church's long role in supporting apartheid but also because Raubenheimer had been a chaplain in the South African Defence Force. The two men had thus been at opposite ends of the theological civil war; now they were to appear together before a congregation of Afrikaner notables.

The service began cautiously, with Raubenheimer speaking of the Afrikaners' role in the past, saying there was much to be proud of but there had also been some mistakes. But after Tutu's sermon, in which the archbishop referred to the "evil deeds" of the past and the need for a leader to step forward and help the people come to terms with what had been done, Raubenheimer unexpectedly stepped forward. "I am not scheduled to speak now, and actually I am not sure what I am going to say," he began. Then, turning to Tutu, he said, "As a minister in the Dutch Reformed Church for twenty years, as a chaplain in the defence force, I want to say to you we are sorry. For what we have done wrong, we ask the Lord for forgiveness."[17] He ended in a whisper, choked by tears. Tutu got up, put his arm around the distraught minister and for a moment the two men stood there hugging each other as the congregation rose to its feet and applauded.

Opposite: A tearful Tutu at the Truth and Reconciliation Commission's last church service, Pretoria, 21 March 2003.

CHAPTER TEN

THE VOICE OF THE VOICELESS

As the work of the Truth and Reconciliation Commission (TRC) drew to a close, it looked as though Tutu's role as a public activist might at last be over. He had retired as archbishop of Cape Town in 1996 to head the TRC. The commission's hearings had been emotionally and physically draining. Tutu was seventy-five years of age and had undergone harsh treatment for prostate cancer. Surely real retirement was beckoning.

But by now Tutu's reputation had spread. Invitations from churches and human rights groups around the world had begun arriving while he was still the archbishop of Cape Town, and Tutu, who loves travelling, tried to squeeze them in to his heavy schedule. One of these was an invitation to address the All Africa Conference of Churches (AACC) in Lomé, Togo, in 1987 – at which he was promptly elected president of this continent-wide council of Protestant churches. Following the massive global media focus on him during the TRC hearings, these invitations swelled from a trickle to a flood, and so began what John Allen, his long-time aide-de-camp, has called Tutu's "international ministry", during which he travelled to Ethiopia, Egypt, Sudan, Rwanda, Israel/Palestine and the United States, preaching and lecturing on themes to do with democracy, human rights and tolerance, and how conflicted societies should strive to resolve their differences through dialogue and accommodation between enemies.[1]

These themes were not always as welcome when people heard them expressed in their own countries as they were when they read about the bold prelate preaching them in South Africa. Typical was when Tutu explained to his audience at that AACC conference in Togo what it meant to be a witness for Christ in Africa. "It pains us," he told them, "to have to admit that there is less freedom and personal liberty in most of independent Africa than there was during the much-maligned colonial days. The gospel of Jesus Christ cannot allow us to keep silent in the face of this … We must be committed to the total liberation of God's children, politically, socially, economically … This is most obviously so for your sisters and brothers in South Africa, but it would be true too for many in independent Africa for whom all that seems to have changed is the complexion of the oppressor."[2]

"Sometimes strident, often tender, never afraid and seldom without humour, Desmond Tutu's voice will always be the voice of the voiceless."

Nelson Mandela

Right: The Elders, Johannesburg, 29 May 2010. From left, back row: former Brazilian president, Fernando H. Cardoso; former US president, Jimmy Carter; former president of Ireland, Mary Robinson; former United Nations secretary-general, Kofi Annan; former prime minister of Norway, Gro Brundtland; former president of Finland, Martti Ahtisaari; United Nations ambassador, Lakhdar Brahimi. From left, front row: Graça Machel; Tutu; Nelson Mandela; and human rights activist, Ela Bhatt.

TUTU: THE AUTHORISED PORTRAIT

So the prospect of retirement melted away. Tutu had been looking forward to some quiet time for contemplation and meditation after the strenuous years of the TRC hearings, but there was to be no rest for the virtuous. As the archbishop likes to express such things, God had once again grabbed him by the scruff of the neck and thrust him into a whole new role in which he became not the moral conscience just of South Africa but of the world. It was a role that was to take another great leap forward nine years after the TRC had submitted its report when, on 18 July 2007, Nelson Mandela's eighty-ninth birthday, the now-retired founding president of the new democratic South Africa announced the formation of a new group of twelve elder statesmen and women, peace activists and human rights campaigners to focus on global trouble spots and "use their political independence to help resolve some of the world's most intractable conflicts". The group included Nobel Peace Prize winners, two former presidents – Jimmy Carter of the United States and Mary Robinson of Ireland – and the former secretary-general of the United Nations, Kofi Annan. Archbishop Emeritus Desmond Tutu was named chairman of the group, to be known as The Elders.

It meant an expansion of his international role that was to engage Tutu in a range of peace initiatives around the globe, from Africa to the Far East, from Northern Ireland to Palestine, from Burma to Tibet, and from Darfur to the Solomon Islands – and ultimately back to his own homeland, the new South Africa. He made waves wherever he went but, as during his years in the apartheid struggle, never let the criticisms or insults daunt him. As Mandela said of him: "Sometimes strident, often tender, never afraid and seldom without humour, Desmond Tutu's voice will always be the voice of the voiceless."[3] And Mandela knew of what he spoke. He had been in power only a few months when he himself felt the sting of Tutu's criticism for allowing the new South African parliamentarians to vote themselves pay increases while the masses of poor people were still struggling. Tutu later accused the African National Congress (ANC) government of "stopping the gravy train just long enough to get on board themselves".[4]

Moreover, Tutu had already dipped his toes into the overheated waters of the Israel-Palestinian conflict even before President F. W. de Klerk had made his watershed speech and while Mandela was still in prison. During a Christmas visit to the Holy Land in 1989, he had lashed out at Israel for practising what he considered to be policies equivalent to apartheid towards the

Bishop Tutu's voice during the fight against apartheid was very important for the movement and for those of us who were engaged and wished to see the end of apartheid. A voice like his – a moral voice that was not afraid to speak up and also inspired others to stand up and fight for their freedom – was extremely important to many of us. And, of course, having been a colonial subject myself, I followed the developments in the country with interest. We did what we could from the UN to support the struggle, including the boycott, and Desmond Tutu was a good rallying point for many of those who fought against apartheid.

I first met him at an event in New York. He was making a statement. He did it in his natural, forth-right, frank manner. That was refreshing, because in some of these international meetings one tends to be diplomatic, cautious, to shave one's words. But when you are dealing with certain issues and moral questions are involved, it is always good to have some-one speaking plainly, clearly and directly to those who have gathered. And that was his style. It is very effective.

There were moments of tension in the world. There were moments of serious conflict. People were lining up on one side or the other and, sometimes, talking past each other. Sometimes Desmond would say something that perhaps others thought. But they couldn't verbalise it the way he could because of situation they were in. And I used to say as secretary-general sometimes people like Desmond and some Non Government Organisations [NGOs] are often ahead of us. They say things we share but, because of the constraints and the positions we occupy, we could not say. So they often lead and eventually we catch up with them. On the question of Iraq, for example, he was quite forthright.

What is a refreshing thing with him is that he doesn't have to be nudged on moral issues. He seems instinctively drawn to them. He is not drawn to them as intellectual curiosity but he wants to see something done about them, either directly, with him doing some-thing about them, or by saying things that empower and encourage others to act. We tend to underestimate the important role of the third party or the bystander. For that individual to say, "This is enough. We can't take it anymore. We cannot accept this." I think often Desmond says things that engender that sort of courage in others who may not have been inclined to act. He mobilises them. That is a very important gift.

We are both members of The Elders. The arch-bishop is a very good chair. He has the capacity to bring everyone together, to encourage each one to make a contribution and to create space for each to talk. And he does it in a way that doesn't lead to contentious or confrontational arguments. He encourages us to speak from our own experience and share our own judgements. He creates an environment where one hardly hears anyone talk out of anger. That exchange, that give and take, is very important. It's not always the case when you bring many strong people together. But he manages to get the group to work effectively and harmoniously and he does it in his way.

For example, when we had the first Elders meeting the public meeting in South Africa, the question of Aung San Suu Kyi's membership arose. How would we handle her membership given the fact that she wasn't there? Would we leave an empty chair to symbolise her presence or her membership or not. You should remember that we also had a member who was there at the time in South Africa who was from China. This was completely new to him. There had been no warning that this question would come. Some of us raised the question if this was the right way or the right approach to it. Desmond managed it well and had his way. We had the chair. And there was no blow-up or violent reaction from our Chinese member.

He explained the fact that she is a member and unfortunately she is placed in a situation because of the politics of the government, that she couldn't be with us. We should symbolise her membership and also send a message to the government that whether she's here or not, she is a member. She's one of us and we support her and we wish they had allowed her to come. When he put it in those terms it was very difficult for others to argue with him. We could not say, "We don't agree. You're talking rubbish. We stick to our posi-tion." His approach was to reason simply and sincerely with the group. After the issue had been settled, during the public deliberations, he was so moved that he even cried.

I think as members of The Elders we have worked very closely together and we have gotten to know each other. There are times when I'm not entirely happy with what is being suggested but he always has a way of not pushing things to a confrontational level. It is remarkable for somebody who had to fight the apartheid regime. I think he learned something from

Above: Tutu with Kofi Annan at the United Nations World Assembly in Vienna, 27 June 1998.

that. Issues can be resolved and you don't have to push it to the level of confrontation to get a yes. And he often has a way of diffusing an issue and then discussing it one on one to try and come to an understanding. The other thing I like about him is he's very encouraging and supportive of the team that works for The Elders. He makes sure he thanks them for their efforts and for what they have done, which we sometimes forget as leaders. We tend to complain when things go wrong but forget to say "thank you" and "well done". He's very good on that, and that's a lesson many people have to learn.

He is very good when others take the lead and he has to follow. You know I often say that a good leader is also a good follower: a good leader has to learn that he cannot always have it his way and he also has to follow

sometimes to hold everything and everybody together. And this is something Desmond understands almost instinctively. He never hesitates to follow if he believes the direction is right. I don't see any ego problems in that situation.

I do think, though, that sometimes he should allow a bit of tension and confrontation to go on, just to clear the air. He is tolerant. He's really a father of us all, and fathers sometimes become indulgent. He is a wonderful man. We all love him dearly.

One thing I have learned from him, or that I take from him, is that he has that constant and persistent faith that things can be better and we can do something about it. We should not find excuses not to act or not to speak out. I think that's important.

JIMMY CARTER

I was president during the days when apartheid was approaching its termination in South Africa. We studied very assiduously what the United States might do to bring enough punishment to the white oppressors that they would someday reconsider their efforts. And, of course, everyone who was involved in that effort began to observe the clarity of expression and the incisiveness of the thoughts and words of Archbishop Tutu. From a religious point of view, that was important to me. My daughter was arrested four times for demonstrating against apartheid and so I had a personal interest as well as a presidential point of view.

I didn't know him well until I saw in the news media his work with the Truth and Reconciliation Commission. He was a fountain of humour, which was extraordinary in those circumstances. His questions were incisive and I think he exhibited, in that respect, the teachings of Christ in a very practical way.

But I didn't really get to know Archbishop Tutu until we had a meeting in the Caribbean with Sir Richard Branson. Branson invited about thirty-five of us to come down for an extended weekend to talk about the possible future of the so-called Elders. Among the three groups, I happened to be in the same group with Archbishop Tutu. So that's where I first got to know Tutu. Branson was exploring the possibility of The Elders. I, and many others, thought it was a sound and practical idea. And I very quickly found that in that diverse group Archbishop Tutu and I basically saw eye to eye and many others didn't agree with some of the things that we put forward. So that's when I first got to know him. Of course, later, when Nelson Mandela and Graça Machel and Archbishop Tutu put together some of the final ideas, working with Richard Branson, and The Elders became an actuality, I was honoured to be invited to join them. Since then I've known him as our chairman. He's been the only chairman we've ever had. In that process he's become a personal friend of mine.

He's an unorthodox chairman. I'm an engineer and when I try to do something I do it on time and with a minimum of digression. I have had some difficulty in accommodating his different style. He looks upon humourous digression or, sometimes, just things that seem to be unrelated to the main subject, as an important part of his leadership. And so I've learned over the last three years or so to appreciate what he does, even though it's quite different from the way I have always done things when I preside. I've also seen a very great commitment to ensuring that nobody forgets he's chair. If there ever is anybody who speaks out

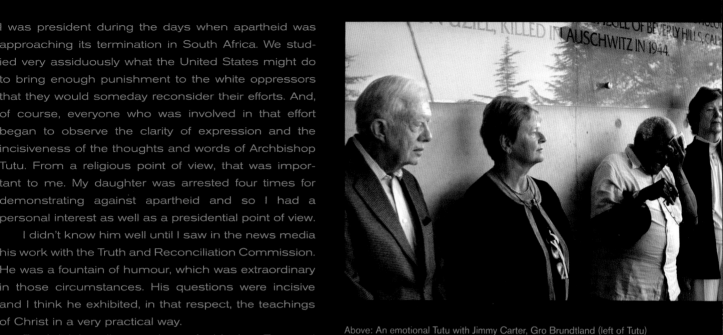

Above: An emotional Tutu with Jimmy Carter, Gro Brundtland (left of Tutu) and Mary Robinson, Jerusalem, 25 August 2009.

without getting recognition and so forth, he chastises them in a very firm and, almost always, human and non-embarrassing way. So I really enjoy him. He adds an element of livelihood and humour to the sometimes dilatory results of his intercessions.

I don't think there is likely to be any more diverse group of ten people that I've ever known than there are among the members of The Elders: we each come from our own geographical area of the world, we had different responsibilities in our earlier lives, we have different priorities in our own existences, we have ancillary duties that we assume when we're not in The Elders meeting. And he's been able to relate equitably and fairly to all of these diverse members. I'm not sure that I could do that as well, so I'm filled with appreciation for him. I think he's taught me a lot about how to deal with other people. He has insisted, whenever possible, to bring in young people, like when we are in the Middle East and when we are in Cyprus. I think he has a particularly vivacious reaction to a crowd of younger people. Whether they are high school age or even elementary school age or even college age, they react to him with a great deal of affection and humour. It sometimes makes me a little jealous, but I've acknowledged his superiority in that respect.

By definition, all The Elders have to be out of politics. We may have been in politics earlier, as was Nelson Mandela, as was his wife, and President Cardoso and Gro Brundtland; all of us have been in politics before, I believe, except him. And this gives him, I think, an advantage over the rest of us in that he has been a man of faith who has had to transcend politics since he was a young person. This is a new experience for most of us. Having been secretary-general of the United Nations, having been president of a great country, having been prime minister of Norway, a head of WHO, president of Ireland, that sort of thing, it's a new element of retirement years for us to adopt a non-political status. It comes naturally to him, because that's where he's been all his life. So that's one thing that I've noticed, and I think the rest of us have learned from him in that respect: how to put aside the political characteristics which are almost inherently part of us in nature. Almost all of us who served in public office have been representatives of a particular political party. He's been able to avoid that. He has not been aligned with a particular group of people. He is aligned with those who suffer instead of those who persecute. And he is aligned with those who are poor rather than those who are rich and powerful. But here's a statesmanship based not on how people vote but on their status in life and their reaction to other people.

There's no way to separate what he has done in his life from politics, and there is no way to separate what we're doing in The Elders, under his leadership, from politics. You can't go into Gaza and see the destruction that the Israelis' bombs and missiles have done to the Gaza people, while seeing the oppression of Palestinians who live under the iron fist of Israeli oppression, without it being involved in politics. The same thing was true when we went to Darfur together. Obviously there was a political element, a political cause of the oppression of the Darfurians by the central government. The route to the alleviation of their suffering also has to go through political circles, from the United Nations to the individual powers that are influential there: Norway, United Kingdom, United States. So you can't separate politics from faith. It's been his life's work to emphasise the religious aspect or the moral aspect without having the political partisanship being a constraint on him that might deter him from doing what's right and honest, and just, fair and peaceful; whereas there are times when anybody who runs for office has to equivocate to some degree to accommodate the special interests of partisan partners.

I remember one vivid occasion when we went to a little village called Bil'in. It was a place where all the cropland and almost all of the surrounding territory had been taken away from the Palestinian farmers and orchid growers by the Israeli occupying force. The Israelis had built a fence adjacent to the village so that the people living there couldn't even get to their former land to graze their sheep or goats, plant their crops or harvest their olives. This place is special, because they hold a peaceful demonstration every week. Not only Palestinians go there, Israelis go there to condemn their own government's policies. People from foreign countries also go to participate. We visited the grave of a young man. He was demonstrating peacefully when he was hit in the chest with a tear gas canister and killed. Tutu was on one side of the grave and I was on the other. Just to stand there on this hilly mountainside, this rocky hillside, across from him on the grave, and to hear him speaking; and then I just had a few words to say which made me feel more of a brother with him, perhaps, than anything else I've ever done in his presence. His obvious grief and anger, as a deeply religious person, reaffirmed my confidence that my grief and anger were not out of place. They were justified.

I don't use the word "epitome" very often. I think he is the epitome of practical application of the Christian faith. In my opinion, Archbishop Tutu always tries to exemplify the teachings of Christ, as he adopts projects on which to speak out, sometimes to his own detriment, or when he takes action that might require several days of his time, like to go to the Middle East with us. It's exhilarating and inspirational to watch how he accommodates these varying pressures. How do you best use a single, individual life and give it a human voice to bring more attention to a human rights deprivation or deviation from Christian morality? He is able to do that in a very effective way. With his wide knowledge of the world and his extensive travel and his early and later studies and his responsibilities in the church, he can see when to condemn his own president. He has done this with Mbeki and also Zuma. He has condemned, as other African leaders don't do, the sustained abuses of Mugabe in Zimbabwe. And he's equally willing, maybe eager, to condemn the policies of the United States when it relates to improper imprisonment of people and the deprivation of basic human rights. He's been able to speak forcefully on behalf of gay people, even in Africa where it's anathema. His willingness to take a chance when he knows he is right, even though he knows it might cause him some grief or criticism from people that he really cares about, shows a special dose of human courage.

was appointed in 1993 to write the UN [United Nations] report on the impact of armed conflict on children. The Arch was one of the eminent persons I asked to give us guidance on how we should approach this. We wanted to know how to understand and then how to make recommendations to this global body on how they should treat children in situations of conflict. Our first meeting was in the US at one of the properties of the Rockefeller family. I remember the guidance he offered us:

"Never base yourself in what you read. You need to meet the real people; you need to listen to them. You need to keep in mind that every conflict has its own historical and cultural background; it doesn't happen in a vacuum. So, although you'll find some similarities, it is always specifics that you have to take into account, so that any recommendations to come of this study will be relevant."

So that's why we structured the study in that way. We visited countries but we also had regional conferences. We brought into one room practitioners, young people themselves and, sometimes, parents, and civil society and government leaders. So we really needed to hear from different perspectives what were the issues we should take into account to prepare the report.

What I understand is important in this is that people like Arch, they take every single human being as a whole. And they also understand that although we are all equal, if you want to be relevant in whatever you do, you have to listen to everyone. Don't talk on behalf of people without listening to them. That was a big lesson for us. It was really a big one.

That was why, in our report, we made sure that we brought not just the faces but the voices of children themselves. We reflected how they felt and what they were expecting from government and also from the global community. And that was what I think made our study make an impact within the UN system.

He was extremely generous with his time in terms of giving us advice, particularly the insights into how we should approach the people – we were dealing with children in situations of suffering. Some of them were refugees. Some of them had been involved in conflict; they had been made perpetrators. It was a very complex situation. He was always keen that we should come to what is essential if you are to talk of children in situations of conflict. I think that for me was the moment when I connected the myth – I grew up knowing him as a myth – with the real person.

As he was advising me on the report, the Arch started to talk to Madiba [Nelson Mandela] and me about the need for us to get married. We were living together and I had made it public that I didn't want to get married. He said that was unacceptable and we were setting a very bad example for young people. While we worked he would concentrate on giving me the guidance I needed on the report I was doing. But at the end he would say, "When?" He didn't need to say much. He would just say, "When?" and I knew what he was talking about. The fact is that I wasn't ready yet. I understood what he meant but I wasn't ready yet. Honestly, I was the one who delayed the decision to get married, and that's why he was the one to bless us. When we finally made the decision it was in this room, precisely this room, that he blessed us. So he has a very special place in our lives as a personal spiritual leader. It's not just what he has been doing for the country and for the world but, even personally, he has been playing a role.

Sometimes when I get a bit overwhelmed with my responsibilities ... with what is expected of me, especially in relation to caring for Madiba ... I know that Madiba's not just anybody – he is a treasure for the country and for the world. Sometimes I feel like I'm too small to know how to do the right thing. At these times, I will approach the Arch and he will give me the guidance I need to make me feel that everything is fine. So he has a very special – a very, very special – place in my life.

Above: Tutu whispers in Graça Machel's ear after telling Mandela he should marry her forthwith, Cape Town, September 1997. Below: Tutu embraces Mayra Avellar Neves, winner of the International Children's Peace Prize 2008, during a ceremony in the Ridderzaal in The Hague, 4 December 2008.

The first time I met him was in early 2008. The Elders had been created in the summer of 2007. Arch was the chairman. The Elders were looking for a CEO. They had decided, after a long process, that they were going to offer the job to me. He had been asked by the collective to convince me to accept their job offer. I met him in Heathrow Airport, I think at about eight in the morning. He had just arrived from I don't know where, and I had to catch a flight forty minutes later to the Netherlands. When he walked in I thought we were going to have some kind of job interview. I had heard a lot about The Elders, but, before I could accept the job, I needed to meet at least some of them. I wanted to hear their story and their commitment to it. He caught me completely by surprise. I guess he catches so many people by surprise when they meet him for the first time. First of all, I was struck by his incredible humanity. You know he is a man of the heart but, when you meet him for the first time in reality, he immediately embraces you in a way, and kind of makes you feel at ease.

He doesn't start any meeting without a moment of silence. I am now well aware of that but, when we were sitting in the business lounge in this airport, it caught me a little bit by surprise.

I was struck by his determination; he was a man with a mission. He had decided that, yes, he was happy to hear a bit about me and he was happy to tell me a bit of what he thought about The Elders. But he was going straight to the goal and he said, "Look, I am going to twist your arm until you say, 'Yes, I accept this job'." When I had to walk to my plane I hadn't said yes yet. He figured, "OK, I am not going to let her loose." So rather than going our separate ways in the business-class lounge, he walked me to my plane. So, here we go, walking through all Heathrow Airport: the blonde girl with this amazing Father and then Mthunzi [Gxashe] walking behind us giggling. And Arch starts asking me: "Do I need to twist your arm a little harder? Should I twist it a little harder?" I think he was a little disappointed that by the time he left me at my gate, I hadn't said yes. But as you see, I did finally say yes. It took me a tiny bit longer than those forty minutes.

But what was so amazing, and that is what I have seen him do so many times since then, is that he can disarm people immediately. When The Elders travel to places, they always try to not just meet politicians but they try to also engage with ordinary people – ordinary people whose lives they are trying to help improve, whose stories they want to listen to, whose voices they want to help amplify and whose concerns they want to bring to the attention of decision makers. I have seen him so often when we meet victims of crimes, or when we meet very courageous human rights activists, when we meet women trying to come together around the peace agenda and when we meet young people. Obviously, for people to meet some of The Elders, who are heroes, who are such eminent individuals – former presidents, former prime ministers, former secretaries general, the most famous archbishop in the whole world – it can be a little daunting. So, often, if I arrive a little before The Elders themselves arrive, or when my colleagues do so, we notice that there is a bit of nervousness in the room. "Wow, we are going to meet these very eminent people; how are we going to talk with them?" As soon as Arch walks in he manages to help to basically defuse all that nervousness and tension immediately, whether it is through giving high fives to young people or by embracing people in the room or by cracking a joke.

The way he does it differs. He has these amazing antennae to read people very quickly. He has this ability to then turn that into very effective communication with whoever. It's at all levels. I have seen it with political leaders, I have seen him do it with the poorest of the poor, I've seen him do it with the journalists, I've seen him do it with The Elders. That's an amazing gift. And it's funny, because he is a very joyful person. Somebody described him as a "joyful warrior for peace". But I think what is not always clear is the fact that there is an incredible knowledge about people. He is obviously super intelligent and very experienced. It's amazing that he uses all those qualities for the betterment of all of us.

On a personal level, working with him is interesting. He is somebody who, when he engages, he truly engages. He doesn't say, "Oh, I will be the chair", and then let's go. He really wants to know what's going on. He is definitely not a micromanager or anything, but he feels a great sense of responsibility. I must say, the only kind of little run-in I had with him was when at one point I said, "Oh, let's not bother him with a certain level of details", and I didn't share some information with him. I learned my lesson. I will never do that again. He is so responsive. You think, "Oh, he is such a busy man and he has so many things on his plate", but if you send him a clear message, tell him, "Look, Arch, that's what's going on", he will get back to you within twenty-four hours, if not sooner, which is an incredibly pleasant way to work with him.

He is also very pleasant to work with in that, although he is demanding, he is also very appreciative

He recognises good-quality work. He will reward you with kind messages back. It's very nice when he acknowledges that good work has been done by the team. And he loves to crack a good joke. I mean, things we work on are sometimes so saddening, and it's very nice that he can sometimes help to put things in perspective.

He was the first chair for The Elders and I find it hard to imagine a better first chair. Here you have ten very eminent individuals whom we brought together to become a star team. It's like you bring the ten best soccer players in the world together and they have to become a star team. That's what The Elders are all about. Their willingness to work together doesn't always translate easily. Some knew each other and worked well together; others have barely worked together or had much contact. I think that he has done an amazing job in bringing them together and helping them to discover their collective power. He does it in very subtle ways: by encouraging people, by acknowledging them individually. He always starts our meetings, our physical meetings – we meet twice a year – by recognising what the different members of the group have done. He is very good at recognising that, even though people can have achieved everything from a professional-career perspective – because they are still humans and they still need recognition, and in the same way that he enjoys it when his fellow Elders or we and our team recognise his achievements. We take it for granted that great people do great things, but you know what? It must be as much of an effort for them as it is for us ordinary human beings.

He is also very good in holding this bunch of individual sheep together (well, they are not sheep; they are much more determined), and he does that with a combination of wit, intelligence and trying to find the shared vision. Sometimes he does it by telling them off. It's hard to imagine, but he is the only one who can say to one or two Elders who come late to a meeting, "Oh, man, should we buy you a watch or what?" I mean, who is going to say that to Kofi Annan or to Ibrahimi? Or who is going to say to a former president of the United States, "Wait, now it's her turn; she is going to go first"? I mean, it's amazing that he not only has the qualities but that he makes them available to all of us.

MARY ROBINSON

I have enjoyed many meetings and events with Arch over a long number of years, including serving with him on the eminent group of AWEPA: the Association of European Parliamentarians with Africa. I recall one enjoyable event in Ireland. Arch came in 1992 to fulfill several events while I was president. We were both given honorary degrees to mark the 400th anniversary of Trinity [College] in Ireland. He had just come from the west of Ireland. He had taken a part in a march to mark the 145th anniversary of the Choctaw people contributing to alleviate Irish potato famine. I have teased him about it since, because when I met him he said, "I will never, never go there again! It was so cold!" And since I come from the west of Ireland, I was not at all pleased. We knew each other well at that stage.

I was very taken with his sense of humour, because humour appeals to the Irish. The first time I met him in South Africa was at the inauguration of Nelson Mandela. The dinner the night before Mandela's inauguration was in the city hall in Pretoria, and there were big crowds. I had my own escort as the Irish president, but somehow we arrived at the town hall a little bit late. As we were being brought up towards the main table of heads of state, I spotted Leah and the Arch at a different table. I immediately waved and they invited me over, so I sat down with them. I vividly recall the conversation we had. I asked the Arch, "What is this like for you? What are you thinking?"

"Well, the first thing I am thinking is that I have never been in this town hall before."

"I can't believe that. You are the archbishop of Cape Town. You are a Nobel Prize winner."

"Well, I've never been here before!"

And then my Irish sense of humour got the better of me. I said, "What are you complaining about? You only voted for the first time a couple of weeks ago!"

He burst out laughing. Then he said, "No, seriously, Mary, I don't think you understand what it is like to have such change come so quickly." And he spoke very eloquently about the very tough struggle.

I also remember the inauguration. Somehow I have a special memory because of the joy and pleasure and honour of sitting beside both Arch and Leah the previous night and seeing through their eyes what an extraordinary situation this now was.

The Elders is the context within which I've worked with Arch the most. He has a tendency to send a lot of emails. I always worry if I don't get an email; I wonder if the ship he is sailing on has sunk or something. He's not the greatest chair, but he is the right chair for The Elders. He gets distracted. He goes off on tangents. He also tends to see certain hands and not others. He's now aware of that and tries to correct it. He has his favourites, so much so that Gro Brundtland pointed this out rather bluntly. He took the point! He is absolutely the right chair of The Elders, and I'm delighted that he has agreed to be the chair until 2013. We'll renegotiate then. He is ideal from every point of view: from the external profile of The Elders to the fact that The Elders begin with a moment of silent prayer or, for those who may not pray in that sense, a silent thought. I think that's important for The Elders. We're not a political think tank; we are Elders. He brings a huge spiritual dimension that I think we all value very highly.

Arch has been keen that The Elders really implement our mandate from Madiba [Nelson Mandela] as well as possible. He used the phrase that we were "punching below our weight" for quite some time. He, as chair, has been chiding us that we – he used a lovely phrase – that we have to "learn to elder". We have to do better, particularly as a team. I think we really do have a huge collective commitment as well as a responsibility to elder. Each time we meet Madiba, which we are very privileged to do, we are renewed in our commitment.

We had lunch together with Madiba when we were in South Africa right before the World Cup. I had the privilege to be seated beside Madiba, and he turned to me, more than once actually, during the lunch and said about Arch, "That is a great man, but I am the oldest here!" Madiba does have terrific respect for Arch. "When I die he will see that I get to heaven. He will say good things about me." They have a great relationship with each other. You can see that.

I also heard a lovely phrase from Leah when we were in Morocco at a meeting of The Elders in a beautiful place that Richard Branson has. We were on the veranda where we would have breakfast looking out on the valley and mountain and beyond, and Arch can be quite arbitrary at times. He's sitting there enjoying his breakfast and suddenly he jumps up and starts being extremely bossy. He wanted us to go to the table to start the meeting. So he jumped up from the table where Leah and myself and my husband Nick were sitting. The terrace carried on around the corner

Above: Tutu receives an honorary degree from Queen's University Belfast, Northern Ireland, 3 July 2007.

....

and we could see Richard Branson and various other people, including Peter Gabriel, out in the sun. And so he went around the corner and was shouting at them, "Come on now, come on. This isn't good enough. Come on." Leah turned to the rest of the table, "You would know that man started life as a cattle herder, wouldn't you?" I don't know if there was some truth in that or she was just having fun at his expense. I am incredibly fond of her as well, as you can tell. She has been the rock of his life. I know what that means, because I am lucky enough to have my own rock. It does make all the difference in what you can do.

Because of The Elders, I have seen Arch more in Leah's company. I realised the strength of the relationship between Arch and Leah, and how extraordinarily complementary they are to each other. I think she does for him what Nick does for me: she's a true friend, the one who tells you what you don't want to hear but need to hear.

I've learned a huge amount from him. I don't know whether I am able to say that I've implemented what I've learned. I've learned that if you really want to reach people you must put them at their ease, and a great way of doing that is humour – humour and warmth and laughter. When people are at their ease, then he comes in with the serious message. I've seen him do it time and again. He starts off by being funny and dressing in a funny hat and doing all these funny expressions just to relax them, and then suddenly the message is a profoundly serious one and people are receptive to it because they've enjoyed him and they've opened up to him and then, bang, in goes the message.

Palestinians. "As a black South African," he said, "if I were to change the names, a description of what is happening in Gaza and the West Bank could describe events in South Africa."[5]

In a speech at Israel's Holocaust Museum during that trip, Tutu delivered a message of forgiveness: "Our Lord would say that in the end the positive thing that can come is the spirit of forgiving, not forgetting, but the spirit of saying – 'God this happened to us. We pray for those who made it happen, help us to forgive them and help us so that we in our turn will not make others suffer.'"[6] Some Israelis found this offensive, with one prominent rabbi calling it "a gratuitous insult to Jews and victims of Nazism everywhere".[7]

Tutu repeated the apartheid comparison in a speech in the United States two years later, when he spoke of seeing "the humiliation of the Palestinians at checkpoints and roadblocks, suffering like us when young white police officers prevented us from moving about". He went on to ask: "Have our Jewish sisters and brothers forgotten their humiliation? Have they forgotten the collective punishment, the home demolitions, in their own history so soon? Have they turned their backs on their profound and noble religious traditions?"[8]

The Elders' first official mission was for Tutu to lead them to Sudan in September 2007 to try to foster peace in the troubled eastern region of Darfur, where four years of fighting between Sudanese government forces – backed by the notorious Janjaweed militia – and a coalition of several non-Arab Muslim groups, called the Justice and Equality Movement (JEM), had already caused more than three hundred thousand deaths and rendered 2.5 million people homeless. The Elders group – which was represented by ex-President Carter, Sir Richard Branson, the colourful British businessman who helped fund the new group and Mandela's wife, Graça Machel – arrived days after Janjaweed fighters had overrun an African peacekeepers' base, killing ten. The Elders flew first to Khartoum for talks with the Sudanese government, then toured Darfur itself where they learned that women and young girls were systematically raped and tortured and that cholera was rampant in the refugee camps. The group ended their tour with a call for sanctions against the Sudanese government. President Omar al-Bashir was subsequently indicted by the International Criminal Court on ten counts of genocide, war crimes and crimes against humanity but, at the time of this writing, has still not been arrested.

Whether The Elders' intervention had a beneficial effect on al-Bashir is hard to tell, but he has moderated since then, first agreeing to a ceasefire with rebels in south Sudan, then to a referendum in which that region voted overwhelmingly for independence from Khartoum, and subsequently to a ceasefire agreement with the JEM – signed in Doha, Qatar, in February 2010 – that observers hope may lead to a similar outcome in Darfur.

Rwanda had presented an equally ghastly African crisis that had grabbed Tutu's attention a few years earlier. The Elders group had not yet been formed, and Tutu was not able to get to Rwanda himself when the carnage began in 1994 – at the moment of South Africa's first democratic election and President Mandela's inauguration in which the archbishop had an important role to perform. The Rwanda genocide was triggered when a jet carrying President Juvénal Habyarimana was hit by a missile that killed all on board. This reignited ancient hostilities between the country's Hutu majority and the elitist Tutsis who had dominated the country's monarchy for centuries until a Hutu coup in 1990. Four years of civil war followed, that ended with an agreement to share power under Habyarimana. Enraged by what they saw as a Tutsi-inspired assassination, the Hutus embarked on a savage campaign of genocidal violence, butchering an estimated eight hundred thousand Tutsis (20 per cent of the population) in a hundred days.

Tutu flew to Kigali, the capital, a year after the genocide, where he broke down and wept uncontrollably at the sight of bodies, inside a church, still wrapped in the rags of clothing they were wearing when killed. Outside, on a makeshift wooden platform, was a huge mound of human skulls. Tutu was equally shattered when he visited Kigali prison, so crowded with prisoners – *genocidaires* accused of the slaughter – that they had to sleep in relays; there was insufficient space for all to lie down at once. Tutu raised his objections to this inhuman situation with members of the Rwandan government. Despite his distress, the archbishop delivered an address in the packed Kigali stadium in which he spoke of the importance of forgiveness if Rwandans were to rebuild their society.

A year later, the presidents of neighbouring Zaire (later the Democratic Republic of Congo) and Uganda asked ex-President Carter to facilitate a meeting of all heads of state in the Great Lakes region of Central Africa to negotiate a regional initiative to combat the climate of genocide and help repatriate 1.7 million Rwandan refugees who had fled to their countries. Carter invited Tutu to join him in this initiative and, after two summit meetings in Egypt and Tunisia, they thrashed out a programme that helped start a slow recovery in the shattered little country.

From there to Northern Ireland. In the autumn of 2005, the British Broadcasting Company (BBC), fascinated by Tutu's role in heading South Africa's TRC, invited him to participate in the making of a three-part television series in which he would bring together perpetrators of violence and their victims in that troubled division of Great Britain. Although the process was unofficial, it was real enough in that it brought about face-to-face confrontations between members on both sides of Northern Ireland's long sectarian conflict. The series, called "Facing the Truth", was given an extra touch of reality by the presence of a victim of the Rwandan violence, Lesley Bilinda, as one of Tutu's fellow panellists. Bilinda's husband, an Anglican clergyman, was murdered in the genocide. She returned to Rwanda and met with those who were linked with her husband's death.

"We had some extraordinary moments in the week or so that we were here," Tutu said in an interview after the filming, "where it was like something divine had intervened. It was exhausting but eminently exhilarating."[9]

The producer of the show, Fergal Keane, a senior BBC correspondent who had been based in South Africa where he had come to know Tutu, said of his star performer: "The Arch ... is a better man than you can imagine. This was never more apparent than when he was dealing with the grief-stricken. His warmth flowed out and over them in a way that made this jaded correspondent feel truly humbled."[10]

Next on Tutu's list of reconciliation missions was the Solomon Islands, an archipelago of nearly a thousand South Pacific islands that had been wracked by five years of ethnic and political tensions that had finally been brought to an end in 2003 by the intervention of an Australian-New Zealand peacekeeping force. Now the time had come to stabilise the situation and an appeal went out to Tutu to help the island state establish a South African-style TRC. Tutu flew to the capital, Honiara, on 29 April 2009 to launch the commission. He also was guest speaker at a conference called "Reconciliation – The Way Forward", which brought together former combatants for reconciliation talks.

One of Tutu's longest and most passionate campaigns has been on behalf of the leader of Burma's democracy movement, the petite but immensely resilient Aung San Suu Kyi, a fellow Nobel laureate who had won a free and fair election but whom the Burmese military then imprisoned and kept under house arrest for fifteen years as they seized power. Tutu first met Aung San Suu Kyi's family in Oslo in 1991 when she was awarded the Nobel Peace Prize in absentia, an occasion which coincided with the ninetieth anniversary of the award, attended by all living recipients. Aung San Suu Kyi's ailing husband, Oxford orientalist Dr Michael Aris, and their children Alexander and Kim were there, but Aung San Suu Kyi herself decided not to leave Burma for fear the military regime would not allow her back.

Tutu greatly admired Aung San Suu Kyi's courage and self-sacrifice in being prepared to separate herself from her family to fight for the liberation of her people. She was driven by a sense of passionate dedication, as the daughter of the founder of modern-day Burma, Aung San, who was assassinated a year after winning independence from Britain for his country, and after whom she was named. Tutu's admiration was deepened and infused with anger when the junta refused to grant Michael Aris a visa to visit his wife one last time when he was dying of cancer, and when she in turn refused to leave Burma to see him because she believed the junta would not allow her back. Aris died in England on his fifty-third birthday, 27 March 1999. Tutu hung Aung San Suu Kyi's picture on his office wall as a token of his admiration and wrote powerful articles in the international media, berating the Western powers for not putting more pressure on the Burmese

dictators while being prepared to go to war in Iraq in pursuit of a more dubious cause.

Even those who had opposed the Iraq war, as Tutu himself had vigorously done, came in for criticism. "They should have shown an equivalent determination to support those at the front line of peace," Tutu wrote. "The coalition of the willing and of the unwilling ultimately have to show each other that something can be done on Burma."[11]

Tutu joined a group of Nobel Peace laureates on a mission to Thailand in the hope of gaining entry to Burma to engage with the military regime, but they were refused visas. The delegation held meetings with some of Aung San Suu Kyi's supporters in Bangkok instead. Tutu again called on the international community to take tougher action. "The United Nations treats the situation in Burma as if it is just a dispute between two sides and they must find a middle ground," he complained. "The reality is that a brutal, criminal and illegal dictatorship is trying, and failing, to crush those who want freedom and justice. The international community cannot be neutral in the face of evil. That evil must be called what it is, and confronted."[12] Four months later, Aung San Suu Kyi was released from detention.

But Tutu's sharpest criticisms have continued to be aimed at Israel and the new South Africa. The two countries closest to his heart: the Holy Land and the homeland. He expected both to behave better than they have, because of their own experiences as victims of racist criminality.

Above: Tutu cries after hearing Peter Gabriel sing "Biko" at a ceremony to launch The Elders, Johannesburg, 18 July 2007.

have to confess that when I heard on the radio that he was going to retire after his birthday, I absolutely protested. I said, "No, he's not to be allowed to retire!"

I can't remember when I first heard of him, because I heard of him way, way back. But I can say that he became personal for me only after I was placed under house arrest from 1989 to 1995. Then, through the BBC, I could hear how loud and clear he was speaking for my release.

Prior to that, I had an impression of him as a political heavyweight. He was someone important who was doing serious and effective work for the anti-apartheid movement. I listened to him very carefully. It was not so much that the circumstances were similar – I don't think I thought of that as much as what lessons I could learn from what he had to say. I learned from him that you have to persevere. Just because there are obstacles, it doesn't mean you can't get over them. We learn that times change, circumstances change and you have to learn to work with circumstances in the best way possible.

Although I have never met him, I feel I know him well because I read his books. After I read his books I discovered that I had found another side of Archbishop Desmond Tutu. He was not just an anti-apartheid worker. He was not just an advocate for human rights. He was somebody who had thought very deeply about spiritual values and had applied them to what he was doing. In some ways that reminded me of Gandhi, because Gandhi always thought spirituality and action have to go together. I was touched by the way in which the Arch linked his faith and his intellect to the removal of apartheid. I think this is one of the reasons he succeeded so well, because his faith (his spirit) and intellect (his mind) were at one when he was working to achieve what he thought was the right thing. I felt that when he was reading the Bible he always had one part of his mind on the question of ending apartheid, and vice versa: when he was involved in fighting apartheid, one part of his mind was with the Bible.

I asked him to write the foreword for my book. I think it was probably my husband's idea. My husband was very, very fond of the Arch – very fond of him. All of us really appreciated what he did for us. My husband always mentioned the fact that the Arch and Václav Havel were two of the most caring people, with regard to what we were trying to do. Michael always spoke very affectionately of him. Actually, he always referred to him as "Desmond". I don't know why. It was rather familiar, I thought, with my conservative Burmese upbringing. I think they met but I'm not sure. My husband always spoke as though he had. A gift of the Arch's – my husband sounded very close to him.

It was that sense of closeness and his political courage that made me ask him to write the foreword. I also liked that he had tremendous fondness and respect for his wife. He talks about her in his book and I liked the way he talked of her.

After he started speaking out for me, I discovered that he was a very warm, a very bubbly person. Recently I spoke with him for the first time. We giggled a lot. I think when I spoke to him I hadn't quite got used to cell-phones as I have now. There was something not quite right, not quite adequate about such small implements. I think he is sort of a giggle-maker, if you like.

What I remember most from our conversation was the overall feeling of warmth and the feeling that he cared. There was a feeling that, although we have never met, we had never spoken to each other, we were not strangers to each other. He expressed his happiness and he talked of a better Burma. He's already demonstrated his commitment to Burma's democracy so the words mattered less to me than the feeling that we were close to each other. I think that probably is a feeling that he gives to other people. I think it's a gift he has.

I've heard that he calls me his pin-up. That's very nice of him. I have just sent him a really nice picture. I believe that the prisoners in the concentration camps who were working on the Burma-Thai Railway, the infamous railway of death, had pin-ups. Their pin-ups were recipes and pictures of cream cakes and so on. There are different sorts of pin-ups. The image that came into my mind is of prisoners of war pinning pin-ups to the walls of their barracks. Now it's the other way round.

People have been asking me who my hero is and I have always said that it's Desmond Tutu. I hope that all of you would be able to come to Burma soon. I would love to come to South Africa, just to see the Arch.

Instead, he felt they were behaving too much like their former persecutors: like an abused child
growing up to become an abusive adult.

When, in November 2006, the United Nations appointed Tutu to lead an investigation into
the Israeli Defence Forces' (IDF) bombardment of a row of houses in the Beit Hanoun sector of
Gaza – in which they killed nineteen Palestinians (thirteen of them being from one family) and
wounded forty – Israel refused Tutu and his co-investigator, British professor Christine Chinkin,
access to the strip. It claimed the IDF had already apologised for a "technical malfunction" of
equipment.[13] A persistent Tutu was turned back three times, but two years later managed to enter
Gaza from Egypt, and with Chinkin undertook the investigation. "In the absence of a well-founded
explanation from the Israeli military, which is in sole possession of the facts," their report stated,
"the mission must conclude that the shelling of Beit Hanoun constituted a war crime."[14]

As Tutu continued to criticise Israel at a conference on racism in Durban and in speeches
at several American universities, a prominent US lawyer, Alan Dershowitz, denounced him as a
"racist and a bigot", while the Zionist Organization of America launched a campaign to protest
his appearances on US campuses.[15] Tutu received strong public support from prominent liberal
Jews at home and in the US, but he riled conservative Jewish groups again when he called on a
Cape Town opera group to cancel plans to perform in Tel Aviv as a protest against Israel's treatment of Palestinians. Some local Jews called for Tutu to be dismissed as patron of Holocaust
museums in Cape Town and Johannesburg, but the governing bodies of those institutions declined.
In the event, the opera group also declined Tutu's boycott appeal, but the archbishop was more
successful when he joined an appeal to the University of Johannesburg (UJ) to cut formal links
with Ben-Gurion University because it had links with the Israeli military. UJ did so on 1 April 2011.

Tutu's criticisms of the new South Africa likewise tended to sharpen over time. He was bluntly
critical of Mandela's successor, President Thabo Mbeki, for allowing denialists to influence him

into neglecting the devastating spread of the AIDS pandemic in South Africa, and for not speaking out more forcefully against the brutal rule of Robert Mugabe in neighbouring Zimbabwe.

Opposite:
Washington DC, 2006.

But it was the rise to power of President Jacob Zuma – after that polygamous leader had faced a charge of raping the young daughter of a deceased comrade (for which he was acquitted after claiming the sex was consensual) and managed to get off the hook for a corruption charge involving kickbacks on a huge, controversial arms deal that had sent his financial manager to jail – that really got under Tutu's skin. "Sometimes, many times, I have wanted to be circumspect, even to be silent," he said in his valedictory address as chancellor of the University of the Western Cape on 10 March 2011. "But it has not been possible. Most of my utterances – no, all of my utterances – are inspired, driven by my love for God and a passionate love for my country and for my compatriots." And so he was compelled to speak out.

"I am fond of President Zuma. He is affable and warm," Tutu went on, before adding pointedly, "but I do believe it would have been better for him to have been pronounced innocent by a court of law rather than through a dubious administrative act and, if indeed there is nothing to hide, the government surely has nothing to fear from a judicial commission of inquiry into the arms deal. It is an unnecessary albatross to carry the huge doubts. Our country, with such tremendous potential, is going to be dragged backwards and downwards by corruption which in some instances is quite blatant."

He slammed the Zuma administration: for neglecting the poor, the unemployed and the homeless while its own members engaged in extravagant expenditure and enriched themselves through cronyism and corruption; for sidelining capable people who had not been directly involved in the liberation struggle "because the first qualification is not calibre or ability but party affiliation"; for threatening to restrict media freedom; and for exploiting the country's party electoral list system to avoid accountability to the people. "But people are not fools," Tutu warned, "they notice things, and one day they will explode."

Harsh criticism from someone who had done so much to bring the new South Africa into existence. But Archbishop Tutu had come to be regarded as the conscience of South Africa. And indeed now of the world.

RICHARD BRANSON

I've been fortunate to have been with the Arch many different places: here on Necker Island when we were working on developing the idea of The Elders; I've been on trips with him to Sudan, to Darfur, to Israel, to Palestine, and I doubt I've met anybody in the world who has such a great sense of humour. It's a wicked sense of humour. When I meet him he makes me grovel, because I'm a white man. I have to lie prostrate on the floor, quite often, and clean his shoes. His jokes are often self-deprecating. He was saying the other day that he's often accused of name-dropping. Someone actually said to him, "Arch, why do you name-drop all the time?" and the Arch responded, "It's funny that you should say that. Only last week I was at Buckingham Palace with the Queen, and she asked me exactly the same question." He's just got such a wonderful, wonderful sense of humour. But he must also be, perhaps, the most caring person I've met in the world.

He can get very emotional. If he talks about Aung San Suu Kyi from Burma, he will sometimes burst into tears: the idea that someone who was elected democratically in an election to run a country is then overthrown by the army and then confined to her home for years and years and years. He literally will weep openly in situations that he feels are just too sad to bear. He'll quietly walk out of the room and then come back a little later. He feels passionately about other people's trials and tribulations that go on in the world. As a result, he works harder than anyone I know though he is a fairly old man, a man who is also suffering from prostate cancer. He'll fly all the way [from South Africa] to an American prison for no obvious reason except for compassion. He will talk to inmates and try to make their lot in prison a little bit better to bear.

He's never missed an Elders meeting. He chairs the meetings with diligence and with humour and makes those meetings enjoyable. He's gone on more Elders' trips than anybody else, and that's after he's done a thousand other trips in between. The idea of The Elders grew from two people: myself and Peter Gabriel, both coming at it from different directions. Peter felt that the world was a global village and the world needed a group of elders that the world could look up to, and that we could use the Internet to communicate from these wise elders to the rest of the world. I felt that in order to resolve conflicts in the world we needed a group of elders. In an African village, people look up to their elders and the world community should look

Above: Tutu and Richard Branson share a joke during a ceremony marking Nelson Mandela's eighty-ninth birthday, Johannesburg, 18 July 2007.

up to their elders, and that if we could get the twelve most respected people in the world together they could go into conflict situations and, hopefully, resolve them. And initially we spoke with Nelson Mandela and his wife, Graça Machel, and asked if they would consider being the founding Elders, which they agreed to be. They then decided to choose the other ten Elders, and their very first choice was Archbishop Tutu. They wanted him, effectively, to chair The Elders, to run The Elders, because Nelson Mandela is that much older than the Arch and that much weaker. And that is the role that the Arch has played, and he's been absolutely magnificent at it. Already, in the two years since they were set up, they've achieved some wonderful things. Perhaps the most notable was when Kenya was falling apart and the civil war was breaking out and the Arch, Kofi Annan and Graça Machel intervened and they knocked the heads of the two warring factions together and managed to get a coalition government formed, and Kenya is now at peace again. They played a very good role in Zimbabwe in trying to get a coalition government formed. So far that's going OK: a little bit more fragile than Kenya. And they are working very hard on the Sudan, Cyprus and Israel/Palestine and other conflict situations. The Arch is very good at making everybody feel at ease, making everybody smile, even in the most serious situations.

He's absolutely wonderful with people. When I'm asked to decide who the person in the world who I most respect is, I have difficulty choosing between him and Nelson Mandela. I think that of the two I would choose the archbishop. He's done more than anyone else in the world to educate people like Nelson Mandela and others into the need for truth and reconciliation and embracing your enemies and making them your friends.

One of the fun experiences that Peter Gabriel and I had was to teach the Arch to swim. He's quite a large man, so he's liable to roll, but he was determined to swim. He forgot to tell me he could walk on water – that would have been a lot easier. And from him I hope I've learned to have a little bit more compassion. He's taught me to make sure I have no enemies in life. Anyone that I've once fallen out with I hope I've rung up and had lunch with or dinner with and befriended. Nobody should go through life having anybody that they've fallen out with. He's also taught me to have a good sense of humour even in the most difficult moments of life.

CHAPTER ELEVEN

A QUICKSILVER SPIRIT

He is a man of many parts: a kaleidoscope man. Ask any South African of any colour what it was that turned Archbishop Emeritus Desmond Mpilo Tutu from public enemy number one into a figure beloved by all, and the answer will likely be his sense of humour. For this deeply religious man, who spends four hours every day on his knees praying and periodically a whole week in silent contemplation, this man of intense moral passion and commitment, is also a gregarious and light-hearted wit. He is a man of fun and laughter.

In fact, his laugh is his most distinctive feature. It is somewhere between a giggle and a cackle that starts in the higher registers of his extraordinary voice and moves through an entire octave, down through his whole body, to end as a deep-throated chuckle in his boots. It is also a weapon – both defensive and offensive. For it can disarm but it can also thrust with the sharpness of a rapier. Tutu likes to say that African people don't laugh with their teeth like white folks, but with their whole bodies. It is a total commitment. An analogy, if you like, of the man himself. For Desmond Tutu, or "the Arch" as he likes to be called, has never done anything by half.

His appearance adds to the image of impish humour. He is short, standing only 1.6 metres (five-feet-four-inches) tall, and his big nose, jutting chin and large eyes behind thick-lensed spectacles combine to prompt cartoonists to depict him as a Punch puppet. But Joseph Lelyveld, the *New York Times* correspondent reporting from South Africa in the

sixties and again in the eighties, who was the first foreign journalist to recognise Tutu as the voice of black leadership inside South Africa, used a different simile in a six-thousand-word profile in his paper's magazine when he wrote that the cleric looked "just a bit like a black leprechaun".[1]

Lelyveld, whose article did much to boost Tutu's image in the United States ahead of the Reagan veto override, was fascinated by his multifaceted personality, his humour and his anguish, his playfulness and his piety, and, above all, his voice – that voice of leadership, which was such a potent instrument of communication. "Sometimes it is sonorous," Lelyveld wrote, when, for instance, he chants *"Bokang Morena"* (praise the Lord) during the Eucharist he is conducting in the Sotho language in the humble [Soweto] church where he has been quietly serving as a parish priest … Sometimes the voice comes across in high-pitched yelps of delight and giggles, as when he dances, literally dances, down the aisle in the middle of the service to evoke the spirit of fellowship by pumping every hand in sight or, later, when he greets the parish's children. Sometimes when it lingers in the lower registers in the course of a reflection or a joke, it penetrates the mind with an edge that is almost metallic. In any given sentence, it can do all of these things, responding to a quicksilver spirit that can be sombre and joyful at once."[2]

The humour and the prayerfulness go together in a single mix: the kaleidoscope factor. The essence of Tutu is that he is still really the street urchin from Sophiatown: the kid who grew up speaking six languages and the earthy Tsotsitaal,

Previous pages: Left:
Tutu reacts prior to
giving a speech at
the Eberhard-Karls
University in Germany,
15 June 2009.

Right: "The Arch",
23 May 1993.

the street slang of the Johannesburg townships; the kid who spent part of his youth earning a few cents as a caddy (a failed one, he says) at a white golf club and even trying his hand at gambling on the trains running between Soweto and the city; and the kid who then grew up to become a high church theologian and a profound intellectual, while never losing that early, earthy way of communicating with blunt words, quick wit and a rich mixture of colloquialisms drawn from all those languages. It made him a great communicator, an intimate one, rather than an orator in the Dr Martin Luther King Jr mould, with a visceral ability to connect with his own people while, at the same time, being a deep thinker and a man of equally deep compassion. It was a mix South Africa desperately needed at the time. As Nelson Mandela once said of Tutu in a birthday tribute: "Desmond Tutu has often spoken about the God in which he believes as a being with a great sense of humour. What he himself brought to our national life is that uplifting touch of lightness and humour amid the most serious messages and teachings."[3] It is a factor that can pop out at the most sacred moments too, as when Tutu stepped into the pulpit of St Mary's Cathedral in Johannesburg after being consecrated as the bishop of Lesotho and opened his solemn, traditional address of acceptance to the prestigious congregation with the words: "In our hotel this morning, Leah said, 'I've woken up in bed with a bishop'."[4]

"Desmond Tutu has often spoken about the God in which he believes as a being with a great sense of humour. What he himself brought to our national life is that uplifting touch of lightness and humour amid the most serious messages and teachings."

Nelson Mandela

The humour is often self-deprecating, which helps put his audiences at ease. He used to enjoy telling a joke, during the darkest days of apartheid, about the Afrikaans media's ingrained bias against him, which has himself, President Botha and Zulu chief Mangosuthu Buthelezi sailing in a small boat off the Cape coast discussing the future of South Africa. The boat springs a leak and is about to sink, at which point Botha takes off his coat, dives into the water and begins swimming for the shore. Buthelezi does likewise. But Tutu stands up, calmly steps off the boat and walks across the water. The next morning's banner headline in the official National Party newspaper, *Die Burger*, is: "Tutu Kan Nie Swem Nie" (Tutu Can't Swim). He can make disarming fun of racial sensitivities too, as when he laughingly offers white audiences an appropriate black response to the perennial question: "Would you want your daughter to marry a Kaffir?" Their answer, he says, is: "Show us your daughter first."

Sometimes it is hilarious. Millions of people around the world saw Tutu's ebullience at its extravagant best when he took the podium to address the crowds which packed the giant stadiums during the 2010 soccer World Cup in South Africa. There he was, wrapped in warm woollies against the southern winter cold, with a silly little yellow-and-green-striped bonnet (the South African national team's colours), looking a little like a clown as he bounced up and down like a jack-in-the-box and waved his arms with enthusiasm. But what Tutu was exulting about at the World Cup was not so much what was happening on the field of play but the great mixed-race

Above: Tutu meets his latex alter ego, as well as that of former president Nelson Mandela, on "ZA News", a satirical news show created by cartoonist Jonathan Shapiro and Thierry Cassuto, 16 July 2010. Below: Children from Milnerton Primary School, Cape Town, visit Tutu in his Milnerton office on his seventy-ninth birthday, 7 October 2010.

Above: Tutu dances off the stage after speaking at a pro-Tibet rally in San Francisco, 8 April 2008. Below: Tutu dances as he addresses a crowd at the Homeless World Cup, Cape Town, 29 September 2006. Right: Tutu returns to his home town of Munsieville, 24 May 1997.

"The thing about the Arch is when he walks into a room it's as if a hundred champagne bottles have been opened and the corks are let loose and the bubbles are flowing."

Deborah Santana

Above: Tutu joins South Africa's "first lady" of satire, Evita Bezuidenhout (played by Pieter-Dirk Uys), on stage for a performance of *Elections and Erections*, 2006.

ALLISTER SPARKS

I had my own experience of Tutu's blend of humour and prayerfulness when I accompanied him on a day visit to South Africa's leading satirist, Pieter-Dirk Uys, in the small town of Darling where Uys lives, some seventy kilometres north of Cape Town. Tutu and Uys became firm friends when Uys, who specialises in impersonations, included Tutu in his one-man show for the first time in the 1980s. Tutu was delighted with the show, and went backstage in Cape Town's Baxter Theatre to meet the comedian afterwards. "It was still illegal for him to be there," Uys told me. "Blacks and whites were not allowed to sit together in a place of entertainment. But we broke the law with relish, and doing Tutu for Tutu was a defining moment in my life. Now he is my friend, and I know he will get me into heaven, because, after all, it's not what you know but who you know, and I know him."

On the occasion of our journey, Tutu was on his way to Darling to open a new preschool, community hall and swimming pool complex in a deprived quarter of the town. Uys had made him a patron of the trust he had founded to raise funds for the project. It was a celebratory occasion and I asked to accompany Tutu on the drive to Darling hoping I could have some informal time to interview him further. But it was not to be. As we slipped into the back seat of his modest chauffeur-driven Toyota Corolla, Tutu spotted my notebook. "Oh, I'm sorry," he murmured, "but I'm afraid I can't talk to you while we're driving, because that's my prayer time." As we took off, he sank into a deep, contemplative silence, occasionally flipping open a leather-bound Bible on his lap to check some reference, then back into prayer mode. When we reached Darling, he bounded out of the car with renewed energy, and spent the day hugging children, listening to a choir of four-year-olds, making a warm impromptu speech, chatting animatedly with everyone and engaging in hilarious banter over lunch with Pieter-Dirk Uys. On the drive back to Cape Town, it was prayer time again.

THE STORY IS TOLD OF HOW A BLACK MAN TOOK GOD
TO TASK FOR CREATING HIM BLACK. HE REALLY WAS
INCENSED AND EXCLAIMED, 'WHAT SORT OF FAILURE
DO YOU THINK THIS IS – SWARTHY AND TOTALLY
UNATTRACTIVE? AND JUST LOOK AT MY HAIR – WHAT IS
THIS CROP OF CRINKLY PEPPERCORNS? AND JUST LOOK
AT MY NOSE – YOU HARDLY TOOK ANY TROUBLE OVER
IT, YOU JUST PLONKED IT IN THE MIDDLE OF MY FACE
DON'T LIKE WHAT YOU HAVE DONE.' WHEN HE HAD
FINISHED HIS TIRADE, A BOOMING VOICE RESPONDED
MY SON, I PLACED YOU IN MY OWN BEAUTIFUL GARDEN
OF EDEN, AFRICA. CAN YOU IMAGINE WHAT WOULD
HAVE HAPPENED TO YOU IF YOU HAD HAD A LIGHTER
COMPLEXION IN THE BEAUTIFUL HOT AFRICAN SUN
AND HOW WOULD YOU HAVE SMELLED THE BEAUTIFUL
SCENTS OF MY GLORIOUS GARDENS IF YOU HAD HAD AN
APOLOGY FOR A NOSE? AND IF YOU HAD HAD FLOWING
LOCKS, HOW WOULD YOU HAVE RUN LIKE A GAZELLE IN
MY THICK AFRICAN FORESTS? YOUR HAIR WOULD HAVE
BEEN CAUGHT IN THE TREE BRANCHES.' THE BLACK MAN
SAID, 'GOD, PLEASE MAY I SAY SOMETHING?' AND GOD
SAID, 'YES.' THE BLACK MAN SAID, 'I'M IN PHILADELPHIA'"

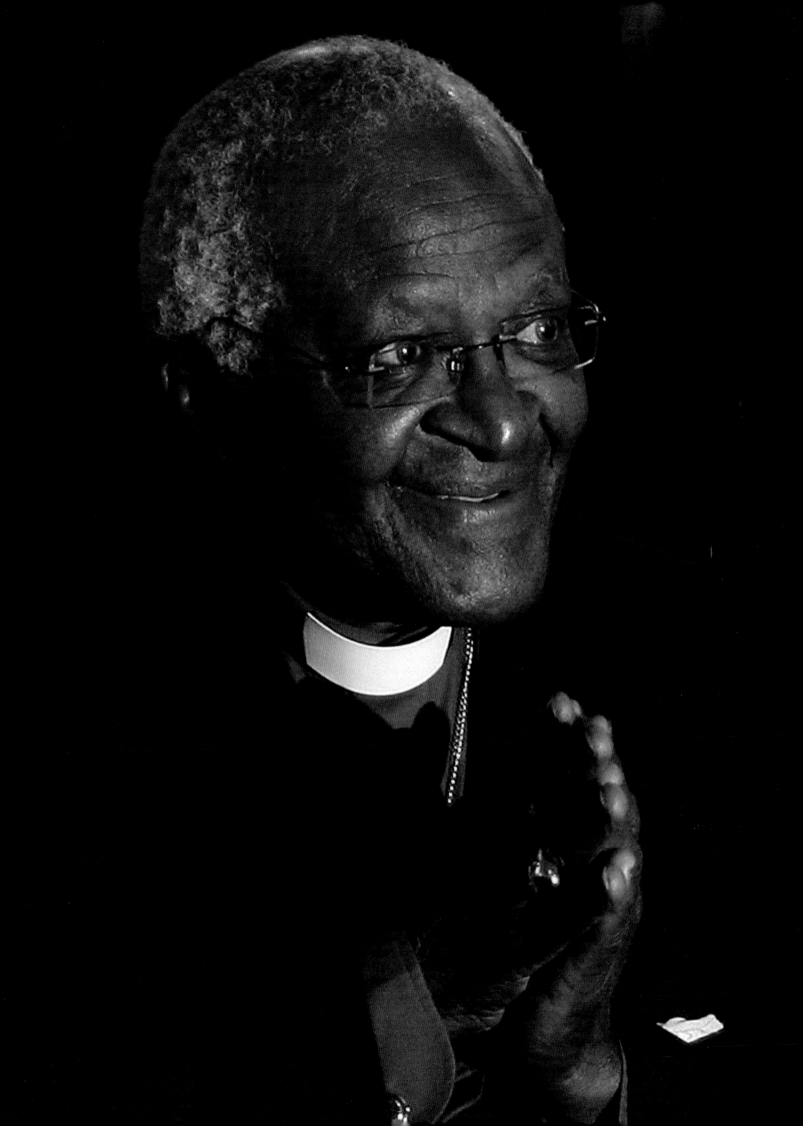

crowds packed together in the grandstands. Here was the manifestation of his long-held dream that South Africa would one day become a "rainbow nation of God".

"I'm dreaming. It's so beautiful – wake me up," he said, making sweeping gestures with his arms at all the black, white and brown faces in the stands. "We want to say to the world, 'Thank you for helping this ugly, ugly worm, or caterpillar, which we were, to become a beautiful, beautiful butterfly'. "[5] he cried. It is that kind of uninhibited spontaneity that has transformed Desmond Tutu from a figure of hatred into one of national affection. He is a consummate performer. As John Allen, who served as his press secretary for thirteen years, says: "I really had the easiest job in the world. I never had to put any spin on anything he did or said. All I had to do was arrange for the press to be there to meet him. He did the rest."[6]

Sometimes the humour has an underside of anguish. Tutu is an emotional man. He can cry as easily as he can laugh, and he has often done so publicly and unashamedly when he has been confronted by the cruelties of apartheid or of poverty.

Although the fun and the piety, the anguish and the tears, all go together in Tutu's life, it is the prayerfulness that is the dominant factor. It is an irreducible part of Tutu's daily routine that has to be maintained whatever the circumstances and wherever he is. Bishop Peter Storey, former president of the Methodist Church, who worked closely with Tutu, recalls that the first time he met Tutu was when the two attended a meeting of the World Council of Churches in Nairobi, Kenya. The Kenyan government had barred South Africans from entering the country because of apartheid, so Tutu had to vouch for Storey as an unofficial guest, which resulted in the two having to share a hotel room. "I woke up about four o'clock in the morning, because I had been sleeping on the floor," Storey recalls, "and I saw this ghostly white apparition in the corner. Then I realised it was Desmond with a bed sheet drawn over himself. He was kneeling, almost in a prostrate position, praying, and he had drawn the sheet over his head to give himself some privacy. I think it was a prophetic encounter, for throughout our relationship it was his spirituality which was the dominant driving force in his life and which impacted most profoundly on me."[7]

Apart from the hours of prayer every day and the week-long retreats, Tutu insisted on opening any meeting he had with a prayer. Another close colleague, Alex Boraine, who was his deputy when Tutu chaired the Truth and Reconciliation Commission (TRC), recalls how Tutu interrupted President Mandela when the three met for an early morning business breakfast. The president was very animated about an issue that had arisen at a commission hearing the previous day and immediately began questioning them about it. "Mr President," Tutu cut in sharply, "we must first pray."[8] Mandela looked startled for a moment, then acceded, bowed his head and the three of them prayed. Boraine also recounts how Tutu celebrated the Eucharist almost every day, even when they were travelling the world on commission business. "Whether we were in a hotel room or on an aeroplane made no difference. The bread and wine would appear, sometimes startling the air crew and passengers who were looking on."[9]

What happens during these deeply contemplative moments of prayer, and especially during the week-long solitary retreats that he undergoes at least once a year? Friends note that he often seems to emerge from them energised, his mind sharper and more decisive. That is when he tends to come up with his inspirational ideas about what action to take. Does he feel he is divinely inspired? Does he actually feel he is in communication with God? Lavinia Crawford-Browne, who was his personal assistant for twenty-two years, once found the temerity to ask him – what was it like? What actually happened? She says there was a long silence before Tutu answered slowly, "It's like sitting before a warm fire on a winter's night."[10]

Many eminent figures have spoken glowingly of Tutu's spontaneous, instinctive humanitarianism. It stems, I believe, from the depth of his Africanness, his commitment to the African cultural ideal of ubuntu. The full phrase is *umntu ngumntu ngabanye abantu*, meaning "a person is a person through other persons". It is the expression of the ideal of communalism in African social life, that each bears a responsibility for the other and that you are not a whole person if you do not bear that responsibility, regardless of who that person is or what that person has done. In Tutu's case it has blended with the Christian concept that you are your brother's

Left: Tutu after receiving the 2005 Gandhi Peace Prize from Indian president Dr A. P. J. Abdul Kalam at a ceremony at the presidential palace in New Delhi, 31 January 2007. Tutu was awarded the prize in recognition of his invaluable contribution towards social and political transformation and forging equality in South Africa through dialogue and tolerance.

I think my first encounter with the Arch was in college. This was in 1986. The state of emergency in South Africa was pretty acute. He gave a sermon in Duke University's chapel. It was one of the most profound things I had heard. It was blending political discourse with spiritual discourse. He was unashamedly a Christian, but he showed how being a Christian doesn't mean you're irrelevant or somehow detached from the problems of the world.

Once I got into the PhD programme at Duke, I was trying to decide what my dissertation was going to be on. One day I was meeting with one of my professors – her name is Susan Keefe and she taught mystical theology – and I said to her, "You know, I was thinking what I really would like to write on is Desmond Tutu's theology. I feel like his theology hasn't really been researched the way it should be. I feel that most people take Tutu seriously as a political agent, not so much as a theologian; and especially in the academy, where everything is so literary, they don't take his corpus of writing and his life-witness seriously as a theologian." When Susan Keefe said to me, "Michael, the best thing you could do is to write on Tutu", that was the voice from heaven. That was the permission that I think an academic, Eurocentric institution gave me to pursue writing on the Arch.

It just so happened that he was in Atlanta, at Emory, on sabbatical. So I set up an appointment, and I drove down to Atlanta and I went into his office. I was a PhD student who did not know what to say. The Arch said, "Before we talk about any of your plans for your PhD dissertation, let us pray."

I told him that I wanted to write this dissertation. I told him the approach that I would be taking: I would be looking at him and doing research on him as a theologian and as someone who was making an impact on the world politically as well as spiritually. I would study how the church, for much of its history, has created dichotomies between the settler and the settled, and how he was able to bridge those gaps through his own spiritual work. I said I would like to be able to do my work in a primary way, being with him in South Africa. So we set up an opportunity for me to come to Cape Town.

I initially stayed at a retreat centre for clergy, and then the Arch invited me to live with him at Bishopscourt and to serve as his chaplain. I would drive him around on the wrong side of the road (as an American, that's the wrong side for me). He trusted me to do chaplaincy sort of work for him and I got to see his

life and leadership first-hand. He also gave me full access to all of his writings: handwritten forewords from books and his own books. He gave me primary access to sitting in his office and reading his books. He and Mrs Tutu were extremely hospitable. They invited me into their home, to be a part of the family. And so, during 1993 and 1994 I lived with the Arch and I was able to do research in a way that was a PhD researcher's dream.

When I was there, South Africa was trying to have the first real democratic election. It was a major threshold. They say it's most dangerous before the dawn, and that was indeed the case for South Africa. The Arch was the "fireman" during all the states of emergency. While I was serving him as the chaplain, he would get unexpected calls to go and put out fires. He may be called to be a peacemaker when a riot was forming. He could be asked to appear on TV to make the statement that could help bring peace – for example, at the time of the Chris Hani assassination.

I remember on one particular day the Arch told me "OK, let's go. We've got to go downtown to Cape Town." We had just finished morning prayer, but we hadn't finished the whole part of morning prayer because the Arch had to leave early. And I got in the car; we were driving down to Cape Town and I heard the Arch in the back seat start to read a canticle. It was the canticle that we'd had right before we had to leave. He was resuming morning prayer to be able to finish it and he was expecting me to be able to give the responses.

In that moment he showed me that if you're going to be a leader, not just in the church but also in the world, you have to do daily things. You have to say your prayers. You've got to treat each person you meet in ways in which you're not pretentious. You've got to have daily habits that accumulate, that give a trajectory toward where you need to end up. If you don't have them in your daily habits, you won't get to where you need to be.

I concluded that one of the hardest things for the Arch was to say his prayers. And as he learned to say his prayers, he gave the habits not only to himself but also to a whole nation. The most difficult things in life are not the grandiose, ultimate problems that we think we have. It's in our daily habits that we find the most difficult things in life. And for me, the Arch gave me the traction to learn how to solve the most difficult problems that we have, and those are daily. The daily habits were the ones that gave him the frame of reference to do the larger things that the world has witnessed.

BRIGALIA NTOMBEMHLOPHE BAM

On the one hand he has an amazing sense of humour. This is very, very important. Because he has humour you feel you have access to him. The second part that is so special is that this person is approachable, sensitive and is so spiritual and so real. Every corner you turn with Desmond you pray. One night I had been in their home with Leah. We were travelling from Soweto back to Johannesburg, where I lived, and we had an accident. We returned to their home after the accident, because we could not proceed to Johannesburg. And the first thing he said when we arrived was, "Let's pray and thank God that you are alive." And I thought, "This person is special."

My family and I remain grateful that we have had this person in our lives, as Anglicans and also as friends. When my brother, Fikile Bam, was imprisoned on Robben Island for ten years, Desmond Tutu and Bishop Huddleston were amongst the people who carried a list of these men who were serving sentences. You should have seen their lists after some years. The pieces of paper had become dirty because as they said their prayers on a daily basis they would open to the page of names. I saw with my own eyes the list of Bishop Tutu. He would call these people by name in his daily prayer.

I was too afraid to return home in 1987. The South African Council of Churches [SACC] was looking for a new general secretary, a replacement for Dr Beyers Naudé. Bishop Tutu phoned me. I was then based in Geneva, Switzerland. He said I should consider a return home and that the Anglican Church was proposing my name as the general secretary of the SACC. It was at the peak of the political problems in South Africa. I can assure you, I spent sleepless nights thinking about it. He reminded me that when he was in Lesotho as a bishop, I had phoned him to say to him, "Please return home. They need you at home. Your voice has to be heard at home. You have to join the people at home in the struggle." I had forgotten that. You know, when you're talking to someone else it's easy to say these things. He said the same words to me in 1987. He said to me, "Pray about this." I tell you that this is one time where I really was very obedient – I prayed about this. I returned home the following year in 1988.

I was hardly home six weeks when they bombed Khotso House, the headquarters of the SACC. The second person I called, because I couldn't think of anyone else I could phone at that time of the night to report the bombing, was Desmond. I phoned my own boss at the time, Rev. Frank Chikane. Then we phoned Desmond. I don't know why. It's just that in that moment I had to think of somebody and I couldn't think of anyone else to tell. The next person I did think of telling was Dr Barney Pityana. Barney Pityana was still at the World Council of Churches and we wanted him to alert the world, the World Council of Churches and all the media people. And, of course, Bishop Tutu came. We were devastated. The building had been blown up. We had nowhere to go. Fortunately, by God's grace, no one was killed.

My final story comes on a lighter note, or perhaps not so light. This happened at the dramatic meeting when we had to sign the National Peace Accord. The accord was between the National Party and the other parties (including the Inkatha Freedom Party and African National Congress) just before the first elections. The Peace Accord was an important accord here, and so in the programme the churches had proposed Bishop Tutu and Reverend Chikane be two of the presenters. These two names were rejected. We had to withdraw them because the give and take in the Peace Accord was important to us. They said, "No, we will not have Bishop Tutu to speak. We will not have Frank Chikane." So we said to Bishop Tutu he must pray. As he was praying, I saw the delegates, especially from the National Party, open their eyes and stare at him. He prayed and prayed in English, then, at some point, switched to praying in Afrikaans. The whole time they stared in disbelief. I never closed my eyes, by the way. In the prayer he had also made his full speech. That's how we got started.

So that was also the wisdom. It's also a comment on Desmond's belief in the power of God and the power of the Spirit. So many of the stories I've told are not just stories of people being clever, activist, articulate, honest, but things that are deeper.

Tutu often repeats his encounter with a little girl while touring one of the so-called "removal camps" where whole communities were relocated in the course of apartheid's futile attempts to consolidate its bantustans by removing black settlements in what was supposed to be "white" South Africa. Poverty was extreme in these primitive camps, usually located far from any prospect of employment.

....

Blessed are the meek for they shall inherit the earth

Once upon a time I went to a resettlement camp, one of those places where black people uprooted from white areas are dumped. I met a little girl coming out of a shack which she shared with her widowed mother and a sister.

I asked her, "Does your mother get a grant or something?"
"No."
"What do you do for food?"
"We borrow food."

And looking round the camp you wondered who could have extra food to lend to others.

"Have you returned any of the food you borrowed?"
"No."
"What do you do when you cannot borrow food?"
"We drink water to fill our stomachs."

keeper: that you must love your neighbour as yourself. Like all noble ideals, of course, it is violated all too frequently throughout Africa, but it remains an ideal nonetheless. For Tutu, it is a living commitment. He responds to it naturally, straightforwardly and with no hint of artificiality or pretence. Nadine Gordimer, the South African writer, political activist and 1991 Nobel Literature laureate, once wrote of him that he was a man with no façade – one never had to revise the impression gained of him at a first meeting.[11] "The open interest, the fellow warmth that radiate from him then are what he *is*. As he has risen to the Himalayas of public life, become world-famous, this hasn't been blunted in any way. I'd call his lack of self-consciousness one of his inherent gifts; the others have been developed by the exercise of character, the spiritual and intellectual muscle-building he has subjected and continues to subject himself to in service to the human congregation."[12] Or as Boraine, who spent more than two years in close association with Tutu, puts it: "To know him is to love him. You cannot spend time in the presence of Desmond Tutu without being profoundly challenged in terms of your own life and purpose."[13]

Yet he can be stern – and demanding. "He is not an easy man to work for," says Crawford-Browne, who during her time as his personal assistant probably became the person closest to him outside his own family, almost an alter ego able to anticipate his every need. "You have to show total loyalty to him, because that is what he does. He shows total loyalty to God first of all, then to his role, his destiny. So you have to show the same to him."[14] And because Tutu is so demanding of himself, he is demanding of all his staff as well. "The demands of the job were so great that it was often difficult to keep up," says Crawford-Browne. "It was a twenty-four/seven job. I ran his home when Leah wasn't there. I ran his financial affairs and took care of his programmes and his office. I felt his role was so critical that it was a huge privilege to be able to support him in performing it."[15]

The sternness shows in his strict insistence that respect be shown, not to him personally, but to the dignity of his office. There was a clear line between the person and the office. As archbishop he preferred to be called "Father" rather than "Your Grace", which reflects the status of an archbishop as the equivalent of a nobleman in British protocol; and while staffers could be relaxed and informal with him in his personal capacity, none dared become overfamiliar, certainly not in his official role. Crawford-Browne recounts how one young clergyman arrived at his office for an appointment, to be told crisply that he was improperly dressed in his casual clothes, and to go away, make a new appointment and return "properly dressed" in his clerical attire. "He can be quite a disciplinarian," says Crawford-Browne. "There is this toughness that comes through that is so much his father", who was a stern school headmaster.[16]

He can also be angry, as he often was when confronting the arrogance and the aggression of the enforcers of apartheid – even though he would then insist that they, too, were the children of God and one should pray for them. John Allen, in the prologue to his biography of Tutu, recounts a blazing row Tutu had with President Botha in the head of state's executive office.[17] Tutu had gone there to plead for the lives of six men who had been sentenced to death for killings committed during one of the uprisings, but the discussion spun into a shouting match as the cantankerous Great Crocodile began waggling a finger in the little archbishop's face and haranguing him for involving himself in politics, for advocating sanctions, for supporting the outlawed ANC and for inviting Western leaders to interfere in South Africa's affairs.

Tutu tried to restrain himself at first, but as Botha raged on he suddenly snapped. As he told his press secretary afterwards, as the anger welled up inside him he thought, "Our people have suffered for so long. I might never get this chance again." So he let fly. "Look here," he yelled at Botha, shaking his finger back at him, "I'm not a small boy. Don't think you're talking to a small boy. I'm not here as if you're my principal. I thought I was talking to a civilised person and there are courtesies involved." As the shouting match raged on, Tutu accused Botha of lying. The president countered that Tutu was following a "wicked path", and when Botha accused him of wanting a socialist dictatorship, Tutu shot back that he loved South Africa more than Botha did because "our people" (meaning black South Africans) "fought against the Nazis; you didn't" – a reference to the fact that in those years many Afrikaner nationalists, including Botha, opposed South Africa's entry into World War II and some formed a pro-German fifth column called the Ossewa Brandwag (Ox-wagon Sentinels).[18]

It was not an edifying affair and, as he drove away, Tutu reflected aloud to his chaplain whether that was the way Jesus would have handled such a situation. "But at that moment," he added, "I didn't actually mind how Jesus would have handled it. I was going to handle it my way."[19] What the outburst did reflect, though, was the extent to which Tutu had freed himself from the emotional and intellectual shackles of second-class citizenship that had crippled so many black people in apartheid South Africa for so long. I can think of few people, of whatever race or colour, who would have had the guts to stand up to the large and overbearing Great Crocodile when he was in full cry, as did this black leprechaun.

Paradoxically, for a man who fought so long and hard for democracy, Tutu can also be quite authoritarian. This is because he is not a strategist who consults his colleagues and considers all the issues before coming to a decision. He acts on instinct and inspiration. This, say some friends in jest, is because "he talks only to God, and his word is final". Alex Boraine recounts an instance when Tutu revealed a glimpse of this authoritarianism during a discussion over dinner with three judges who were to form part of the amnesty committee of the TRC.[20] The judges were unhappy with a decision to allow television cameras into the amnesty hearings. Judges are accustomed to being lords in their own courts, and the idea of TV cameras being there was anathema to these three. But from Tutu's perspective, the very essence of the commission's work was to enable the whole country to be witness to the evil deeds and confessions of apartheid's criminality. To prevent that in any way would defeat the whole purpose of the exercise.

"We had a really nice dinner," Boraine writes of the incident. "We talked about this and we argued and he [Tutu] used all his skill and humour, but the judges were unmoved. Suddenly, to

RICHARD BURRIDGE

I grew up in a politically active left-wing family. I was a student activist in the seventies. I was leader of a young political party, even in my school days. When I was at Oxford in the seventies, I was part of the anti-apartheid movement, and we were agitating against Barclays Bank's investment in South Africa and all that kind of stuff. And then I was a school teacher for a number of years. Then I went and did my ordination training. I continued working a lot on justice issues and concern for Africa and concern for the poor and all that sort of thing. So I became aware of the Arch somewhere along the way.

In 1987, I became the university chaplain at Exeter university in the south-west [of England], and we had been trying to give the Arch an honorary degree and have him give a major lecture for several years. The [South African] authorities each time refused to grant him a passport. It was May 1990 when he was finally able to come. We'd been planning this for years. Of course in the intervening time, Nelson Mandela was released. We had seen the extraordinary footage of him standing on the balcony with Desmond Tutu. That was only a couple of weeks beforehand. The day we had him in Exeter was the day of the first-phase meeting between Nelson Mandela and De Klerk. Suddenly this was the top story in the world and we had Desmond Tutu in Exeter.

Of course security-wise it was a total nightmare. Any right-winger that wanted to disrupt could just take a pot-shot at the Tutus when they were with us. And so, suddenly, I had the archbishop of Canterbury on the phone, I had the special branch, the armed police and so on. So I literally had to arrive at Heathrow at six o'clock in the morning. The plane came in, everybody else was told to keep their seatbelts on and stay in their seats, and Matt Esau, John Allen and the archbishop and Mrs Tutu were escorted off the plane.

Of course the first thing the archbishop wanted to do was to celebrate Eucharist. And we were rushing him through customs and John was saying, "We haven't got the time to do it here, we'll do it when we get to the station." So we bumbled into armoured cars and were driven to Reading Station where we were going to get the train to Exeter. The university wanted absolutely no press before we got to Exeter because they wanted to have him with "University of Exeter" behind, you know.

We had the front half of the dining-car, and there was this guy who was told he wasn't allowed to speak to the South African party. He had to talk to me only. He said, "Do you want to order anything?"

"I need a small bottle of red wine and a piece of bread."

"Bread for everybody?"

"No, no, one piece of bread."

"Would you like me to cut it out for you?"

"No, I think the archbishop will break it."

The poor guy, you could see he obviously hadn't got a clue. His last attempt was, "Would you like it buttered?"

As we went to Exeter, John Allen looked at the programmes and said, "Yes, you'll do that. No, you won't do that. Yes, if he's going to speak here he has to be quiet there. If he's going to give out here he's got to take in there. If he's going to lead the series there, he has to pray first, you know." It had an enormous effect on me, in part because I had suddenly realised what John Allen had said: If you're going to give out, you've got to take in. If you're going to lead, you've got to follow. If you're going to speak, you've got to pray. And that rhythm, that discipline, that spirituality hit me very hard. I remember it really clearly.

So that was the start. When I became the dean of King's we discovered that he was one of our alumni and I was invited to come out to Cape Town for the retirement service in 1996. We started talking about what was going to happen post-retirement, and we said, "Would you like to come back to King's as a visiting professor, have some time, etcetera, etcetera?" The next thing that happened was that Madiba [Nelson Mandela] asked him to come and chair the TRC so that post-poned it for a couple years.

So over the years he kept saying that it would be nice to come back to King's. And so in 2004 he was the distinguished visiting professor here. He was here for the best part of three months.

Having him here was crazier, much crazier than Exeter. Exeter was a small visit and John was in control. Having him here for three months, well, it gave me heart trouble. Alison, who had been my secretary, worked as his PA. So Alison was in the outer office and he was in the inner office. The problem is that every-body wants a piece of him. We had Cherie Blair on the phone, we had David Frost on the phone, and of course we had come down to South Africa to spend some time with Lavinia [Crawford-Browne] to be trained on how to look after him. He would get up in the morning and go up to the early Eucharist and be happy, and then we'd have a car bring him here. I once tried to walk with him from St Martin-in-the-Fields to here. It took us an hour because he stopped to say hello to everyone, and everybody wanted to say hello and give him big hugs. So we'd have to have a limousine to bring him. That was only two hundred yards. It was the only way to get him here safely.

But it was also an incredible privilege being with

prayed together. We were able to have Desmond and Leah up to our house and they'd have dinner with us. But also seeing again this extraordinary commitment to early morning Eucharist: prayer, silence, listening to God, taking in. Now he's a little bit older than he was when I first met him. The early-morning call when I first met him was 4:30 a.m. He wanted to go running along the towpath with armed police escorting him before Eucharist. And that commitment to spirituality is the private side. People see the international-media superstar stuff; they don't see that, and for me the gift was seeing that.

The ability, the willingness to give out, to want to encapsulate the love of God for the world in a great big bear hug, that's another gift. But there's also a steely side underneath all of that, which is an absolutely determined commitment. He's first and foremost a priest trained in the rigid disciplines of the Community of the Resurrection. The impact of Trevor Huddlestor and then Timothy Stanton and then many others shows in his commitment to prayer and his commitment to spirituality which undergirds that and is often not seen. That's what's kept him sane, kept him human, kept him holy, and stopped him most of the time from being taken in by too much of the razzmatazz and the circus when it hits town. And that means underneath all that is a rock-solid commitment to the basic idea that God loves everybody regardless of their size, their shape, their colour, their background, their education, or even of the size of their nose – and therefore a determination to oppose anything that demeans a child of God. That was the rigid hard edge that drove his opposition to apartheid. That drives his passion for justice right now.

Right, above: Tutu with
Leah, 5 September 1977.

Right, below: Tutu with
Leah at Jan Smuts
International Airport (now
O. R. Tambo International
Airport), Johannesburg,
26 September 1977.

my astonishment and theirs, he got up – he was dressed in a tracksuit, the rest of us somewhat more formal – and declared that the meeting was over, that the hearings would be open, that the television cameras would be allowed and that he couldn't continue the discussion any longer because he had to go upstairs to watch a very important soccer match." Boraine says the judges were taken aback, somewhat angry, and one of them declared: "So this is the new democracy in South Africa." But they talked on after Tutu had left, the judges finally agreed to give the television cameras a trial, and today Boraine believes they would all agree that the televising of the hearings to all parts of South Africa was a vital part of the commission's work.[21]

What is it like to live with this mercurial man, so committed to his mission? "It's a challenge," says his wife Leah. "Yes, there's definitely a challenge living with Desmond." But she is quick to add that he is loving and caring, slow to anger and quick to apologise – sometimes too quick, she adds laughingly, because sometimes you need a good row to get the resentment out of you and here is Desmond cutting it off with his apology "when there are still things you haven't said that you would like to say".[22] The challenge has been in keeping up with him in his hectic life. She married a man expecting to be the wife of a schoolmaster, leading a fairly tranquil life until retirement, then looking after grandchildren. "That's not what happened," she chuckles with heavy understatement.[23] One senses that she would not have enjoyed that lifestyle at all. Leah Tutu exudes too much strength of character to have been content with such a dull existence. She is dynamic, every bit as self-confident and forceful as her husband, although in a more direct and less flamboyant way.

In many respects she has been an ideal partner. Leah's own sharp wit and intelligence has complemented Tutu's effervescent personality. It was as his most resolute supporter during his most difficult years, when he was threatened by the government and vilified by most whites, that Leah played her main role, urging him to speak out and not be intimidated. "I would rather you were happy on Robben Island than unhappy outside," she once told him, referring to the Alcatraz off Cape Town where Mandela and other key political prisoners were incarcerated.[24] Such firm family support was vital for the struggle leaders. As Mandela often said, the feeling of guilt at having abandoned one's wife and children in the interests of the struggle was one of the most painful aspects of their long imprisonment.

Although Leah denies ever having been an adviser to Desmond, friends say he would invariably bounce things off her and take her advice seriously (perhaps she was the only one besides God he did consult). Even when he was abroad, which was often, he would telephone Leah every day. Without her, the friends say, Desmond might have become isolated in an ivory tower, cut off from the people. Leah, a skilful community organiser, kept him in touch. While they lived in Johannesburg she founded and organised the South African Domestic Workers Association, a support body for what is probably the most vulnerable group of workers in South Africa.

Tutu's long and far-travelling mission no doubt took its toll on their marriage and family. "I think she was angry with the world for taking Desmond away from her," says Crawford-Browne. "She resented all the comings and goings, the invasion of her privacy. I think she found that hard to bear. This was expressive of a very strong woman."[25] She particularly resented the people who would gawk over her fence from the top of tourist buses when she was home. "I've stoned another bus today," she wrote tersely to a friend.[26] It turned out that she had been gardening when a tourist bus came by and she had hurled clods of earth at it when the tourists peered at her. When I asked Leah about this, she laughed heartily. "Oh it wasn't only clods," she said, "I sometimes threw apricots and peaches from my trees."[27]

Leah sometimes accompanied Desmond on his foreign trips. Although she disliked the celebrity life, which Desmond charmingly admits to loving, she enjoyed seeing new places and meeting interesting people with whom she could converse and share stories. "But I don't enjoy photographs, having cameras pointed at me, or people interrogating me."[28] At first, she says, they were really "protest travellers" telling the South African story abroad, and when they returned home they had to run a gauntlet, at Johannesburg airport, of shouted insults, dirty looks and stares of pure hatred. That was not pleasant.

"I'VE ALWAYS LONGED FOR MORE CONTEMPLATING, FOR MORE QUIET, TO CATCH UP ON MY READING. THE TIME HAS NOW COME TO SLOW DOWN, TO SIP *ROOIBOS* [RED BUSH] TEA TOGETHER WITH MY BELOVED WIFE IN THE AFTERNOONS, TO WATCH CRICKET, TO TRAVEL TO VISIT MY CHILDREN AND GRANDCHILDREN RATHER THAN TO CONFERENCES AND UNIVERSITY CAMPUSES."

DESMOND TUTU

Above: Cartoon by
Jonathan Shapiro,
Sunday Times,
25 July 2010.

Left: Tutu kisses Leah
at a church service for
their fiftieth wedding
anniversary, 2 July 2005.

Now that Tutu has announced his retirement from public life early in 2011, the two are looking forward to more time and a quieter life together. "I've always longed for more contemplating, for more quiet, to catch up on my reading," Tutu said in a press conference after making the announcement. "The time has now come to slow down, to sip *rooibos* [red bush] tea together with my beloved wife in the afternoons, to watch cricket, to travel to visit my children and grandchildren rather than to conferences and university campuses."[29]

Sounds like the retirement of the old school teacher couple after all. But I wouldn't bet on it. A silent Tutu is an oxymoron.

CHAPTER TWELVE

WE ARE ALL GOD'S CHILDREN

When a prince of the Church tells you that "God is not a Christian", you must know you are dealing with an unusual prelate.[1] But that is vintage Tutu: full of mischief but at the same time deeply profound. For what Tutu is expressing, even in wit, is the essence of his all-faith ecumenism, which I believe makes him not just a hero of South Africa's historical transformation but also a figure of singular relevance in the post-Cold War world – the world of Marshall McLuhan's "global village" in which all faiths and creeds and races are neighbours and had better learn to live together amicably if they are not to destroy the entire village in this nuclear age. A world in which, as Tutu said so often during the Truth and Reconciliation (TRC) hearings, there can be no peace without forgiveness: without recognising that for all our differences of race and faith, languages and cultures, between black and white, Jew and Arab, Christian and Muslim, Hutu and Tutsi, rich and poor, gay and straight, we are all members of the human race – God's children, as he puts it, made in his image. There can be no outsiders, no "other".

In historical terms, of course, the archbishop's statement is factually correct for, as he points out still in this mischievous vein, although God is eternal, the Christian religion is a relative latecomer on the theological scene as compared to many others that were there long before it, such as Hinduism, Buddhism, Judaism and any number of indigenous faiths around the globe, from Africa to the ancient world of Mesopotamia. "Christianity is quite new on the block," Tutu says with a chuckle.[2] But the profundity that lies behind this bit of jocularity is that Tutu respects and acknowledges the validity of all these faiths. It is a concept so deeply at odds with the traditional notion held by nearly all religions through the ages – not least by Christianity –

that theirs is the only true faith, that Tutu's remark comes as a conversation-stopper.

The Dalai Lama, he will tell you, is the holiest man he knows – to which the temporal and spiritual leader of Buddhist Tibet responds that Tutu is "a good friend and religious brother".[3] Brothers in faith? Indeed. When I asked Tutu whether, in the light of his belief that there is only one God, that his God and the Dalai Lama's are one and the same, his reply was as riveting as the notion of God not being Christian. "Ultimately I say yes," he said. "I mean, for me there is one supreme transcendent deity whom we call God, but we come at God from different perspectives."[4]

For Tutu, there is something terribly wrong about the doctrine that says one cannot enter into the kingdom of heaven if one has not been baptised as a Christian. "God wouldn't say to the Dalai Lama: 'You've led a good life; normally you'd be coming into heaven but what a shame you are not a Christian.' I mean, that's lousy! That's unacceptable. We Christians can't claim to have a corner of the market on anything."[5]

It is equally unthinkable in the case of Mohandas Gandhi, a Hindu who committed himself to working for the poor and unleashed a wave of moral enlightenment that ultimately swept across the whole colonial world.

"I am a Christian, but the books that we hold provide for how we should be thinking about God," says Tutu. "I mean, right at the beginning the gospel of John tells about 'the light that lightens everyone'. It doesn't say, 'the light that lightens those who are going to become Christians'; it says 'everyone who comes into the world'."[6]

With that, Tutu digs out a little prayer from a collection of papers in his desk, saying he doesn't know its provenance but believes firmly in the essence of what it says, which is that no religion holds all the truth about God, only God himself knows that, while the religions are all seeking to

TUTU: THE AUTHORISED PORTRAIT

understand it from their own perspectives. "Our theologies are human attempts at putting into human terms what is ultimately ineffable," Tutu explains. "We are talking about the infinite in terms that apply really to finite creatures. The truth about God for us Christians is in fact what is contained in Jesus Christ, but there is no one among us who can claim his understanding is comprehensive and infinite."[7]

Thus all faiths are groping, each in its own context, towards an understanding of the one ineffable truth that is known only to God himself. Therefore all have their own validity.

Suddenly the full impact on Tutu of those earlier years of working for the World Council of Churches' Theological Education Fund becomes clear. For it was during this time that he steeped himself in the concept of contextual theology as he travelled across Africa and talked to his colleagues specialising in the variants of Christian theology as they appear in different socio-historical contexts in different parts of the world. But for the fully evolved Desmond Tutu, contextual theology is no longer confined to variants of Christian belief. Now it is pan-theological, it encompasses all faiths. "What faith you belong to," says Tutu, "is very largely an accident of birth and geography." It is the faith you were born into or that your parents chose for you. But the important thing is that "it is not the faith that comes first, it is the fact of being human together, the revolutionary truth being that we are all loved equally by God," even though our perceptions of God may begin from different historical perspectives.[8]

As usual, Tutu has a simple parable to illustrate this profound insight. It is the story of a group of blind people coming upon an elephant and trying to describe what it is they have encountered. One feels a leg and says, "Oh, it's like a tree". Another touches its trunk and says, "No, it's like a snake". "For us Christians," says Tutu, "the truth about God is contained in Jesus Christ because he is the effulgence of God for us. But we can't say, 'Ah God, now we have you tapped!' We can never say that because, in the true sense of understanding Jesus, we can see that things change. There was a time when Christians believed in slavery; they thought there was nothing wrong with it and that it was compatible with Christianity. Then someone comes along with a different understanding, maybe a deeper understanding, and says, 'Sorry this can't be compatible with what we have found to be the truth about God.' And so I myself say the God I believe in doesn't sit around apprehensively and worry that human beings are going to be making all sorts of discoveries and making God redundant. My God is not that kind of God. My God says, 'Aaaah, aren't they wonderful! Now they've found out this other truth.'"[9]

So Tutu's theology is not only contextual, it is also evolutionary. It can accommodate not only other faiths but science as well. Knowledge of the truth known only to God is not static. It unfolds incrementally with each new discovery, each new insight, as humanity itself evolves in its different social contexts. Nor does Darwinism, so problematic for the fundamentalists, present any difficulties for this deeply prayerful Christian and Old Testament specialist who grew up close to the Cradle of Humankind, where the earliest fossil finds of the human species have been unearthed. To him there is no essential difference between the message conveyed by the findings there and the biblical story of the creation. The first chapters of Genesis, the story of Adam and Eve in the Garden of Eden, Tutu says, are written as poetic imagery to convey the essence of the Judaeo-Christian message of the ultimate unity of all humankind, of our common origin derived from the imagery that we are all descended from one set of parents. The findings at the Cradle confirm that common origin.

South Africa's celebrated author Nadine Gordimer, who describes herself as a Jew and an atheist, says of her long-time friend that "if anyone could have launched me into the leap of a religious faith – any denomination – it would have been Archbishop Desmond Tutu," but that he has always been too respectful of others' rights to try. "If Desmond hasn't caused by his matchless example as a man of faith to lead me to find my own humble way to one, he has certainly influenced my life."[10]

Yet however broad his acknowledgement of the validity of other faiths, or even the respect he shows to those of no belief, Tutu himself remains firmly rooted in his own deep faith. Faith and theology, remember, are not the same thing. Tutu is an ardent Anglo-Catholic. There is no

Left, above: Tutu and His Holiness the Dalai Lama, Vancouver, 19 April 2004. Both men were there to take part in a round-table dialogue on the theme "Balancing Educating the Mind with Educating the Heart" and received honorary degrees from the University of British Columbia.

Left, below: Tutu and His Holiness the Dalai Lama at a conference on teaching compassion to youth, University of Washington, Seattle, 15 April 2008.

When I first met Bishop Tutu, he told me that once he got the Nobel Peace Prize, that actually opened the door for him to visit Washington. Later, after I also received the Nobel Peace Prize, it was really confirmed. I also felt I made some sort of impact. Meeting with different people became a little bit easier. And those people who invited me, they also said they invited me not as a dalai lama but as a Nobel Peace Prize laureate.

Bishop Tutu and I had more and more meetings. It became very clear that he's, firstly, a very, very spiritually minded person. He follows God, in his own way, very sincerely. When we are together to talk with an audience, he emphasises faith. I usually do not put emphasis on faith; I usually put more emphasis on secular ethics. Whether we are believers or non-believers, we should be warm-hearted persons. Warm-heartedness is biological. It does not necessarily come from religious faith. But he and I are very similar – each one devoted to his own faith.

Emotionally and mentally, Bishop Tutu and I are very close. I call him my spiritual older brother. We are both fully committed to the value of spirituality. We both belong to the camp of people who believe in spirituality. He not only believes, he practises and has gained some experience. In age, I'm younger. So, naturally, he's my elder brother!

In front of an audience, he praises me. He says long praises in many sentences. Then he states, "Unfortunately he is not Christian!" The audience always laughs at this. They understand that he's saying that he respects different religious traditions. So here, also, we are similar. We each have faith in one form of religion, but respect all religions.

On one occasion in South Africa, I had some lengthy discussions about methods to promote harmony among the religions. It has been my practice, since 1975, to meet with scholars of different religious traditions and discuss the similarities and differences between our practices. When we find differences, we ask, "What's the purpose?" since religions have the same intent: the promotion of basic human values. We have different views, different philosophies, but

the same purpose. When I have met with religious practitioners we find more or less the same qualities in them. They are using different methods or practices, they are of different religious traditions, but they exhibit more or less the same qualities. People like Mother Teresa and Bishop Tutu himself and many others, through their own Christian faith, really transformed their lives. Their lives were more meaningful. They were more compassionate, more sensible and more responsible. So meeting and speaking with religious practitioners, that's a second method to promote closer understanding. Then the third way is pilgrimage. People of different races and different religious traditions can make pilgrimages to each other's holy sites. People of different faiths can meet together. They can share a message of peace and spirituality.

Archbishop Tutu added another idea. When disasters happen, people from different organisations can come together and help. Since then, on many occasions when I speak of ways to enhance harmony, I add his suggestion. And actually, we experienced that in 1959 when large numbers of people from the Tibetan community arrived in India. Many Catholic organisations and Protestant organisations offered us lots of help. That also created positive feelings toward each other.

He is always playful, always jovial, always teasing. He is such a nice person. On one occasion, I think in America, a few Nobel laureates were moving from one place to another. In the hall we walked in a procession. I always push him ahead because he is the older spiritual leader. So I was behind him. I pretended to choke him. He turned back. "Dalai Lama, I will inform the police that I need protection!" We are always teasing each other. In any meeting of the Nobel laureates, he always brings a very jovial atmosphere. Of course he can be very serious. But generally, whenever he joins, the atmosphere completely changes. He is an easy-going, open, wonderful person.

He is a freedom fighter but the fight is carried on with compassion, forgiveness and a full commit-ment to non-violence. He is a wonderful person. His

...ommitment to reconciliation in South Africa is wonder-ul. He did not just say nice words, but he actually carried out committed action. I really admire him, and of course Mr Mandela also, for that. Besides his spiritual practice, his commitment has been a lesson to me. In South Africa he committed the practice and provided the teaching. He made an example to others of forgiveness. He showed the basis for the work of reconciliation and forgiveness. When I have spoken to audiences I have sometimes said: "After democracy was achieved, Bishop Tutu and the black people became the leaders in reconciliation. They carried out his work very sincerely. For black South Africans, once they got the power it would have been easy to forget about reconciliation. But they did not. This was really wonderful." So I learnt. In the same sort of spirit that Bishop Tutu implemented reconciliation, we can learn from his experience. In the future we may have that kind of work when the time comes [for Tibet].

He is the elder spiritual brother. That means mentally he is the elder, the senior, the more experienced. I'm his junior, so logically the junior can learn more from the senior. The senior may learn from the junior. I never expect he should learn something from me.

He is my friend. Once a person is a very close friend and develops respect, then the other's problem you feel as your own problem; the other's happiness you feel in your own. That's quite natural. In our case, it is not just a friendship but it is a friendship with deep admiration, deep respect and, I think, no barrier; we can be quite frank with each other. That's very nice.

Politically, in the initial period he did not touch on the Tibetan problem. But then later, actually at one meeting in New York, he mentioned the Tibetan problem. He used his moral authority to bring attention to the issue. Then also in Delhi, when he was awarded the Gandhi Peace Prize, he said that the government of India looks after the Dalai Lama and this makes him very happy. He added that the government of India should also support Tibetan freedom. We appreciate his support. Last year, before the World Cup, the South

African embassy in New Delhi declined a visa for the Bishop Tutu publicly expressed his unhappiness and displeasure about this. He really showed solidarity. I'm very impressed. I am very impressed.

Jointly Bishop Tutu and President Havel wrote an article about Liu Xiaobo. I think it appeared in the *Guardian*. It was a very strong statement. I heard about it through the BBC, although I didn't see the article itself. It is very helpful to have someone like him, someone with moral authority, to make clear what is wrong and what is right. That's very important. I think spiritual leaders should do more. They should speak out. The politicians and leaders of government have to take into consideration various other factors: the economy and many, many things. But spiritual leaders are supposed to stand firm on moral principle. Even if there are some immediate consequences, it doesn't matter.

On this planet everybody says, "Peace, peace, peace." Even North Korea says, "Peace, peace, peace." But reality is just the opposite. The United Nations is supposed to be the highest world body, but sometimes it looks like a trade centre: "If you do this, I will do that." Someone must make clear that right is right and wrong is wrong fearlessly, truthfully, honestly. Although Bishop Tutu is retired, whenever there is an issue of humanity, I think he must speak. His voice is important. He should stand firm as he has done. He must continue, please, till his last breath. He should stand firm. It's very important. And also [the fact that he is] a black person from the African continent is very helpful. Maybe it's a little selfish of me. If some Europeans make a statement then the Chinese communists say, "Oh, it's Western imperialist anti-Chinese forces speaking!" They can easily dismiss it.

South Africans suffered a lot under white coloni-als, under apartheid. When he speaks strongly, it is difficult to say that he's the instrument of Western anti-Chinese forces. I guess the Chinese may try to say that Archbishop Tutu is the instrument of Western anti-Chinese forces. After all, they described me as an instrument of Western anti-Chinese forces.

wavering in his total devotion to its rituals and doctrines. John Allen likens this apparent duality to Tutu's analogy of "the rainbow nation of God". Each colour of the rainbow has its own authenticity, its own truth, yet it is the combination of all, side by side, that gives the whole its beauty. So, too, with the multiracial nation of Tutu's dreams. It is not a melting pot of homogenised uniformity: each race, each colour, each culture has its own intrinsic value and justifiable self-pride, but it is the totality of all together in mutual love and recognition of their common humanity that makes the whole rainbow so vibrant and attractive. The same goes for faith. Take pride in the religion to which you belong and be true to its revelation of the truth as perceived in its context, but recognise as you do so the validity of all others and the truths they have revealed to their adherents in their contexts.

"WHAT FAITH YOU BELONG
TO IS VERY LARGELY
AN ACCIDENT OF BIRTH
AND GEOGRAPHY ...
IT IS NOT THE FAITH
THAT COMES FIRST,
IT IS THE FACT OF BEING
HUMAN TOGETHER,
THE REVOLUTIONARY
TRUTH BEING THAT
WE ARE ALL LOVED
EQUALLY BY GOD."

DESMOND TUTU

My very first dealing with Archbishop Tutu was when was trying to get him to come to a conference that was running. I called his office in South Africa, and his secretary said to me, "I'm sorry, the archbishop is praying right now." It was right then that I knew that he was the real deal. This is a man deeply rooted in prayer. In this last seven years of my own life, I was in the midst of controversy and so on, and I know you can only withstand such a thing when you are walking very, very closely with God. It was always clear to me that this must be a man who walks very closely with God, and I had proof of it right on the telephone in my first interaction with him.

It was years later, just a couple of years ago, that I was writing a book, and without having ever met me, he agreed to write the foreword. I have to say, it was maybe the greatest honour of my life. It's a wonderful introduction to my book. The thing about it that I felt was so gracious was that he declared himself to be proud to be in a church with Gene Robinson. This is someone whom I not only admire, but whom I look to as a model of how to conduct oneself in a way that speaks louder than all the important words that might be said. You don't have to wonder what Desmond Tutu believes, because he lives it in such a public way. You know the medium is the message. He is the incarnation of all the values that we preach in Christianity. I have to say, in a world where nearly everyone has clay feet, and obviously no one is perfect, this is the person I have looked up to, who has inspired me on those days when I wonder if I can keep going. I think of him and his powerful witness to all of us, despite astounding odds, and I'm buoyed up by that.

You know, so many people have this sentimental notion of Christianity. Anybody who really reads the scriptures knows that Jesus laid out a pretty tough road. It is a road that involves integrity and honesty and truth-telling. The Truth and Reconciliation Commission was, I think, a living-out of what I understand to be the gospel in the most realistic and naked of terms. It's "We're gonna tell the truth here no matter how much it hurts, and we are not going to punish anyone at the end. What we are going to do is tell the truth and deal with that."

I think that the truth and reconciliation process put together two things that are very important to the gospel that Archbishop Tutu and we all try to preach: we have to be responsible for what we do in our lives, and we can actually begin to reflect the forgiving, reconciling love God has for us. I don't know that I have ever seen that lived out so dramatically as in that process.

You know, Martin Luther King was always fond of quoting that the arc of history is long and difficult but it bends towards justice. I think one of the reasons that Archbishop Tutu's witness is so powerful is that not even around the issue of race has he neglected the bigger picture that what God wants for all of God's people is integrity, dignity, freedom and liberation. No matter what particular fight he is engaged in at the moment, he never loses sight of that overarching bend towards justice for all of God's children. So each of these fights, whether it's on racial issues or ethnic issues or gay and lesbian issues, each one of those becomes an example of the way in which God wants justice for all of God's people.

To have someone of the stature and reputation and unassailable sainthood of Desmond Tutu speak out on the gay and lesbian and transgender issue, has just offered amazing comfort and support to those of us in that movement, and to me especially. I think about all the things that have come his way and how he has never returned hate for hate, but lets it stop with him.

when I'm tempted to return hate for hate, I think, "By golly, if Desmond Tutu can do this, I can too!" And I see the power of that, you know. I have learned that when you do that people don't remember what you said, but that you treated your enemy with dignity and respect. You never treated them as less than the child of God that they are, and that just speaks so much louder than words. So I think for those of us in the LGBT [lesbian, gay, bisexual and transgender] movement, and then for me quite personally, just being in the front lines of this, his example has been of enormous importance to us.

When I finally got to meet him – you know, a person like Bishop Tutu is so big in your mind. He's just so big. And then I saw him, and he was so compact. I thought how could all of this power be coming out of this little package? I think the other thing I have always admired about him that I experienced in meeting him is this contagious joy. I can't believe there is anyone who has ever met him who wouldn't name that about him. You

know, there was a seminary dean who in an address to the students said to them, "You know, I see so little joy in you. I know you do your studies, you make good grades, you write good papers, but I don't see any joy. I wonder how it will be that people will experience that the news you have for them is good news." There is no question with Desmond Tutu that the good news he's got is good news because he himself is joyful. The other thing that I so cherished about meeting him is that no matter whether he is laughing or he's being serious, there is this peacefulness. The Bible talks about the peace that passes all understanding and you know it when you meet Bishop Tutu. There is a peace that comes from having no doubt that you are loved by God. It doesn't matter whether you are in the midst of a struggle or you are salvaging someone's marriage or you are laughing at a joke, that peace that passes understanding, comes through, and it's the thing that I want most for my own life. I will be forever grateful to Bishop Tutu for demonstrating that to me.

NIGEL CRISP

I didn't really know Archbishop Tutu except for smallish encounters.

He chaired a session for us on telemedicine. We were in one of the committee rooms in the Houses of Parliament. It was filled with about sixty people, probably fifty of them Brits and the rest Africans living in England. We were talking seriously and rather ponderously about how to make this work. You will have been in meetings where people talk seriously about stuff in a

sort of depressing way, and you can feel yourself wind down. I cannot remember exactly what the archbishop said, but it would have been along the lines of God smiling and reminding us of our virtue. He brightened the whole atmosphere. He reminded us all that this was about people talking to people, heart to heart, not organisation to organisation. It changed the atmosphere in the room. It helped the people to once again become enthusiastic and energised.

Above: Archbishop
Tutu, 1988.

Our other perceptive author, Antjie Krog, adds a further dimension to any understanding of the *weltanschauung* (world view) of this great humanitarian. Krog believes the essence of Tutu's vision is to be found in his African spirituality; in the concept of ubuntu, or *motho ke motho ka batho* as it is called in the Sotho-Tswana language group of Tutu's mother, that "a person is a person through other persons", which is central to traditional African communal life and religiosity. Yes, she concedes, Tutu is obviously a highly educated and sophisticated theologian, a modern man of the modern world in every respect, yet there is still this other factor deep within him, rooted in his antecedent culture that enables, compels, him to see humanity in its collective whole rather than as a set of free individuals as Westerners do. "It is that factor of African spirituality," she says, "of seeing every person as being interconnected with you – if you are hungry or being harmed, it affects me profoundly – that makes the difference, that broadens and deepens and makes his Christianity extraordinary."[11] It enables him, as she puts it, to see Christianity through the lens of his African spirituality.

Antjie Krog's sense of Tutu is derived almost entirely from observing him intensely at the TRC for the two and a half years that she was a radio reporter covering its hearings. She was fascinated by the visceral interconnectedness Tutu was able to establish, especially with black victims as they poured out their painful stories, and since the hearings she has examined the testimonies carefully for the cultural lessons she believes they contain. Her first observation is that a great many more black victims, about 80 per cent, were prepared to forgive their torturers and the killers of their loved ones than white victims were. Secondly, among those who were prepared to forgive, whites and blacks tended to forgive for different reasons. Whites tended to say they would forgive "because Jesus has forgiven". None of the forgiving blacks said that: their reasoning, almost invariably, was that "I also have to live", sometimes that "I hope you can change" (said to the torturer or murderer), or simply, "We have to change this country".[12]

In other words, in Krog's thesis, blacks were motivated by the ubuntu concept of the interconnectedness of humanity. "Every time," she says, "it was this thing that we are all linked to one another. For you to become fully humane, you need me, but I also need you for my full humaneness. If I am hurt or my child is killed, I cannot be whole so I affect your humaneness. So it's a constant effort to make the world whole so that this wholeness can restore all of us to be what we're actually meant to be."[13]

Krog takes umbrage at the fact that many critics of the TRC process have accused Tutu of making it too much of a religious process, of forcing Christianity down people's throats. This, she feels, reflects a failure of whites in the main to comprehend the African psyche, not recognising its spiritual interconnectedness but simply assuming that all humanity is individualistic as Westerners are – and as she admits she is. "No black audience ever protested at the way Tutu ran the hearings," Krog notes. "This is because he and those audiences understood one another perfectly. When Tutu was speaking he was not saying something alien to them, he was speaking something they deeply understood. It was that which made our TRC unique, different from all the others that have been held in the world. It made people capable of interpreting the whole process, the whole notion of amnesty, of forgiveness and reconciliation, differently."[14] She also feels that is the reason the amnesty hearings were less successful, because Tutu was not part of that special TRC committee whose proceedings were more like a court of law: factual, impersonal and legalistic.

Viewed overall, Krog, Max du Preez and nearly all others who were close to those TRC hearings believe the process encapsulated the essence of South Africa's political miracle in that it brought sworn enemies together to engage one another face to face; and that through a process of acknowledging one another's pain and fears and recognising one another's identity imperatives, they were able to arrive at a compromise deal that was eventually captured in a new constitution. For them, Tutu's handling of that quintessential aspect of the whole process was vital.

There are two focal points, touchstones for me, when I think of Desmond Tutu and the world view of Desmond Tutu. It's almost too small a word to use the word "theology" of Desmond Tutu – it's a world perspective. One has to do with ubuntu, which I think is the centre of his life. It has become the centre of my life. It has become the centre of our theology here at All Saints Church. That word is too magnificent to be translated into "community" or "it takes another person to be a person". It is just ethereal, supernal in what it means about a person's soul. A person understands that he or she needs the person in front of them to be who they are. It is totally synonymous and resonant with the theology of Dr Martin Luther King Jr. I grew up in the state of Georgia; Dr King was a son of Georgia. He was very influential in my life. I got to meet him. Dr King said: "In order for me to be who I am, you have to be who you are. And in order for you to be who you are, I have to be who I am." It's that kind of mystical interconnectedness of all of us that ubuntu describes and that Archbishop Desmond Tutu embodies.

The other touchstone that is so important to me, is that God needs us. God needs our "yes". And our "yes" is just as important as was Mary's "yes". That wonderful story of Gabriel coming to call on Mary and asking her to do this rather surprising and impossible and radical thing, and she says, "What?" and finally she says, "Yes." To hear him tell that story with all that giggly ebullience that is in the heart of Desmond Tutu is to transform you to say, "I, too, can be Mary. I, too, am Mary." It reminds me of that very important place in Florence, Italy, at the convent of San Marco, where that great artist Fra Angelico painted all of those marvellous paintings on the walls throughout that monastery. The most prominent one is "The Annunciation". There is Gabriel coming to call on Mary. The great thing about that painting is it is set in the garden of that monastery. So those monks who would see it knew that the artist

Fra Angelico was trying to say, "It is happening right here." They would go two by two every night to their cells and the last painting they saw before they went into their own cells was this one. The idea being that if God is gonna call on you tonight to say that you are pregnant with God's will, will you say yes? So ubuntu and our collaboration with God are just so central.

As a result of being the new rector, the new guy on the block, I was invited to his retirement festivities in Cape Town. That was when he retired as the archbishop of South Africa. My wife and I went for our first trip to South Africa. I came off this long flight with my wife and we were just overwhelmed. The first thing that we had to do was to go to the cathedral in Cape Town for the rehearsal for the event that was going to happen the next day. All of my exposure to him during that trip was rather grand and awfully public and filled with a lot of crowds.

This was during the TRC [Truth and Reconciliation Commission] hearings and so he invited us to accompany him to one of the hearings. We sat and heard a woman describe the phenomenon of a man who was seated across from her having taken a jackhammer to her son's abdomen. She told it in the detail that Archbishop Desmond invited people to tell their stories. All of us were crying, including the archbishop. Then he thanked her for her testimony and said, "Now I ask you if you will forgive him. Your testimony and your forgiveness will mean that our country has a future." He said it much more eloquently than that. It was the most memorable experience of my life. For him to receive that pain, to hold in his soul her trauma, and then to speak this word of truth that is even greater than any trauma any of us can have – "We have hope for humanity and for our community and we have a future when we forgive." She began weeping.

The beautiful thing about the TRC hearings was how well cared for everyone was. She had been there with members of her family, but immediately professionals from the TRC staff came and surrounded her. She said, "I do. I do forgive him." At that point there was another flood of weeping from all of us. We knew we were in the presence of the greatness of the Arch and of the greatness of this woman. We were also in the presence of the divinity of an exchange. We knew that something sacred had happened and that we had been witnesses to it.

A former member of the Psychological Operations Unit of the apartheid government told a moving story. His job was to go into the Arch's office to mess with his mind, to tell him to cower and be fearful and to stop his revolutionary liberatory ministry. And, as the man tells the story, he was the person that was changed. The Arch had told him that his true self was to be a man of reconciliation and truth and peace, not of division. And there is something about Desmond Tutu that has the power to tell us our true self is to be this person of justice and deep spirituality that God made us. So to be free is to come back to your true self – you.

I've been at my church for fifteen years, and the third year I was here I was invited to consider being a bishop somewhere. The Arch had been here on Sunday and had gone to a beach house to rest for the week, and then came back. I claimed the responsibility and the privilege of driving him from here to the airport. The reason was that I wanted some pastoral counselling. I will never forget it. We got into the car and we were on our way. The traffic was slow, as it can be in Los Angeles. I said, "Archbishop, I need to ask you to be with me in something and help me to discern." So I laid out this thing about the diocese and the call. And, I will never forget, his first words were: "Thank you for inviting me in." I thought, how lovely, how grace-filled not to start with advice but to start with saying thank you. So I knew at that moment that he was a person of gratitude. That kind of grounding in gratitude probably was – is – a secret.

I've had the great honour of being with the Arch physically many times, both hosting him here and being a guest in his and Leah's home in Cape Town. I have had the honour to be in the presence of a very small meeting with the Dalai Lama. What's striking is that they both have this bubbly youthfulness about them. I think that's because the Holy Spirit is always new and young, and that when people allow God's spirit to come in their lives that they are very youthful.

He tells a wonderful story about how in Anglo-Catholic parishes and in Catholic churches there is the reservation of the sacrament and there in the presence light above the aumbry or tabernacle. Those who are practising in that religion genuflect when they come in. They are genuflecting to the fact that God is in this reserved consecrated host. He believes we should genuflect for one another, because God is dwelling in every human being. There is that deep, passionate belief of his. He can be playful in the way he acts it out.

I got my Master's in divinity from Candler School of Theology at Emory University. They had asked me to come and receive a preaching award and to preach. Desmond was a professor in residence there, and I knew that. I was just so anxious because I was going to be preaching with Desmond Tutu in the congregation. Usually the preference is to have things the other way. I flew from Los Angeles to Atlanta. A taxi dropped me off on campus and I went to the dean's office. He called Archbishop Tutu to say that Bacon was there. The Arch came in and he knelt, he genuflected in front of me. I was so touched and so I genuflected in response. Well, he got lower on the ground. I got lower on the ground. He got lower. So we had a contest on who can genuflect the most dramatically in front of the other. He's playful.

So what does all this add up to? What kind of person do we have here in this humble high-school teacher who became a lukewarm priest and eventually grew into a turbulent peace activist and Nobel laureate and is now entering his octogenarian years not just as a man for all seasons but for all faiths and all humanity? He is, I believe, a man whose expanded world view is extraordinarily relevant in the bewildering times in which we live.

The central feature of these times is the shrinkage of time and space in a technologically driven world, creating the global village in which the forces of human proximity and instant communication are homogenising cultures. This in turn has produced a fundamentalist religious and ethnic backlash that the major Western powers have failed to understand adequately, since they have viewed these responses through Western eyes as they habitually do. As a result, their ill-considered attempts to impose democratic order on these unappreciative societies have not only failed but have sown further destabilisation and confusion. Now the world is at a crossroads: do the major powers continue with their failed military strategies or do they try something different – and, if so, what? This is where I believe Tutu's vision of the world has relevance.

In an age where ideological conflict has receded from the world stage, issues of identity, of culture, religion, language grouping and so on have come to the fore as rallying points to mobilise people around issues of grievance, real or imagined. This is not to say all members of these groups are susceptible to such rallying cries, but it certainly is true that fundamentalists and the leaders of even lesser radical groups use them. Thus we have heard Osama bin Laden, Iran's President Mahmoud Ahmadinejad and other Muslim fundamentalists describe the United States as the "great Satan", while ex-President Bush in turn spoke of waging a "crusade" against the "axis of evil" and against the "evil-doers". Such loaded language is obviously intended to arouse cultural and religious passions which in turn become instruments of aggressive mobilisation in our inflammable global village. Their potency is what needs to be countered and that can be done only by inculcating a deeper understanding of the complexity and validity of other major religions and cultures – of "otherness" generally.

This is where the global relevance of Tutu becomes apparent. The essence of Tutuism, if one may coin such a word, is precisely that need to understand other faiths and cultures and accept their validity. While stressing that there is one God whom all faiths are seeking to understand in their own contexts, this must never convey the impression that all are actually covert Christians. "Don't insult people of other faiths," John Allen recalls him saying during a conference of interfaith leaders, "by saying, 'Oh, actually our God is your God too.' In other words, you're Christians without knowing it. Don't insult people by reducing their faith to that."[15] A delicate line to tread but, for Tutu, an important one that illustrates his sensitivity on interfaith matters.

In the rainbow nation that Tutu helped create, I am who I am in all the glory of my tradition, while I respect you for who you are in all the glory of your tradition. In the rainbow nation we all live beside each other. It's not the red or the yellow that makes the rainbow beautiful. It's when you put all the colours together that it becomes beautiful. Beautiful because of its diversity. Surely there is a profound lesson here for our fractious and diverse global village which can trace its origins back to a place not far from where this once sickly Sophiatown street kid was born.

Right: Tutu waves
to members of the
media at the United
Nations headquarters
in New York,
24 September 2007.

PERSPECTIVES

TREVOR THAMSANQA TUTU

What I learned from my father that I would want to pass on to my children would be the love of sport. I would want to give them the love of education, reading and self-improvement. I would want to make sure that they respect all people. I would want to make sure that they respect all religions and all sexual orientations. I want to ensure that they know how to laugh at themselves, that they know how to see the funny side of life. I would want them to appreciate their blessings, such as they are, and be aware of their responsibility to other people, particularly to those less fortunate than themselves. I would say that those are the core values I think that he tried to make sure that we had. Yes, those are his core values and I think that's what he's tried to live by.

....

THANDEKA TUTU-GXASHE

On our return to South Africa we went off to boarding school. I don't know how it affected them but I know how it affected me: I hated it. I was always the home-body type. I was the quiet one, the bookworm-type child. So, for me, it was very traumatic. Fortunately Naomi [her younger sister] was at St Michael's with me and so she kind of looked after me, rather than the other way round. She was the little fighter and I was the timid one. I got accustomed to it. You get accustomed to anything you have to. I know it was very difficult on them. They would have to drive all the way from Alice, in the Eastern Cape, to Johannesburg. That is a good twelve to fourteen hours. Then they would drive the five hours to Swaziland, pick us up, drive all the way back. They had to do this six times a year. There were three semesters. They would have to drive there to get us, drive back. Then drive there to take us back and drive back. It had to have been hard on them. But it was that or Bantu education, and Bantu education was not happening.

To avoid going to shops and being ill-treated, my mum used to make breakfast and lunch. We stopped on the side of the road and ate, as opposed to trying to buy food in little towns. We would buy cold drinks and things like that but not food. If you even found a place that would serve black people, you couldn't be too sure that anything was going to be fresh.

I remember there was a lot of singing and a lot of fighting on the drives. With four kids in a car for that length of time, the fighting was almost inevitable. There were four of us and only two windows in the cars that we were in. There was always a fight over who got to sit at the window. Then we also had arguments when it would be: "He's looking out of my window."

When we were driving, there would be times when my dad was praying. We could talk among ourselves but we wouldn't talk to him. He was praying. The discipline of his quiet time, he insisted on it. It's been part of our lives. He has to have his quiet time for praying and meditating and what have you. Even when we were little kids driving those long, long distances, we knew there were parts of the journey when we could talk, but we had to talk softly. That was not the time to be fighting. If we wanted to fight, we had to wait until he had finished praying.

When my father was a chaplain at Fort Hare, sometimes we would come home for holidays and there would be a huge picnic with students. We would all go along, and he would be dancing. He was always the life and soul of the party. The Eastern Cape is a very beautiful place. We would drive and park near a river and have a picnic there. People would bring their own music. There would be dancing. I remember that. Life seemed to be fun. That was what life was. That was who he was. As I grew older, I found out that, actually, the person who was the life and soul of the party was my mum. She's the more social person. She has better stories than he does. People think he has better stories but, actually, she's the one who sets everybody off laughing. We would have concerts in the house. There wasn't a whole lot of enter-tainment. There weren't places to go for entertainment, and so we would have concerts in the house. They would all do their little performance. They would dance or sing. He and my mum would do choruses and sing. I just think I had a really blessed childhood.

NONTOMBI NAOMI TUTU

As a parent, I think my father to be a much gentler person than my grandfather was. I think, even apart from being a parent, I think he tried to be different from his father, even in terms of his relationship with my mum. My grandfather was very disdainful of my grandmother. I think my father has made sure that he is the opposite of that with my mother. He goes out of his way to make sure that she knows that he values and cherishes her, and everybody else knows it too. I think that that comes out of seeing my grandfather's fairly disrespectful treatment of my grandmother. I think that he has definitely taken from my grandmother the idea of the importance of hospitality. I talked about our house being a place where people came together – that was my grandmother's house growing up. Apart from all the grandchildren that she took in, there was always somebody there who had come for a meal or for a get-together. It was a house of hospitality. I think that he definitely took that from them.

There are times when you see this little, patriarchal African thing coming out of my dad. On the one hand, he makes tea, washes dishes and the rest of it but, on the other hand, if there are children in the house, and by children I mean even us (you know, I'm fifty now but that's a child in the house as far as he is concerned),

then it should not be his place to go and get himself a glass. There are children in the house and that's what children do: they get you your drink and your whatever else you need. But my grandfather was contradictory too. One of the things that I remember growing up, is that my grandfather always made tea for everybody in the house in the morning. In our culture that is the work of the women and, normally, daughters-in-law. He would make tea and bring it to people in their beds. My grandfather would always cook breakfast, you know. I think that all people are contradictions but I think that my dad definitely tried to be as far from that rigid patriarchal perspective as he could.

One thing that I don't think many people would know is that my dad has good taste in women's clothes – he really does. When we were growing up – in fact, when we lived in England and he travelled a lot – he would buy most of our special clothes. He would buy stuff on his trips and he had a really good eye. I mean he doesn't seem like the kind of guy who would have a good eye but he really did. Even now he will go out and buy clothes for us. If he is travelling and sees something, he is quite willing to say, "Oh that would look good on one of them" and he will buy it. He has very good taste in women's clothes.

....

MPHO A. TUTU

I am an Episcopal priest. I studied and was ordained in the United States. When I got to seminary, I found that my father was ubiquitous: he'd written the foreword for this text, the afterword for that text, and he was quoted in another text, and his speech is excerpted in yet another text ... and so on, so on, so forth.

I'm not sure whether it was a pain or an inspiration. It was a curiosity. I think I had taken him much more lightly than was warranted. I think that as I engaged in my own theological studies, and found him quoted and excerpted all over the place, I recognised him as much more of a heavyweight than I had given him credit for. He wears his accomplishments very lightly. He's not the person who is constantly hammering you over the head with his achievements and what he's managed to do against the odds. He doesn't assault you with what it is that you have to live up to; that is not at all who he is. He was incredibly respectful of my process. He let me find my way, the way I needed to. When I told my mother that I wanted to go to seminary and I wanted

to become a priest, my mum was a mum: she was thrilled and enthusiastic and excited. My dad prayed with me.

The day that I graduated from seminary at the Episcopal Divinity School in Cambridge, Massachusetts, my father was the commencement speaker at Virginia Theological Seminary in Alexandria, Virginia. He had agreed to the engagement before he knew my graduation date. I was really disappointed that he wasn't going to be with me but I had made peace with it. My mum was going to be there and that was wonderful. He called me the morning of my graduation to apologise again and I was trying to be really fine although I wasn't really, really fine. I didn't want to make him feel bad, because he was doing what he had to do. At the beginning of the ceremony, all the graduates marched in and then we were all seated. Suddenly I heard a small rush of sound like waves on pebbles. I turned around and my dad was getting into the seat next to my mother. She was as surprised as I was. He had made his speech

Above: With daughter Naomi, Cape Town, 26 April 1998.
Below: With granddaughters Nompumelelo (daughter of Naomi) and Nyaniso (daughter of Mpho), 8 October 2001.

Above: Desmond and Leah with daughters Mpho, Naomi and Thandi.
Right: With newly ordained daughter Mpho, Christ Church, Alexandria, Virginia, 17 January 2004.

and jumped off the podium, run to a waiting car, got a flight to get up to Boston, got a police escort from the airport to the chapel to come and be at my graduation. He's not just a father: he is a daddy. He says so.

Last year my older sister celebrated her fiftieth birthday. My father and I concelebrated the Eucharist. Many of the women said how deeply moved they were to see the two of us at the altar together.

We had shared the liturgy before but on those times one of us was preaching and the other presiding. This time we presided together and for me it was lovely – more than lovely. It was amazing and sacred and wonderful and all of those things. But afterwards I had

an additional piece of context. I had a conversation afterwards with Brigalia Bam. She had argued for the ordination of women at the provincial synod that finally decided to ordain women to the priesthood in South Africa. She spoke about how important that was. She and others talked about how hard my father had worked for women's ordination and how he had prayed for it. She said, "He never knew when he was struggling for the right of women to become priests that one of the outcomes would be that he would one day be able to stand at the altar with his own daughter and concelebrate the Eucharist." That, in retrospect, made the moment even more momentous.

Following page: Tutu and family with the Obamas after Tutu is presented with the Presidential Medal of Freedom at the White House, 12 August 2009.
From left to right: Mpho's daughter, Nyaniso; Naomi's daughter, Nompumelelo Ngomane; Naomi; President Obama; Leah; Tutu; Michelle Obama;

As a crusader for freedom, a spiritual leader, chair of the Truth and Reconciliation Commission, and a respected statesman, he has become a symbol of kindness and hope far beyond the borders of his native land. Through it all, he has been guided by the belief that, in his words, "My humanity is bound up in yours and we can only be human together."

The glint in the eye and the lilt in the voice are familiar to us all, but the signature quality of Archbishop Desmond Tutu, says Nelson Mandela, is the readiness to take unpopular stands without fear. He played a pivotal role in his country's struggle against apartheid and is an extraordinary example of pursuing a path to forgiveness and reconciliation in the new South Africa. Tribune of the downtrodden, voice of the oppressed, cantor of our conscience: Desmond Tutu possesses that sense of generosity, that spirit of unity, that essence of humanity that South Africans know simply as ubuntu.

NELSON MANDELA AND GRAÇA MACHEL

Madiba [Nelson Mandela]: I believe that God is waiting for the archbishop. He is waiting to welcome Desmond with open arms. If Desmond gets to heaven and is denied entry, then none of the rest of us will get in!

I remember so much about the archbishop. I didn't always agree with him. Even when I disagreed with the archbishop I kept quiet. I never disagreed with him in public.

Graça Machel: [laughs] Except that one time ... and I thought the archbishop was right. The archbishop criticised you for wearing those printed shirts like this one you're wearing now. He said a head of state should wear a suit, not all the time, but ... I agreed with him. I think you look so nice in a suit. But you stopped wearing suits, except when you went to Parliament. You said that you "shouldn't be criticised for wearing wild-print shirts by a man who wears dresses!"

Madiba: [smiles] Well, on that occasion, he criticised me in public first!

BILL CLINTON

When I was a young man, I began to follow Archbishop Tutu's efforts to end apartheid and achieve equality for his people. His work inspired me then, and continues to do so.

In 1993, I invited him to the White House to highlight the continuing importance of his work: to emphasise our determination to work with him, Nelson Mandela and others to help the new South Africa succeed and to include him in the United States' recognition of the government of Angola, acknowledging the impact of Archbishop Tutu's influence beyond the border of his homeland. Archbishop Tutu was both a moral and a political force. When I first met him I was struck by the energy and passion that seemed to pour out of him – in words, gestures, looks. He exuded conviction and a good-natured but aggressive determination. He had no interest in dwelling on what he and others had already accomplished. All the talk was about what we needed to do next. In all our encounters since, that hasn't changed.

South Africa's Truth and Reconciliation Commission [TRC] proved that the truth can set us free and empower people to build different and better tomorrows. When I asked John Hope Franklin to lead the One America Initiative in 1997, I was very aware of what the TRC had done. What the US needed was not so much to unearth the past as to face the uncomfortable truth about our continuing racial divides, and work together to overcome them. In 1998, when I went to South Africa for the first time, I saw first-hand the power that comes from moving beyond the roles of oppressor and victim to genuine partnership. Both our nations still have problems and divisions, but the life and lessons of Desmond Tutu show us how to overcome them.

I think if the US had continued the One America Initiative, with its grass-roots outreach, specific reports, and concrete policy recommendations, it would help us to reduce inequality, racial, ethnic and religious tensions, and the collective insecurity which has prevented us from enacting immigration reform and other steps consistent with our own mission. *E pluribus unum* (out of many, one). I try to advance these words through my foundation and the Clinton Global Initiative [CGI] as we focus on turning good intentions into positive results. In the interdependent world of the twenty-first century, it is essential that we embrace our common humanity.

Since his retirement from the church in 1996, Archbishop Tutu continues to inspire people around the world through his efforts to combat HIV/AIDS, reduce poverty and protect human rights, and extend the reach of peace. I love having him at the CGI, because he lifts our spirits, increases our understanding and pushes us

to do something, whatever we can, to leave a better world for our children. At his first CGI appearance, he said something especially remarkable for an archbishop. He said, "Religion is like a knife. If you use it to slice bread it's good. If you use it to slice your neighbour's arm off it's bad." That's what I admire about him. He is saying we shouldn't be judged just by our title, talents or possessions but by the fruits of our labour.

Archbishop Tutu has the ability to see our shared humanity in each person he meets, and to get us to do the same. He makes life interesting, effort noble, failure bearable, progress possible – all because he has brought his unique gifts to bear as our common humanity.

Above, left: Tutu with Nelson Mandela who is holding the Jules Rimet World Cup trophy at the FIFA headquarters in Zurich, 15 May 2004, the day after FIFA announced that the 2010 World Cup would be hosted by South Africa.
Above, right: With President Clinton in the Oval Office of the White House, May 1993.

SHARON GELMAN

In 1979, I was living in Washington, taking a weekly art class at the Smithsonian with my father. We were driving there one night and he said something in an off-the-cuff way about Bishop Tutu. I'd never heard that name before. I said, "Who's he? Is he friends with Rabbi Tap Shoes?" I thought he was making up a character with a cute name. He said, "No, no ... He's a leader of the anti-apartheid movement." I was embarrassed that I was so ignorant so I decided to find out about this Bishop Tutu and I started learning about a heroic, courageous, truth-telling man.

The first time I saw him was about a decade later at the University of California in Los Angeles. And he was all those things I'd read: brave, noble, articulate, wise. Yet he was also impish and adorable, jumping around the stage like a holy rascal. I was a young activist in

my twenties who wanted to change the world. I already knew enough about myself to know I would never become like Nelson Mandela – he's tall and dignified, restrained and powerful.

But I remember seeing Desmond Tutu and thinking about being an activist, thinking about who I was and who I wanted to become. He was so warm and goofy and funny. I thought, "Oh, maybe I can be like him!" He was just so accessible and human. I thought maybe I could be a leader if you're allowed to be silly and goofy ... and short.

He was also electrifying. I remember sitting there electrified. I was already involved in the anti-apartheid movement, and being in the presence of someone who was doing the real work was just so thrilling. But at the same time, because he was so human and milanos, he just knocked himself off of any pedestal I tried to put him on in my head. One of the gifts of someone like that – one of the gifts and one of the challenges – is that then you have to think, "Well, if he can do those things, then I also have to try and do those things. I have to find the courage to stand up and be brave and be truthful and forgiving and not see the people on the other side as enemies. I have to try and live this too."

The first time I began to get to know him was when we hosted him in 1999. We produced this big event called Jabulani, a celebration of the tenth anniversary of Artists for a New South Africa's [ANSA] existence and the fifth anniversary of South Africa's freedom. He was our keynote speaker and he was everything that I hoped he would be but even more than I could have imagined. A writer from the *Los Angeles Times* wrote that if Desmond Tutu ever wants to quit the God business, he could definitely have a career doing stand-up. It's true: he has the best sense of humour.

The theatre was full of renowned people from the entertainment community: actors and musicians. Many of the people sitting in the audience were as famous as the ones who were performing.

We'd put together a children's dance troupe and spent a month teaching them the *toyi-toyi* and what it meant: how the youth in South Africa danced and sang when they protested apartheid. The group included activists' children and children who were activists themselves. It also included the children of celebrities – Denzel Washington and Samuel L. Jackson and Alfre Woodard – and kids from gang-prevention groups and the inner-city. These kids spent a month together learning and dancing. And we invited all of their parents that night, from Pauletta and Denzel Washington to parents who had never been to that kind of show before. We also invited one hundred people living with HIV and AIDS to come as our guests. So the audience was this big, wonderful swathe of humanity: black and white, young and old, rich and poor, famous and unheard of. The crowd represented the equality we were talking about and what South Africa had been fighting for.

Alfre performed an extraordinarily beautiful rendition of a Don Mattera poem: "This land, this whole land, must be free, shall be free." No description can do her performance justice. And in the stanzas that call out the names of African heroes, we added the names of many of the heroes we'd worked with: "This is Ahmed Kathrada's land and Albertina Sisulu's land. This is Desmond Tutu's land." And at the very end, Alfre said, "And this is Hugh Masekela's land!" The curtain shot up and Hugh and his band were there, playing

Bring Back Nelson Mandela". The Arch, who was sitting in the front row, let out a loud whoop and hopped out of his seat and started dancing up and down the aisles. He was pulling people out of their seats to join him. It was so joyous and he made it more joyous because that's just the kind of person he is.

At one point later that night we lost him. I found him backstage with the kids who had danced the *toyi-toyi*. He had hugged and kissed every one of those children, every single one of them.

It was a beautiful night. There were actors performing poetry and theatre pieces: Samuel L. Jackson, Sidney Poitier, Julia Ormond, Blair Underwood, Mary Steenburgen, Ted Danson and many more. And gifted musicians like Stevie Wonder and Joan Baez, who sang "Biko", played. It was just incredible but the Arch took it to a whole other level. He stood on that stage and made us laugh and then made us cry. He acknowledged everyone, thanking us as if we'd all hung up the stars and the moon and freed South Africa and then baked a really great cake. He got everyone to move their arms back and forth above their heads, saying "We are all here together, black and white together", and the room really was that. I remember looking up and there were people standing on their seats, not just in front of their seats but actually on their seats, waving their arms along with him. We were artists and activists and common folk and rich folk and every folk. Folk in power and folk without power and, in that moment, I think everyone there truly believed that we could build a freer and more equal and better world. It was transcendent.

The thing about Desmond Tutu is that he speaks the truth so well you can really hear him. He gets into your heart and awakens that truth in you. Whenever I listen to him talk, I feel a deep part of me, the best part of me, wake up and come out. He acts like he expects everyone to be as loving as he is, and so who are we to disagree?

I first met Mama Leah in South Africa in 1994. I was in Cape Town at the Parliament buildings for the opening of an exhibit of fine art against apartheid that had been created by artists from all around the world. I was awestruck, thinking, "Oh my God, I'm in Parliament and it's now run by Nelson Mandela and ex-prisoners and even activists who used to sleep on my floor. It was very moving and exciting. I was talking with a group of women and one of them said something about, "Oh my husband!" And I said, "I don't know who your husband is. Who's your husband?" She said, "He's the only man at this party wearing a pink dress." And I just fell in love with her. I thought, "No wonder he's main-

Above: With Leah in New York, 16 October 1984.

tained such fabulous humility and sweetness. He's got a strong partner who, if he ever got full of himself, would keep him in line." She was loving and yet you could just tell that she was not going to be impressed by the whole shebang that accompanies being a global hero. She was also incredibly funny and warm and down-to-earth, like he is.

For Tutu's seventy-fifth birthday, we produced a remarkable event with the Arch in Los Angeles and then we led a delegation of some of ANSA's core supporters to South Africa to visit our programmes and attend his party there. About thirty of us went: Carlos Santana, Deborah Santana, Samuel L. Jackson, LaTanya Richardson, Alfre Woodard, Roderick Spencer, C. C. H. Pounder, Jurnee Smollett and family and friends. There we were, in Johannesburg, at this huge birthday party, sitting in a room with the Arch and Nelson Mandela and Ahmed Kathrada and Cheryl Carolus and Cyril Ramaphosa and Barbara Hogan, a whole pantheon of heroes and the who's who of South Africa. At that time, Mr Mandela was doing very little in public and it was so intensely meaningful to be in a room with both the Arch and him. He looked very dapper and he said to the Arch "I've come to officially welcome you into a very exclusive club: the club of old men." And then he chided him in this very loving, familiar way: "Now you better start acting like a proper old man. No more jumping around laughing all the time." And they laughed and the Arch clapped his hands and we all laughed. It was such a legendary moment, I felt as if I was in Camelot.

I am cognisant of how privileged we've been to witness these profound times in history, this powerful movement and the birth of a nation. This all will be remembered as history, but I think it also will become a legend: "There once was a country on the very southern tip of Africa, the most racially oppressed place in all the world. But then the people rose up and their leader came forth from prison to become the president. And a new democracy was born with the most progressive constitution in the world and the people chose a path of reconciliation over revenge." It really is the stuff of myth and legend, yet it is so real. These are very real human beings who sacrificed so much and suffered such enormous losses to bring this transformation about. And we've been able to stand among them, to get to know them and work alongside them, helping and watching history unfold. It has been a powerful, humbling, sacred and inebriating experience and, through it all, I have come to realise the most challenging and rewarding part is to try and follow the example of Desmond Tutu: to try to walk through the world full of courage and joy and love.

DEBORAH SANTANA

The wondrous quality about the Arch is when he walks into a room it's as if a hundred champagne bottles have been opened, the corks are let loose and the bubbles are flowing. His effervescence and his joy take over any space with a fierce love for all of life. One of the things that I most respect is that he walks through life with complete humility not because he's trying to be humble, but because he knows that we are all humans here together. Spending time with him has reinforced what I believe we humans should be like.

I feel like the Arch is my dad. I lost my dad in 2000 and it has been wonderful to have someone come into my life who holds a great mantle of peace and generosity of spirit, someone who acts as though I'm his daughter also.

During a difficult time in my life, Sharon [Gelman, executive director of Artists for a New South Africa] and I attended an event at Grace Cathedral where the Arch was being honoured with the International Gay and Lesbian Human Rights Commission's Outspoken Award. Even with the large crowd pushing to speak with him, he took the time to ask me how I was doing. He knew I was suffering in my spirit and his kind words comforted me.

I named my foundation "Do A Little" after a quote I read in *Guideposts* magazine attributed to the Arch. "Do your little bit of good where you are. It's those little bits of good put together that will overwhelm the world." "Do A Little" affirms my belief that each of us has a significant role to play in healing our universe. I want to make sure people know we do not need to have thousands upon thousands of dollars to produce an effective change in the global consciousness, or to help eradicate poverty, or to inspire someone to lift their chin up and know that you care about them. Each of us can do something. I'm so proud every time someone asks me why I named my non-profit "Do A Little" and I can say that this is something the Arch said.

In 2003, Carlos and I were fortunate to be able to donate the proceeds from a tour to start the Amandla AIDS Fund with ANSA [Artists for a New South Africa]. We asked the Arch to be the honorary chair, knowing that his presence in administration and management of the fund would ensure that every penny would go exactly where it was intended. We met in the dining-room of the Peninsula Hotel to talk a little bit before the press conference to announce the fund. In walked the bubbly Arch carrying a bright blue plastic pillow. He had had his prostate surgery not too long before, and he needed the pillow for comfort. I was struck by his modesty to carry this blue pillow, set it on his chair and sit down as if he didn't have a care about such an insignificant act. It was a great man doing something very ordinary.

During our breakfast, he spoke about how South Africa and the world would be better places if more women leaders held positions of authority in the governments and were listened to for their wise, integrated wisdom. With his amazing insights in my heart, we went into the press conference. He talked about children with HIV/AIDS and the work to be done to make antiretroviral medicines available for everyone. It seemed that as he was talking, the klieg lights of the press dimmed, and his light shone. It's true – after the press conference the press was silent and stunned, and then gave him a standing ovation.

BLAIR UNDERWOOD

My introduction to Artists for a New South Africa [ANSA] came through Alfre Woodard. It was my introduction to this world of South Africa and what was happening there. It was through her I learned about Nelson Mandela and Archbishop Desmond Tutu and the work that was being done in South Africa. I have always been so inspired by these leaders. I think one of the reasons I was so open to what Alfre had presented to me was that I had just finished doing a film. It was a TV movie of the week for NBC, where I played a character named James Chaney. So, I had taken this journey in my mind, in my spirit, of James Chaney and our civil rights movement. And, truly, what was happening in South Africa in 1989–90 was very similar in many ways to what was happening in the United States in the 1960s. What I saw in Archbishop Tutu and Nelson Mandela at that time was the very palpable, very real, very relevant, very current struggle of civil rights and also of life and death. I have always been, and will always continue to be, inspired by that. I got to questioning how could a human being do that? How could a human being still be loving, still be caring, still be empathetic? So I went on this path to learn more about them. Of course, in the archbishop's case, you understand he is a man of God, so it starts there.

Above, left: With the "Tutu Tester", a mobile unit that tests people for diabetes, obesity and HIV/AIDS, Cape Town, 22 October 2009. Above, right: With Blair Underwood and LaTanya Richardson at Artists for a New South Africa's tenth anniversary celebration (Jabulani), Los Angeles, 1999.

May 24, 1999 was ANSA's ten-year anniversary and we had a big event called Jabulani (be joyful), in celebration of those ten years. Archbishop Desmond Tutu was there that evening and, as you can imagine, it was loud. It was raucous. It was poignant. It was just great fun. I had the opportunity to meet him that evening at the after-party. There are certain human beings who you can only hope and pray to be as open, as selfless, as giving as they are. He is way up there in my eyes. It was incredibly humbling to make his acquaintance and to meet him. I just remember him coming up to say hello. There is a picture that is one of my favourite pictures that shows him putting his hands on my face and smiling. I don't remember what he even said at the moment, because I was just glazed over in regard and respect. It was just a wonderful moment.

Anyone who is conscientious aspires to do the right thing and treat people right and live a good life. When you meet those people who have accomplished that in the face of so much adversity, it's tremendous.

What surprised me most in meeting Archbishop Desmond Tutu was his sense of humour. What surprised me was his humanity. He's filled with joy. He's filled with incredible joy. When you mention his name, the first thing people do is smile. It's because of the joy that he possesses. It emanates from him and it's reflected in the people who speak and interact and engage with him. An ancient tradition says God tolerates humanity despite our many transgressions. He does that by making sure that at any given time there are thirty-six souls who, without knowing they have made this deal, redeem mankind. When I think of the bishop, I think of him as one of those thirty-six.

He is so brilliant and I love listening to him speak because he is always poetic. But he's speaking from experience, and that is much more than poetry. His is a life well lived and hard fought. I'm always just blown away by knowing his history and seeing that sense of love and that sense of godliness, the sense of joy. I want to be like that when I grow up.

LATANYA RICHARDSON AND SAMUEL L. JACKSON

LaTanya: Our friend, Alfre Woodard, had asked us to become a part of Artists for a New South Africa [ANSA]. By this time apartheid had been abolished. We had moved from Georgia to New York to California. When we got to California and Alfre presented me with this opportunity, I started to involve myself in the organisation. I really had no thoughts of meeting Desmond Tutu or Nelson Mandela or any of the other iconic architects

[of the new South Africa] like Ahmed Kathrada, whom I came to meet. It's an overwhelming feeling to know that so many of the people who changed the world can actually be in your sphere, let alone be in your presence. And to meet them, and have them say your name, is an overwhelming experience. When I met the Archbishop I could barely speak. I was so overjoyed I wanted to jump up and down and laugh.

Above: Tutu with performing artists Idrissa Diop (far left), Naomi Striemer (second from right) and Shawn King (far right) at the launch of the Internet site www.welovefreemusic.com in conjunction with SOS Records, New York, 6 May 2008.

We had Jabulani, an event that we did to raise money for ANSA. And he was dancing. And, honest, that's not what we're used to in this country. Really, we're not used to our icons just being a part of everyone else. They're always set apart. I think that night we tried to set him apart but he was like, "Oh no! Come along, come along!" And he pulled us all in to dance. It's like his spirit. He pulls you in and you just want to work for him. You want to help make the vision plain. You just want to do it his way. You trust him, because here's something about what he says and how he says it, so that at the end of the day you know you can trust him. You know that he hasn't led you down a wrong path.

Samuel: This is the difference between him and any other politician-type person that you can imagine. There's believability in the Arch. There's a familiarity with the Arch. I honestly can't remember when I didn't know him. Once you meet him, it's hard to imagine ever not knowing him. Sure, I meet a lot of people. Sometimes

I'm kind of like, "Yeah, oh yeah. I remember you." But to be overwhelmed by a person's personality, for me, it's pretty difficult. But I was infected by his joy. You meet him and he makes you feel like you've been talking together all your life. He talks to you in a way that lets you know that he's been through what you've been through, or lived in the same situation you've lived in.

LaTanya: And that he understands.

Samuel: Yeah, and that he totally understands. The politicians and our elected officials, whoever they are, he's not like them. He's not some person that's turning away from you. He's in you and he's of you.

We saw him at the airport in London last year. We were just there and I heard the laugh. I knew the laugh before I saw the face. And I just turned around and I said something silly like, "ABDT" and he went "Sam-u-el!" and just laughed. And he was dead tired and we could see that.

LaTanya: He was tired.

Samuel: And you could see that.

LaTanya: He was coming from the Jimmy Carter conference that he does with the heads of state.

Samuel: The Elders.

LaTanya: Yes.

Samuel: And he was dead tired and we could see it but all of a sudden he said, "Come, come! We must eat. Let's talk!" We had three hours to kill. He was planning to sleep, because he had six hours to kill. But we went and ate at the lounge at British Air. We talked and laughed. And then we came back out and we put him down in a chair and covered him up and left him to sleep. And it was like, "All right Uncle Desmond, go to sleep. Thanks for talking to us and brightening our day." Look whom we made it to, we made it to the Arch! And we were like that, you know. And we don't get like that about people. But that's who he is and he is an integral part of the fabric of us as African people. That's what we should be. That's what we could be. That's what we are.

LaTanya: Like to be.

Samuel: He is that person that we should be, because he's a pure example of anti-hate. If we could all look at each other and gather each other together and have a healthy conversation that's about what's good and what's right about us as people; about how we are all the same, instead of what's different and what's wrong. Let's figure out what we all do believe in and make that work. It doesn't have to be a love fest. It just has to have the joy of life that he has, that he gives you when he sees you. It makes you say, "Aren't you glad you woke up today? Aren't you glad you're in this moment today?"

LaTanya: He really does believe it. He says it because he believes that this is a moral universe. He really does believe that in the end good will triumph. He's not just giving it lip service. We can't thank his family enough, because we all embrace him so. But only because he makes you feel as though his arms are wide open to you. So we just take him as if he's ours. Thanks to his family for allowing him such breadth and such space. We want to claim him. I think that if he, if he ran all of our countries ...

You know what? I want him to retire, I really do. I think he should go and do whatever he wants to do. If he wants to sit outside by the ocean and fan himself, what-ever, do nothing. He's done enough. He continues to be the person that we all look to for spiritual guidance too.

Samuel: If he is supposed to retire, he has a right to do just what you said, to sit by the ocean and fan. He doesn't have to do anything. He's done what he needs to do. If you can end up in his orbit, you'll be all the better for it wherever you are. My life is just better because I came into contact with him.

LaTanya: I know mine is. I know I'm different. I know I'm different.

Samuel: I'm glad your sister came into contact with him. Your sister, Deborah, is like your average person, you know, in America. I mean, he transformed her in a very real kind of way. You wish you could take what he has and put it in a bottle and open it up in the middle of this country and just let it run out so people could look to the person next to them and go, "We're not different. We're just human beings who need to do what we need to do."

LaTanya: In the face of everything that is negative that happens in the world, I promise you that he is my touchstone for things that can occur that are correct, and for the correct thing to do. What would he do? What would he say? What's he already said? I can follow that.

Samuel: Right. We get angry every day. We look at something and get angry. But then we just stop and say, "Wait." And the words, the writings, just being in the presence of the Arch, allow you to say, "Wait, I don't need to be angry with this person. I don't need to hate these people." Once you've met him, you've been blessed. And, like I said ...

LaTanya: I love him.

Samuel: We're some pretty jaded people in an interesting sort of way. But ...

LaTanya: I'm not jaded.

Samuel: ... I walk into a room and he looks at me and says, "Sam." It makes me feel like the most privileged person in the world.

ALFRE WOODARD

He is one of those people that you feel you've known forever. I feel that I have known him since I was a child. That's impossible, but I think it's because of a quality that the Arch has that has no timeline. He's a man that you actually believe is living in the middle of eternity.

I used to think that the struggle was very serious. You struggled and it was hard and it was terrible. You had to have your game face on, because what you were struggling against was so unfathomably immoral that it required a kind of seriousness and sternness.

I think the first time I ever saw the Arch, and in every encounter that I have had with him since, I just immediately became joyful and exuberant. He puts into action the idea that you struggle joyfully because you know you're on the side of good and truth. There is no reason to be down about it and you don't have to posture about it.

The Arch demonstrates that when you are standing for what's right, you've already got freedom. It's a privilege to be in your right mind and have the wherewithal and the clarity to know what needs to be taken down and what needs to be built up. And that's great.

More than once I have heard friends and comrades of the Arch laughingly tell this story: "There was one time in Cape Town when we were getting ready to march. We were all very scared and serious. We thought we were all going to get shot by the police and die. People were getting arrested. We didn't know whether we would get thrown in jail or disappear. We were terrified. Suddenly the Arch turned around and pointed down at his feet and said, "Look at my new Tekkies!" He was showing us his bright, new, white sneakers. We all cracked up!"

That's something that we say about South Africans. As they have waged their struggle for liberation, there have been very sober moments and proper decorum, but there was always celebration at the same time. When I see him, he seems like the personification of "rejoice!" When I look at him it's like, "Yes, that's 'rejoice' standing right there!" And even in those moments when he does get pointedly direct and serious, there isn't anything closed off about it. It's just factual, pragmatic.

It's so interesting, because spirituality is very accessible, it's practical. Everybody has it, everybody. With a lot of other clerical leaders it's almost as if they demonstrate their religiosity by distance. I call him "the Arch" because I never think of him as "the archbishop". I don't know him in a "religious" context – I have studied religion and I have joined religions – but I've been taken deeper as a spiritual person by my interactions with him. He's a demonstration of how it is impossible to usurp any person's godliness. He tells us we are all equal children of God and God looks on us all in the same way. That gives you power and that power becomes political. He takes it right out of the scriptures into everyday life. There is not a big jump from standing up before the apartheid government and calling them to task, to the true gospel of the prophet Jesus. It is the radical doctrine of the gospel of love and he lives it! That's what I think he does. He demonstrates that you get to make that decision every day, every moment. He brings active holiness to everybody. It has to demonstrate that good has all the power, has the only power. It has to shout down evil.

One of the great things is that, in any encounter that you have with him, you feel his light and it ignites a light in you as well. So he is a very special man, because he makes everybody see their own light. Working with him, especially in terms of sociopolitical things, you understand that the light can't be put out. It can never be put out and you are in charge of it. I spent a lot of time as a Catholic. You go to ask a priest for a blessing or you go to other churches and the person lays a hand on you or on your head. Whenever you have an encounter with the Arch you just feel like the blessing comes because he is one of those places that God shines through. The validation when he looks at you, lets you know that a blessing is there. And a blessing is something that we must pass around. I've never encountered a person whose path it is to be a spiritual leader ever give so much power to people. He gives it directly to people. It doesn't matter who you are, what your faith, even if you don't have any, you know he does that. He empowers but from a spiritual aspect, just in terms of his joy. But it's revolutionary, because he's empowering people's social consciousness and he's empowering them to take action.

Right before the Jabulani fund-raising event [for Artists for a New South Africa (ANSA)] we heard that he was ill. He had been given a diagnosis of cancer. We were alarmed. But, as he is wont to do, he still said, "I'm gonna come. I will be at the Jabulani." We were told that he was really tired. He was unwell. We expected that he was going to be really down. Our first thought was, "He is the archbishop. Take care of him." A lot of people around here had never met him. They had read things he said. They expected to be genuflecting to Archbishop Tutu. So he came. We wanted to make it as easy as possible for him.

Above: Tutu addresses a press conference at a United Nations' conference on racism, Durban, South Africa, 5 September 2001.

He was sitting [at the dinner] in the Wiltern and as soon as Hugh Masekela struck up, he hopped up! He hopped up and started running up and down the front of the stage just boogieing! And, of course, people were astonished. Then they were just giggling. First of all, they had never seen an archbishop, or any kind of bishop, dancing like that. Then there were those of us We were like, "Stop him! Stop him!" What's interesting is that the only people who didn't think it was unusual were the children. The young people, the teenagers just thought it was fabulous. I will forever remember that. Just by being who he is, by being how he is, he gives everybody else possibility. I will always remember and cherish that experience.

Above: Tutu on stage at the FIFA World Cup Kick-off Celebration Concert at Orlando Stadium, Soweto, Johannesburg, 10 June 2010.

Previous page: At the inaugural One Young World Summit, London, 8 February 2010.

NONTOMBI NAOMI TUTU

I remember my dad playing soccer. It's so weird now, that I remember that he was very sporty. He played cricket for fun but I remember, particularly when we moved back to Alice, that he played soccer with the theological seminary staff and students. His nickname was "the Wizard". I remember going to watch the soccer matches. I never asked where he got the name; I decided that my dad had magic footwork and magic skills – that's why everybody called him the Wizard.

TREVOR THAMSANQA TUTU

I remember he took me with him to watch England play Portugal in the 1966 World Cup semifinal. How he managed to get tickets I have never to this day understood, because they were like rare jewels. But he got us tickets and we sat right behind the goal. It was fantastic for me. The England side was made up of players, three or four of whom were my favourites because they played for West Ham: Bobby Moore, Geoff Hurst, Martin Peters and I can't remember the other one.

I can always remember going to the cricket with him, my mother making sandwiches so that we could afford going to the Oval. I can remember going to Lord's to watch the great West Indies cricket team playing their test games. My father is a very enthusiastic spectator. He kicks the ball for players and tackles the opposition when it's rugby. He takes the catches in cricket and thinks every kind of driver is the most beautiful he has ever seen. He is a very enthusiastic spectator. A friend of mine remarked that he used to think that I was a crazy spectator but now that he's seen my father he's realised that it was purely hereditary.

RICHARD GOLDSTONE

Desmond and I really became friendly watching cricket at Newlands. We were both invited by the South African Cricket Union. That was when he was archbishop. I must tell you one incident that occurs to me. At one of the cricket games at Newlands, it was international and we were playing against Australia or England. The president of the South African Cricket Union came up to me at the tea adjournment. He said that SABC [South African Broadcasting Corporation] had suggested it would be a good thing and make good television if he were to lead Archbishop Tutu around the ground at lunchtime. He asked for my advice on the advisability of his doing so. I was a bit terrified at the thought: 95 per cent of the forty thousand people were white South Africans, and this was before 1994. But I said if security was not a problem then I would leave the decision to Archbishop Tutu. They said that security didn't seem to be a problem. In the end, the president of the union led him around the ground at Newlands. He got a standing ovation. Every person in that stadium stood to applaud him. That really was an amazing sight.

BILL COSBY

What struck me about him when I first met him was that he sounded like Barry Fitzgerald, the Irish actor. I've never been close to a black person who was really rolling 'r's and wasn't speaking Spanish. I had to really back off a bit, as a comedian, to keep from highlighting that kind of thing. And then it was exciting that, while at the dinner table, we found out that his favourite desert was ice cream and his favourite flavour was rum raisin. I just never let him forget it. For years, my wife and I have always wanted to receive in our home those who are agents of change. Some of it is so that our children will be able to say, "Yes I saw and heard, etc. etc." Because we want our children to have a part of it all. And what has struck me so wonderfully about Desmond Tutu – and it is parallel and perpendicular to Mandela and those men who were on the island, Robben Island, something that I've always seen and admired, and he had it. Tutu had it, and it was something that I cannot understand in human behaviour, period. It is front-line people having the ability to have a sense of humour. It's not a sense of humour that people write and put in plays. It's a sense of humour about seeing death. It's a sense of humour about seeing the oppressor and the stupidity of it all. He is able to tell the story and laugh.

I don't know how many great, great, great leaders, on purpose, can get up and actually be funny, and he can.

RICKY RICHARDSON

I've watched him in quite difficult situations. He launched the global e-health programme in Geneva at the World Health Assembly. There were quite a lot of cynics in the room. By the time that he had spoken to them for five minutes, or ten minutes, they were all on board. You could have heard a pin drop. He has this extraordinary capacity of persuasion through conviction, because his own conviction shines through. He carries his audience, even if, to begin with, they're doubting Thomases.

It's not often that one can say that one knows someone who has changed history in our time.

JEFFREY ARCHER

I first heard of Desmond Tutu when I was in South Africa some thirty years ago. I was there for a book I'd written called *Kane and Abel*. I was very nearly thrown out of South Africa for saying how much I disapproved of the regime. When I came back to England, I heard him address a gathering at Southwark Cathedral. It was absolutely packed out. Having been a member of Parliament, oratory is very important to me and he is a most unusual speaker. He does not rely on notes, or he doesn't appear to. He darts from subject to subject, feeling to feeling, with immense passion. And it's the passion that you can't resist. If you took the words just as they were spoken, they would not have the same power. But because the man has such clear passion, his words struck me tremendously.

His voice is wonderful – I mean, if you hear it, you know straightaway who it is, and that's very rare. This is true of some actors and a lot of interesting people I know: I can tell you who they are, even with my eyes closed; you just know their voice straightaway. But his voice is almost as well known as his face. If you hear that voice on the radio you go, "Oh, Archbishop Tutu." It has a sort of sing-song quality and a sincerity about it you can't miss.

I thank God that he was put on earth. I think Mandela played an amazing role and is a giant of history, but Archbishop Tutu isn't far behind. He's a great man on several levels. I think his strength – that so few of us ever master if we acquire fame or fortune or whatever it might be – is remaining simple. He is, above all, a simple man. And that, funnily enough, is his strength. He's not a king or a great sportsman. He's this simple man, like Mother Teresa, who sort of rides above we normal mortals.

JACKSON BROWNE

To me, Father is a figure that has been a beacon to people all round the world. He was so visible. He was able to transmit the struggle of South Africa around the entire world. His moral standing was so unquestionably sound. His sense of humour and his humanity also allowed people into the struggles. It gave people a face and a person to find. This incredibly courageous person, often dressed in scarlet, was in the middle of this incredibly dangerous conflict. With the violence going on all around him, he held the moral centre. It was stunning, stunning really. It's impossible to convey to him the kind of impact that he had.

The forces arrayed against the people of South Africa preserved apartheid by marginalising people. They called them the enemies of society. They said that to destroy property was the same thing as destroying people's lives. So a person like Desmond Tutu – well, there is no other person like Desmond Tutu – from the righteous centre of Christendom was able to speak and to communicate and to remind people of their own humanity.

There is a handful of white South Africans who stood arm in arm with Archbishop Tutu. It always brought me to tears to know that there were people who took the courageous stand to do the right thing in spite of incredible danger to themselves.

I've had the pleasure of seeing him address a room full of supporters after the triumph of having ended apartheid. There was such an outpouring of love and gratitude and friendship. He rekindled the spark, the flame that to this day has them continuing to do the work that he inspired them to do.

Every time he is interviewed he is so funny that you feel this intimacy with him that you really don't have. When I got to meet him, I wanted to say something silly like, "You know you put a spell on me." I wasn't referring only to that night and what he had to say to the people assembled, but also the accumulated glimpses of him. He never forgets to let us see him, the human being.

BOB GELDOF

The apartheid regime in South Africa was abysmally evil and wrong; and therefore the anti-apartheid struggle, while concretely political for its combatants, was equally glaringly, and more powerfully and truthfully, a moral fight. Archbishop Tutu framed that empirical political fight with the necessary moral voice, authority and perspective that extended from his country at the tip of the African continent to encompass a far wider audience and argument about humanity. That is his great, enduring legacy.

The Dalai Lama says, "It is more important to be a good person than a spiritual person." Arch is both. He is, quite clearly, an exceptionally good person. He is also a spiritual person. Perhaps it is his spirituality that allowed him to speak with a heightened rhetoric that would have seemed out of place, and would simply not be allowed, to a politician. He then exemplified this with a concrete example of his faith and his morality by stepping, at great danger to his own person, into the midst of the Sharpeville riots. It is this combination of moral conviction and fearless bravery that made him so heroic to the great global public – and is what inspired me.

When I was thirteen, my friend and I organised the anti-apartheid movement in our area of South Dublin. My school was a big rugby school. In fact, it was the big rugby school in Ireland and our main job was to supply the Irish rugby team with players. Rugby is a huge sport in Ireland. So when the South African team, the Springboks, came over, my friends were part of the group that tried to organise a boycott of the games. Even back then it was Tutu's voice we would quote, and now today in this modern, changed world, he is still making an impact on young people.

In fact, Tutu is accepted by young people everywhere, from all walks of life. When he talks to them, they

Above: With Bob Geldof at the One Young World Summit, London, 8 February 2010.

love it; they listen and they want more. He is as valid and valuable to them as are any of their other heroes in popular culture. That's an extraordinary accomplishment. I've seen the U2 tour a couple of times and there is a point at which Tutu appears on the big screen with a message, from the ONE Campaign [against extreme poverty and preventable diseases], of positivity about modern Africa. When his on-screen self finishes speaking, the crowd erupts with cheering and applause, because, actually, he is a bigger star than the people on that stage. He is, you see, like all the great preachers, a consummate showman, and why not? The pulpit is after all a stage or it is nothing. Do you want people bored and leaving the church or do you want them coming back next week? You want them coming back. But the point with Desmond, of course, is that offstage the show must continue. It must be exhausting for him, and while I have seen him weary and worn out, he will not stop, he will not flag. The Arch speaks way above the overwhelming ruckus of noisome and useless political sterility. And, crucially, he tells you what he expects of you, and because of who he is and what he represents, you really, genuinely do not want to let this man down.

Historically, he reminds me of Thomas à Becket, England's iconoclastic twelfth-century archbishop of whom King Henry II despairingly roared: "Will no one rid me of this turbulent priest?" For those in power, Arch is a complete pain in the arse; he is our "turbulent priest". He calls it as he sees it and he never shuts up. I mean, I'm Irish and we never shut up, but we're sort of allowed to keep going. But he operates on a whole other level of irritating power because his is such an unassailable position. The title "archbishop" alone means he speaks on behalf of something greater. Politics is easy: it's left or right. The moral sense is above those often spurious and meaningless distinctions, and he speaks to that. He speaks of, and to, every single human. It's almost impossible to attack that, never mind put it in prison. It would be ruinous, as it was when King Henry II killed his archbishop. Becket, too, spoke out against the corruption and great iniquities of his time, and nothing would silence him. The difference is that Thomas looks quite tall and Desmond Tutu is this small, feisty fellow. And he never stops laughing. I'm never quite sure if he's laughing out of the sheer joy of living or at the whole mad absurdity of it all. I suspect both.

He is the smallest giant I've ever met. The fact that he is a little, feisty man is actually part of the whole Tutu shtick. And being a great showman he knows how to use whatever he's got to put over what he's got to say. This is shtick. You want to go up and embrace him because he has embraced you with his language and his laughter. He has this amazing trick he learned a long time ago that's specifically his: namely, giggling at the absurdity of position. Though proud and aware of its value, he constantly makes light of his esteemed position within the church hierarchy, for example, and yet his reach goes far beyond his constituency in Cape Town to the entire world. No one – and I really mean that – nobody can or would gainsay him, whether it's a pope, president, king, despot or tyrant. He is a tiny

joyful bubble of life.

I've seen him with Leah, his wife, and you see the tolerance she must need. It reminds me of the expression "Behind every great man is a surprised woman". She tolerates and loves this impish character because I suspect only she must see the private exhaustion and fear that surely must be this man's constant private companions. Leah loves the complex, contradictory figure that we don't see because she understands it is that complexity, and the struggle it involves, that gives us the public person that we love too, but in a wholly different way.

The first time I met him was in the early 1990s, when I interviewed Madiba [Nelson Mandela], Buthelezi, De Klerk and the Boss [Tutu]. He was such an overwhelmingly interesting man. We just spent the afternoon chatting. Of course I was a bit freaked out in his presence, but you must remember that since I was a boy I've been reading and watching this man. He had no idea who I was, but completely accepted that I was interested and he didn't patronise me, which a lot of

people in those days tended to do. I've seen him many times since and it's incredible to me how I have ended up being a friend of this amazing man. I can honestly say it continues to be one of the great privileges of my life.

I think the nicest time I had with him was in Galway on the west coast of Ireland. We spent a long time together, talking very seriously about Africa. To spend a night talking with Desmond is like spending a night in the park with one of your friends. He talks and tells great stories that I could sit and listen to for hours. He's a great raconteur, like the Irish are, laughing at his own jokes, which the Irish always do, but all the while he's giving you invaluable insights into Africa and Man. I love his company and it's easy to forget that you are in the company of one of the great figures of our age. That's the singular pleasure. The guy may know that he's going down in history but I don't think he cares. He's living absolutely in this moment. He's not particularly interested in the past. He is living now and articulating a vision of the future that, for all our sakes, one hopes is correct.

Left: Tutu announces he will retire after his seventy-ninth birthday in October 2010, 22 July 2010.

QUINCY JONES

I feel I've known him all my life, him and Madiba [Nelson Mandela]. He took over very graciously while Madiba was incarcerated. I'll never forget the grace with which he held the position and the grace with which he stepped aside when Madiba got out. It touched me so much, because you know how politics works. They had none of that.

The man is a 360 human being. That's what I love about him. He doesn't need to flaunt his ego. He knows who he is. He's my favourite kind of human being 360 – a sense of humour, a sense of leadership, a sense of fairness.

That's the way God planned it: for a man to have that kind of humility and still have that kind of authority and the confidence of knowing who he is. He's one of my true heroes. He is the totality of what a human being should be.

HARRY BELAFONTE

One day I got a letter from my friends, Arthur and Mathilde Krim, saying that a wonderful man from South Africa was coming here for a short visit and they would love it if I would be able to come to dinner and be part of the group. They felt that this individual had important things to tell us as Americans and to inform us in some really significant way and in some great detail about what was going on in South Africa, not only from the point of view of a powerful religious voice but also from the point of view of a citizen and from the point of view of an African. I had already heard of Desmond Tutu – I think many of us had – but the opportunity to meet him personally and to get to hear him speak was an opportunity that only death could deny me.

And when I went to my friends' house I went prepared for a very sober, conservative social evening; I went prepared to sit in some kind of ceremonial, sacred gathering. I mean, you're meeting a man who was not only revered and respected but he's a sacred man – his aura preceded him.

When I walked into the room: "Ahhaa! So you're Harry!" And this force leapt out of the seat and came towards me and gave me an embrace. I was kind of just caught off guard. I didn't know what to do – hug or lick him or what to do. Here was this armful of energy and delight and such power for life. I said, "Oh my God!"

And I knew one thing when I saw him – not only while I was talking to him but at the end of that first meeting this is going to cost me dearly!

I said, "I will never be able to say no to this man – ever – on anything!"

The greatest expense so far? Sleep! My greatest expense has only been in my capacity to stay accessible whenever he called and I've gotten to where that isn't a big problem. But I have had calls from him on several occasions at odd hours – a conflict of time zone. But, of course, he, by example, keeps you attuned to how to serve well. So he not only becomes the activator of things, he also becomes the principal definition of how those things are done.

I was given an award at the Kennedy Center – the Kennedy Center Honours. It was quite filled with pomp and ceremony and celebrity and everything else. You're not permitted to say anything except to thank the crowd and sit in a box next to the president of the United States of America. At that time it was the Father Bush. When Desmond walked out on the stage to present me with the honours, I wept – I was absolutely blown away. And then I wanted to rush backstage to see him without stepping all over the president. By the time I got there, he was gone. "What do you mean he's gone?" "He got back on the plane to go back to South Africa." I said, "Desmond came all the way from South Africa for this moment and just had to go right back?" I was told "Yes!" What a generosity. He validated me in such remarkable ways.

He spoke in many places where he asked me to come and I would perform or sing a song or do things with him. Having said all of this, Archbishop Desmond Tutu is one of the mysteries in my life. I don't know why people of his cloth, of his fabric, of his generosity, of his

intellect, I don't know what made them pause at the crossroads of my life and say, "Come."

I was there to give him support. If advice was sought and I had the wherewithal to say something to contribute I would. I would try to influence Archbishop Tutu, to introduce him to people I thought he should meet or know. I thought a lot of people came to the table in great disguise – they were really of the devil – and did much of the devil's work. There were a lot of people who claimed to be friends who in fact were foe. In talking to Desmond I would say things that would just counsel him to be careful. I would say, "This is what I think. I'm not too sure this is the best way or this is the best person."

In the final analysis I found something in Desmond about this issue I'm talking about that was really quite fascinating. He was so deeply rooted in his own spiritual purpose and meaning that you hardly felt your counsel was necessary because his spiritual being transcended all that stuff. And I also felt a sense of some kind of spiritual immortality – not physical immortality. But I felt that he would walk into these dens of corruption and purify the evil-doers. He walked into places with a lot of money people, a lot of money people. These men did much to corrupt the freedom movement. They corrupted the goals of the revolution. These people who now come and give you airplanes and put fortunes at your disposal, yesterday were your mortal enemy – and still are your enemy. But they use you now to their advantage. And I think Desmond understood that we may all have a role to play but his role was to be the redeemer. He was to make room for redemption. Even though people came as evil-doers to destroy him and his platform and this image in their circle, I think he also felt that "I will win them over".

I think that the purpose of this mission is to go among the lepers, to go among those who are cursed, go among those who are most in need and do his thing. Well, you know, I'm not quite anointed that way. I saw a lot of guys who worked vigorously against the boycott, who were making a lot of money – a lot of money. They were black people and white people. When we had beat them at the gate, they then turned and slyly made their way into places where they found opportunity or willingness. And certainly Desmond became one of the figures of leadership that stepped over that line and said, "I will go among them." You have to hold your breath and ask, "Who will prevail in this struggle?"

I don't think I ever had as great a sense of privilege and an act of generosity quite as great as when Desmond Tutu invited me to preach in his church on Christmas Eve in Cape Town a couple of years ago, and he said, "You must come to the church and just come

Above: Tutu addresses the Challenge Future Peace Conference in Bochum, Germany, 30 June 2007. The conference was conceived to stimulate multicultural and interfaith dialogues and address global issues including initiatives to end poverty, promote social justice, strengthen children and women's rights and protect the environment.

to the pulpit and speak to us". And I was quite over-whelmed by the generosity and by Desmond himself. He challenged me in a very interesting way, because when he gave me the platform on that Christmas Eve night, from the pew to the pulpit was the longest walk in my life! Because what was upon me was: "What do you do with this moment? What do you say to this willing throng of people standing in the room?" (The church was packed.) And all I could do was to ask the peoples of Africa to pray for the souls of the people of America. And then I said: "We stood – many of us stood – by you in your struggle to end apartheid. We prayed with you. We fought with you. We died with you. And now we come humbled by the experience of this treaty. And now we come to beg you to help us and pray for us in this very dark moment in our lives with George W. Bush and where our nation was led astray." So I took this moment to say, "Pray for us. Help bring light to what we might be able to achieve if we can get past this very dangerous time."

So that was what I did. I think it worked. I didn't expect the reward to be quite that big! Not only do we see Bush get out but, my God, what you replaced him with – Barack Obama! That's what I get for asking those Africans to pray.

Every day, I experience joy, knowing that Desmond is in the world. I experience particular joy and particular privilege in knowing that I can pick up a phone and make a call and more often than not his voice will be at the other end when I'm seeking him. And that would be a voice that would be generous in whatever it is that we will discuss. There is nothing more to be desired, there's nothing more to need. That's an anointing in itself.

I was in Hollywood not too long ago and a very well-known actor – a black actor – said to me, "You have paid such a price. I couldn't do it. What you've given up, the hits you've taken, what you've done for justice."

And I said, "I have to accept what you're saying is a genuine concern for my well-being and what you perceive to be the sacrifices that I have made. But I have to look at another side of this coin. Let me tell you something: don't weep for me. I wake up every morning and I can get on the phone and talk to Nelson Mandela and Archbishop Desmond Tutu. You wake up every morning and talk to your agent and your lawyer and you count your money. And let me ask you something: in the life's journey, which one has the better deal?"

BONO

The first time I met Archbishop Tutu was with the band in South Africa. We had served in the anti-apartheid movement, been a part of Band Aid, the Sun City boycott, that kind of thing. We liked to think we were committed, but really we were a bunch of tourists. This was the first thing he taught us.

The lot of us – band members, managers, entourage – turned up at the archbishop's office in Cape Town, and he looked at us and said, "Let's bow our heads, shall we?" He was hushed in tone, but the simple statement spoke volumes. It said, very plainly: "You are stepping on our ground now. You may indeed be well-intentioned. You may or may not be believers. But you have to understand what we are trying to do here, and you must start with prayer and meditation." Having begun on that note, he told us about Truth and Reconciliation, which was why we had wanted to visit. When he finished, I had questions, but the archbishop had another agenda. "Now, look," he said, "there are a couple of people I would like you to meet. Will you come with me?" "Yes sir," we said.

He led us up the stairs to a large hall. It was filled with hundreds of people sitting and waiting for us it appeared. I looked nervously at the rest of the band, hoping I was not expected to speak. Well, I wasn't. The Arch smiled his smile and said to the crowd, "Here are U2 to sing for you."

Our very organised manager, Paul, seeing a total lack of any equipment (guitars, amps, the things that make a rock band rock) managed only to say, "You have got to be joking!" The Arch was not joking. "No, no," he replied. "Sing – you are singers, aren't you?"

So we sang, unprepared and unplugged. In a country where everyone I've ever met has perfect pitch, we sang *a cappella*. First, one of ours, "I Still Haven't Found What I'm Looking For", then one of the Lord's (with a little help from John Newton), "Amazing Grace". As we were singing "Amazing Grace", it occurred to me that this most powerful word – "grace" – is my favourite in the spiritual lexicon, and as good a description of the Arch as any that a thousand poets could write.

Grace, I have found, is a very hard thing to get your head around – I've spent my life trying. It flies in the face of what most humans would call just. All physical laws would suggest that for every action there is and ought to be an equal and opposite reaction: an eye for an eye, a tooth for a tooth. What you put out there, you get back … cosmic balance, karma, if you like. Grace turns it all on its head. Grace short-circuits karma. And when grace is put in motion, in action, its power is unmatched.

– to wit, the idea of Truth and Reconciliation. At first, it seemed so counter-intuitive, maybe even counter-productive. The Arch puts more faith in people than we tend to put in ourselves. But that faith is catching.

South Africa could have been a tinderbox. Instead it has been a lesson in grace: difficult then, difficult now – the way they have dealt with the horrors of apartheid. Tutu believed that the truth was more important than recompense, and requires openness and light — the daylight that doubles as an astringent for the wounds of their history. So jail sentences were put aside; black families learned how their sons and brothers died, from, in some cases, the very Afrikaners who had tortured and shot them. It was a searing sort of truth, but as Tutu taught us, knowing is a precondition of healing. "Making the truth public," he has said, "is a form of justice."

Tutu helped create a model – a moral and practical model – that will be needed and studied and, we hope, replicated in conflict zones for the rest of the millennium, an antibiotic to revenge, grown in a culture of tough love under the roof we were trying to sing off. We should have done more than bow our heads; we should have taken off our shoes, for this was holy ground, and music our sacrament.

That day, as we sang a song we had chosen mainly because it sounds good without instruments, grace reordered the way I saw the world. This is what the Arch and his great friend up the road, Madiba [Nelson Mandela], are all about.

That was also the day of my first reproach. In my nervousness, I was doing what Irish people do, which is to talk and talk, and in my talking I said one of the stupidest things anyone could have said to this man. "With all this work you are doing on Truth and Reconciliation, with everything you've got going on, how do men like you get any time for prayer and meditation?"

He turned to me, perplexed, then shot me a really, really dirty look. It felt like a slap. "How do you think we can do any of this without prayer and meditation?" he said. My heart sank like a stone. Of course he was right – I could see it immediately.

Years later, when our movement of activists was working on the Jubilee 2000 Drop the Debt campaign, I told that story to the people around me (and still tell it to myself regularly). I said, "Be very careful that you never run empty. You've got to refill the well." This is Tutu's wisdom. He knows from experience that people who are passionate, who rail against injustice in whatever form, can get so fired up they burn out.

The Arch never has. I will never forget the fierce

Above: Tutu celebrates with family and friends at a church service for Leah's seventieth birthday, Soweto, 18 October 2003.

discomfort of keeping him waiting for a joint interview and photo shoot while I was stuck in Manhattan traffic. And when I finally rushed into the hotel where we were meeting, he was nowhere around. "Where's he gone?" I asked. He was praying in his room. Refilling the well. When he returned, he made relentless fun of my anxiety.

Even that was a lesson. If you decide to enlist in his fight against extreme poverty, for freedom and human rights, you'll find no place for piety or self-righteousness. The Arch himself is full of love and joy and laughter and irreverence. This is not in any way at odds with his seriousness of purpose. It is, like his faith, a source of strength.

The archbishop is the real rock star. I have seen the crowds go wild. U2 asked him to do a filmed piece to play every night on our 360 tour. By the time it finishes, the tour will have been seen in person by seven million people and by even more on TV and DVD. We wanted to inspire those fans with a sense of their own power on the journey of equality. It seemed clear to us that the Arch was the only person to carry this off – this mad notion of talking about equality and justice in the middle of a loud, high-tech rock show. It is a mad idea. His authority on this is unmatched, of course, and he's a hero, but that doesn't mean he could hold the attention

of eighty thousand people who've exchanged their hard-earned cash for a night of entertainment. Some were worried the whole thing would bomb.

Not me – I had seen the showman in him. He agreed without hesitation, though I don't know if he fully realised what he was signing up for. I am sure he'd never been to a U2 show. In the segment, his head is projected onto screens 25 feet high; his voice booms around the stadium. And what he tells the crowd is that they are part of the same movement that defeated apartheid. They are the same people who fought for civil rights. They are the same people who fought against violence in Northern Ireland. And by joining the ONE Campaign, they are part of equality's onward march.

It's a very powerful piece, but the reason it works in that setting is because of his mischief. His refusal to take himself seriously is what led him to agree to this, and that comes through very strongly. When the film opens, the stadium goes quiet out of respect for him. Then, when the Arch speaks, there's an electricity as his words send shivers down the spine. Then the crowds fully go crazy, shouting and cheering as if it's him, not the band, they've come here to see. Quite an act to follow. He did his bit in one take, by the way.

Every meeting with the Arch, every speech, every

statement makes its mark. His air of grace does not lift him above this earthly realm. He does not seek sanctification. He is exactly where he wants to be – right down on the ground with the rest of us, as close to the poorest and most vulnerable and most reviled criminal as he is close to God.

....

WILMA JAKOBSEN

Desmond Tutu was instrumental in my whole ordination process. When I first began seminary I had no particular notion about becoming a priest, because we did not have either women deacons or women priests in the Anglican Church at that time. So it was not an issue. But in my first year, the Anglican Church decided, at the Provincial Synod, to ordain women as deacons. I felt at that time that my vocation was campus ministry, not particularly anything to do with ordination. But I was in the US and I was attending church at All Saints Pasadena. Of the six priests working there at the time, two were women. I had never met a woman priest before. One of them I particularly connected with; we worked together with the youth ministry, I became close to her and learned such a lot from her. And I think my own understanding of my own possibility of wanting to be ordained came one day in church, out of the blue, when I sat watching her. Her name was Franny and I said to myself, the thought popped into my head: If Franny can do this, why not me? A year or so later, Bishop Tutu was elected as the archbishop and, because he was archbishop, he was also the bishop of the diocese of Cape Town. So he became, at the end of my second year, my diocesan bishop. And I realised that, if I was thinking in any way about this ordination thing, I needed to speak to my "bishop to be". It wasn't clear whether or not he supported the ordination of women. I went home to Cape Town for the summer, the winter there. My aim was to get an appointment with him at some or other time. My rector told me, "Wilma, that is simply impossible. He's too busy, he has too much going on. It won't be possible." A friend of mine said, "Wilma, I'm on a committee to organise his enthronement. If you write him a letter, I'll give him the letter." So I wrote this letter and said would it be possible to have an appointment with you, and would it be possible to get two tickets to the enthronement? Everybody wanted one. They were like gold dust. You couldn't get them. The week before the enthronement, my mother came running to me and said, "Wilma, there's a telegram for you." Those old-fashioned things: telegrams! A telegram from Bishopscourt that said, "Contact Lavinia

Above: Tutu takes an afternoon nap at Bishopscourt, Cape Town, 24 December 1986.

....

Browne at Bishopscourt for an appointment with the archbishop and tickets to the enthronement." I was delighted! I went with a friend, it was absolutely fantastic.

On his fifth day of work, I walked up to Bishopscourt to have an interview with him. I don't really even know what I wanted to do except to ask him this question. It was winter and it was cold. He had a little fire in the grate. And you know, the very first thing he said to me was, "I suppose you want to know what I think about women priests?" and then of course all I could say was yes, because it was exactly what I wanted to know, nothing else really. He was outstanding. He just expressed his support for women being ordained as priests and then said, "You know, the church has to help you explore your vocation," and he said, "You know I can't ordain you as a priest, because we have not yet passed the legislation and until that time I can't do that." But he

see that he was pained by the fact that the church had not ordained women as priests, and he was pained that he couldn't ordain me. He did so much within the Anglican Church of southern Africa to keep the issue alive when it could've died. He had this as a priority. He gave both resources and time to convene conferences where we could bring people together to talk about the issue. I think that without his support it may not have happened by now, but we don't know. We think he was the instrument that God used for all of us women who are now priests and deacons in southern Africa.

When the vote went through at our Provincial Synod, he was overcome with emotion and left the central hall. But he found me afterwards and he just came with this bear hug and said, "I'm going to ordain you!"

And he did it four times, stepped back and said, "I'm going to ordain you!"

A few years later, I was at the cathedral for ordinations. It was a beautiful service. When it came to the part in the service where we pass the peace, I walked towards the archbishop to say, "The peace of the Lord be with you," and he said, "Where were you last night? I tried to call you. I wanted to ask you to be my chaplain." And I don't even know what I said.

And that started one of my most challenging jobs. I was his last chaplain before he retired. Simply amazing! I prayed with him even as I drove him. It was quite challenging sometimes, negotiating peak-hour traffic and praying morning prayer and remembering the responses all at once. I prayed with him at the chapel of Bishopscourt. That was, for me, one of the highlights of the year and a half I served as chaplain. When I walked into the chapel of an evening, he would already have been there for some time. And you could just feel electricity in the air. You could feel that he was a man of God at prayer. You could watch him as a man of prayer and see the impact of that on his life – prayer for him is the source and resource of all that he does.

I learned he was giving and also hard to work with sometimes, like anyone in a big, high-profile position. He has this iron intellect and his intuition. Let's just say there were ten tasks I was working on simultaneously. Nine of them are going great. I mean they are just done and they're amazing and little miracles have been achieved. But let's say one was not possible, for reasons way beyond my control. He would never ask about the nine that I did. He'd only ask about the one that I didn't do. I learned just don't make excuses, just say, "I'm sorry, it's not done yet". I think he called on us all, all of us who worked for him, to raise the bar. I never said, "It's not possible." God is a big god. Everything is possible with God. God and hard work are a good combination.

added, "You need to go back to seminary, finish your degree. We'll write to you. We'll talk about this and write to you and we'll let you know." So that was exciting. It was very exciting! It was amazing!

The next year I wasn't sure and I prayed for certainty. I'll never forget: it was Good Friday and I had gone up to Nevada to take part in a protest about underground nuclear bombs. I came back on a Saturday and there was a letter waiting for me. It said, "When you finish your degree, come back home. We'll send you to a theological college here in South Africa and we'll ordain you." So I just felt that the hand of God was in this process.

I went back home to theological college. In 1988, I was ordained to the diaconate along with Wilfred Meyer. I always had Father's support along a sometimes painful and exciting journey. Of course, my male colleague Wilfred, who had been ordained deacon, was ordained priest six months later. I was ordained priest almost five years later. I think that was the reason I got to be so close to him. I was the permanent deacon, as it were; I didn't get ordained priest, like the men. I could

One of the lessons that stands out is his prayer life, his spirituality. I watched him pray for other people. In the days before email, people would send these prayer letters. He would have his blue drawstring bag that had the Bible, the prayer book and all these letters. When we were driving between places, he would just ask, "Where's my bag?" I had to be the keeper of the bag. He would get into the car and he would take out the stack of letters. He would read through the letter, pray for the person, put it at the bottom, read through the next one, pray for the person, put it at the bottom. I mean, in so many different ways he was praying and he knew all these people. He responds to people. No matter who you are, he has a place for you in his heart. His heart seems to be so large, so full of love, so full of the grace that he has experienced in his own spiritual journey. His own heart has been enlarged, as it were, so he can fit everybody in. You know he doesn't just fit in the kings and queens and the presidents or the bishops. You know he fits in so-called smaller people. He's always praying for arbitrary people who wrote to him and said, "Please pray for me." He prays for them. At regular intervals throughout the day he prays. I still think about that. I am challenged by that in my own life. I can never ever say, "I'm too busy to pray" because he was much busier than I ever am and that's what he did.

KAREN HAYES

I went to Rwanda with him and saw him in action practising reconciliation work. The archbishop was the chair of the All Africa Conference of Churches at that time. He was initially invited by churches in Rwanda to come and help provide some support for them during this difficult time. I think what he had in mind was to really try and help in the process of bringing people together.

One of the things that we did was to visit a massacre site where hundreds of people, primarily women and children, had been slaughtered by the militias. Up to then, Father Desmond had been very clear, strong in his voice, asking survivors to think about putting in place an amnesty process, to think about reconciliation instead of revenge. He was really unwavering in his commitment to that. Then we visited the massacre site, Ntarama. When you visit a place like that yourself, it's unlike anything anybody can tell you. It's unlike anything you see on television. We drove to the site and we could see, from a distance, a bunch of white circular objects piled on tables. As we got closer we realised that those were skulls. We got out of the car and it was just unspeakable, what we saw. We saw one skull that still had a spear going through it. We saw children's skulls. And then, when we moved forward into the church, there were the remains of many, many people.

What had happened was that when the militias came, the men had run away into the bush. I think that many of those men were killed. The women and children ran into the church thinking that they were going to have safety there. Instead, the militias threw hand grenades inside and set fire to the church.

We saw clothing, shoes ... We were all very quiet. Father, in his role as archbishop and leader, to help all of us in this experience, started to pray. But he lost his words. He seemed so overcome by the enormity of all of these things. He lost his words and he broke down into tears and needed to be consoled himself. I felt for him. I had felt for the victims first and for all the Rwandan people who were struggling with this. I felt for Father because I wondered if he had had a loss of hope in that moment. The remarkable thing about him is that he allows himself to be human. In that moment, he was a man and a pastor. He is willing to allow his vulnerability to just be what it is in a situation like that. It gave us all permission, really, to grieve in that moment for all of the horrible things that were in that place, that happened there.

One of the other things we did was visit the prison in Kigali where people who had been implicated in the genocide were being held. The way in which the prisoners were being treated was also unspeakable. I think something like ten times the capacity of prisoners were being kept there. When we went and visited, there was only room for the prisoners to stand. People had to make a little path for Father to go through and for us to follow. We could see that these people, mostly men but they had women in there as well, would have to take turns in order to sit down. What had happened was that there was no judicial process in place. If somebody just pointed their finger and said, "I saw you ..." you would be rounded up and put in prison. One of the prisoners actually handed Father a letter asking him for help.

When we got back to the hotel after that experience, we talked about it. There was no doubt that some of those people, maybe many of them, were murderers. But, when you walked in there, you saw how malnourished they were and how desperate they were. Father was very, very outraged by that. There was to be

Above: Tutu addresses the Challenge Future Peace Conference, Bochum, Germany, 30 June 2007.

a high-profile dinner that night with the Rwandan government. He was struggling to figure out what to say to these leaders who were survivors of the genocide. He felt that he needed to be critical of the way that they were treating the accused. He said that if it were publicised how the Tutsi government was treating the accused, they were going to lose support for their cause. That's the message I think he really wanted to give to them. He worried that if there were an outbreak of disease, all of those people would be wiped out. He was very disturbed by seeing women in there. From his point of view, no matter what you've been through, you don't want to take on the behaviour of your enemy, your opponent, your oppressor.

But he worried about what to say and what they could hear. One of the things that he does when he wants to deliver a difficult message is he starts with humour. He disarms people with those jokes. Usually his public speaking starts with these jokes. It does allow people to let down their guard. Maybe they are a little more receptive. What he did that night in Rwanda was that he told a joke. He made it preposterous. He

referred back to South Africa and talked about how ridiculous racism is. Father Desmond has a large nose, so he talked about how ridiculous it would be if people with large noses were in power, and so if you wanted to go to a university for small noses you would have to apply to the Ministry of Small Nose Affairs. So he got all the people in the dining-room, mostly Tutsis, laughing. Then he said, "Oh, I hear that in Rwanda you tell whether you are Tutsi or Hutu by the shape of your nose." He said, "You know, you kill this one because his nose is like this. You kill that one because the nose is like that. You kill God, and God is in every person sitting next to you." His message to the survivors was: "Don't do the same thing they did. Don't imprison and treat like animals those whose noses are shaped differently than yours." Then the laughter got nervous. You could hear a pin drop. It was very powerful.

At the time people felt it was too early for people in Rwanda to start talking about forgiveness. I guess they expected Father Desmond to come and remind them about how bad the situation was and how horrible what they had gone through was, and to acknowledge and affirm that. I think he did that. But I think what they didn't expect him to do was to even think about forgiveness at that stage. In one of the responses at that dinner one of the Rwandan leaders said, "Well, we are Christians but even Jesus didn't say you have to reconcile with the devil. We are dealing with the devil here."

Towards the end of our visit he was meeting with certain church leaders. Some of those folks had actually been implicated as well. Father was saying to the church leaders that if the people of faith can't get together as religious leaders, how could they ask the rest of the country to start coming to the table and talk? He was quite frustrated with their resistance. During one of the last meetings we had, he was really pleading. He was saying, "If we are saying we are Christians, then actually Jesus did say, 'Father, forgive them.'" Then he took it to another level. He said, "If you can't deal with it on a spiritual level, let's talk about the practical level. Forgiveness is practical politics. Your country will go down the drain if somebody doesn't make a radical move. This cycle has been going on in Rwanda for decades, since colonial times. There have been times when the Hutu people were persecuted by the Tutsi people and times when the Tutsi people were persecuted by the Hutu people. Somebody has just got to stop it. Stop the cycle." Within the next few years Rwanda did start its Gacaca practice.

How does he do it? How does he go to all of these places and not tire? How does he talk to group after group, to people on both sides? How does he hold all of that? I think that prayer time he reserves for himself – hours and hours of prayer time everyday – that's how he does it.

My observation after filming him off and on for many years is that what he does is he plants a seed. Maybe they couldn't hear it at that time, but it seems to me that seeds were planted. He didn't go there knowing that he was going to have a tangible outcome. He doesn't, he's just so committed and passionate. I think, many years from now, people will look back and say, "Oh, I see that trajectory. You know, Tutu did talk about stopping the cycle way back then. He was one of the early voices talking about that, and this is the way it went."

JODY WILLIAMS

I was at the University of Virginia. It was a conference of the Nobel Peace laureates. The most memorable were Archbishop Tutu and the Dalai Lama. His Holiness and the archbishop are often referred to as the "super laureates". They are in a tier of their own. It makes sense, you know; they are super close to God. These two spiritual leaders from different traditions have the same energy or vibe. Watching them interact, just the joy you could feel between them, it was really outstanding. I felt I was in the presence of – I don't like the word "great" – magic, spiritual magic, if there is such a thing. I love the rare times that I have seen them together; they are great.

Archbishop Tutu, as we all know, is gracious. When I watch him speak, when I listen to him speak, he is full of an amazing energy. It's calm and musical. I tend to get a little agitated and loud and I use language that some people find shocking. I do push, you know. Push, push, push in ways some people find controversial. He's been supportive in recognising that sometimes you have to really push. There have to be people to really push to make people open their eyes or their ears and start thinking. We have different ways of trying to make people think. I think his is more commonly accepted.

Archbishop Tutu is one of a handful of activist Nobel laureates – I think there are about a dozen or so – who you can pretty much always count on to speak together on issues. We've had many, many email exchanges. We've even had one email fight. That instance was related to Burma. He thought I was being unkind to an individual. Well, not me personally, but the Nobel Women's Initiative, and he let me know that. It wasn't fun. I didn't like to be in that state of disarray with the archbishop. I really treasure his friendship. I really really do. He's such an outstanding human being. He's kind and fun and funny. He's an outstanding human being.

Archbishop Tutu, Betty Williams and I did a session with youth at a conference. Whenever he stood up, you just felt kindness. You felt a human being who really understands the capability for good of every single human being. He almost makes me want to believe that, because I don't. I think there are some people who are just fundamentally evil. Of course, one would get into robust discussion of that with the archbishop.

We got into it a little bit, not about good and evil per se. In Bali, for PeaceJam as a matter of fact, there was a discussion about spirituality or religion, because of course he's the Arch and Betty is Northern Irish Protestant and I was raised Catholic. I now consider myself to be a spiritual vagabond. I'm not sure what that means. On militant days, I consider myself an atheist, on days when I'm weak, to be agnostic.

When I speak of atheism it's a rejection of the concept of God as taught in Catholicism when I was growing up. A male figure that actually really cares every minute what you are doing is just beyond my comprehension. It's just not a concept of creation and energy and spirit in the universe that I can accept at all.

So the three of us went at that for a while, and I purposely wore my Ganesh necklace. I consider Ganesh, the overcomer of obstacles, to be the Hindu equivalent of St Jude. I could somehow relate to this elephant-headed god in a way that I couldn't relate to St Jude.

I wore my Ganesh necklace as a statement when he and Betty and I were discussing these things. He responded to the statement in his customary way: he laughed. He said, "Oh, I can see that you actually do believe. I'll pray for you." That's how he's kind. I have never seen him belittle anyone or make someone feel ashamed or bad because they don't decide to share the same vision. That's kindness, that's real compassion. It's something that I have struggled with my whole life, because I tend not to be particularly tolerant, although I think I have gotten much more so in my adult age.

You know he is human. He will let you have fun with him and that makes him profoundly marvellous. I have a picture of him from Bali that is hilarious. It was rainy and muggy and hideously hot. I think it started to rain when we were being taped. The archbishop had yellow rain gear, one of those rubbery things. He put it on and he put his hood over his head and tied it under his chin. He let me take a picture of him. He looked ridiculous. I love that picture. Every time I think of the human archbishop, I think of him in that ridiculous, absolutely ridiculous thing.

I think about him a lot, I really do, in terms of how he views the world and compassion, which of course is a big theme of His Holiness. When I do something obnoxious, I think, "Oh, if the archbishop were behind

Above: Tutu in Bali for PeaceJam, 2006.

297

me he would be shaking his head and thinking, 'She could have done it quite a bit differently. The point is well taken, but she could have done it a tad differently." I do think he is around all the time. I'm serious. I don't quite understand why I think he is around more than His Holiness, whom I adore. But the Arch seems to be there, you know, like the good and the bad angels perched on my shoulders. My good is the Arch; I don't know who the bad is. The Arch is saying, "Jody, you know you could do this in this way. Why did you have to use that ugly language? Why did you have to call that person a moron?" – which I did do in a speech in front of him once. At that moment, I was so charged up I thought I was cool. Years later I thought, "Oh dear, I could have said it a little differently and still made the same point."

He has taught me a little more grace, he really has. When I received the Nobel Peace Prize, it was really difficult for me. When I was coordinating the landmine campaign, I took very seriously the term "coordinate". It wasn't to make myself first; it was my job to make sure that everybody in the campaign around the world had access to the same information, because that made us all equally powerful in trying to address this problem. I didn't ever care if I was interviewed. In fact, there were organisations and individuals who liked that and sought it, and so they did the talking. And then after the prize the only person they wanted to talk to was me. That really made me very angry actually.

One of the things that Archbishop Tutu said when asked the question: "How has the Nobel Prize changed your life?" was that before the prize he would say things and people listened or they didn't; after the Peace Prize he would say the same things and suddenly everything

was a pearl of wisdom. It didn't feel like suddenly everything I said was a pearl of wisdom but, with anything related to the landmine campaign, the only person they wanted to talk to was me and that really made me angry. We had worked together to make this happen. You were happy talking to them yesterday. I'm still the same person. I'm still the same grass-roots activist today ... I found it very difficult and I was not always gracious. I think I have struggled with that and I think the archbishop has played a role in making me become a little more gracious. Just thinking about him, watching him, thinking about how he does it – his impact has been bigger than I realised.

I would say that the greatest gift of our friendship feels almost like unconditional love – that's a pretty awesome gift. I feel like he is one of those people that, no matter what, if I need anything he will be there. That's a gift. I'm going to weep. Oh goodness, I will ruin my mascara! I had not thought about the Arch on unconditional love; maybe that's presumption on my part. Dear Archbishop, if I'm presuming unconditional love, I apologise. I would then appeal to you as an archbishop to offer unconditional spiritual love and guidance. But anyway, I do presume unconditional love and support from the archbishop.

I've just been thinking about how my first time when I was ever arrested was when I was protesting against apartheid South Africa here in Washington. It was when, every day, people were arrested and arrested, and it went on for years, I recall. That was my first arrest. It was in front of the apartheid South African embassy. Little did I know then that I would have a different relationship with South Africa through Archbishop Tutu. It's an honour and a privilege to call him a friend.

TOM HAYDEN

I was a student activist against apartheid in the sixties and there was a big movement in the seventies. We had a group called the Campaign for Economic Democracy, a student branch.

My wife Jane Fonda and I ventured to make a trip to South Africa during a time when it was very, very difficult to get visas from the authoritarian government. We took our two children, Vanessa and Troy. I believe it was around '81. We had elaborate plans to meet Tutu. By this time his name was known, and we corresponded. It turns out the state had other intentions. We were held at the airport and were not allowed to leave. During that time, while we were in the airport, Desmond Tutu called

us or we called him. It was the first time I ever heard that jolly little voice: "Are we having breakfast?" He already knew that the police were at the airport and we weren't having breakfast. I just made a note to invite him to the States. I thought it might be easier for him to come to see us. That eventually led to one of his trips to the States.

I don't remember if he had difficulty getting a visa but he did get here and it was a multi-purpose trip. We had a Hollywood event at our house in Santa Monica. We were trying to get young Hollywood actors and activists to focus on films about apartheid and to take a stand for social justice with the celebrity that they had acquired. It was billed as a Hollywood party. I guess it was that, but it was really to introduce Bishop Tutu to the liberals of the motion picture and television industries, and musicians. It was quite an event. Today's Hollywood establishment, then in its youth, was there: Bono and a young Alec Baldwin.

The other purpose of the trip was to create an encounter, a meeting for Bishop Tutu with the president of the University of California David Gardner and the governor of California George Deukmejian.

Speaker Willie Brown and Assemblywoman Maxine Waters were quite committed to doing something about South Africa. The Speaker was a regent at the university. He had great power over the budget. Maxine Waters was the leading African American voice in the assembly. I was a mere newcomer to this battle. Maxine and the Speaker had introduced a seemingly hopeless measure to divest state pension funds and university funds from any companies doing business in South Africa. It was a non-violent way to try to break the financial underpinnings, the economic underpinnings of the apartheid system. I became a co-author.

At stake were three or four, or more than that, billion dollars of UC [University of California] investment in companies doing business in South Africa. This issue was stirred up all round the country on campuses and state legislatures. Remember, cities, states and universities all have billions and billions of pension funds invested under the, so-called, fiduciary principle, which was to get the best returns for your investment and leave moral questions out.

I set up a meeting between Tutu and one or two university officials. He met for hours with David Gardner, and as a result of that meeting the university regency decided to divest. That was a real tipping point, as university after university divested. It also led to the State of California divesting. Maxine Waters's bill was signed by Governor Deukmejian. That had an enormous effect in undermining the economic structure that was supporting the South African apartheid state.

I think the civil rights movement here laid the ground for this success. That and the fact that it was a clear moral question of right or wrong and that there were emissaries like Bishop Tutu who could come here and make the case.

Desmond Tutu was a black man with a white collar and that goes a long way here. Our civil rights movement was led by black men with white collars: Martin Luther King being one. It's a familiar, somewhat comforting image if you are trying to persuade constituencies in the United States who are Christian. He was in that mainstream framework, so his message would resonate. It put people on the defensive, since this man was making the moral arguments that we already believed.

I think in his preparation to talk to Gardner at the university and Deukmejian, he knew whom he was talking to. In the first case, a conservative Mormon and a Republican. In the second case, a conservative Republican governor of the state who was not exactly elected on a civil rights platform. So he had to somehow craft an argument that was in their interests and what I found very interesting, was that he didn't flinch from the moral argument. He knew that if he appealed to their faith traditions he would win the moral argument.

I think that he is a very shrewd and crafty man who has thought it all through. He thinks strategically. Now, he has his own natural gifts; I don't think that he was conducting a charade. He is quite funny. He's quite impish. He's quite non-threatening. And he knew that his crazy laugh was bound to disarm people much more effectively than a machete because, once he made you laugh and everybody was laughing, it simply made it much easier to discuss very important and heart-wrenching issues.

But I imagine he also can become very threatening to the conservative president of an international university when he raises his finger and his voice becomes suddenly shrill. But I think his evident good nature and kindly demeanour, graciousness and sense of humour were all conducive to persuading the man that it was better to give up to this bishop than to give up to an armed phalanx of Mau Mau terrorists or whatever they thought was coming if Tutu wasn't honoured. I think Tutu knew all this and he knew how to play a certain role. Would somebody else have come along if he hadn't been there? Perhaps, but sometimes individuals make a decisive difference in the outcome of social movements. I think he was such a person, is such a person.

Archbishop Tutu came into my life because I am a member of the human family. I've been a political activist and human rights defender for as long as I can remember. I met him in New York in 1981 or 1982. We met while I was still working on Tibet, but it was my work on Burma that brought him even closer to me.

The archbishop: Father; teacher; my dad, after my dad's passing; mentor; political adviser; justice seeker; non-violence advocate; a moral compass for humanity; a moral compass to me. Father reminds me that the impossible is oftentimes possible, we are made for goodness; all are God's children. He taught me the meaning of ubuntu. He teaches by example.

I recall when Father and former president of the Czech Republic Václav Havel agreed to commission a report that Burma activists thought would serve as an entrée to the UN Security Council. As events evolved, I became distressed that I would be working with a government official whose views were so contrary to my own and, I thought, to Father's too. I queried Father about this person: is this person also a child of God? Father sent me an email stating without equivocation: "Dear child, he is a child of God." I resisted this big time. I replied with something like, "Now, I've gone along with you, Father, for decades on this goodness business, but not this time!" Father would not give up. He told me to go to the zoo and pray. I obeyed; I know an admonishment when I hear it. Every morning I would walk at Washington National Zoo to a specific place near the bird sanctuary where I would meditate about this. Despite decades of attending teachings by His Holiness the Dalai Lama, who radiates compassion and teaches the benefit of kindness, it was Father's insistence that I take this particularly difficult person into my heart which turned a spiritual corner for me.

Incredibly, I hear from him all the time, as do others. I don't know how he finds the time to deal with the endless justice struggles that he supports, or the "naughty children" throughout the world whom he loves. He is indefatigable. He responds to every email. He replies to my Burma emails with pithy, wise zingers: "abominable", "wonderful", "God help them" and such. On the rare occasions when I send good news about Burma, such as when Daw Aung San Suu Kyi was released from house arrest last year, I always receive: "God be praised."

When I am asked who provides me with political insights and advice, I always say, without hesitation, "The archbishop!" He allows me to vent thoughts, ideas, strategies, tactics, initiatives and queries. He has, with great generosity, afforded me unfettered access to his political acumen. He has taught, guided and inspired me spiritually, emotionally, politically, even fatherly, whereby words to describe what he means to me will always fall short.

What a blessing to have Archbishop Tutu and His Holiness the Dalai Lama in my life, and what a joy to see them at events together: two spiritual brothers bursting with laughter at each other's jokes, hugging and beaming, sharing their faiths and experiences, their love for one another and for humanity. I keep a picture from one such event on my desktop. It is a daily reminder that goodness, kindness, forgiveness and tolerance have exemplars amongst us.

If I had to express a frustration with the archbishop, it would be that he rarely rests. He was to retire after the Truth and Reconciliation Commission but we met weeks later, at a conference in Virginia, with His Holiness the Dalai Lama and other Nobel Peace laureates. He was hardly retired. Over a decade later, the archbishop officially announced his retirement. His definition of retirement is not in Webster's. Just when I think Father is truly winding down, I will get an email that he is off to promote reconciliation in yet another country fraught with violence and conflict. Though officially retired, he continues to provide hope to suffering beings, people living with HIV/AIDS, to those whose rights have been denied.

On the occasion of his last birthday, the Burmese exile community wanted to express their collective gratitude for his decades-long support of his sister Nobel Peace laureate Daw Aung San Suu Kyi. Email messages, gifts, plaques, paintings were all designed to say thank you to the person whom the Burmese exiles call "their" archbishop. How many people worldwide consider Father to be "their" archbishop?

Archbishop Tutu, whom I address in emails as "Father Dearest", has blessed me with an abundance of riches. His personal counsel to me is usually summed up in two-word emails: "Be good".

I was probably in my teens when I first encountered Desmond Tutu's name. He had such a moral presence that I can remember that, even long before my interest in international politics. He was just a very charismatic and attractive figure. When I was at Stanford [University], the anti-apartheid struggles were not as full-blown as what would come later but I remember that people were trying to figure how to get a handle on this problem. How could you bring pressure on the apartheid government in South Africa? What was an appropriate set of tools for a university? Was it divestment? Was it moral suasion? Was it simply bringing students here from South Africa? And I think that the third of those turned out to be the most important. It was to give students, particularly black students from South Africa, a place where they could come, interact and tell their story, but where they could also have the benefit of education here in the United States.

I first met Archbishop Tutu when I was the national security adviser. So the struggle in that sense had been achieved, but there was so much work to do. He came to see me and this man for whom I'd had great reverence – had really revered from afar – was suddenly standing in my office at the White House. It was quite a wonderful experience. I remember his moral bearing. This was someone who obviously had gone through a lot.

I myself am a child of Birmingham, Alabama, and even though the struggle was somewhat different in the United States than in South Africa, it had also been a struggle for justice, it had also been a struggle about the colour of your skin. I remember talking with him about that. He is in a small group of very, very important moral figures who brought to bear that most important asset in struggles for justice: moral authority.

Later we worked together on Burma. He came to the State Department. The First Lady Laura Bush had been very outspoken about Aung San Suu Kyi and on Burma. We needed voices from outside the European and American context. I told him that I was very grateful that he had been such a powerful voice for the people of Burma. The question of how you bring justice to people who are under the terrible scourge of tyranny is a major one. People say you can't impose democracy. Well that's true, but you don't have to impose democracy. You have to impose tyranny. You don't have to impose

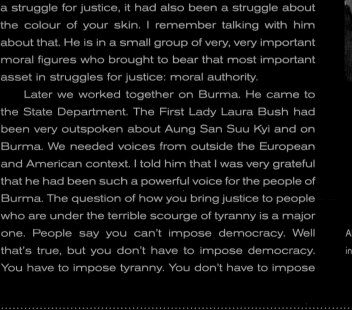

Above: Tutu and other Nobel laureates are welcomed to a camp for Karen refugees in Mae Sot on the Thai-Burmese border, 18 February 1993.

democracy. People, given the choice, will choose to govern. They will choose to have a say in their own future. They will choose to be free from the knock of the secret police at night. They will choose to be able to say what they think and to worship whom they please. You have to impose tyranny. So when it comes to an issue like Burma or, for that matter, Zimbabwe, there's a lot of common ground.

We disagreed on Iraq. I placed a call to him from then-president Bush and told him that I didn't think the president would agree to delay the war. Any time you are dealing with someone for whom you have enormous respect, you respect their opinions. You don't have to agree with them. He was a man who had certain views about how one carried out struggles for justice. Of course in South Africa it had largely been a non-violent struggle. But the fact is that South Africans were fortunate to have F. W. de Klerk alongside Nelson Mandela. That was not Saddam Hussein. And so Iraqis didn't have the option to be free from tyranny that South Africans ultimately had. I just thought we had a disagreement about the importance of how to do it. And in this respect we didn't agree. But I never felt that it was personal. I believed that the Iraqis deserved the same freedom from tyranny that everyone else deserved.

On so many other things we had common ground, like in the struggle for AIDS relief. He was a great spokesman for that important issue and I think when the Bush administration is viewed in history, that programme, the US President's Emergency Plan for AIDS Relief, will be remembered as the largest single-country programme for a pandemic in human history and for the millions of lives that it would probably have saved. And so we had common goals and common views as well. We talked about it and he was a very important proponent, particularly in South Africa, where even the question of what caused AIDS was a delicate and controversial one. It was good to have somebody who was willing and able to speak on those issues in a clear and, I think, correct voice.

I have learned that the arc of history is long, not short. It is hard from our vantage point – from today – to know how we will be judged by history. Still, I believe history will say that Desmond Tutu was a man whose integrity and strength helped liberate a people.

"MY HUMANITY IS BOUND UP
IN YOURS AND WE CAN ONLY BE
HUMAN TOGETHER."

DESMOND TUTU

CONTRIBUTOR BIOGRAPHIES
NOTES
FURTHER REFERENCES
SELECT BIBLIOGRAPHY
INDEX
ACKNOWLEDGEMENTS

CONTRIBUTOR BIOGRAPHIES

Malcolm Alexander is the managing director of Interregna Limited. He is one of the founding trustees of the Tutu Foundation UK.

John Allen was Desmond Tutu's press secretary for over a decade, also serving under him as director of media communications for the Truth and Reconciliation Commission. From 1998 to 2000, he assisted Tutu in running his office from the Candler School of Theology at Emory University in Atlanta, United States. His biography of Tutu, *Rabble-Rouser for Peace*, was shortlisted for South Africa's Alan Paton Award for non-fiction in 2007.

Kofi Annan was secretary-general of the United Nations (UN) from 1997 to 2006, serving two terms. His efforts to invigorate the UN were recognised in 2001 when he and the UN were jointly awarded the Nobel Peace Prize. He is involved in a number of political and humanitarian initiatives, including The Elders, and is president of the Kofi Annan Foundation, which develops programmes and partnerships in sustainable development and peace and security globally, and also supports Kofi Annan in his role as chairman of the African Union Panel of Eminent African Personalities.

Lord Jeffrey Archer is a charity auctioneer, an athlete, a playwright and a best-selling author. He served as a member of Parliament and deputy chairman of the British Conservative Party and has been a member of the House of Lords for the past nineteen years.

Aung San Suu Kyi is a Burmese political activist and the leader of the National League for Democracy. Her party won 392 out of 495 seats in Burma's parliamentary elections in 1990, but the military seized control. Aung San Suu Kyi, who was placed under house arrest prior to the elections, continued to be subjected to various forms of detention for twenty-one years, and was released in November 2010. She was awarded the Nobel Peace Prize in 1991.

The Reverend Ed Bacon is the rector of All Saints Church in Pasadena, California. All Saints is a 3,500-member multi-ethnic Episcopal congregation. The recipient of several honorary doctorates, in 2005 Rev. Bacon was awarded the Islamic Center of Southern California's Peace and Compassion Award, and in 2006 the Religious Freedom Award by the American Civil Liberties Union of Southern California.

Dr Brigalia Ntombemhlope Bam is the chairperson of the Independent Electoral Commission of South Africa. She was the first female general secretary of the South African Council of Churches, a founding member and president of the Women's Development Foundation, and has also been a member of the South African Human Rights Commission.

The Reverend Dr Michael Battle is the rector of Church of Our Saviour in Los Angeles, California. He was ordained by Archbishop Tutu in South Africa in 1993 following two years in residence as his chaplain while he wrote his doctoral thesis on Tutu's theology.

Harry Belafonte is an award-winning musician, producer and composer and a political and social activist. He was appointed as cultural adviser to the Peace Corps by President John F. Kennedy in 1962. He initiated and organised the recording of the charity single "We Are the World", released by the supergroup USA for Africa in 1985, which went on to win a Grammy Award and raise over US$63 million for humanitarian aid in both Africa and the United States. A UNICEF Goodwill Ambassador, in 1997 he was honoured by the United Nations for his work on behalf of children around the world.

Michele Bohana was the founding director of the International Campaign for Tibet. She is now the director of the Institute for Asian Democracy. She represents Burmese leader Aung San Suu Kyi on the board of PeaceJam and is the government advocate for the Johns Hopkins Center for Public Health and Human Rights.

Bono is the lead singer of the Irish rock group U2. He is well known for his humanitarian work in Africa, and co-founded the aid organisations DATA (Debt, AIDS, Trade, Africa), Edun, the ONE Campaign and Red. He has been nominated for the Nobel Peace Prize three times.

Sir Richard Branson is the founder and chairman of the Virgin Group of companies, which encompasses businesses from the entertainment industries to the airline Virgin Atlantic and the Virgin train networks. Sir Richard is a trustee of several charities and, with his friend Peter Gabriel, he conceived the idea for a model of global leadership that has become The Elders.

Jackson Browne is an American singer-songwriter and an environmental and social activist. In 1979, with other musicians, he co-founded Musicians United for Safe Energy to protest against the use of nuclear energy. He has performed at numerous benefit concerts, and his humanitarian efforts have been recognised with the John Steinbeck Award and the Harry Chapin Humanitarian Award.

The Reverend Professor Richard Burridge is dean of King's College London. He is the author of several books on Jesus and the gospels, and serves as a representative of the Church Commissioners on the Ethical Investment Advisory Group.

Jimmy Carter was president of the United States from 1977 to 1981 and is a Democrat. In 1982, he founded the Carter Center, which addresses national and international issues of public policy. In 2002, he was awarded the Nobel Peace Prize for his efforts towards finding peaceful solutions to international conflicts and for advancing democracy and human rights.

Susan Cheshire was born and raised in Bletchingley, Surrey, United Kingdom. She was invited to attend Sadler's Wells, one of the UK's leading dance schools, but her career was interrupted by World War II, and she joined the Women's Royal Naval Service, serving in South-east Asia as a cypher officer on Lord Mountbatten's command. She was a parishioner at St Mary the Virgin in Bletchingley, Surrey, and became friends with the Tutu family when Desmond Tutu was appointed assistant curate there in the mid-1960s. She is the mother of Ricky Richardson.

Bill Clinton was president of the United States from 1993 to 2001, serving two terms. He has been a lifelong advocate for civil rights and racial equality. Through the Clinton Foundation, he has launched a number of initiatives which include providing treatment for HIV/AIDS sufferers, fighting climate change and developing sustainable economic growth in Africa and Latin America. The Clinton Global Initiative brings world leaders together to find innovative solutions to pressing global issues.

Bill Cosby is an American comedian, actor, author, producer, educator and activist. His television series *The Cosby Show*, which screened from 1984 to 1992, was one of the most-watched sitcoms of all time. He has been the recipient of over a dozen honorary doctorates, and his awards include the Presidential Medal of Freedom for his contribution to television, and the Bob Hope Humanitarian Award.

Lord Nigel Crisp was chief executive of the United Kingdom (UK) National Health Service, the largest health organisation in the world, and also the permanent secretary of the Department of Health. An expert on international development and global health, in 2007 he published *Global Health Partnerships*, a report for the British prime minister on how the UK can provide health support to developing countries.

Frederik Willem de Klerk was the last apartheid-era president of South Africa. In the early nineties, he unbanned anti-apartheid organisations and released Nelson Mandela from prison. He was awarded the Nobel Peace Prize in 1993 and served as deputy president, with Thabo Mbeki, under Nelson Mandela from 1994 to 1996.

Bob Geldof is an Irish rock musician, activist and entrepreneur. In 1984, he co-founded the charity supergroup Band Aid, whose hit song "Do They Know It's Christmas?" became one of the biggest-selling singles in United Kingdom history. He went on to organise Live Aid in 1985, a benefit concert which raised over US$150 million towards famine relief in Africa, and then Live 8 in 2005 to help pressurise the G8 into making significant poverty-alleviation pledges. Live 8's series of ten benefit concerts is estimated to have attracted three billion viewers worldwide. He co-founded DATA (Debt, AIDS, Trade, Africa), sat on the Commission for Africa and is currently a member of the Africa Progress Panel.

Sharon Gelman is the long-time executive director of Artists for a New South Africa as well as a writer. A dedicated human rights and social activist, she was previously the director of human rights programmes for the Hollywood Policy Center and has worked in partnership with numerous charitable organisations, including Treatment Action Campaign, Amnesty International, the AIDS Foundation of South Africa and Young Artists United.

Justice Richard Goldstone is a former judge who served in South Africa's highest courts including the Constitutional Court of South Africa. In the early nineties he chaired South Africa's Commission of Inquiry Regarding Public Violence and Intimidation, which became known as the Goldstone Commission. He was the first chief prosecutor of the United Nations International Criminal Tribunals for war crimes in the former Yugoslavia and Rwanda. He is the recipient of numerous awards, including the International Human Rights Award of the American Bar.

Chris Green is an arts consultant based in London. He was popular events director of the City of London Festival from 1978 to 1991, director of the Poetry Society from 1989 to 1993 and chief executive of the British Academy of Songwriters, Composers and Authors from 1998 to 2008. He is currently chair of the Learning Skills Foundation, a director of the Courtyard Arts Centre in Hereford and president of the Hereford and South Herefordshire Liberal Democrats. He contested six UK general elections as a Liberal for the Liberals.

His Holiness the Fourteenth Dalai Lama, Tenzin Gyatso, is the spiritual leader of Tibet and its former head of state. He has lived in exile in Dharamsala in northern India since 1959 when a potential Tibetan national uprising was crushed by Chinese troops. He has consistently advocated non-violent policies for the liberation of Tibet, and has been a spokesperson on international conflicts, environmental concerns and human rights issues. His Holiness has been the recipient of over eighty-four awards, honorary doctorates and prizes, including the Nobel Peace Prize, which he was awarded in 1989.

Tom Hayden is regarded as one of the strongest student voices of the anti-war and civil rights movements in the United States in the 1960s. A political and social activist, writer and educator, he served in the California State Assembly and the state senate and is the director of the Peace and Justice Resource Center in Culver City, California.

Karen Hayes is an independent film-maker and the director and producer of *The Foolishness of God: Desmond Tutu and Reconciliation*, an authorised documentary feature film. She serves on the staff of Global AIDS Interfaith Alliance, which partners with religious organisations in resource-poor countries to support communities in AIDS prevention and care.

Samuel L. Jackson is an American film and television actor and film producer. He became involved in the civil rights movement while he was at college, and was an usher at the funeral of Martin Luther King in 1968.

The Reverend Wilma Jakobsen is a senior associate rector at All Saints Church in Pasadena, California. She was the first woman deacon and priest to be ordained in the Anglican Church in southern Africa, and served as chaplain for Archbishop Tutu for two years prior to his retirement. Before taking up her current post, she was the university chaplain at the University of Cape Town.

Quincy Jones is an award-winning American musician, composer, producer, conductor and arranger. He produced the hit charity single "We Are The World" in 1985 to raise funds for humanitarian aid. An active human rights campaigner, in 2004 he launched We Are The Future, an initiative to raise funds for the development of child health centres in African countries. His personal foundation, the Quincy Jones Foundation, supports initiatives towards global issues affecting children.

Martin Kenyon was the general secretary of the Overseas Student Trust in the United Kingdom. He is a lifetime member of the Council for Education in the Commonwealth, an NGO based at Parliament that works with the appropriate authorities to promote educational development in the Commonwealth.

Graça Machel is a social and political activist and an international advocate for the rights of women and children. She was responsible for producing the United Nations' report on the impact of armed conflict on children between 1994 and 1996. Among other awards, she has received the UN's Nansen Medal for her contribution to the welfare of refugee children. Machel is a member of The Elders. She is the third wife of former South African president Nelson Mandela and the widow of Samora Machel, the former president of Mozambique.

Archbishop Walter Khotso Makhulu served as bishop of Botswana and then archbishop of the Church of the Province of Central Africa. He is past president of the World Council of Churches and the All Africa Conference of Churches, as well as an Ordinary Companion of the Order of St Michael and St George. He is a recipient of France's Ordre des Palmes Académiques, and Botswana's highest civilian honour, the Presidential Order of Honour.

Nelson Mandela is probably the world's most revered statesman. In 1964, he was convicted of sabotage for his resistance activities as leader of Umkhonto we Sizwe, the armed wing of the African National Congress. During his twenty-seven-and-a-half years of incarceration, he became an icon of the anti-apartheid movement and, following his release from prison in 1990, he became the first democratically elected president of the new South Africa in 1994. He was awarded the Nobel Peace Prize in 1993. After stepping down as president in 1999, he was a spokesperson for the fight against HIV/AIDS and also participated in peace negotiations in Burundi, the Democratic Republic of Congo and other countries. He is a founder and honorary member of The Elders, and is married to Graça Machel.

Hugh Masekela is a South African musician and composer. He was one of the founding members of South Africa's first youth orchestra, the Huddleston Jazz Band, and later went on to play with many famous musicians, including Bob Marley and Paul Simon. His 1987 hit single "Bring Him Home" became an anthem for the movement to free Nelson Mandela.

Sylvia Funeka Morrison is Archbishop Tutu's elder sister.

Sally Muggeridge is the former chief executive of the Industry and Parliament Trust. She is an elected member of the General Synod to the Church of England, representing the Diocese of Canterbury, and is a founding member of the Tutu Foundation UK.

Barack Obama was elected the forty-fourth president of the United States (US) in November 2008 and is its first African American president. He was elected to the Illinois Senate in 1996 and then to the US Senate in 2004, winning by 70 per cent of the vote. In 2009, he was awarded the Nobel Peace Prize for his extraordinary efforts to strengthen international diplomacy and cooperation between peoples.

Joyce Piliso-Seroke was the South African national secretary of the Young Women's Christian Association (YWCA) and was later appointed to the World YWCA's executive committee in Geneva. She served as a committee member of the Human Rights Committee of the Truth and Reconciliation Commission. In 1999, the South African president appointed her to serve as the chairperson of the Commission on Gender Equality.

The Reverend Dr Bernice Powell Jackson is an ordained minister of the United Church of Christ in the United States. She has been a member of the World Council of Churches Central Committee since 1998, and the council's president for North America since 2004.

Gloria Radebe is Archbishop Tutu's younger sister.

Condoleezza Rice was the sixty-sixth United States secretary of state and the first African American woman to hold this position. Prior to this, she held positions as President Bush's national security and foreign policy advisor. Before entering the Bush administration she was provost of Stanford University.

LaTanya Richardson is an American actress who serves on the board of Artists for a New South Africa. She is married to Samuel L. Jackson, and the couple supports a number of charities, including Champions for Children, the Twenty-first Century Leaders Foundation and Make-A-Wish Foundation.

Professor Ricky Richardson is a paediatrician and an acknowledged authority on e-health and telemedicine. He is honorary consultant physician at Great Ormond Street Hospital for Children, a consultant at Portland Hospital for Women and Children, and the group clinical director of HealthSystems Group, one of the largest health information technology consulting practices in the United Kingdom. He is the son of Susan Cheshire.

The Right Reverend Venerable Gene Robinson is the ninth bishop of the Episcopal Diocese of New Hampshire, United States. He is most widely known for being the first openly gay, non-celibate priest to be ordained a bishop in the Anglican Communion. In 2009, he was awarded the Stephen F. Kolzak Award for his work advocating equal rights for the lesbian, gay, bisexual and transgender community.

Mary Robinson served as the seventh president of Ireland from 1990 to 1997, and was the first woman to hold the office. She was the United Nations high commissioner for human rights from 1997 until 2002, and is a member of The Elders. A human rights advocate, she is the president of the Mary Robinson Foundation – Climate Justice, which works to secure justice for victims of climate change.

Justice Albie Sachs is a human rights activist and anti-apartheid hero. While in exile in Mozambique during the apartheid era, he lost an arm and the sight in one eye after South African security agents planted a bomb in his car in 1988. As a member of the Constitutional Committee and the National Executive of the African National Congress, he was involved in the negotiations leading to South Africa becoming a constitutional democracy. Following South Africa's first democratic elections in 1994, he was appointed as a judge on the South African Constitutional Court by Nelson Mandela.

Carlos Santana is a Mexican-born American rock icon. His musical signature is internationally recognised. He is dedicated to humanitarian outreach and social activism. With his family, he created the Milagro Foundation, which supports programmes for disadvantaged children in the areas of arts, education and health.

Deborah Santana is an author, philanthropist, activist for peace and social justice, and founder of Do A Little, a non-profit organisation that serves women and girls. She is also a board member for Artists for a New South Africa.

Allister Sparks is a South African journalist, author and political commentator. He was the editor of the *Rand Daily Mail* from 1977 to 1981, and South African correspondent for the *Washington Post*, the *Observer*, *NRC Handelsblad* and the *Economist*. In 1985, he was nominated for a Pulitzer Prize for his reporting of racial unrest in South Africa.

Brother Timothy Stanton is a monk of the Community of the Resurrection in Mirfield, West Yorkshire, United Kingdom.

The Reverend Dr Peter Storey is a former president of both the Methodist Church of southern Africa and the South African Council of Churches. He was Nelson Mandela's prison chaplain on Robben Island and, later, was appointed by Mandela to help select the Truth and Reconciliation Commission. Reverend Storey is a founder and patron of Gun Free South Africa and a founder of LifeLine Southern Africa.

The Reverend Mpho Andrea Tutu is the youngest daughter of Archbishop Desmond and Leah Tutu.

Nomalizo Leah Tutu is married to Archbishop Desmond Tutu and is the mother of their four children. She championed the cause for better working conditions for domestic workers in South Africa and, in 1983, she helped found the South African Domestic Workers Association. In 2010, together with her husband, she was awarded the Inyathelo Indima-Tema Philanthropy Award.

Nontombi Naomi Tutu is the third child of Archbishop Desmond and Leah Tutu.

Trevor Thamsanqa Tutu is the eldest child of Archbishop Desmond and Leah Tutu.

Thandeka Tutu-Gxashe is Archbishop Desmond and Leah Tutu's second child and eldest daughter.

Blair Underwood is an American film and television actor. Throughout his career, he has supported a number of charities, including the Muscular Dystrophy Association, YouthAIDS and Love Our Children USA. He is also a co-founder and director of Artists for a New South Africa.

Mabel van Oranje has been the chief executive officer of The Elders since 2008. A human rights advocate from the Netherlands, she has co-founded several humanitarian organisations and is a former international advocacy director of the Open Society Institute. In 2005, the World Economic Forum named her a Young Global Leader.

Dan Vaughan was an aide to Archbishop Tutu.

Brother Dominic Whitnall is a professed member of the Community of the Resurrection based in Mirfield, West Yorkshire, United Kingdom.

Professor Jody Williams was the founding coordinator of the International Campaign to Ban Landmines and, with the campaign, she was jointly awarded the Nobel Peace Prize in 1997. In 2007, she was appointed by the United Nations Human Rights Council to lead a high-level mission to report on the war in Darfur. Professor Williams co-founded and currently chairs the Nobel Women's Initiative, and she has been the recipient of fifteen honorary degrees.

Alfre Woodard is an award-winning actress and social activist. She is a founding member and director of Artists for a New South Africa, a non-profit organisation working in the United States and South Africa to combat AIDS, educate and empower youth, and build bonds between the two nations through arts, culture and the shared pursuit of social justice.

NOTES

Chapter One – Our Real Leaders Are in Prison and in Exile
1 Joseph Lelyveld, "South Africa's Bishop Tutu", New York Times Magazine, 14 March 1982; 2 Alan Paton to Bishop Tutu, Sunday Times (Johannesburg), 21 October 1984, quoted in John Allen, Rabble-Rouser for Peace, 214; 3 Transcript of Danish interview, Ecunews, 14 September 1979, quoted in Rabble-Rouser for Peace, 178; 4 Citizen (Johannesburg), 7 September 1979, quoted in Rabble-Rouser for Peace, 178; 5 Nelson Mandela describes how Tutu became "public enemy number one to the powers-that-be", foreword, Desmond Tutu, The Rainbow People of God, xiv; 6 W. H. Njongonkulu Ndungane, "Reckless Courage", in Tutu As I Know Him , 147; 7 See note 5 above.

Chapter Two – Liberator of the Exodus
1 Desmond Tutu, God Has a Dream, 63; 2 The Rainbow People of God, 72; 3 Desmond Tutu, interview by Trevor McDonald, Paths of Inspiration, BBC Radio 2, 1996, quoted in Rabble-Rouser for Peace, 26; 4 Lewis Nkosi, Home and Exile, 13; 5 "Archbishop Trevor Huddleston Dies at 84", BBC News, 21 April 1998.

Chapter Three – A Man of Almost Unique Value
1 Hendrik Verwoerd's speech to the Senate, 7 June 1954; 2 AB2414 student file, Church of the Province of Southern Africa Archives, Historical Papers, William Cullen Library, University of the Witwatersrand, Johannesburg, quoted in Rabble-Rouser for Peace, 73; 3 Ibid; 4 Rabble-Rouser for Peace is the title of John Allen's biography of Tutu. (see bibliography); 5 Harold Macmillan's speech to the Parliament of South Africa, 3 February 1960; 6 Joseph Lelyveld, Move Your Shadow, 315; 7 Tom Lodge, Black Politics in South Africa since 1945, 215.

Chapter Four – How Can You Love God and Hate Your Brother?
1 Desmond Tutu, interview by Carina le Grange, 8 June 1995, quoted in Rabble-Rouser for Peace, 72; 2 Desmond Tutu, interview by Allister Sparks, 15 June 2010; 3 Ibid; 4 Enoch Powell's speech to the annual general meeting of the West Midlands Conservative Political Centre, 20 April 1968; 5 "Our Image of God Must Go", Observer, 17 March 1963; 6 Desmond Tutu, interview by Allister Sparks, 15 June 2010; 7 Joseph Lelyveld, "South Africa's Bishop Tutu", New York Times Magazine, 14 March 1982; 8 Desmond Tutu, interview by Allister Sparks, 15 June 2010; 9 Ibid; 10 Ibid; 11 Rabble-Rouser for Peace, 105; 12 Ibid, 108; 13 Desmond Tutu, interview by Allister Sparks, 15 June 2010; 14 Desmond Tutu, interview by Allister Sparks, 9 April 2010; 15 Steve Biko, I Write What I Like, 29; 16 Shirley du Boulay, Tutu: Voice of the Voiceless, 79; 17 Desmond Tutu, interview by Allister Sparks, 9 April 2010; 18 Ibid; 19 Desmond Tutu, foreword, G. C. Oosthuizen, M. C. Kitshoff, and S. W. D. Dube (eds), Afro-Christianity at the Grassroots, vii–viii; 20 Desmond Tutu, Hope and Suffering, Sermons and Speeches, 51; 21 Desmond Tutu, "Black Theology", September 1973, in ASATI Staff Institute, January 1975, Drawer 2, Theological Education Fund Archives, World Council of Churches Library and Archives, Geneva, quoted in Rabble-Rouser for Peace, 139; 22 Ibid.

Chapter Five – I Do Not Fear Them

1 Allister Sparks's notes from reporting on Desmond Tutu's evidence to the South African Government Commission of Inquiry into the South African Council of Churches, September 1982; 2 Ibid; 3 Geoff Cronjé, *'n Tuiste vir die Nageslag – Die Blywende Oplossing van Suid-Afrika se Rassevraagstuk*, quoted in Allister Sparks, *The Mind of South Africa*, 147; 4 Abraham Kuyper, Jr, *Lectures on Calvinism*, 91–2; 5 Allister Sparks's transcription of Desmond Tutu's evidence to the South African Government Commission of Inquiry into the South African Council of Churches, September 1982; 6 Ibid; 7 Ibid; 8 Ibid; 9 Ibid; 10 Ibid; 11 Email from Dan Vaughan to John Allen, 16 January 2006, quoted in *Rabble-Rouser for Peace*, 199; 12 Leslie A. Hewson (ed.), *Cottesloe Consultation: The Report of the Consultation*, 74; 13 International Commission of Jurists (ed.), *The Trial of Beyers Naudé*, 73; 14 John de Gruchy and Charles Villa-Vicencio (eds), *Apartheid is a Heresy*, 161; 15 J. W. Hofmeyr, J. A. Millard, and C. J. J. Froneman (eds), *History of the Church in South Africa*, 333; 16 Nicholas Wroe, "God's Showman", *Guardian*, 20 November 1999; 17 *US News and World Report*, vol. 97, issues 14–27, 1984, 13; 18 Desmond Tutu's speech at Khotso House, Johannesburg, 18 October 1984; 19 Ibid; 20 Allister Sparks's notes from reporting on Desmond Tutu's charge on enthronement as archbishop of Cape Town, St George's Cathedral, Cape Town, 7 September 1986; 21 Ibid; 22 Ibid; 23 Hays Rockwell, interview by John Allen, quoted in *Rabble-Rouser for Peace*, 240; 24 Fred Williams, interview by John Allen, quoted in *Rabble-Rouser for Peace*, 240; 25 Desmond Tutu, "The Current Crisis in South Africa" hearing before the Subcommittee on Africa of Committee on Foreign Affairs of the House of Representatives, Washington, DC, 4 December 1984.

Chapter Six – Faith and Revolution

1 *Hope and Suffering, Sermons and Speeches*, 32; 2 *Rabble-Rouser for Peace*, 155; 3 Peter Storey, interview by Allister Sparks, 16 June 2010; 4 *The Rainbow People of God*, 19; 5 Ibid, 20; 6 Ibid, 20; 7 *I Write What I Like*, 101; 8 Simon Jenkins, "The Great Evation. South Africa: A Survey", *Economist*, 21 June 1980; 9 Ameen Akhalwaya, *Sunday Express*, 26 August 1984; 10 William E. Smith, "South Africa: Gathering Hints of Change", *Time*, 19 August 1985; 11 "Crisis in South Africa", *Newsweek*, 19 August 1985; 12 Commonwealth Group of Eminent Persons, *Mission to South Africa*, 20, 102–3; 13 De Wet Potgieter, *Total Onslaught*, 93; 14 Ibid, 78; 15 *Government Gazette*, vol. 272, nos 11156 and 11157, Pretoria, Government Printers, 24 February 1988, quoted in *Rabble-Rouser for Peace*, 290; 16 Jim Wallis and Joyce Hollyday, *Crucible of Fire*, 28; Ibid 34; 17 *Journal of Theology for Southern Africa*, no. 63, June 1988, 72–4, quoted in *Rabble-Rouser for Peace*, 291–2; 18 *Journal of Theology for Southern Africa*, no. 63, June 1988, 82–87, quoted in *Rabble-Rouser for Peace*, 292.

Chapter Seven – We Can't Argue with God

1 South African Democracy Education Trust, *The Road to Democracy in South Africa*, 1038; 2 Desmond Tutu, interview by John Freeth, 11 July 2003, Desmond Mpilo Tutu office records, quoted in *Rabble-Rouser for Peace*, 308; 3 Interview, Lt. Gregory Rockman, SAPA Press Release, September 1989; 4 Statement by acting state president, AB2701, C3 (5), Church of the Province of Southern Africa Archives, Historical Papers, William Cullen Library, University of the Witwatersrand, Johannesburg, quoted in *Rabble-Rouser for Peace*, 310; 5 *The Rainbow People of God*, 182; 6 F. W. de Klerk, *The Last Trek*, 159; 7 Ibid; 8 Statement by Walter Sisulu at a press conference on his release from prison, Holy Cross Anglican Church, Soweto, 15 October 1989; 9 *The Rainbow People of God*, 185; 10 *The Last Trek*, 157–8; 11 Ibid; 12 Nelson Mandela's address following his release from prison, Cape Town, 11 February 1990.

Chapter Eight – We Are Unstoppable

1 Antonio Gramsci, *Selections from the Prison Notebooks*, 275–6; 2 Ben Temkin, *Buthelezi: A Biography*, 224; 3 Allister Sparks, *Tomorrow is Another Country*, 146; 4 Ibid, 146; 5 Ibid, 151; 6 Address to the nation by Nelson Mandela in a televised broadcast, 13 April 1993; 7 Allister Sparks's notes from his reporting of the funeral of Chris Hani, Soweto, 19 April 1993; 8 *Tomorrow is Another Country*, 189; 9 *Sunday Times* (Johannesburg), 13 March 1994; 10 Desmond Tutu, comments at Union Buildings, Pretoria, 19 April 1994, quoted in *Rabble-Rouser for Peace*, 336.

Chapter Nine – There Are Things That Went Wrong

1 Antjie Krog, *Country of My Skull*, 57; 2 Alex Boraine, *A Country Unmasked: Inside South Africa's Truth and Reconciliation Commission*, 90; 3 Max du Preez, interview by Allister Sparks, 10 April 2010; 4 *Country of My Skull*, 57; 5 Allan Boesak's address at the funeral of the Cradock Four, Lingelihle Stadium, Eastern Cape, 20 July 1985; 6 *A Country Unmasked*, 103; 7 *Country of My Skull*, 80; 8 Almond Nofomela before the Truth and Reconciliation Commission's Amnesty Committee, Durban, 3 September 1999; 9 Eugene de Kock before the Truth and Reconciliation Commission's Amnesty Committee, Port Elizabeth, 6 March 1998; 10 Mohammed Allie, "Jailed Policeman Accuses De Klerk", BBC News, 27 July 2007; 11 *A Country Unmasked*, 145; 12 *Country of My Skull*, 45; 13 Ibid, 336; 14 Ibid, 338; 15 Ibid, 339; 16 Desmond Tutu, foreword, *Report of the Truth and Reconciliation Commission*, vol. 1, chpt. 1, 23; 17 Allister Sparks, *Beyond the Miracle*, 169.

Chapter Ten – The Voice of the Voiceless

1 *Rabble-Rouser for Peace*, 374; 2 Ibid, 374–5; 3 Dave Andrews, "People of Faith, Desmond Tutu", *Target* (Tear Fund) 3, 2004; 4 Desmond Tutu, interview by John Carlin, PBS Frontline, date unknown; 5 Walter Ruby, "Tutu Says Israel's Policy in Territories Remind Him of SA". *Jerusalem Post*, 1 February 1989; 6 "Tutu Urges Jews to Forgive The Nazis", *San Francisco Chronicle*, 27 December 1989; 7 Rabbi Marvin Hier of the Simon Wiesenthal Center was quoted as saying this in "Tutu Assailed", *Chicago Sun-Times*, 30 December 1989; 8 Desmond Tutu, "Apartheid in the Holy Land", *Guardian*, 29 April 2002; 9 *Facing the Truth* press release, BBC News, 14 February 2006; 10 Fergal Keane, "Facing the Truth", BBC News, 14 March 2006; 11 *International Herald Tribune*, 7 October 2004; 12 Desmond Tutu, "Desmond Tutu: My Tribute to Burma's Opposition Leader, Aung San Suu Kyi", *Guardian*, 2 August 2009; 13 Ian Fisher, "Palestinians Mourn Civilians Killed by Israel", *New York Times*, 10 November 2006; 14 Report of the Fact-finding Mission to Beit-Hanoun, Established under the United Nations Human Rights Council, 1 September 2008; 15 Dershowitz made the statement on the sidelines of the Durban Review conference on Racism in Geneva, reported by the South African Press Association, Associated Press and the German news agency DPA, 20 April 2009.

Chapter Eleven – A Quicksilver Spirit

1 Joseph Lelyveld, "South Africa's Bishop Tutu", *New York Times Magazine*, 14 March 1982; 2 Ibid; 3 Speech by Nelson Mandela at Desmond Tutu's seventy-fifth birthday party, Johannesburg, 7 October, 2006; 4 *Tutu As I Know Him*, 111; 5 Desmond Tutu's address to the crowd at the FIFA World Cup Kick-off Celebration Concert, Orlando Stadium, Johannesburg, 10 June 2010; 6 John Allen, interview by Allister Sparks, 16 June 2010; 7 Peter Storey, interview by Allister Sparks, 16 June 2010; 8 Alex Boraine, "To Know Him is to Love Him", in *Tutu As I Know Him*, 183; 9 Ibid; 10 Lavinia Crawford-Browne, interview by Allister Sparks, 7 April 2010; 11 Nadine Gordimer, "The Man of Wholeness", in *Tutu As I Know Him*, 110; 12 Ibid; 13 Alex Boraine, "To Know Him is to Love Him", in *Tutu As I Know Him*, 182; 14 Lavinia Crawford-Browne, interview by Allister Sparks, 7 April 2010; 15 Ibid; 16 Ibid; 17 *Rabble-Rouser for Peace*, 5–6; 18 Ibid; 19 Ibid; 20 Alex Boraine, "To Know Him is to Love

Him", in *Tutu As I Know Him*, 271; 21 Ibid; 22 Leah Tutu, interview by Allister Sparks, 15 June 2010; 23 Ibid; 24 Desmond Tutu, interview by Allister Sparks, 9 April 2010; 25 Lavinia Crawford-Browne, interview by Allister Sparks, 7 April 2010; 26 *Rabble-Rouser for Peace*, 271; 27 Leah Tutu, interview by Allister Sparks, 15 June 2010; 28 Ibid; 29 Statement by Desmond Tutu at a press conference announcing his retirement, Cape Town, 22 July 2010.

Chapter Twelve – We Are All God's Children
1 Desmond Tutu, interview by Allister Sparks, 9 April 2010; 2 Ibid; 3 *Tutu As I Know Him*, 165; 4 Desmond Tutu, interview by Allister Sparks, 9 April 2010; 5 Ibid; 6 Ibid; 7 Ibid; 8 Ibid; 9 Ibid; 10 "The Man of Wholeness", in *Tutu As I Know Him*, 110; 11 Antjie Krog, interview by Allister Sparks, 1 July 2010; 12 Ibid; 13 Ibid; 14 Ibid; 15 John Allen, interview by Allister Sparks, 16 June 2010.

FURTHER REFERENCES

p. 17: An English-language version of Ntsikana's "Great Hymn" which appears as "Great Shield" in *An African Prayer Book* by Desmond Tutu.
p. 21: Excerpt from *uMama: Recollections of South African Mothers and Grandmothers* by Marion Kleim (ed.).
p. 87: Excerpt from Desmond Tutu's speech entitled "Rediscovering Justice" at the University of San Francisco, June 1995.
p. 93: Excerpt from Desmond Tutu's Nobel lecture, Oslo, 11 December 1984.
p. 113: Desmond Tutu, press statement, 2 April 1986.
p. 179: Excerpt from *No Future Without Forgiveness* by Desmond Tutu, p. 5.
p. 231: Excerpt from Desmond Tutu's speech to the Cape Town Press Club about scapegoatism, 17 March 1987.

SELECT BIBLIOGRAPHY

Allen, John. *Rabble-Rouser for Peace: The Authorized Biography of Desmond Tutu*. New York: Free Press, 2006/London: Rider, 2007.
Biko, Steve. *I Write What I Like*. Johannesburg: Picador Africa, 2004.
Boraine, Alex. *A Country Unmasked: Inside South Africa's Truth and Reconciliation Commission*. Oxford: Oxford University Press, 2001.
Commonwealth Group of Eminent Persons. *Mission to South Africa: The Commonwealth Report*. Harmondsworth: Penguin/New York: Viking Penguin, 1986.
Crawford-Browne, Lavinia, and Piet Meiring, eds. *Tutu As I Know Him: On a Personal Note*. Cape Town: Umuzi, 2006.
Cronjé, Geoff. *'n Tuiste vir die Nageslag – Die Blywende Oplossing van Suid-Afrika se Rassevraagstuk*, Johannesburg: Publicite Handelsreklamediens (Edms.) Bpk, 1945.
De Gruchy, John W., and Charles Villa-Vicencio, eds. *Apartheid is a Heresy*. Cape Town: Eerdmans, 1983.
De Klerk, F. W. *The Last Trek: A New Beginning*. London: Pan, 2000.
Du Boulay, Shirley. *Tutu: Voice of the Voiceless*. London: Penguin Books, 1989.
Gramsci, Antonio. *Selections from the Prison Notebooks*. New York: International Publishers, 1971.
Hofmeyr, J. A., J. A. Millard, and C. J. J. Froneman, eds. *History of the Church in South Africa: A Document and Source Book*. Pretoria: University of South Africa, 1991.
Huddleston, Trevor. *Naught for Your Comfort*. London: Collins, 1956.
International Commission of Jurists, ed. *The Trial of Beyers Naudé: Christian Witness and the Rule of Law*. London: Search Press, 1975.
Kleim, Marion, ed. *uMama: Recollections of South African Mothers and Grandmothers*. Cape Town: Umuzi, 2009.
Krog, Antjie. *Country of My Skull*. Johannesburg: Random House, 1998.
Kuyper, Abraham, Jr. *Lectures on Calvinism: The Stone Foundation Lectures*. Grand Rapids: Eerdmans, 1931.
Lelyveld, Joseph. *Move Your Shadow: South Africa, Black and White*. London: Abacus, 1987.
Lodge, Tom. *Black Politics in South Africa since 1945*. Johannesburg: Ravan, 1983.
Nkosi, Lewis. *Home and Exile: And Other Selections*, London: Longman, 1965.
Oosthuizen, G. C., M. C. Kitshoff, and S. W. D. Dube, eds. *Afro-Christianity at the Grassroots: Its Dynamics and Strategies*, foreword by Desmond Tutu. Leiden: E. J. Brill, 1994.
Paton, Alan. *Cry the Beloved Country*. London: Jonathan Cape/New York: Charles Scribner's Sons, 1948.
Potgieter, De Wet. *Total Onslaught: Apartheid's Dirty Tricks Exposed*. Cape Town: Zebra Press, 2007.
South African Democracy Education Trust. *The Road to Democracy in South Africa*, vol. 3: *International Solidarity*. Cape Town: Zebra Press, 2008.
Sparks, Allister. *The Mind of South Africa*. London: William Heinemann/New York: Knopf, 1990.
Sparks, Allister. *Tomorrow is Another Country: The Inside Story of South Africa's Road to Change*. Sandton: Struik, 1994.
Sparks, Allister. *Beyond the Miracle: Inside the New South Africa*. Chicago: University of Chicago Press/London: Profile Books/Johannesburg and Cape Town: Jonathan Ball, 2003.
Temkin, Ben. *Buthelezi: A Biography*. London: Frank Cass/Balgowan: J. B. Publishers.
Truth and Reconciliation Commission of South Africa. *Report of the Truth and Reconciliation Commission:* vols. 1–5. Cape Town: Truth and Reconciliation Commission, 1998.
Tutu, Desmond. *Hope and Suffering, Sermons and Speeches*, compiled by Mothobi Mutloatse and edited by John Webster. Johannesburg: Skotaville, 1983.
Tutu, Desmond. *The Rainbow People of God: South Africa's Victory Over Apartheid*, edited by John Allen. London: Transworld/New York: Doubleday, 1994.
Tutu, Desmond. *An African Prayer Book*. New York: Doubleday, 1995.
Tutu, Desmond. *No Future Without Forgiveness*. London: Rider/New York: Doubleday, 2000.
Tutu, Desmond. *God Has a Dream: A Vision of Hope for Our Time*, with Doug Abrams. London: Rider/New York: Doubleday, 2004.
Wallis, Jim, and Joyce Hollyday, eds. *Crucible of Fire: The Church Confronts Apartheid*. New York: Orbis, 1989.
World Council of Churches. *Cottesloe Consultation: The Report of the Consultation Among South African Member Churches of the World Council of Churches, 7–14 December 1960 at Cottesloe, Johannesburg*, edited by Leslie A. Hewson. Johannesburg, 1961.

ACKNOWLEDGEMENTS

Additional Image Captions and Credits

Front cover and case: Portrait of Archbishop Tutu by Stephen Voss, courtesy Stephen Voss/Redux Pictures.

Back cover: Tutu dances off the stage after speaking at a pro-Tibet rally in San Francisco, California, US, 8 April 2008, courtesy Mario Anzuoni/Reuters.

Back flap (top to bottom): Allister Sparks, courtesy Allister Sparks; Mpho A. Tutu, by Andrew Zuckerman, copyright Desmond M. Tutu; Doug Abrams, courtesy Dina Scoppertone.

Endpapers: Detail from weavings handmade at the Philani Health & Nutrition Project, a community-based non-governmental organisation (NGO) operating in the informal settlements of Khayelitsha, Crossroads, Brown's Farm, Mfuleni, Nyanga and Delft outside Cape Town, of which Tutu is patron. Visit www.philani.org.za for details. Courtesy Anton Crone.

pp. viii and 305: Tutu during the Truth and Reconciliation Commission, Cape Town, 1997, by Jillian Edelstein, courtesy CameraPress.

p. x: Portrait of Archbishop Tutu by Andrew Zuckerman, copyright Desmond M. Tutu.

p. xii: An original mixed-media fresco by Igshaan Adams, resident artist at Philani, and other Philani artists. The artwork was commissioned especially for *Tutu: The Authorised Portrait* and is based on the cover photograph by Stephen Voss. Courtesy Anton Crone.

Photographic Sources and Permissions

Every effort has been made to trace the copyright holders of the images reproduced in this book and the publisher apologises for any unintentional omission. We would be pleased to hear from any who are not acknowledged here and undertake to make all reasonable efforts to include the appropriate acknowledgement in any subsequent editions.

Africa Media Online: 12; 5 (both) and 33 Shadrack Nkomo/Baileys African History Archive; 10 Museum Africa; 36, 38 and 39 Baileys African History Archive; 116, 154 and 159 Eric Miller; 137 Santu Mofokeng.

AP Photographs: 204 Jeff Moore; 214 Findley Kember; 224 Daniel Maurer; 259 Mary Altaffer; 275 (left) Schalk van Zuydam

Avusa Media: 74, 76, 78, 94, 96, 131, 225, 262 and 266; 14 (top), 143 and 157 R. Botha; 14 (bottom) and 92 Robert Tshabalala; 28, 29 and 31 Vikki Perreira; 83 John Parkin; 88 Margo Williams; 90 Noel Watson; 150 Terry Shean; 163 (top) James Soullier; 169 Herbert Mabuza; 188 and 189 Raymond Preston; 222–3 Martin Rhodes; 227 (top) Essa Alexander; 229 Elizabeth Sejane; 241 (both) Joel Sefface.

Corbis: 3, 34–5, 104, 126, 156, 163 (bottom) and 298 David Turnley; 6 (both) and 128–9 Gideon Mendel; 13, 160–1 and 162 Patrick Durand/Sygma; 48 William Campbell/Sygma; 106 Tim Clary; 177 Greg Marinovich/Sygma; 202–3 Benedicte Kurzan/EPA; 205 Jim Hollander/EPA; 207 and 208 Ulrich Schnarr/EPA; 211 (bottom) Robin Utrecht/EPA; 246 (bottom) Dan Levine/EPA; 255 Orlando Barria/EPA; 273 Kapoor Baldev/Sygma; 280–1, 285 Felipe Trueba/EPA.

Camera Press: 186–7, 197 and 199 Jillian Edelstein.

Gille de Vlieg: xiv and 85

Getty Images: 86 Hulton Archive; 101 (right) and 148 Selwyn Tait; 108 Robert Abbott Sengstacke; 178, 181, 184, 200, 219, 227 (bottom), 230, 242, 265 (bottom) and 286–7 Oryx Media; 217 Alexander Joe/AFP; 232 Prakash Singh/AFP; 271 (left) Franck Fife/AFP; 271 (right) Cynthia Johnson; 282 Paul Gilham/FIFA; 289 Berthold Staeller/AFP; 295 Michael Gottschalk/AFP; 302–3 Pongasak Chaiyanuwong.

Louise Gubb: 124–5, 138, 166, 173, 211 (top), 265 (top), 291 and 292–3

Independent Newspapers (South Africa): 130

Michael Jacobs: 275 (right)

Carey Linde: 246 (top)

Rashid Lombard: 102–3, 110, 121 (top), 158 and 164–5.

Magnum Photos/Snapper Media: 8–9 Ian Berry.

Mpilo Foundation Archives: 20, 21, 30, 56 and 57 courtesy Tutu family; 42–3, 68, 69, 107 and 236 Mpilo Archive; 65 and 73 Conrad Guelke.

John Muafangejo: 82

Museum Africa: 44

PictureNET Africa: 195 Peter Andrews; 244 Henner Frankenfeld; 250 (all) Shayne Robinson; 276 Bebeto Matthews; 279 Obed Zilwa.

PQ Blackwell: 220 Matt Hoyle.

Reuters: 142 Greg English; 228 (top) Mario Anzuoni; 228 (bottom) Mike Hutchings; 267 Mannie Garcia.

Jurgen Schadeburg: 26

Jonathan Shapiro: 172, 182, 193, 194 and 243

South African History Archives: 190 and 191

South African National Archives: 95 and 104 (bottom)

Thembinkosi Dwayisa: 18

UCT Archive: 89 and 121 (bottom) Guy Tillim; 100, 101 (left), 118–9, 132 (both), 133, 134–5 and 140–1 Paul Weinberg; 105 and 254 (both) David Goldblatt; 114–5 and 122 (bottom) Gideon Mendel; 122 (top) Themba Nkosi; 123 Steve Hilton-Barber.

United Pictures International: 62

UWC/RIM/Mayibuye Archive: 11, 93, 145 and 147 Desmond Tutu papers.

The White House photographer: 268–9

Graeme Williams: 168

Jody Williams: 297

Literary Permissions

Excerpts from Desmond Tutu's speeches and sermons reprinted by kind permission of Desmond Tutu (unless otherwise specified).

Quotations on pp. 4, 56, 225 from "South Africa's Bishop Tutu" by Joseph Lelyveld. From *The New York Times*, 14 March 1982 © 1982 *The New York Times*. All rights reserved. Used by permission and protected by the Copyright Laws of the United States. The printing, copying, redistribution, or retransmission of this Content without express written permission is prohibited. Excerpt on p. 93 from Desmond Tutu's Nobel lecture © The Nobel Foundation 1984. Quotations on pp. 183, 192, 196 from *A Country Unmasked: Inside South Africa's Truth and Reconciliation Commission* reprinted with the permission of Alex Boraine. Quotations on pp. 183, 188, 192, 196, 198, 199 from *Country of My Skull* reprinted with the permission of Antjie Krog and Zebra Press.

First produced and originated in 2011 by PQ Blackwell Limited
116 Symonds Street, Auckland 1010, New Zealand

This edition published in 2011 by
Pan Macmillan South Africa
Private Bag X19
Northlands
Johannesburg
2116
South Africa

www.panmacmillan.co.za

SA ISBN 978-1-77010-140-1
UK ISBN 978-0-230-75995-4

Publisher: Geoff Blackwell
Editor-in-Chief: Ruth Hobday
Designer: Cameron Gibb
Production Manager: Sarah Anderson
Additional Design: Helene Dehmer
Image Research: Gail Behrmann
Copy-editor: Rachel Clare
Editor: Lisette du Plessis
Proofreaders: Mary Dobbyn Proofreading Services
Indexer: Sam Hill

www.pqblackwell.com

Printed through 1010 International Limited. Printed in Hong Kong